Paths to
Political
Reform

Paths to Political Reform

Edited by
William J. Crotty
Northwestern University

LexingtonBooks
D.C. Heath and Company
Lexington, Massachusetts
Toronto

Library of Congress Cataloging in Publication Data

Main entry under title:
  Paths to political reform.

  1. Elections—United States—Addresses, essays, lectures. 2. Political
parties—United States—Addresses, essays, lectures. I. Crotty, William J.
JK1967.P37   324.973   78-9439
ISBN 0-669-02395-7

Published simultaneously in Canada.

Printed in the United States of America.

International Standard Book Number: 0-669-02395-7

Library of Congress Catalog Card Number: 78-9439

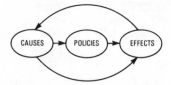

Policy Studies Organization Series

General Approaches to Policy Studies

Policy Studies in America and Elsewhere
    edited by Stuart S. Nagel
Policy Studies and the Social Studies
    edited by Stuart S. Nagel
Methodology for Analyzing Public Policies
    edited by Frank P. Scioli, Jr., and Thomas J. Cook
Urban Problems and Public Policy
    edited by Robert L. Lineberry and Louis H. Masotti
Problems of Theory in Policy Analysis
    edited by Philip M. Gregg
Using Social Research for Public Policy-Making
    edited by Carol H. Weiss
Public Administration and Public Policy
    edited by H. George Frederickson and Charles Wise
Policy Analysis and Deductive Reasoning
    edited by Gordon Tullock and Richard Wagner
Legislative Reform
    edited by Leroy N. Rieselbach
Teaching Policy Studies
    edited by William D. Coplin
Paths to Political Reform
    edited by William J. Crotty
Determinants of Public Policy
    edited by Thomas Dye and Virginia Gray
Effective Policy Implementation
    edited by Daniel Mazmanian and Paul Sabatier
Taxes and Spending Policy
    edited by Warren J. Samuels and Larry L. Wade
Causes and Effects of Inequality in Urban Services
    edited by Richard C. Rich
Analyzing Inequality in Urban Services
    edited by Richard C. Rich
The Analysis of Policy Impact
    edited by John Grumm and Stephen Wasby
Public Policies for Distressed Communities
    edited by F. Stevens Redburn and Terry F. Buss

Specific Policy Problems

Analyzing Poverty Policy
    edited by Dorothy Buckton James
Crime and Criminal Justice
    edited by John A. Gardiner and Michael Mulkey
Civil Liberties
    edited by Stephen L. Wasby

Contents

Acknowledgments

The editor wishes to thank Stuart Nagel who suggested this volume and helped greatly in bringing it to fruition.

Introduction: Political Reform in the Late Twentieth Century

William J. Crotty

Reform movements tend to run in cycles. They arise normally from an unusual act—something modest and traditionally of local concern (such as the refusal of a black woman to sit in the back of a bus in Montgomery, Alabama) or something spectacular that grabs the nation's attention (the involvement of the White House and the president's reelection committee in a burglary of the opposition party's headquarters). The incident receives extended public attention and, in turn, sets off a related series of events that trigger the national conscience and eventually lead to significant reform. The civil-rights revolution of the late 1950s and the 1960s and the Watergate-related reforms in electoral-financing and campaign practices epitomize the process. The problems exposed were fundamental and serious. One (civil rights and the treatment of blacks) was of long-standing concern to the society. The other (the expansion and abuse of governmental and specifically presidential powers), although a topic of debate among academicians and commentators, was little appreciated by the public at large.

The civil-rights movement addressed problems of long duration. Few would question that blacks had inferior economic and social opportunities and a political influence that was negligible in relation to their numbers in the society. In many areas of the country, legal and governmental sanctions were used to enforce black political impotence. Yet the courts, the Congress, the federal government, and the states—in response to the prevalent attitudes of the day, the structure of political power within the society, and a close reading of what the Constitution allowed and hence what a government agency could or could not do—tolerated the situation and, in many respects, encouraged it. Meaningful change appeared hopeless; all the constitutional avenues to normal reform—the government, the courts, the media, the public in general—seemed resigned to the situation. Blacks appeared to lack the political muscle necessary to force significant changes. Consequently, most Americans shut their eyes to the situation.

All this was to change. The impetus for a renewed and ultimately extraordinarily successful struggle came from minor incidents at the local level: black college students denied service at a dining counter in Greensboro, N.C., a black woman's refusal to sit in the rear of a Montgomery bus.

The aftermath of these incidents—one involving a sit-in and the other revolving around a subsequent bus boycott and the mobilization of a civil-rights coalition in support of the Montgomery blacks—caught the national attention. They pricked the American conscience. In turn, they led to other, more militant encounters: the mobilization of blacks and sympathetic whites behind the leadership of the Rev. Martin Luther King, Jr., the Student Nonviolent Coordinating Committee (SNCC), and others; the police dogs and cattle prods used on demonstrators in Birmingham; the bombings of black churches and the killing of black children; the emergence and national prominence of racist states-rights proponents such as Governor George Wallace of Alabama; the rebirth of the Ku Klux Klan; cities burning nationwide; and the use of federal troops to maintain order and integrate schools. The experience was a traumatic one, and its ramifications continue to this day. But it did lead to impressive gains.

Beginning in the late 1950s, a series of civil-rights acts were passed that attempted to ensure the equal treatment of blacks. The most impressive of these, the Voting Rights Act of 1965 (and its successors), was to force the enfranchisement of blacks in the South.[1] The result has been the transformation of American politics. Southern politics have become more competitive, segregationist politicians in the region now have a limited political base and declining support, and blacks have become a significant political force, both in the South and nationwide.[2] With political clout come the social and political rewards long enjoyed by other groups in the society. Instead of government being a handmaiden of discriminatory practices, as it had been since the last quarter of the nineteenth century, it now became the ally and chief sponsor of black advancement. The battle would not be won quickly, but the entire nation had been mobilized, albeit somewhat reluctantly, and its energies redirected toward the full integration of blacks into American society. All this was the outgrowth of a few single acts in scattered communities that eventually culminated in the civil-rights revolution.

Watergate also has had a profound impact. The break-in at the Democratic party's national headquarters eventually was linked both to Richard Nixon's Committee to Re-Elect the President (CREEP) and to the Nixon White House. Under extended investigation, the Nixon administration was shown to have engaged in a series of abuses of official power—from the illegal use of government office to the unauthorized invasion of a neutral country—a number of which were criminal and several of which were unconstitutional. The revelations led to confrontations between the administration, the press, the courts, the Congress, and even special prosecutors appointed by the White House. After two tumultuous years, and with his impeachment pending before the Congress, Nixon resigned.

In the wake of the Watergate scandals, a number of efforts were made to limit government discretion in everything from the exercise of its war-power functions to its influence over federal agencies such as the Federal Bureau of Investigation (FBI), the Central Intelligence Agency (CIA), the Securities and Exchange Commission, and the civil service. Attempts were made to open up federal decision-making and contract-awarding processes through sunshine laws, new codes for official conduct, the detailed revelation of administrative (and legislative) financial practices, and efforts to identify and restrain conflicts of interest. These initiatives were only partially successful, but they did focus attention on the existing problems and, if nothing else, they began to educate the public to the potential for abuse of power in high places.

In a series of related developments, the Congress—enjoying renewed attention from the public and, correspondingly, higher expectations of performance—continued to modify its procedures to enable it to contend more successfully with its enormous workload and the conflicting pressures placed on its membership. Congress also began to consider—and eventually reluctantly passed—a series of reforms in campaign-finance laws that have revolutionized the pursuit of the presidency. A Federal Election Commission was established to monitor campaign expenditures; detailed, publicly accessible records of all significant campaign expenditures were required; and the federal financing of presidential-nomination and general-election races was instituted. The government funding of electoral contests to free them from the influence of special-interest monies has long been a reformers' dream that until the 1970s appeared too extreme to receive serious legislative attention. After the Watergate revelations on campaign abuse, such funding seemed a natural and reasonable step. It has proved popular with the public and has been greeted with enthusiasm by those seeking the nation's highest office. None of this would have been likely to occur without the police apprehension of what, at the time, appeared to be some petty criminals in a burglary at the Watergate building in June 1972.

These are only illustrations of the approaches to reform. One constitutes a reaction to a nagging and chronic problem that has existed for generations. The movement began with an obscure act that fed a national sense of uneasiness and that in time led to improvements. Most of the changes are incremental in nature, but cumulatively they begin to resolve the issues at stake.

The second approach to reform involves some type of abuse that comes to the public consciousness dramatically and instantaneously. The public is incensed; its quick, strong reaction forces political office holders to find some satisfactory resolution to the problem. The solutions that are proposed and enacted may not actually deal with the problem. Official agencies find dramatic changes difficult to tolerate. If some action is absolutely essential, a period of political fencing and false starts is likely to be the first response. Reform proposals may be watered down to lessen their impact or may focus on subsidiary, more easily changed areas. If pressures persist, then the governing agencies can be forced to deal in a meaningful way with the basic causes of the problem; in the process, fundamentally new departures can be initiated. Either way, a sense of movement and action must emerge that is sufficient to placate the public and the media and to create the impression that the public's elected representatives are leading the fight for change.

Watergate has been used as an example of the second type of approach. The events of Watergate did lead to important immediate and long-run changes. A president was ousted from office and another (Gerald Ford) sworn in, an abrupt and significant break in political continuity. Public attitudes toward the presidency and politics in general are less trusting and more cynical.[3] The public is more likely to be sensitive to abuses of office and of the public trust, although the results of this are yet to be shown. More specific limits of authority were proposed, and to some extent adopted, for government agencies such as the FBI, the Internal Revenue Service, and the CIA. How effective these will prove to be again must await the evidence of future decades. Civil-service reform was introduced and implemented at least partly in response to Watergate. Controls over the awarding of contracts were improved. The impeachment process was dusted off and put in motion. Despite the awkwardness of the procedures, the impeachment of a president is no longer as unthinkable as it once was. And the federal funding of presidential campaigns became a reality, a noteworthy advance in making presidential candidates more representative of—and indebted to—the broader public than special interests. Less impressive have been the series of administrative changes, intended to ensure a more open and accountable executive branch. These are unlikely to change the workings of the bureaucracy significantly, although they did permit office holders to present a sense of leadership and responsiveness to the public when it was politically necessary.

In the reform process, a specific visible act dramatizes the problem and leads to a general public awareness of it—fashionably called consciousness raising—and to support for change. This is followed by elite bargaining that, in turn, can lead to meaningful reform. The political (congressional, executive-branch, and interest-group) give and take over the various civil-rights statutes and presidential-campaign proposals are examples. Many of the initial changes contemplated and introduced, as indicated, may be symbolic: a tinkering with the system, such as the earliest civil-rights acts or the tentative proposals adopted to halt bureaucratic abuses, intended to show a responsiveness to the public concern but not designed to alter the established patterns of business significantly. The political elites nibble at the edges of the problem. Most reform dies at this stage. It takes an unusually aroused (Watergate) or persistent (civil rights) public and an intensely concerned body of office holders to institute meaningful change. Reform does not come easily.

The process can be schematically presented (table I-1). The impetus for change usually arises from a broad public concern with a problem, although on occasion (as with the later efforts at registration reform) political elites can initiate the proposals or, more often, sustain and expand the scope and impact of the changes. These same elites, of course, can kill reform in- itiatives or channel them into fairly harmless outlets.

Whatever the elite reaction—superficial changes to calm the public or fundamental redefinitions of political structures—the initial impetus for reform soon falters and is followed by long periods of inactivity. As public demand falls off; as the reform coalition (an odd assortment of groups held together by one concern) dissipates; as the media loses interest and the public becomes either insensitive to the remaining issues, antagonistic to further changes (for example, busing to achieve integration), or convinced that the problem has been basically resolved; attention shifts elsewhere. New issues arise—most recently inflation, the declining standard of living, and the threat of recession—and the public and its elected representatives move on to new agendas. As the convulsions of reform end, the nation wearily returns to more placid pursuits and a period of regeneration.

Nevertheless, the changes introduced do condition, often in subtle ways, the response to the new political concerns. And the problems themselves, if not adequately resolved, do not disappear. They smolder and, over time, the pressures begin to build, and with them the impetus for a new reform era.

Table I-1
Schematic Depiction of Reform Process

Support	Awareness of Problem	
	Chronic (Long-Running Concern)	Short-Term (Incident Dramatizes Need for Change)
Broad (public)	Civil rights First wave of registration reform Electoral college reform	Watergate (campaign reform) Presidential nominating changes (post-1968 period)
Limited (elite bargaining)	Congressional reform Current efforts at franchise expansion Political party reform	Current efforts to expand campaign financing Current (limited) efforts to reform administrative agencies and practices

Reform in Contemporary Politics

The foregoing lends perspective to the continuing reform controversies. Before discussing the issues involved in each of the areas of proposed change, however, it is necessary to say something about the public mood. The context in which reform takes place is as important to its successful implementation as are the issues associated with the individual problems.

The Setting

Redefining the American Electorate. One thing that has changed significantly over the last two decades has been the American electorate. In chapter 1, Kagay and Caldeira show this by charting six of the major components that enter into voter decision making: attitudes toward the Democratic and Republican candidate, group-benefit issues, domestic policies, foreign concerns, and evaluations of party performance and government management. They examine the importance of each group of concerns during the period from 1952 to 1976, the extent to which the attitudes favored one party or the other, and the degree of consensus or polarization found among voters on each dimension.

The authors find that policy concerns play a role in political decision making above that often anticipated (especially for what has often been called the issueless 1950s). In the earlier elections (1952-1960), voter perceptions of candidates appeared more important than issue stands. The gap between these perceptions closed during the period after 1964 until by the 1972 presidential election issues were more important to voters than candidate evaluations.

The Democrats generally benefited from domestic-policy stands and those relating to group concerns. The Republicans gained the most from candidate evaluations and from their positions on foreign policy and government management. Perceptions of the candidates polarized voters the most. Interestingly, the pattern of responses in 1976 in many respects resembled those found in the 1950s.

Kagay and Caldeira's study has importance for an understanding of the attachments and motivations of an electorate in flux. If their findings are correct—and their general emphases have been supported by other researchers—issues are replacing party loyalties as the major influence on the vote.[4] If so, the ability of the voters to make independent decisions on matters of policy consequence rather than meekly following party-line positions will be influenced even more by factors that structure the choices they are offered (registration practices, redefinitions of nominating and campaign approaches).[5]

The role of the political parties is changing. Not only does party influence appear to be on the wane, but the parties have historically been uncomfortable in presenting the voters with well-defined issue positions of contemporary relevance as a basis for choosing between them. This inadequacy, in turn, relates to the transformations in party structures—both those underway and those proposed—that are presently being debated.[6] A changing electorate will have to develop new bonds between itself and its elected representatives.

The Public Mood. Public confidence in American institutions has declined. In chapter 2 Dennis, who has done extensive research on the topic, argues that there has been a decrease in public esteem for the parties that parallels the erosion of their base of popular support. Trust in political institutions in general is decaying, a condition that—while understandable in light of the problems brought on by Vietnam, Watergate, and a sick economy—could have serious consequences for the operation and structure of American parties.

Dennis makes his point by reviewing over time the institutions most and least trusted by Americans (none do particularly well, but political parties rank first or second in trustworthiness with no more than 7 percent of the electorate and are considered least trustworthy by 70 percent); the institutions in which voters have the greatest confidence; the extent to which people believe parties respond to their concerns; the degree to which parties are perceived as differing significantly on issues; the importance of parties to the voter; and the nature of support (attitudinal and material) given to the parties. Dennis demonstrates that partisan voting declined between 1952 and 1976 (in 1952, only 34 percent voted for a party different from their own in presidential election; by 1976, the figure was 53 percent). He also shows that the norm of partisanship—the belief that people should vote for the party rather than the "best" candidate regardless of party—has never been held strongly by Americans. In the 1970s, about 90 percent of the voters believed they should vote for the candidate, rather than the party.

Dennis believes that the public mood he has characterized and the trends he has analyzed indicate difficult times ahead. If serious institutional reforms to bolster the parties and reintroduce confidence into the political system are not undertaken, the future may witness even greater electoral instability.

Defining the Electorate. One of the main influences on voter turnout is registration procedures. The first and possibly most important obstacle an individual must face before voting is registration. The requirements are obscure, and enrollment procedures are often poorly understood. In addition, most public officials charged with enrolling voters do little to publicize the requirements the prospective voter must meet or to facilitate anything approaching universal enrollment. The United States is one of the most backward countries in this respect, and this is one reason its electoral turn-out ranks at the bottom of those for democratic nations.

In chapter 3, Crotty reviews the difficulties with registration practices and the relationship between these and voter turnout. Much has been done in the last twenty years to alleviate some of the more arbitrary aspects of registration hurdles; this was one offshoot of the civil-rights movement and the concern (during the Vietnam War) with permitting eighteen- to twenty-year-olds to participate in elections. Nonetheless, much remains to be done.

There are two major plans presently before the nation: one would allow election-day registration for federal elections and the other, the Universal Voter Enrollment plan, would require the government to register voters in a door-to-door preelection canvass, much like those conducted in other na-tions. Both plans would reduce qualifying criteria (age, residency, and so forth) to the bare minimum.

Registration improvements do not excite popular interest. They are basically technical concerns that, while of enormous significance to the operation of a democratic polity, are fully appreciated only by the politi-cians who must introduce the changes. Many elective office holders fear the redefinition through registration reform of an electorate with which they now feel comfortable. Nonetheless, change will have to come through some type of elite bargaining, a difficult avenue through which to achieve anything of fundamental consequence.

Changing the Way in Which a President Is Elected. Electoral-college reform serves as an example of an area—the manner in which presidents are elected—with which there has been chronic dissatisfaction. It can be argued that the electoral college has never worked as intended and that since the ad-vent of the two-party system in 1800, an event the Founding Fathers did not envision, the electoral college has been unable to serve the functions for which it was created. Today, the electoral-college system appears to many to be out of step with democratic traditions and contemporary values. It is also open to abuse, and this is a subject of concern.

In chapter 4 Lawrence D. Longley, an expert on the operations of the electoral college, identifies five basic problems implicit in the process: the "faithless" elector; the winner-take-all electoral vote at the state level; the equal representation of states (two electoral votes per state) regardless of size within the electoral college; contingency plans for selecting a president if the electoral-college vote is indecisive; and the uncertainty that the winner of the popular vote in presidential contests will also win the electoral-college vote. The electoral college adds a strange and poorly understood dimension to presidential contests.

Longley analyzes empirically and in depth the problems associated with the electoral college and the strengths and weaknesses of the four major

plans—the automatic, proportional, district, and direct-vote proposals—put forward as reform alternatives.

Support for fundamental alterations in, or a replacement of, the
electoral-college system appeared to be increasing up to 1970. Since then,
although there has been activity, no changes have been instituted. Reform
would involve amending the Constitution, a procedure that is not invoked
frivolously. There is considerable uneasiness with the present system, and
popular opinion (as measured by the polls) appears to support modifying it.
Building a coalition behind electoral-college reform with the intensity and
concern necessary to bring about significant change is a difficult undertaking. It may take a single, critical abuse of the electoral-college system to
mobilize the public. Meanwhile, the system is likely to continue much the
same as in the past.

Issues and Institutions in Contemporary Reform

The chapters previously mentioned deal in one way or another with the mass
public, their perceptions of the political system, the changes in the electorate
and the manner in which it relates to the polity, and some of the institutional
arrangements that structure this relationship and the public's direct impact on
political decisions. Another related aspect of reform deals with the concerns
relevant to significant institutions that serve important democratic purposes.
These include the political party and the manner in which it performs its functions; the process through which presidents are nominated; the manner in
which campaigns for public office are conducted, especially who pays for
these campaigns and how; and the way in which the Congress operates in
responding to the public will. Each will be addressed in turn.

Reforming the Political Parties. After an organizational and institutional
stability that lasted for more than a century, political parties have begun to
undergo what could turn out to be drastic changes. This has occurred mostly in the last decade. Based on Dennis's analysis, it could perhaps be said
that no institution was more in need of reform. Party structures appeared to
be archaic, out of touch with modern concerns, and threatened by a host of
new developments. These include a changing electorate (as detailed in
chapter 1); the rise of "single-issue" politics; the advent of Political Action Committees (PACs) and their increasingly significant role in American
politics; the new technology of campaigning; the increasing significance of
the media; the popularity of candidate-centered organizations and campaigns; and, most ominously, the continuing loss of public support (as
shown in chapter 2). To many, the parties seemed unresponsive to the
public will.

The parties have made an effort to improve. Many believe that the parties' very existence as a vital force in American politics depends on their ability to adapt to the new and basically hostile environment in which they must compete. The parties have made an effort to reform their procedures in order better to serve their constituencies.[7] In fact, the 1970s were years of constant experimentation and change for both the major political parties.[8] The approach taken by the Democrats to the modernization of their procedures was quite different from that of the Republicans.[9] Exactly how the parties changed, and the implications of these new departures, is the subject of chapter 5 by Charles Longley.

Longley examines changes in four areas: party rules, party law, party finance, and the representativeness of party elites. He details the structural and policy-implementing experimentation within the parties. He pays particular attention to such changes as the institution of a party charter to govern all party activities and the creation of midterm policy conventions within the Democratic party, and he attempts to assess the impact of these and other reforms on the party system.

Longley concludes that in some areas (the representativeness of party elites or the manner in which the national party functions) little significant change is discernible. Yet a decade of turmoil has left its impact, primarily in the tentative move toward nationalization of the parties. If this trend should continue—and the chances are that it will—the traditional emphasis in American politics on a state-based, loose, and uncohesive organizational structure will be reversed. Whether a stronger national party will better serve the needs of a representative democracy and reinstitute the party as a critically significant force in American life has yet to be shown.

Selecting a Presidential Nominee. David, in chapter 6, calls on his long experience in analyzing presidential-selection procedures to place the recent party reforms in historical perspective.[10] He reviews the evolution of nominating practices from the Antimasons' introduction of the national convention through the critical election year of 1968. He develops the background of major questions concerning nominations, such as the controversies over apportionment formulas, the infighting over credentials and standards of party loyalty, the generally unassertive role of national parties in nominating politics, and the use and subsequent decline of presidential primaries, which have increased in importance once again in the post-1968 period.

With the work of the McGovern-Fraser commission, in particular, the rules governing presidential nominations within the Democratic party were completely rewritten. As a consequence, the power distributions within the party were reshuffled, with the dislocations that ensued causing a great deal of bitterness within the party ranks.[11]

David traces the work of the major reform commissions and evaluates the implications of the changes they introduced for the operations of primary and caucus selection procedures and in producing a streamlined national convention.[12] He pays particular attention to the most recent of the reform bodies, the Winograd commission, that introduced a new set of rules to govern the 1980 nominations. Among other things, an attempt was made to shorten the nominating season and to raise the level of support a candidate needed before he could claim any national-convention delegate votes.

The Winograd commission's proposals were controversial, although not for the same reasons as those of their predecessors (such as the McGovern-Fraser and Mikulski commissions' recommendations). Basically, it was argued that the new commission's rules attempted to close the nominating system, in effect repudiating the work of the earlier reformers. Be that as it may, the ability of the Winograd commission, backed by the Carter administration, to enact the rules it preferred demonstrated the power of the national party to control the most important aspects of presidential-nomination procedures. This development may be the most fundamental single change to emerge from the politics of the reform era.

David also evaluates the more limited reforms in the Republican party and assesses potential congressional action on questions affecting presidential nominations. Many who desire a more standardized set of nominating procedures—in their eyes, a more rational system—are looking to Congress for help. Congressional initiatives in this area would be a new, and not totally welcome, departure for the federal government.

David concludes by suggesting that experimentation with convention procedures and presidential-nominating forms is likely to continue into the foreseeable future. There is no consensus in sight at present as to what would best serve the interests of the party, its members, or the nation.

Financing Campaigns. A revolution in campaign-finance practices has occurred over the last decade. Spurred by the Watergate revelations, particularly those concerning the seemingly inexhaustible funds available to the Nixon presidency for campaign and other purposes, the laws regulating the use of money to seek federal elective office have been overhauled. A number of changes thought impossible a decade ago are now federal law. A Federal Election Commission has been created to oversee the financial operations of campaigns, stringent new reporting regulations have been introduced and enforced, spending limits have been placed on individual and group contributions and on campaign expenditures, and, most significant of all, federal funding is now available to subsidize presidential candidates in prenomination and general-election races.

In chapter 7 Jacobson reviews these developments. He analyzes the limits placed on campaigns; the reasoning behind, and partisan debate over, the changes; the social and political ramifications of the new departures; and the likely course of future reform. In the process, he points out the rise of new and unexpected funding agents—the Political Action Committees (PACs)—that have caused concern for many legislators.

The 1970s were a decade of swift and unprecedented change in political-financing practices. The reforms introduced, as Jacobson shows, did not resolve all the problems and, in fact, created new ones in several areas. Nonetheless, the reforms are popular and do represent an improvement over the old practices. There will be pressure in the 1980s for the Congress to expand federal financing to House and Senate elections (a move they have resisted) and to limit the increasingly influential role of the PACs. There will also be a call to extend government funding to state elections. On the other hand, many legislators and interest groups can be expected to work through the legislative process in an attempt to weaken the role of the Federal Election Commission and to prevent any further extensions of the reforms. The fight will be carried out among legislative and interest-group elites, with relatively little public or media attention (barring another political scandal). The implications, nonetheless, are broadly significant for the conduct of American campaigns. The last thing the majority of office holders want to do is to encourage competition through subsidized elections or limit their advantage in attracting campaign funds. Nonetheless, over time, it is likely that initiatives undertaken in the 1970s to subsidize campaigns and to control expenditures more tightly will be expanded.

Reforming the Congress. Another institution under continuing attack has been the Congress. Criticism of Congress is not new, but it has assumed a sense of urgency in the last decade. Since the imperial presidency has begun to fall into disfavor, critics have looked to the Congress to assume a more aggressive role in national leadership. To do so, the Congress would have to reform both its internal structures and its relationship to its constituents. Under the most favorable conditions, it is unlikely that Congress can exert effective national leadership. This is not its role. An improvement in its operating procedures and a modernization and, to an extent, democratization of its decision-making processes could, nonetheless, have beneficial results. The Congress could set some effective limits on the exercise of presidential power as well as making itself a more effective partner in national policy making. Such changes could increase its public esteem.

There has been movement in these directions. Davidson, in chapter 8, reviews the background of change and the forces working to restructure an institution often perceived as "sleazy" and "irresponsible." A number of reforms have already been instituted, and Davidson argues that these are formidable and that Congress may be our most changed institution. Membership, structures, procedures, and staffs have all been altered in one way or another. As a consequence, much of the common wisdom about the Congress and its operation needs rethinking.

The "two Congresses" Davidson talks about represent the dichotomy between institutional forms and pressures, on the one hand, and individual activities and constituency pressures on the other. He discusses the changes in both and the reasons for these changes. Institutionally, Congress has seen modifications in its workload, in the proliferation of committees and subcommittees, in the expansion of staff bureaucracies, and in the democratization of the House and Senate in reaction to the seniority system.

In relation to its membership pressures (and, not incidentally, to the decline of the political party as a force in campaigns), Congress has seen the rise of the "incumbency party"—the ability of congressmen to maintain themselves in office—through the increasing emphasis on a constituency-service role for members. The prospect of a more assertive Congress on national-policy questions would mean tension between a congressman devoting his energies towards educating himself on national-policy questions and one fulfilling errand-boy functions for his constituents. The pull in competing directions has led to disillusionment and exhaustion among members and may be the reason that voluntary retirements have increased until they now constitute the chief source of turnover in Congress.

Davidson concludes by suggesting that the pressures between legislative tasks and constituent errand-running place congressmen in an untenable situation. The job required of the congressional office holder may exceed human capabilities.

This problem is one of many that Congress must begin to come to grips with in future decades. The institution will continue to change. The pressures will continue to increase. And the public's expectations are, if anything, likely to become more demanding and harder to satisfy. Congress can play an increasingly important role in American politics. To do so, however, it will first have to resolve the tensions implicit in its representative role.

Problems with Reform. This book concludes on a properly cautionary note. The arguments advanced by Janda in chapter 9 could apply to any area of contemplated reform. In this case, political parties are used to illustrate the potential pitfalls of change.

Janda has studied political-party organization cross-nationally. He finds that American parties are highly decentralized and organizationally ineffectual in comparison with parties in other nations. These results were anticipated (they fulfill the expectations held by political parties' scholars). Janda's contribution has been to show empirically how American parties compare with those in other nations. This, in itself, has been a singular achievement.[13]

The process can be taken one step further, however, and this is the point of Janda's chapter. If American parties are organizationally inchoate, would it not be reasonable to improve their operations and strengthen their organization in such a manner as to enable them better to execute their functions in a democratic society? In short, it would appear that they represent prime candidates for reform. In fact, the parties have been the object of numerous reform initiatives over the last decade.

It is at this point that Janda asks us to consider the implications of what we contemplate doing. Political "engineering," the desire to transform an institution to correspond better to idealized criteria, is rooted in Western culture. The problem, however, is that while the weaknesses of an institution may be evident, reformers often have a poor understanding of the causal factors within the environment that account for the conditions they find (that is, what social and political functions explain the ways in which the institution operates). Furthermore, reformers usually have inexplicit assumptions; they often hold broadly symbolic value positions that may be unrelated or even antagonistic to a realistic achievement of a political institution's goals. Since the factors conditioning an institution's performance may be poorly appreciated and the reform goals and value standards vague, the reforms, once enacted, may be ineffective or even counterproductive. In the latter case, the changes implemented could undermine, rather than improve, the institution's operations, in effect further weakening it—the opposite of what was intended.

Janda develops these themes in relation to political-party reform. He argues that recent party reforms have been anything but ineffective. In gaining adoption, however, they may actually have contributed to the continuing demise of the parties. In particular, Janda believes that the reforms have weakened the parties organizationally.

The reformers desired an issue-oriented party. A programmatic party must depend on a strong organizational base to be effective. Intraparty democracy and a decisive, independent party presence may well be incompatible.

In the same vein, many of the representational objectives sought by reformers appear to work against the centralization of authority needed for effective decision implementation. A "representative" party may not be compatible with the "consensual" party approach that has dominated American politics in response to the nation's social and cultural pluralism and its federated governing structures.

Janda sees the four theoretical reform objectives that he has developed as weakening the party fabric. In turn, he argues that the way to improve party performance is to maximize organizational strength and to centralize political power within the party structure to a far greater degree than has previously been the case. These changes, he believes, would lead to many of the social and political objectives sought by the reformers.

The argument is a powerful one. Reformers often do have a poor comprehension of the factors conditioning an institution's operations and of the ramifications of their own proposals. They may be blinded by the immediate problems they encounter, and the changes they advocate may do more harm than good. A cautious approach to reform is advisable. The next decade is likely to witness such an approach.

Environments change, and institutions and their roles in society must respond. As a need manifests itself, intelligent efforts directed toward the improved operating of an institution so that it better serves the society's democratic goals would appear a reasonable risk to take.

Conclusion

Reform movements have their own momentum. Times of robust activity are followed by long periods of seeming passivity. A single incident, volatile, dramatic, and well publicized, can set off a chain reaction of events that lead to a pressure for change. The modifications introduced in response to the public outcry may be merely cosmetic in effort to pacify the public and head off meaningful change. Or they can lead to fundamental and innovative efforts to restructure approaches to a problem. The problem dealt with, in turn, may be one of long-standing concern or it may be one that has received little immediate attention, the public having been drawn to the area by some incendiary event.

The United States has gone through a recent period of intense turmoil. Beginning in the late 1950s and early 1960s, and fueled by the discontent over the Vietnam War and Watergate, this tumultuous era came to a close in the mid-1970s (roughly terminating with the 1976 election). In a number of respects, these years could be compared to the political-reform phase of the Progressive Era of the early twentieth century (1900-1916). During the last fifteen years or so, fundamental changes have been implemented in the manner in which the nation transacts its political business. In many areas—the way in which presidents are chosen, government financing of campaigns, the redefinition (both attitudinally and legally) of the electorate, the continuing modernization of congressional forms—the changes have been substantial and will affect the manner in which future generations conduct their political affairs. In other areas—the inability to halt the slide in party fortunes, for example—the results have been less pronounced.

Reform in the 1960s and 1970s did not enjoy the intellectual and ideological cohesion or the strong public support from prominent figures found in the earlier period (in fact, in contrast with attitudes in the Progressive Era, most of the media commentators, political figures, and academicians tended to oppose it as an unwarranted disruption of the way in which political business should be done). Reform thrusts tended to creep up in scattered areas. The broad-scale assault on public institutions seen during the Progressive Era was also absent. The present-day reforms were supported and eventually enacted because they attempted to deal with real problems—from the abuse of official power to the feelings of impotence and rage on the part of people who felt unrepresented by their governing institutions. If there were a central theme in the contemporary reform period, it would lie in the efforts to open, democratize, and make more relevant the political institutions of major concern to the society.

The present era has not had the solid base of middle-class support that mobilized behind the Progressive movement's reform proposals. The tendency in the contemporary period has been to attack problems in important but isolated areas. Links among the reform publics have been tenuous or nonexistent. What these publics have shared is a strong disillusionment with business as usual, a desire to update and make more responsive institutions of vital concern to the American polity, and a vague, populistic belief that democratic government should, as directly as possible, represent the concerns of its citizenry. What has happened in the principal areas of concern, and what may need to be done, is the subject of this book.

The nation is presently in a period of respite with respect to change. After a period of explosive, if fragmented, change and of constant social and political upheaval, Americans are tired. From the mid-1970s on, there has been a post-Watergate depression. Attention has shifted. There is little continuing interest at present in reform. Not surprisingly, as economic conditions have worsened, the public's attention has turned to pocketbook issues: inflation, recession, a declining standard of living, and the cost of energy.

This is a period of passivity and regeneration. The present decade, barring some unforseen political scandal of national proportions, is likely to be a period of tinkering, making adjustments, and smoothing the operations of institutions transformed by the changes of the previous decades as well as a time for incremental advancements and extensions of reform programs. The changes introduced are likely to be modest, brought about by political elites in the absence of public concern. Nonetheless, should the problems continue—as they are likely to—and should discontent slowly grow (which is also likely), the seeds for a new reform era will have been planted. In time, these also will push to the surface, and a new period of social upheaval and political change will be in the offing.

Notes

1. Crotty (1977), pp. 60-69.
2. For different perspectives on these developments, see: William Havard, ed., *The Changing Politics of the South* (Baton Rouge: Louisiana

State University Press, 1972); Jack Bass and Walter De Vries, *The Transformation of Southern Politics* (New York: New American Library, 1977); Reg Murphy and Hal Gulliver, *The Southern Strategy* (New York: Charles Scribner's Sons, 1971); Robert Sherill, *Gothic Politics in the Deep South* (New York: Ballantine, 1969); and, for a baseline for comparison, V.O. Key, Jr., *Southern Politics* (New York: Alfred A. Knopf, 1949).

3. See Dennis (chapter 2, this volume).

4. See Kagay and Caldeira (chapter 1 this volume); Herbert Asher, *Presidential Elections and American Politics* (Homewood, Ill.: Dorsey, 1976); Norman H. Nie, Sidney Verba, and John Petrocik, *The Changing American Voter* (Cambridge, Mass.: Harvard University Press, 1976); and Richard G. Niemi and Herbert F. Weisberg, eds., *Controversies in American Voting Behavior* (San Francisco: W.H. Freeman, 1976).

5. See the Crotty, David, and Jacobson chapters (chaps. 3, 6, and 7) in this volume.

6. See the Charles Longley, David, and Janda chapters (chaps. 5, 6, and 9) in this volume.

7. Cornelius P. Cotter and John F. Bibby, "The Impact of Reform on the National Party Organizations: The Long-Term Determinants of Party Reform" (Paper presented at the Annual Meeting of the American Political Science Association, Washington, D.C., 1979.)

8. William Crotty, *Decision for the Democrats* (Baltimore, Md.: The Johns Hopkins Press, 1978).

9. Crotty (1977), pp. 255-261; Charles Longley, "Party Reform in the Republican Party" (Paper presented at the Annual Meeting of the American Political Science Association, New York, 1978); and Cotter and Bibby "The Impact of Reform on the National Party Organizations."

10. Paul T. David, Malcolm Moose, and Ralph M. Goldman, eds., *Presidential Nominating Politics in 1952*, 5 vols. (Baltimore: The Johns Hopkins University Press, 1954); and Paul T. David, Ralph M. Goldman, and Richard C. Bain, *The Politics of National Party Conventions* (Washington, D.C.: The Brookings Institution, 1960, 1964).

11. Crotty *Decision for the Democrats*; Crotty, "Building a 'Philosophy' of Party Reform" (Paper presented at the Annual Meeting of the American Political Science Association, New York, 1978); and Austin Ranney, "The Political Parties: Reform and Decline," in *The New American Political System*, ed. Anthony King (Washington, D.C.: American Enterprise Institute, 1978), pp. 213-247.

12. For differing assessments, see Jeane Kirkpatrick, "Representation in American National Conventions: The Case of 1972," *British Journal of Political Science* 5 (July 1975):265-322; idem, *Dismantling the Parties* (Washington, D.C.: American Enterprise Institute, 1978); Ranney, "The Political Parties: Reform and Decline"; and William Crotty, "Assessing A

Decade of Reform" (Paper presented at the Annual Meeting of the American Political Science Association, Washington, D.C., 1979).

13. Kenneth Janda, "A Comparative Analysis of Party Organizations: The United States, Europe, and the World," in *The Party Symbol*, ed. William Crotty (San Francisco: W.H. Freeman, 1980), pp. 339-358; and Kenneth Janda, *Political Parties: A Cross-National Survey* (New York: The Free Press, 1980).

References

American Political Science Association. *Toward A More Responsible Two-Party System*. New York: Rinehart, 1950.

Agranoff, Robert. *The Management of Election Campaigns*. Boston: Holbrook Press, 1976.

———— , ed. *The New Style in Election Campaigns*, 2nd ed. Boston: Holbrook Press, 1976.

Bickel, Alexander M. *Reform and Continuity*. New York: Harper and Row, 1971.

Boorstin, Daniel J. *Democracy and Its Discontents*. New York: Random House, 1971.

Broder, David S. *The Party's Over*. New York: Random House, 1972.

Commager, Henry Steele. *The American Mind: An Interpretation of American Thought and Character Since the 1880s*. New Haven: Yale University Press, 1950.

Crotty, William. *Political Reform and the American Experiment*. New York: Thomas Y. Crowell, 1977.

Crotty, William, and Jacobson, Gary C. *American Parties in Decline*. Boston: Little, Brown and Company, 1980.

Forcey, Charles. *The Crossroads of Liberalism: Croly, Weyl, Lippman and the Progressive Era, 1900-1925*. New York: Oxford University Press, 1961.

Hofstadter, Richard. *The Age of Reform*. New York: Random House, 1960.

———— . *The Idea of a Party System*. Berkeley: University of California Press, 1969.

Kolko, Gabriel. *The Triumph of Conservatism*. Glencoe, Ill.: Free Press, 1963.

Lazarus, Simon. *The Genteel Populists*. New York: McGraw-Hill, 1974.

Noble, David W. *The Paradox of Progressive Thought*. Minneapolis: University of Minnesota, 1958.

Olson, Mancur. *The Logic of Collective Action*. Cambridge, Mass.: Harvard University Press, 1965.

Pateman, Carole. *Participation and Democratic Theory*. Cambridge: Cambridge University Press, 1970.

Pomper, Gerald, ed. *Party Renewal in America*. New York: Praeger, forthcoming.

Rubin, Richard L. *Party Dynamics*. New York: Oxford University Press, 1976.

Schattschneider, E.E. *Party Government*. New York: Holt, Rinehart and Winston, 1942.

_____ . *The Semisovereign People*. New York: Holt, Rinehart and Winston, 1960.

Stewart, John G. *One Last Chance*. New York: Praeger, 1974.

Wiebe, Robert H. *Businessmen and Reform*. Cambridge, Mass.: Harvard University Press, 1962.

_____ . *The Search for Order: 1877-1920*. New York: Hill and Wang, 1967.

Wilson, R. Jackson. *In Quest of Community: Social Philosophy in the United States, 1860-1920*. New York: John Wiley and Sons, 1968.

Part I
The Electorate:
Its Contemporary
Status and
Efforts at Redefining
Its Influence

1

A "Reformed" Electorate? Well, at Least a Changed Electorate, 1952-1976

Michael R. Kagay and
Greg A. Caldeira

Introduction

In this chapter we examine the stability and change of partisan attitudes in presidential elections from 1952 through 1976. For the 1952-1972 period, the results of each of the six presidential elections are decomposed into a series of attitudinal components, which are then analyzed with respect to the following questions:

1. Which considerations have been on the voters' minds most frequently?
2. Which considerations have benefited which of the political parties?
3. On which considerations has the electorate experienced the most partisan polarization?

Following this analysis, we present some findings from the 1976 presidential election. Finally, we decompose the presidential vote during the entire 1952-1976 period into long- and short-term political forces and comment on the implications for the future.

The findings of this chapter provide a sketch of both the statics and the dynamics of electoral choice over these twenty-four years. They constitute a people's portrait of this era in American politics—the subjective reactions of members of the mass public to events, leaders, issues, and other objects on the political landscape. These results should provide a basic factual backdrop for the other chapters in this book. Changes in institutional forms and formats must, of course, contend with the changes in presidential voting behavior that have occurred in the past twenty-four years.

We are grateful to the following colleagues for suggestions and assistance at various stages: Roberta S. Cohen, Victor Crain, William J. Crotty, Jan Juran, Stanley Kelley, Jr., David Seidman, Donald E. Stokes, Edward R. Tufte. The Woodrow Wilson School of Public and International Affairs of Princeton University provided funds to support the data analysis. The data utilized were made available by the Inter-University Consortium for Political and Social Research (ICPSR) and originally collected by the Survey Research Center and the Center for Political Studies of the Institute for Social Research (CPS/ISR), University of Michigan. Arthur Miller graciously provided us with data that had been excluded from the ICPSR's tapes of the 1972 election. Parts of this chapter come from a paper presented at the 1975 Annual Meeting of the American Political Science Association, San Francisco, California.

The Six-Component Model Revisited

Since 1952 the Survey Research Center and the Center for Political Studies of the University of Michigan have recorded the "partisan attitudes" of respondents in each of their national preelection surveys. These partisan attitudes are elicited by a series of eight open-ended questions that invite respondents to cite their "likes" and "dislikes" with respect to each major political party and each presidential candidate. Using probes, interviewers record and then coders retain up to five positive and five negative reactions to each of the four stimuli, for a maximum of forty possible comments. Coders assign each response to one of several hundred master themes according to the substance of the remark.

In 1958 Stokes and his colleagues introduced the "six components" of electoral decision.[1] In this approach the multitude of individual master codes or themes are sorted and reduced into six broadly based substantive categories:

1. *attitude toward the Democratic candidate*, including all references to the candidate's personality, background, experience, leadership abilities, character, competence, and role as party representative;
2. *attitude toward the Republican candidate*, including similar references;
3. *attitude toward group benefits*, including all references to economic and social groupings, group threats, group ambitions, group vulnerabilities, and group connections;
4. *attitude on domestic-policy issues*, including all references to domestic conditions, economics and welfare, and civil rights, and to philosophies of government such as liberalism and conservatism;
5. *attitude on foreign-policy issues*, including all references to foreign affairs and to the themes of war, peace, and defense;
6. *attitude toward party performance and management of government*, including references to efficiency versus corruption, profligacy versus thrift, previous administrations as teams, and other remarks suggesting that one or another party would be better at running the government.

For each of these categories, one can compute a "net partisan score" for each voter. The number of comments favorable to the Democrats or their candidate is added to the number unfavorable to the Republicans. Similarly, the number of comments favorable to the Republicans or their candidate is added to the number unfavorable to the Democrats. Subtraction of one sum from the other yields the net partisan score. The sign of each component's score indicates which party an individual favored with respect to a particular class of considerations; the size of each score indicates how much the individual, on balance, favored that party. Potentially, scores on a component can range from $+20$ to -20; the effective range of each component has usually been about one-third of that distance. A score of 0 indicates either that none of the individual's likes and dislikes fell into a particular category or that the number of his comments favoring one party exactly equalled that of his comments favoring the other party. Thus, a score of 0 represents the point of partisan neutrality—a meaningful origin for each of the six attitudinal scales. Each scale also has an easily interpretable metric—the number of expressed attitudes favoring one party over the other.

Once one has created the six component scores for each respondent, several descriptive statistics are of interest. The sheer frequency of reference to each component, for instance, constitutes an indicator of the salience of each class of considerations vis-à-vis other considerations; it suggests which of the broad topics dominated the voters' minds. The mean net score of a component indicates which party was, on balance, favored by the electorate as a whole, and by how much. The dispersion of a set of scores may serve as an indicator of partisan consensus versus partisan polarization of public attitudes.

One may also wish to talk about the weight of a class of considerations in the electorate's calculus or the relative impact of a component on the outcome of an election. This demands some technique for fitting an equation to the data—usually multiple regression analysis, but possibly another approach such as probit analysis. In regression analysis, the partisan choice of each voter, as revealed in the postelection survey, is coded either 0 or 1 according to political party and then is regressed on the six-component scores by the method of ordinary least squares. The linear probability equation, then, is:

$$Y = a + b_1X_1 + b_2X_2 + b_3X_3 + b_4X_4 + b_5X_5 + b_6X_6$$

where Y is the probability of voting Democratic, a is the constant term (always close to the neutral breakpoint of 0.5), each X_i is one of the six net partisan scores, and each b_i is the unstandardized weight appropriate to a component as determined by regression. Over the five elections of the 1952-1968 period, the R^2 (variance explained) of this model hovered around 0.55, and the actual proportion of individual votes correctly accounted for was about 88 percent of those voting. These figures dipped just slightly in 1972.

The regression coefficient indicates the increment in the probability of voting for a party that accrues from an individual's holding one additional net partisan attitude. Other statistics can be derived from these regression weights. The regression coefficient multiplied by the mean score of a component indicates the partisan advantage (in terms of percentage of the two-party vote) that a party derived from public attitudes about a particular consideration. The regression coefficient multiplied by a measure of dispersion indicates the effects of attitudinal polarization. In the following discussion, we shall use these transformed statistics as well as descriptive statistics.

**Which Considerations Have Been on
Voters' Minds Most Frequently?**

How salient are the major considerations with respect to one another at
each presidential election? Do these considerations remain stable in salience
or do they fluctuate across time? The most straightforward measure of the
cognitive salience of the six components is the sheer frequency of comments
made by respondents about each of the categories. (For the remainder of
this section, we use interchangeably the terms *salience, importance, prominence*, and *frequency of reference*.)

When pressed for partisan reactions to the current political landscape,
the average voter has usually volunteered nine or ten considerations that
have been on his or her mind. As a rule, over two-thirds of the voters expressed a total number of likes and dislikes that ranged between four and
fifteen. We now turn to the major categories or themes under which these
considerations can fall.

Overview: Candidates versus Issues

Figure 1-1 is a visual presentation of much of what we have found. For this
purpose we have summed the references to the two presidential candidates
as well as all references to policy issues, both foreign and domestic. The fre-
quencies are then presented as a percentage of all comments made to the
open-ended questions. It is apparent at a glance that in all three elections of
the earlier (1952-1960) period, presidential candidates were much more
salient than were policy issues. During the later (1964-1972) electoral
period, however, this gap seems to have closed until in 1972, for the first
time, issues as a whole superseded the presidential candidates in the public
consciousness.

We hasten to point out, of course, that the trend is not fully monotonic.
Issues were more important in the 1952 contest, for example, than in either
of the next two races. The stereotype of the issueless 1950s and the personal
figure of General Eisenhower can obscure the issue orientation of the 1952
campaign—when many voters, urged on by Democratic leaders, feared that
the New Deal might be dismantled. Within the second era, on the other
hand, candidates staged a slight comeback in salience in 1968.[2] On the
whole, however, our examination of the frequency with which various considerations were on the electorate's collective mind supports the following
generalization: a relatively candidate-oriented period spanning the 1952,
1956, and 1960 elections preceded a more issue-oriented era that encom-
passed the elections of 1964, 1968, and 1972. The high point of issue
salience during the entire period was in 1972, when a spurt in the partisan

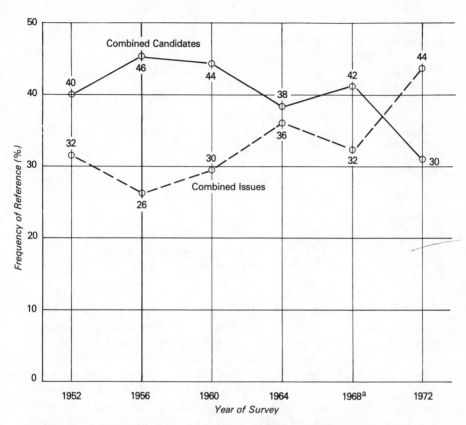

Figure 1-1. Relative Salience of Presidential Candidates and Policy Issues

relevance of foreign issues was added to the already heightened salience of domestic issues. Table 1-1 presents our findings in more detail.

Presidential Candidates: Reduced Dominance

Candidates' images were highly salient throughout the 1952-1972 period. Considerations of personality, character, experience, competence, and the like were much on the minds of voters. In comparing the two candidate components for each of these years, it is striking that—without fail—the more salient candidate proved to be the winner of the contest. Since three of the victors were incumbent presidents, this finding is not particularly surprising: the incumbent enjoys enormous advantages in name recognition,

Table 1-1
Frequency of Reference to Each of the Six-Component Themes

Component	1952	1956	1960	1964	1968[a]	1972
Democratic candidate	17.2%	18.4%	24.8%	22.1%	20.4%	14.6%
Republican candidate	22.9	27.2	19.5	16.1	21.1	15.7
Group benefits	9.9	13.4	11.6	10.9	9.6	13.2
Domestic issues	22.8	17.4	20.2	28.4	23.7	28.1
Foreign issues	8.7	8.7	9.3	7.8	8.5	15.9
Party management	18.5	14.9	14.7	14.7	16.7	12.5
Total	100%	100%	100%	100%	100%	100%
Average number of comments per voter	10.2	9.2	8.9	9.1	10.4	8.6
Sample size (voters only)	1181	1266	1406	1111	911	827

[a]Wallace voters are excluded from the 1968 figures; effect is minimal.

press coverage, and the visibility of his actions. In each of the other three contests, however, when neither candidate was an incumbent president, the eventual winner was also the more salient figure. In two of these three contests, of course, one candidate was an incumbent vice-president, but in both cases he proved to be the less salient figure and eventually lost the contest. It would appear, therefore, that achieving a higher public salience than one's opponent is, if not a prerequisite, then at least a concomitant of winning the presidency. In political contests at lower levels this phenomenon probably involves sheer name recognition; at the presidential level it surely includes much more—public familiarity with a candidate's achievements, stature, and promises.[3]

Issues of Public Policy: Increased Importance

Throughout this twenty-year period, domestic issues—wages, jobs, taxes, welfare, civil rights, and the like—were uniformly more salient than foreign issues, such as war and peace. In fact, in each of the five contests from 1952 through 1968, the foreign-issues component received the fewest references of any of the six components. That foreign affairs should be relatively remote from the electorate's consciousness even in 1952 and 1968, when U.S. soldiers were fighting bloody land wars in Asia, is perhaps not so surprising. A number of investigators have commented on the lack of "centrality" of foreign events to citizens' day-to-day lives.[4] Citizens have fewer "reality checks" when it comes to distant events. Even the most disturbing foreign issues, such as Vietnam, seldom coincide with major domestic cleavages. The bipartisanship of much of our foreign policy during the Cold War also served to depress citizens' awareness of partisan differences in the arena of foreign affairs. Because of all these influences, foreign events simply spring to mind less frequently when a voter cites his or her reasons for preferring one party or candidate to the other. It is possible, of course, that references to the candidates' trustworthiness and general capacities for leadership do reflect foreign concerns, even when these references seem entirely personal and unrelated to issues of policy.

The most remarkable feature of the foreign component is that, although its salience remained low and stable across five elections, its frequency of reference rose dramatically—almost doubling—to a high in the campaign of 1972. Study of the marginals for the master codes relevant to the foreign-issues component reveals that the sudden rise in the salience of foreign considerations in 1972 was stimulated mainly by the global diplomacy of Nixon and Kissinger—in Vietnam, China, the Soviet Union, and the Middle East. Senator McGovern's campaign also broke with the usual bipartisan consensus in the foreign field and made this area of policy more contentious than usual in 1972.

For the component of domestic issues, we observe what is probably a longer-term and more consistent trend. Beginning with the Johnson-Goldwater contest in 1964 and continuing through 1968 and 1972, references to domestic concerns appear to have reached a new and higher level. The salience of domestic issues in *each* of these three recent elections was higher than in *any* contest during the 1952-1960 period. To the extent that the frequency with which a consideration is expressed constitutes a reliable index of the importance of that consideration, issues of domestic policy have become more important since the early 1960s.

The steep climb in salience of domestic issues from the low point of this time series (1956) to the high (1964) is particularly dramatic, representing an increase in importance of more than 60 percent. Data from the 1956 contest figured prominently in Campbell et al. (1960), and data from the 1964 contest have been central to later "revisionist" analyses of the orientations and behavior of members of the mass public.[5] One can all too easily forget that the salience of domestic issues in 1952 approached that for 1968. We do, however, find some corroboration for a characterization of the late 1960s and early 1970s as a more issue-oriented period.[6] By the time of the 1964 contest, the domestic-issues component had become the single most salient of the six. Domestic issues maintained their preeminence during the next two contests in 1968 and 1972 as well. Thus, since the mid-1960s and early 1970s, voters have had more to say about domestic-policy issues than about any other single political object.

Group Benefits and Party
Performance: Steadier Salience

The salience of group considerations has been remarkably stable. Its range of fluctuation over time has been quite small, and its rank order in relation to the other five components has been the same at each election—second from the bottom. An inspection of the individual master codes relevant to the group component suggests that tension between "common people" and "big business" has been the major reference about groups during the 1952-1972 period. The staying power of these New Deal images is quite impressive. Such images have suffered only a minor displacement by group threats and group ambitions of more recent vintage, such as black power, feminism, the youthful counterculture, and ethnic revivalism.

Assessments of party performance and party management of government, as stated earlier, include themes of corruption versus efficiency, profligacy versus thrift, praise or blame of incumbents as a team, and similar judgments that one of the political parties is better suited than the other for running the government. The salience of such themes was highest in 1952, when Republicans emphasized the "mess in Washington"; among the six components that year, such considerations ranked third in importance. Their salience was lowest in 1972, when Nixon's reelection campaign under the Committee to Re-Elect the President went out of its way to avoid party ties and party rhetoric and when McGovern's candidacy appeared to break continuity with earlier Democratic "teams"; among the six components that year, references to party management ranked last in frequency. During the four contests between 1952 and 1972, however, the prominence of party performance remained remarkable in its steadiness, routinely ranking below the candidates and domestic issues but ahead of group benefits and foreign issues.

Which Considerations Have Benefited Which Party?

One might also think about stability and change in presidential elections in terms of the net partisan benefit accruing from each of the six components. Each of the six scores of the six-component model indicates the *direction* as well as the *intensity* of a voter's evaluations. It indicates *which party* he favored, on balance, and by *how much*. Aggregated across all voters, the arithmetic mean of each component indicates which political party, on balance, was favored by the electorate as a whole and by how much. These means answer the question, "In terms of this particular consideration, how much more was there to be said for one party than for the other?" Only as the value of a component's mean net score diverges either positively or negatively from zero, that is, from partisan neutrality, can a party be said to have benefited from a class of attitudes.

Overview: Candidates versus Issues

Of course, it is to be expected that the political objects that change the most from election to election—the candidates—should evoke the most changeable response from the electorate. Although party and group associations are relatively stable—with public-policy issues only somewhat less so—the personal attributes of the candidates introduce strong short-term stimuli that can either reinforce or potentially modify the longer-term standing of the political parties. Moreover, enormous quantities of campaign resources are deliberately invested in communicating to the mass public the attributes of each candidate. Much of the dynamism that we observe in American presidential elections, according to both academicians and practical campaigners, accrues from public reaction to the images of candidates.[7]

Figure 1-2 illustrates this well, presenting mean scores of the combined candidate components and the combined issue components while omitting group benefits and party performance. We ignore sign—that is, which party benefited—folding each scale over on itself and considering simply the degree to which the electorate's evaluation diverged from neutrality. Evaluations of candidates do indeed fluctuate the most. There also appears to be a strong incumbency effect; each peak was achieved by an incumbent successfully running for reelection in a landslide year, whereas each trough records a more even match between two nonincumbents. This is eloquent testimony to the image-making power of incumbent presidents.

Figure 1-2 also shows the rise in issue advantage during the mid-1960s. The electorate's distance from partisan neutrality on all issues of public policy doubled between the 1952-1960 era and the 1964-1972 era. To ignore the beneficiary and to focus just on the amount of the benefit, as figure 1-2 does, reveals a clear change in the impact of issues. Each of the three points in the later period is higher than *any* of the points in the earlier period. This rise is due in large measure to the fact that domestic issues and foreign issues became mutually reinforcing in their partisan advantage. In the earlier three elections the two sorts of issues favored *opposite* parties; in the second three elections both kinds of issues favored the *same* party—the Democrats in 1964 and the Republicans in 1968 and 1972.

Table 1-2 presents the mean score of each of the six components for each election year. There are revealing patterns in these data. Some considerations have consistently benefited a particular party in a way that enables us to draw a stable profile of partisan images— the strengths or abilities of each party as fixed in the public mind.[8] Some other considera-

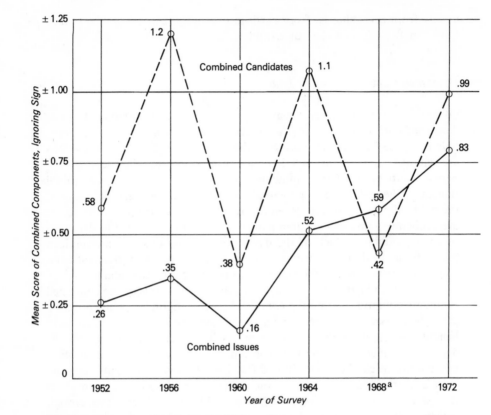

Figure 1-2. Distance of Candidate and Issue Evaluations from Neutrality

tions appear to have been more dynamic, benefiting first one of the parties and then the other as the electorate responded to the current political atmosphere. To chart these mean values over the six elections is to sketch a portrait of partisan images over the recent historical era. These values help to indicate *why* elections turned out as they did.

Transformation of these mean scores aids discussion. The mean of a component multiplied by the unstandardized multiple regression coefficient of that component yields the value that we refer to as net partisan advantage or the vote shift.[9] One may conceptualize the regression coefficient in terms of an "if . . . then" statement: if the score of a component changes by one attitude, then the vote will change by an amount equal to the regression coefficient. In a sense, multiplication of a component's regression coefficient by the mean score of that component actualizes the "if" statement. At the aggregate level the resulting value represents the percentage of the two-

Table 1-2
Mean Net Evaluations within the Six-Component Categories

Component	1952	1956	1960	1964	1968[a]	1972
Democratic candidate	+0.349	-0.034	+0.373	+0.724	-0.049	-0.551
Republican candidate	-0.927	-1.176	-0.753	+0.353	-0.373	-0.443
Group benefits	+0.711	+0.879	+0.698	+0.749	+0.641	+0.742
Domestic issues	+0.268	+0.187	+0.137	+0.442	-0.175	-0.324
Foreign issues	-0.531	-0.533	-0.295	+0.076	-0.411	-0.502
Party management	-0.907	-0.231	-0.256	+0.055	-0.402	-0.193
Overall mean	-1.036	-0.908	-0.094	+2.398	-0.768	-1.271
Sample size (voters only)	1181	1266	1406	1111	911	827

Note: Positive values denote a pro-Democratic balance; negative values represent a pro-Republican balance.
[a]Wallace voters are not included in the 1968 figures.

party vote shifted as a result of public attitudes toward a consideration. At the individual level the value represents the increment in the probability of the average elector's voting for a party. Thus the transformation encompasses the degree to which public attitudes diverge from neutrality as well as the degree of importance that a class of considerations has in the electorate's voting calculus. Most important, it rescales the mean values into a more interpretable metric; instead of stating the fraction of an attitude that a party was, on balance, benefited, we may discuss the actual portion of the two-party vote shifted by those attitudes. These transformed values ($b \cdot \bar{X}$) are discussed next.

The Presidential Candidates: Often a Republican Edge

Figure 1-3 reveals the considerable popular appeal of Republican candidates over this twenty-year period. With the exception of the Goldwater debacle, Republican presidential candidates have proved of greater help to their party's fortunes than Democratic candidates have been to their own party's standing at the polls. Eisenhower's 1956 candidacy dominates the series; the General's image and personal qualities swung almost 8 percent of the total vote to the Republican column in that year. But in his three national campaigns Nixon moved, on balance, beween 2 and 6 percent of the vote in the Republicans' direction, in each case a better personal showing than that of his Democratic rival.

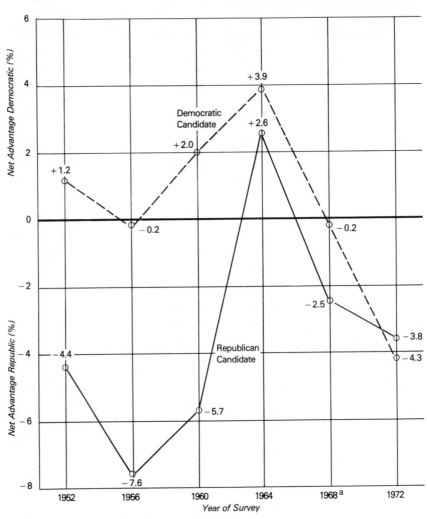

Figure 1-3. Partisan Advantage ($b \cdot \overline{x}$) Accruing From Candidate Evaluations

Undoubtedly minority political parties everywhere have a special incentive to put forward attractive candidates. At a disadvantage because of longer-term partisan forces affecting the electorate, the minority party can hope to capitalize only on short-term opportunities—a scandal or fissure within the majority party, some new issue that cuts across old cleavages, or the relative appeal of the candidates themselves. Of these variables, only the nature of the candidate is genuinely within the minority party's control.

One might also argue that it is in the nature not just of minority parties but of conservative parties everywhere to focus special attention on their candidate's capacities for leadership—moral reputation or administrative experience or ability to inspire faith, or perhaps prestige in the councils of foreign nations. Often at a disadvantage on domestic economic issues and on group associations as well, conservative parties may have a special interest in stressing the integrative aspects of political life. In the choice of their candidates and in the conduct of their campaigns, conservative parties have the greatest opportunities to focus public attention in this potentially beneficial direction. Certainly the popular rection to Goldwater's candidacy demonstrates the devastating consequences that can attend a campaign in which the minority party's candidate is also personally controversial.

The mass public's response to Democratic presidential candidates has been mixed, as indicated in figure 1-3. Only three of the six Democratic candidacies under examination have stimulated more positive than negative evaluations from the public. Stevenson in 1956 and Humphrey in 1968 evoked approximately as many "cons" as "pros." McGovern in 1972 actually helped to shift more of the total vote into the Republican column than did President Nixon himself! McGovern's candidacy proved even more catastrophic for the Democrats than Goldwater's did for the Republicans in 1964.

The corollary to the argument previously advanced is that it may be an occupational hazard of liberal parties everywhere to offer the more divisive candidate. Usually activists, often pressing for unsettling or at least novel programs and perhaps associated with salient domestic conflicts and contentious groups as well, liberal candidates should perhaps be expected to stimulate more mixed reactions than their conservative rivals. Throughout the entire period examined here, only Johnson's appeal in 1964 even approaches that usually enjoyed by Republican hopefuls—and Johnson, unusually for a Democrat, ran in that campaign as a "consensus" candidate, president of "all of the people," against a controversial Republican. When the Democrats have won, as in the campaigns of 1960 and 1964, their candidate has definitely helped, but none appears to deserve quite the personal credit for his party's victory that Republican winners can usually claim.

Issues of Public Policy: The Democrats
Upstaged during the Nixon Years

Democrats have enjoyed a traditional advantage among the mass public when matters of domestic public policy are at stake. From 1952 through 1964 the public consistently rewarded the Democrats as the party of economic prosperity, social security, and concern for the welfare of the common man. The high point of Democratic advantage occurred in 1964 when Goldwater took explicit issue with many of these domestic accomplishments, thereby increasing the salience of such concerns and allowing the contest to be fought on terrain favorable to the Democrats. In the two following presidential elections, however, the Democrats were clearly upstaged in domestic-policy matters. In both 1968 and 1972 it was the Republicans who, on balance, gained votes from domestic issues. In fact, Goldwaterite deviationism in 1964 may simply represent a temporary disturbance in a secular trend that has benefited the Republicans. It is tempting to see in figure 1-4 an almost steady twenty-year decay in the evocative power of Depression-related themes and a concomitant rise of newer domestic issues that cut across the aging cleavages of the New Deal and that worked increasingly to the advantage of the Republicans. From the mid-1960s on, the public's evaluations actually crossed the neutral point and began to favor the minority party.

Prophets of a new Republican majority saw in this trend evidence of and opportunity for partisan realignment.[10] Partisans of a continuing Democratic majority could argue, however, that the Nixon years may prove to be the disturbance in the long-term curve and that, as their own McGovernite deviationism fades from the party, the Democrats can possibly regain their traditional advantage in domestic matters.[11]

Evidence that such a rebound could occur is shown in the curve for foreign issues over this twenty-year period. In the case of foreign issues, the Republicans enjoyed the usual advantage, benefiting from their public image as a party of peace, preparedness, and diplomatic competence. But this advantage, too, seemed to decay steadily between 1952 and 1964. During the Johnson-Goldwater contest, the Democrats for the first time in this era succeeded in winning more votes because of foreign-policy issues than did the Republicans. Hopeful Democrats in the mid-1960s might have discerned in this event the culmination of a secular trend, a long awaited reversal of Republican advantage, and the beginning of Democratic hegemony in the area of foreign affairs.

But, as figure 1-4 shows, the trend did not persist but, in fact, reversed itself in the next election. In the 1968 contest the Republicans had regained their advantage in foreign issues, and by 1972 they had rebounded fully to their level of 1952. Nixon's gradual liquidation of the Vietnam War and his dramatic global diplomacy served to revive in the public mind some of the images of peace versus war from which the early Eisenhower administration had also benefited. This cycle of decay and revival, driven by events as well as by leadership, provides in the field of foreign affairs an example of what might occur in the area of domestic political issues. The Democrats, by virtue of events as well as of their own efforts, may likewise succeed in reviving previously beneficial public images and in regaining an edge in popular evaluation of performance on domestic issues.

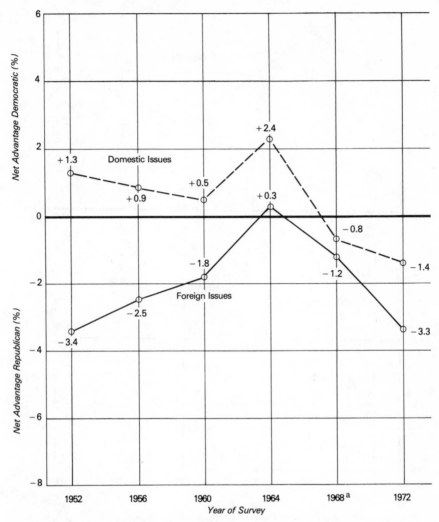

Figure 1-4. Partisan Advantage ($b \cdot \overline{x}$) Accruing from Issues of Public Policy

Group Benefits and Party
Performance: Steadier Advantage

In figure 1-5 we represent the partisan advantage that has accrued from
public images on themes of group benefits as well as of party management.
In each case public evaluation has been somewhat more consistent. Without
exception, the Democrats have benefited from group associations throughout the entire six-election period, netting between 2.5 and 6.0 percent of the
vote at each election because of their perceived image as benefactors of the

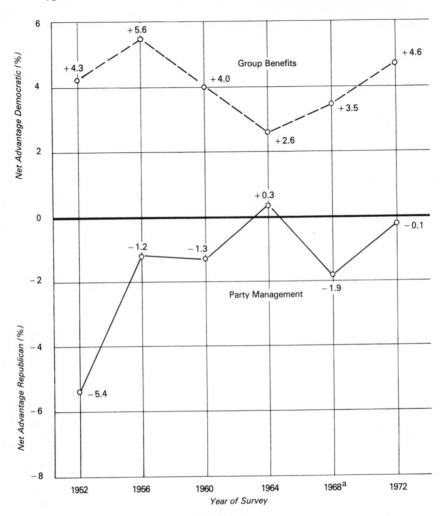

Figure 1-5. Partisan Advantage ($b \cdot \overline{x}$) Accruing from Group Benefits and Party Management

common man. One might suspect that group-benefit images favor the Democrats simply because that party's supporters are more inclined to think and talk about politics in terms of groups.[12] These images have been so persistent and so strong, however, that *in all six contests even Republican voters gave the edge to the Democrats on group-related themes.* This is the sole instance in our data in which the voters for one party consistently saw more to be said for the opposition than for the party they chose at the polls. Clearly the Republican party has suffered a long-term disadvantage in its group associations, and this negative image affects even its own voters. Moreover, this electoral liability has shown no sign of lessening during our period of study, even during the Nixon years.

The theme of party performance and party management of government has almost as consistently benefited the Republicans, but not by nearly as much. Republicans have enjoyed a traditional advantage in images of administrative competence, particularly in 1952, when alleged corruption in the federal government was a liability of the outgoing Truman administration—a debit that cost Governor Stevenson 5 percent of the vote. Conservative parties everywhere may have a better public image when it comes to running an efficient, thrifty, "businesslike" administration, staffed by men of conventional wisdom and seeming respectability.

Which Considerations Have Caused the Most Polarization among the Electorate?

Is there a relative consensus among voters in their evaluations of political objects? Or do voters sharply disgree as they survey the political landscape? Although it is the electorate's center of gravity that is important for the outcome of the election, the degree of their dispersion about this center is an additional index of some interest, one that alerts us to the *intensity* or *temperature* of the contest. The degree of partisan "heat" generated over a component influences the size of measures of association such as the partial correlation coefficient and the standardized beta weight.

The concept of *partisan polarization* versus convergence clearly expresses our meaning. This widely employed notion can be defined in several different ways, and some users do not define it at all rigorously.[13] In the context of our data, we conceive of polarization as the degree to which the two parties' voters disagree in their evaluations of political objects. We have calculated the interparty range as an indicator of such disagreement. This measure is the absolute difference between the mean evaluation reached by Democratic voters and the mean evaluation reached by Republican voters $(\bar{X}_D - \bar{X}_R)$.[14] The value of the interparty range for a component, such as domestic issues in 1964, can be thought of as the average distance separating all Democratic voters from all Republican voters on that consideration. The interparty range is expressed in the same units as the component, that is, the net number of likes or dislikes. This value may be compared with the interparty range for other components and for other election years.[15]

When Democratic voters and Republican voters evaluated a particular political object in a particular election year, how much attitudinal distance separated them? Do some political objects tend to evoke more partisan disagreement than others? And has partisan polarization remained stable over time, or have clear trends appeared?

Overview: Candidates versus Issues

In figure 1-6 we summarize our main argument in this section. We have combined the two candidate components and the two issue components into two summary scores. We have then computed the interparty range for each

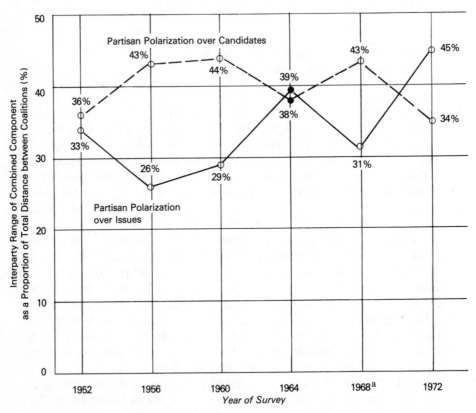

aWallace voters are not included in the 1968 sample.

Figure 1-6. The Relative Magnitude of Candidate Polarization and Issue Polarization

combination in each election year. In figure 1-6 these values are expressed as the proportion of the *total* distance that separated the two voting coalitions in each year.

In this six-election series, 1964 and 1972 are the only years in which the two voting coalitions were more polarized on evaluation of issues than they were on assessments of candidates. After the early 1960s the *salience* of issues heightened, first on the domestic front and then in the foreign sphere. By the late 1960s the Republicans regained their traditional advantage on foreign issues and finally succeeded in wresting advantage on domestic issues away from the Democrats. The result of increased salience and of the congruent or mutually reinforcing partisan advantage was that a relatively unusual amount of *issue distance* separated the two voting coalitions. This development generated much of the heat of these latter three presidential elections.

Presidential Candidates: Relative Polarization

Table 1-3 presents absolute interparty range for each of the six components in each of the six elections. Attitudes toward the two candidates are typi-

Table 1-3
Absolute Interparty Range as an Index of Partisan Polarization
$\overline{X}_D - \overline{X}_R$

Component	1952	1956	1960	1964	1968[a]	1972[b]
Democratic candidate	1.76	1.70	2.28	2.09	2.19	1.14
Republican candidate	2.03	2.25	2.17	1.74	2.52	1.47
Group benefits	1.23	1.60	1.41	1.08	1.31	1.23
Domestic issues	2.59	1.68	2.05	3.20	2.56	2.20
Foreign issues	0.91	0.75	0.92	0.81	0.75	1.26
Party management	1.97	1.25	1.41	1.28	1.49	0.45
Total Distance Between the Two Coalitions	10.48	9.23	10.23	10.18	10.83	7.75
Sample sizes						
(Democratic voters)	494	511	693	750	421	296
(Republican voters)	687	755	713	361	490	531

[a]Wallace voters are not included in the 1968 figures. This exclusion slightly exaggerates partisan polarization for 1968 shown above.

[b]Partisan polarization in 1972 may be underestimated due to a minor change in the format of the questions. The CPS added a filter to the series of likes-dislikes.

cally among the most polarized components of the vote for each election. This is not surprising since, as previously observed, images of the candidates are, as short-term forces, particularly salient and dynamic components of the vote. The candidates, as the principal combatants in the electoral battle, also embody in their persons a major portion of the tension and polarity that characterize the contest. The candidates stimulate a relatively high level of disagreement among the electorate, then, because the campaign makes the candidates especially salient and because these actors personify for the voter much of what the electoral conflict is about.

Issues of Public Policy: Differential Polarization

The most striking fact about issues is that the American electorate has been consistently more polarized on domestic issues than on foreign issues. In fact, the usual pattern at each election across the twenty years has been for public evaluations of domestic issues to be among the *most* polarized of all six components of the vote and for public attitudes on foreign issues to be the *least* polarized. Even when the great issues of war and peace and of the United States' international role have divided elites and have been part of the campaign's rhetoric—as in 1952, 1960, and 1968—there has been little partisan disagreement on such issues among the mass public. This generalization parallels our earlier findings about the relative salience of the two categories of issues. Foreign issues have not often sprung to mind when voters revealed their likes and dislikes about objects in the partisan political arena. Concerns about domestic issues, however, have usually ranked with the candidates themselves in frequency of mention.

These data do not support a simple picture of two level plateaus at different altitudes—an issueless politics of consensus in the 1950s versus a politics of turmoil in the 1960s. Nor is it correct to sketch an unbroken slope, climbing from valley to hilltop, over this period. There does seem to have been genuine change, however. There is marked difference in levels of polarization between the 1956 and 1960 contests, on the one hand, and the 1964 and 1968 elections, on the other. In particular, the difference between the nadir of domestic polarization in 1956 and its apex in 1964 is akin to a quantum leap. Nevertheless, one should not use the high and low points of the series to define either the slope or the two plateaus. A more refined picture would feature 1956 as a valley, surrounded by somewhat higher ground on both sides, and 1964 as a peak, surrounded by relatively lower terrain all around. Domestic policy polarization is clearly a variable whose value is subject to contextual and social influence—not a constant constrained by inherent capacities of the electorate.

Group Benefits and Party Performance: Steadier Consensus

The group-benefits and party-performance components tend to capture some of the longer-term forces at work among the electorate, and, accordingly, show somewhat steadier and less volatile levels of polarization—levels that are also of similar magnitude. In no election year during this period has either component been the most polarized of the six; in only one year has either theme been the least polarized component.

Strikingly, the level of polarization over group benefits has been inversely related to the level of partisan discord over domestic policies: when polarization on policy has risen, disagreement over group benefits has declined, and vice versa. This relationship promises insights into the interaction between the external political environment on the one hand and the electorate's internal conceptualization of politics on the other hand. It may be that when leaders are more than usually divided on issues of policy, the electorate becomes aware of this and voters are permitted and encouraged to see the connection between private troubles and public policies. When the gap on issues between leaders is small or ambiguous, however, many voters may fall back to a lower, group-related level of conceptualization—what Philip Converse has termed "ideology by proxy."[16]

In the area of party management, an interesting pattern also emerges. Conflict over party management has been high in each of the three contests between nonincumbents—1952, 1960, and 1968; disagreement has given way to greater consensus in each of the other three contests (1956, 1964, and 1972), when incumbents were running. Our interpretation is that when an incumbent is running, public disagreement is focused more personally on the president himself as the head of both party and government. In races between two nonincumbents, on the other hand, controversy tends to be directed more at the occupants of the White House during the previous four years and at the opposition's likelihood of doing better—themes that tend to be coded as "party management."

Recapitulation: 1952-1972

This report has charted some major considerations that enter into electoral choice in six presidential contests. We have treated the salience of each class of concerns, the partisan advantage reaped from each by the Democratic and Republican parties, and the degree of voter consensus or polarization over each. We have paid particular attention to the rise—or perhaps simply the return—of "issue politics" after the early 1960s. The findings present a moving picture of the American electorate in the 1952-1972 era, highlighting both the statics and the dynamics of mass political perceptions of presidential campaigns.

Several major findings concerning issue politics in presidential campaigns deserve reemphasis. First, during the 1952-1960 period, candidates were much more salient than were issues; but during the 1964-1972 era, the gap between these two considerations closed until in 1972, for the first time, issues overtook the presidential candidates in the public consciousness. The trend is not monotonic, of course; but our examination supports the generalization that a relatively candidate-oriented period, 1952-1960, preceded a more issue-oriented era, 1964-1972.

Second, in terms of the partisan advantage of the various considerations, over the twenty-year period issues of public policy also have come to have increased impact. In its considerations of domestic policies from 1952 through 1964, the public consistently rewarded the Democrats. The pinnacle of Democratic advantage on domestic issues came in 1964. In the next two presidential contests, however, it was the Republicans who profited from the public's response to domestic themes. Foreign issues, of course, have been the mainstay of the Republicans; the Goldwater debacle, again, was the exception to the rule. In 1964, 1968, and 1972 a single party reaped advantage from both types of issues.

In this six-election series, the greatest partisan polarization has usually been over the presidential candidates. But the 1964 and 1972 elections, both landslides, found the voting coalitions more polarized over issues than over candidates. Presidential candidates, as we noted, are the very embodiment of powerful and partisan short-term forces, and it follows that voters should usually manifest less consensus on these political objects.

Some Comments on the 1976 Presidential Election

Did the trends that we have isolated in the previous pages continue in 1976? We now make some observations about the partisan advantage reaped by each of the political parties from the six components of the vote in 1976. First, we pose a series of questions: Did the Democrats continue to suffer from public evaluations of their presidential candidates? Did the Republicans, as usual, receive considerable benefit from their nominee? Did the Democrats retain their almost invariable hold over the electorate's evaluations of their connections with groups? Did the Republicans hold their gains on the dimension of domestic policies, or did the Democrats regain their traditional advantage on that component? Did the GOP continue to reap votes from its handling of foreign-policy issues? Finally, which of the political parties profited from the public's evaluations of management of government?[17]

First of all, it is clear that the Democratic candidate, Jimmy Carter, did better personally than his two immediate predecessors, but not so well as his opponent, Gerald R. Ford. Governor Carter's candidacy, on balance, moved about 0.1 percent of the two-party vote into the Democratic column in November 1976; President Ford moved 2.5 percent into the Republican column. Once again, the GOP's nominee proved much more helpful in his capacity to draw votes than did the Democrats' nominee in aiding their drawing power. President Ford made one of the weaker showings by a Republican presidential nominee in the last twenty-four years. But, quite apart from his pardon of Nixon, his reputation for clumsiness, and his debate gaffe over Eastern Europe, Ford's decency and other personal attributes clearly helped him.

In 1976, group-related considerations continued to benefit the Democratic party; considerations of a group nature netted the Democrats 4.6 percent of the vote. Once again, the Democrats capitalized on their ties with some of the larger social and economic groupings in American society. The Democrats' advantage on this dimension remains a near constant in American presidential politics.

In 1976 the Democratic party regained its hold on the public's evaluations of issues of domestic policies. In 1968 and 1972, domestic considerations had benefited the GOP, but 1976 marked a return of Democratic partisan advantage on domestic issues. On balance, the Democrats gained 0.6 percent of the vote from these issues. Governor Carter clearly recognized the strategy needed to recapture the electorate's favor on domestic issues. Having stressed his image as an outsider and having avoided linking himself with previous party figures prior to the convention, nominee Carter—in the tradition of Democratic winners—in the end emphasized his connections with the "great men" and policies of the Democratic party—FDR, Truman, Kennedy, and LBJ.

Foreign issues netted the GOP about 0.4 percent of the two-party vote. Thus the Republicans continued to benefit from their reputation as the "party of peace and preparedness," although they gained fewer votes from this dimension than in any other year except 1964.

The Republican party barely continued to gain votes from the public's evaluations of its performance in management of government; the margin was narrow, but the GOP gained 0.1 percent of the vote from these evaluations. This finding is surprising in view of the events surrounding and preceding the 1976 presidential election: Watergate, Agnew's and then Nixon's resignation, Governor Reagan's near victory over President Ford in a heated intra-party battle. The voters do not seem to have punished the Republican party as a party as much as they might have in 1976 for the sins of Agnew, Nixon, and Watergate.

Perhaps the most impressive aspect of our analyses of these data from 1976 is their resemblance to the results from the elections of the Eisenhower era—1952, 1956, and 1960. In the presidential elections during the 1952-1960 period, the GOP also made gains from the voters' evaluations of its candidates, of its performance on foreign issues, and of its management of government. The Democrats in the three elections of the 1950s also made gains from their stands on domestic issues, and from group-related attitudes. As a result of a peculiar confluence of events and circumstances, the Democrats, behind Jimmy Carter, managed in 1976 to restore several familiar patterns—in political geography, in voting coalitions, and in the directionality of the six components of the vote.

Long-Term Versus Short-Term Political Forces

We have considered the various forces that affect the voters' evaluations of the candidates and parties. But for some purposes it is also useful to separate the impact of short-term and long-term forces on presidential voting. Thus we conclude this chapter with an analysis of data on long-term versus sho.t-term forces in presidential elections for the 1952-1976 period. To estimate the relative importance of these two sets of forces, we have decomposed the presidential vote for the twenty-four year period into a long-term effect (partisan identification) and a short-term effect (a summation of the six components). We have used stepwise regression, forcing partisan identification into the equation first. (The rationale for entering partisan identification first is that much theory and evidence indicate that it temporally precedes and therefore potentially structures the voter's short-term evaluations of candidates and parties.[18]) To operationalize the relative impact of the two forces on the vote, we use the percentage of the variance explained by each effect. The results are presented in figure 1-7.

For the first five elections during this period, the long-term component—partisan identification—explained more of the variation in voting than did the short-term forces; in 1956 and 1960 it accounted for more than twice as much variance as did the summary measure of the six components of the vote. In 1964 and 1968, partisan identification continued to dominate voting decisions, although the margin grew smaller. Finally, in the 1972 presidential election, short-term forces overtook partisanship as the more crucial determinant of the vote. The 1972 presidential election, as we have noted, was characterized by a cluster of major short-term forces—the "Eagleton incident"; the issue of McGovern's "competence"; non-traditional issues such as the "three A's" (acid, amnesty, and abortion); and the failure of McGovern to reunite the divided factions of the Democratic party after the strife-torn convention in Miami. Also during the late 1960s and the early 1970s fewer and fewer Americans claimed any tie to a political party.[19] Thus, after the 1972 presidential contest, one might well have questioned the continued relevance of traditional partisan attachments to voters' deci-

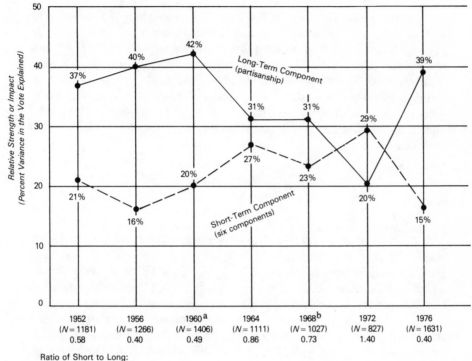

Model: Vote $= a + b_1 \cdot \text{PID} + \overset{7}{\underset{i=2}{\Sigma}} b_i \cdot x_i$

step 1: party identification
step 2: Stokes' six-component model

[a]1960 sample weighted due to panel decay; same for 1976.
[b]1968 sample includes Wallace voters with vote coded as "0".

Figure 1-7. Long-Term Forces versus Short-Term Forces on U.S. Voting Behavior

sions on presidential candidates. The election of presidents, one might have argued, could in the future be the outcome of a constellation of short-term forces, with few stabilizing influences (as there had been during the 1950s); the electorate could swing wildly back and forth between Democratic and Republican candidates, with party loyalty becoming largely irrelevant to choice.

In the 1976 election, however, we saw a return to a pattern of voting behavior much like that observed during the 1950s. Partisan identification explained more than twice as much variance in voting as did short-term forces. Thus, after a twenty-year period in which short-term forces gradually overtook partisan identification as a determinant of presidential voting, partisan attachments in 1976 once again dominated. Does this herald a return to 1950s-style politics? It depends. These results indicate, at least from our viewpoint, that elite behavior is a most important determinant of whether the electorate votes on the basis of partisanship. If political elites and, of course, the political issues and circumstances of the day present the American voter with the opportunity to use his or her partisanship as a reliable cue to choosing a president, then the results can look much like those reported for 1952-1960 and for 1976. But, if, as happened from 1964 through 1972—and as might happen again—elites and events prevent a congruent alignment of issues and parties, then the voters of the 1980s seem more than ready to seize on the short-term forces present in the election for their decisions.

Notes

1. See Stokes (1958) and Stokes, Campbell, and Miller (1958). The model also figures prominently in Campbell et al. (1960), chaps. 3, 4, 6, 19 (in the abridged version, chaps. 2, 3, 4, 16). Stokes's most recent report, which includes a methodological appendix, is "Some Dynamic Elements of Contests for the Presidency" (1966).

For recent variations on the six-component model, see Pomper (1975), chaps. 7, 9; Declercq, Hurley, and Luttbeg (1975); Kirkpatrick, Lyons, and Fitzgerald (1975); Asher (1976), chaps. 5, 6; Popkin et al. (1976); and Miller and Miller (1976).

2. The comeback in the salience of candidates in 1968 is apparent whether or not Wallace's voters are included in the sample. The six components, however, do not capture comments about Wallace himself as offered by either pro-Wallace or anti-Wallace voters. Our figures therefore underreport the salience of candidates in 1968. We can estimate the amount of underreporting since the Center for Political Studies did ask open-ended questions about Wallace that year. Respondents emphasized Wallace's personal qualities over his issue positions by a ratio of 1.66 to 1.

3. See, for instance, Hinckley (1970).

4. For example, see Converse (1964).

5. See, for instance, Field and Anderson (1969); Pierce (1970); RePass (1971); and Pomper (1972). Also see Pomper (1975), chap. 8.

6. See especially Pomper (1972) and Nie, Verba, and Petrocik (1976). But for some evidence that contradicts this characterization, see Brunk (1978).

7. For the work of practical campaigners, consult Shadegge (1964); Napolitan (1972); and Nimmo and Savage (1976).

8. See Trilling (1976).

9. This mode of calculating net partisan advantage was previously used by Stokes (1966). Our findings replicate his earlier ones and extend the time series. For some purposes it is also useful to separate the short-term

and long-term portions of partisan advantage and to recalculate the values with the effects of partisan identification removed. See Campbell et al. (1960), pp. 524-531. See the section of this chapter on long-term versus short-term political forces.

10. See, for instance, Phillips (1969).

11. See, for example, Stewart (1974); and Scammon and Wattenberg (1970).

12. See Converse (1964). Although Converse does not present data on levels of conceptualization separately for Democrats and Republicans, it is likely from the data he does array about levels of education—and from what we know about the relationship between education and partisanship—that Democrats are more inclined than Republicans to think of politics in terms of "groups."

13. The standard deviation has been used as a measure of polarization by Herbert McClosky, Paul Hoffman, and Rosemary O'Hara, "Issue Conflict and Consensus Among Party Leaders and Followers," *American Political Science Review* 54 (June 1960): 406-427; and by Philip E. Converse and Georges Dupeux, "The Politicization of the Electorate in France and the United States," *Public Opinion Quarterly* 26 (Spring 1962):1-23. Black and Rabinowitz (1974), creating a nine-component model from the "likes" and "dislikes" items, graph mean values for Southerners, non-Southerners, blacks, and whites in their discussion of "polarization" versus "convergence."

14. Campbell and his collaborators, although not speaking in terms of "polarization," do graph the attitudinal distances between groups of partisan identifiers using standard units; see Campbell et al. (1960), pp. 129-130. Pomper (1975, p. 158) offers similar data for his model in 1972.

15. Note that this measure of polarization captures only *partisan* conflict. Many important disagreements between social classes, the generations, or the sexes may be irrelevant to partisan politics, or may cut across current partisan cleavages or be deliberately skirted or obscured by the political parties. These factors act as constraints on the amount of *partisan* polarization that social groups can demonstrate.

16. See Converse (1964).

17. For some initial commentaries by others on the 1976 presidential election, see Miller (1977); Miller (1978); Miller and MacKuen (1978); and Miller and Miller (1977).

18. See, for instance, Fred I. Greenstein, *Children and Politics* (New Haven, Conn.: Yale University Press, 1965), chap. 4. See also the causal model in Arthur S. Goldberg, "Discerning a Causal Pattern Among Data on Voting Behavior," *American Political Science Review* 60 (December 1966):913-922; and Mark A. Schulman and Gerald M. Pomper, "Variability in Electoral Behavior: Longitudinal Perspectives from Causal Modelling," *American Journal of Political Science* 19 (February 1975):1-18.

19. See the following article and the literature on which it draws: Paul Abramson, "Generational Change and the Decline of Party Identification in America: 1952-1974," *American Political Science Review* 70 (June 1976):469-478.

References

Books

Asher, Herbert B. *Presidential Elections and American Politics: Voters, Candidates, and Campaigns Since 1952.* Homewood, Ill.: Dorsey Press, 1976.

Campbell, Angus; Converse, Philip E.; Miller, Warren E.; and Stokes, Donald E. *The American Voter.* New York: John Wiley and Sons, 1960.

Key, V.O., Jr. *The Responsible Electorate: Rationality in Presidential Voting, 1936-1960.* Cambridge, Mass.: Harvard University Press, Belknap Press, 1966.

Miller, Warren E., and Levitan, Teresa E. *Leadership and Change: The New Politics and the American Electorate.* Cambridge, Mass.: Winthrop Publishing, 1976.

Napolitan, Joseph. *The Election Game and How To Win It.* Garden City, N.Y.: Doubleday and Company, 1972.

Nie, Norman; Verba, Sidney; and Petrocik, John. *The Changing American Voter.* Cambridge, Mass.: Harvard University Press, 1976.

Nimmo, Dan, and Savage, Robert. *Candidates and Their Images: Concepts, Methods, and Findings.* Pacific Palisades, Calif.: Goodyear Publishing, 1976.

Phillips, Kevin P. *The Emerging Republican Majority.* New Rochelle, N.Y.: Arlington House, 1969.

Pomper, Gerald M. *Voters' Choice: Varieties of American Electoral Behavior.* New York: Dodd, Mead, 1975.

Scammon, Richard M., and Wattenberg, Ben J. *The Real Majority.* New York: Coward-McCann, Inc., 1970.

Shadegg, Stephen C. *How To Win an Election.* New York: Taplinger Publishing, 1964.

Stewart, John G. *One Last Chance: The Democratic Party, 1974-1976.* New York: Praeger Publishers, 1974.

Trilling, Richard J. *Party Image and Electoral Behavior.* New York: John Wiley and Sons, 1976.

Articles, Reports, and Papers

Black, Merle, and Rabinowitz, George. "An Overview of American Electoral Change: 1952-1972." Prepared for delivery at the Annual Meeting of the Southern Political Science Association, New Orleans, La., 1974.
_____ . "American Electoral Change: 1952-1972 (With a Note on 1976)." In *The Party Symbol*, edited by William Crotty. San Francisco: W.H. Freeman, 1980.
Boyd, Richard W. "Popular Control of Public Policy: A Normal Vote Analysis of the 1968 Election." *American Political Science Review* 66 (June 1972):429-449.
Brody, Richard A., and Page, Benjamin I. "Policy Voting and the Electoral Process: The Vietnam War Issue." *American Political Science Review* 66 (September 1972):979-995.
_____ . "Comment: The Assessment of Policy Voting." *American Political Science Review* 66 (June 1972):450-458.
_____ . "Indifference, Alienation, and Rational Decisions: The Effects of Candidate Evaluations on Turnout and the Vote." *Public Choice* 15 (Summer 1973):1-17.
Brunk, Gregory. "The 1964 Attitude Consistency Leap Reconsidered." *Political Methodology* 5 (Summer 1978):347-359.
Campbell, Angus, and Stokes, Donald E. "Partisan Attitudes and the Presidential Vote." In *American Voting Behavior*, edited by Eugene Burdick and Arthur Brodbeck. Glencoe, Ill.: The Free Press, 1959.
Converse, Philip E. "The Nature of Belief Systems in Mass Publics." In *Ideology and Discontent*, edited by David E. Apter. New York: The Free Press, 1964.
_____ . "Public Opinion and Voting Behavior." In *The Handbook of Political Science*, Vol. 4, edited by Fred I. Greenstein and Nelson W. Polsby. Reading, Mass.: Addison-Wesley, 1975.
Converse, Philip E.; Clausen, Aagge R.; and Miller, Warren E. "Electoral Myth and Reality: The 1964 Election." *American Political Science Review* 59 (June 1965):321-336.
Converse, Philip E.; Miller, Warren E.; Rusk, Jerrold G.; and Wolfe, Arthur C. "Continuity and Change in American Politics: Parties and Issues in the 1968 Election." *American Political Science Review* 63 (December 1969):1083-1105.
Declercq, Eugene; Hurley, Thomas L.; and Luttbeg, Norman. "Voting in American Presidential Elections: 1956-1972." *American Politics Quarterly* 3 (July 1975):222-246.
Field, John Osgood, and Anderson, Ronald E. "Ideology in the Public's

Conceptualization of the 1964 Election." *Public Opinion Quarterly* 33 (Fall 1969):380-398.

Hinckley, Barbara. "Incumbency and the Presidential Vote in Senate Elections: Defining Parameters of Subpresidential Voting." *American Political Science Review* 64 (September 1970):836-842.

Jackson, John E. "Issues, Party Choice, and Presidential Votes." *American Journal of Political Science* 19 (May 1975):161-186.

Kagay, Michael R., and Caldeira, Greg A. " 'I Like the Looks of His Face . . .': Elements of Electoral Choice, 1952-1972." Prepared for delivery at the Annual Meeting of the American Political Science Association, San Francisco, Calif., 1975.

Kelley, Stanley, Jr., and Mirer, Thad W. "The Simple Act of Voting." *American Political Science Review* 68 (June 1974):572-591.

Kessel, John H. "Comment: The Issues in Issue Voting." *American Political Science Review* 66 (June 1972):459-465.

Kirkpatrick, Samuel; Lyons, William; and Fitzgerald, Michael R. "Candidates, Parties, and Issues in the American Electorate: Two Decades of Change." *American Politics Quarterly* 3 (July 1975):247-283.

Margolis, Michael. "From Confusion to Confusion: Issues and the American Voter (1956-1972)." *American Political Science Review* 71 (March 1977):31-43.

Miller, Arthur H. "The Majority Party Reunited? A Summary Comparison of the 1972 and 1976 Elections." In *Parties and Elections in an Anti-Party Age*, edited by Jeffrey Fisher. Bloomington: Indiana University Press, 1977.

_____. "Partisanship Reinstated? A Comparison of the 1972 and 1976 U.S. Presidential Elections." *British Journal of Political Science* 8 (April 1978):129-152.

Miller, Arthur H., and MacKuen, Michael. "Informing the Electorate: Effects of the 1976 Presidential Debates." In *The Great Debates, Carter Versus Ford*, edited by Sidney Kraus. Bloomington: Indiana University Press, 1978.

Miller, Arthur H., and Miller, Warren E. "Issues, Candidates and Partisan Divisions in the 1972 American Presidential Election." *British Journal of Political Science* 5 (October 1975):393-434.

_____. "Ideology in the 1972 Election: Myth or Reality? A Rejoinder." *American Political Science Review* 70 (September 1976):832-849.

_____. "Partisanship and Performance: 'Rational' Choice in the 1976 Presidential Election." Prepared for delivery at the Annual Meeting of the American Political Science Association, Washington, D.C., 1977.

Miller, Arthur H.; Raine, Alden S.; and Brown, Thad A. "A Majority Party in Disarray: Policy Polarization in the 1972 Election." *American Political Science Review* 70 (September 1976):753-778.

Natchez, Peter B., and Bupp, Irvin C. "Candidates, Issues, and Voters." *Public Policy* 17:409-437.

Nie, Norman, and Andersen, Kristi. "Mass Belief Systems Revisited: Political Change and Attitude Structure." *Journal of Politics* 36 (August 1974):540-591.

Pierce, John G. "Party Identification and the Changing Role of Ideology in American Politics." *Midwest Journal of Political Science* 14 (February 1970):25-42.

Pomper, Gerald M. "From Confusion to Clarity: Issues and American Voters, 1956-1968." *American Political Science Review* 66 (June 1972):415-428.

Popkin, Samuel L.; Gorman, John W.; Phillips, Charles; and Smith, Jeffrey A. "Comment: What Have You Done For Me Lately? Toward an Investment Theory of Voting." *American Political Science Review* 70 (September 1976):779-805.

RePass, David E. "Issue Salience and Party Choice." *American Political Science Review* 65 (June 1971):389-400.

Stimson, James. "Belief Systems: Constraint, Complexity, and the 1972 Election." *American Journal of Political Science* 19 (August 1975):393-418.

Stokes, Donald E. "Partisan Attitudes and Electoral Decision." Ph.D. dissertation, Yale University, 1958.

_____ . "Some Dynamic Elements of Contests for the Presidency." *American Political Science Review* 60 (March 1966):19-28.

Stokes, Donald E.; Campbell, Angus; and Miller, Warren E. "Components of Electoral Decision." *American Political Science Review* 52 (June 1958):367-387.

Weisberg, Herbert, and Jerrold G. Rusk. "Dimensions of Candidate Evaluation." *American Political Science Review* 64 (December 1970):1167-1185.

2

Changing Public Support for the American Party System

Jack Dennis

Introduction

A recurring theme of the present era in American politics is that public confidence in institutions has declined. This general sense of malaise is said to have spread throughout the institutional structure of government. The people of America in the late 1970s show a marked unwillingness to accord leadership automatic acceptance and legitimacy. All of the major political institutions at the national level have suffered in terms of this erosion of positive public sentiment that began in the mid-1960s. Indeed, the political recession that started at that time—especially with the urban riots and the Vietnam War—continued through the Watergate period until today. This downturn in public trust has proved to be remarkably difficult for new leaders and reformers to reverse.

While this phenomenon of public mistrust is probably a good deal more complex and less well understood than is usually thought, it is obviously relevant to any consideration of the state of public sentiment toward any particular institution of government. The question of the present state of public legitimation of the American party system, for example, will be necessarily answered in part by the more generalized forms of alienation affecting the whole range of basic institutions of American society. The party system does not exist apart from the complex of interrelated institutions that make up the American political system. Thus, the apparent decline in public confidence in government over the past decade poses difficulties for analysis of the state and trends of public esteem or disregard for the parties. Such a depressed level of general institutional trust may well serve to mask what is possibly a longer-term and more fundamental state of decay of the political party system.

In earlier work, going back to 1964, I have argued that the political party system has indeed suffered a long-term erosion of positive public feeling. I have proposed that at the most basic level the parties have been

This is a revised version of a paper presented at the Conference on Political Parties in Western Societies, Northwestern University, September 21-22, 1978. The author is grateful for financial support for the data collection and computer analysis to the Research Committee of The Graduate School, University of Wisconsin, Madison, and for help in data processing to Suzann Thomas. Michael Mezey and Carole Uhlaner offered helpful criticisms of the original draft.

35

subject to deinstitutionalization.[1] In the past decade other observers, using a variety of methodologies and evidence, have arrived at similar conclusions. Burnham (1970), Broder (1971), and Nie et al. (1976), to name but a few, have found evidence that the party system has lost some of its popular base of support, particularly with respect to the extent of citizen identification with one or the other of the two major parties.[2] The general conclusions drawn from such analysis are that not only does the decay in the party system greatly affect the way elections are organized and decided, but more generally, it also is beginning to have a serious impact on the whole present operation and structure of American government.

Not everyone agrees either with these conclusions or with their empirical assumptions, especially that of partisan decomposition. Indeed, there is some recent evidence on the state of aggregate party identification that suggests the possibility of greater stability and salience of partisanship than is apparent on the surface. Many people who identify themselves initially as Independents nonetheless show, in their reported voting behavior, substantial partisan consistency.[3] Furthermore, Brody's recent work suggests that the major changes have come more in the realm of intensity of partisan commitment than in its direction.[4] Thus, some part of the attitudinal decline so apparent in the various indicators of partisan decomposition has been not fully or immediately translated into "partyless" voting or into a complete severance of psychological ties with the Republicans or the Democrats. At present we do not know whether such phenomena represent a transitional phase, whether partisanship is presently not being measured in a way that adequately represents its complexity, or whether people are changing merely the form and expression, not the substance, of their partisan identification.

We should also note in this connection that, although national tickets were led by an antipartisan Democrat and a partially concealed Republican in 1976, there was a detectable upturn in the electoral impact of partisanship in the presidential election.[5] Thus, more recent events and investigations have given those who argue that the death of partisanship has been greatly exaggerated at least some confirmation of their view.

This raises an important problem that is not easily resolved on the basis of an analysis of party identification alone. Given the increasingly well-known ambiguities inherent in the present modes of measurement of party affiliation, the prospect of an immediate resolution of questions about the state of public legitimation of the parties, based on trends in party identification alone, is in doubt.[6]

The approach that I have proposed is to take multiple indicators of party system support into account. I have argued also that one needs to consider a variety of dimensions of public response to the political parties, including a fairly general level of public evaluation that I have termed, following Easton (1964), "diffuse support." If we are to understand fully the changes that occur in public feelings about the party system, as well as the causes and consequences of such feelings, then it is important to go beyond party identification. We need to achieve a fuller understanding of the complex of public attitudes and perceptions about the role of parties in the American political system.

I shall attempt here to bring to bear some new evidence on the state of public sentiment toward the party system, to determine whether recent changes are of the kind that would reverse the long-term trend toward institutional decay or whether the modest upsurge of party relevance in 1976 voting conceals the fact that citizen support for the parties is still being eroded. I will update my earlier discussions of this problem and see what changes have occurred since the last reported data point in early 1974. Has there been some marked reversal of the tendency toward delegitimation, or has it remained as a strong negative tide still running against the institution of the political party?

In the report of the initial wave of my series of Wisconsin surveys (1964), I detected an irresolute state of public support, with a mixture of both positive and negative feelings about the operation and role of the parties. Putting these earlier data together with subsequent evidence, however, I found a distinctly negative trend of public opinion with respect to the parties.[7] As indicated in the second of these reports, a variety of indicators showed falling levels of positive public thought and action vis-à-vis the parties. The present analysis is focused only on a selected subset of this potential array of indicators. Those indicators for which new data have been collected in the late-1974 to mid-1978 period will be used.

Diffuse Support

From the perspective of a generalized response to the institution of party, the most strategic area of inquiry is what has been termed *diffuse support* for the party system. Diffuse support is a reservoir of good will, presumably generated over a long period; it is therefore not easily depleted or increased in the short run. A number of specific feelings might be included in such a generalized sentiment. At the most abstract level are the norms that support pluralism and the importance of maintaining some form of organized partisan competition in elections and in other areas of democratic participation.

In 1964 a question was posed to a probability sample of Wisconsin adults that was designed to tap this very general, normative level of feelings about the party system. The pattern of response to this question is shown in table 2-1, which presents the marginal percentages not only for 1964, but also for late 1974 and for 1976—two instances when this question was

Table 2-1
Support for Pluralism: The Norm of Organized Partisan Competition in a Democracy, Wisconsin 1964, 1974, and 1976

Question: "Democracy works best where competition between political parties is strong".

	1964	1974	1976
Agree	74%[a]	73%	66%
Both agree and disagree	13	16	16
Disagree	13	11	17
Total	100%	100%	99%
Base *N*	645	506	529
Total *N*	702	548	581

[a]Percentages were adjusted by removing missing data.

repeated for similar probability samples of Wisconsin adults. We find that this abstract norm was endorsed almost by consensus in both 1964 and 1974; it held up well even in a period during which more specific elements of diffuse support were steadily declining.[8] In the 1974-1976 period, however, we detect some decline—perhaps a delayed response to earlier erosion along less abstract dimensions of diffuse support. Whatever the explanation, this small recent drop runs counter to the small increase in the salience of partisanship in 1976 detected in the voting studies.

Are the levels of diffuse support dropping for other indicators as well? Three items that I have had the greatest success in carrying through the whole series of Wisconsin surveys from 1964 through 1976 are relevant here. These are shown in figure 2-1 which reveals a continuation of essentially the same levels of public support shown earlier for each indicator. By 1976 only 37 percent of respondents agreed that party labels should be kept on the ballot, in sharp contrast to the 67 percent who had agreed with this in 1964. The drop in diffuse support in these terms over the twelve years is considerable, and is suggestive of a marked impetus toward institutional delegitimation.

For the two trend items that had indicated a markedly unfavorable image of the parties even in 1964, 1976 shows no real improvement. About 20 percent of respondents in 1964 had disagreed that the parties fail to provide a clear choice on issues; with the exception of 1972, this is about the level of negative sentiment that persisted throughout the period. On the question of whether the parties create unnecessary conflicts, the result is roughly similar. In 1964, 15 percent had disagreed that the parties create unnecessary conflicts, and this level stayed about the same through 1976. Thus, on the two time-series questions that had elicited highly negative responses even in 1964, one finds roughly comparable, high levels of public disapproval—with only around 20 percent holding a favorable image of the operation of the party system at any time. On the one item carried through all of the available data points where opin-

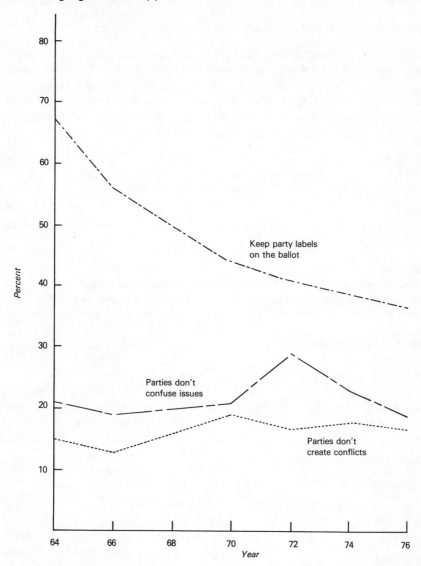

Figure 2-1. Diffuse Support for the Party System, Wisconsin 1964-1976
            (Percent Supportive)

ion had been initially rather favorable to the parties, the same kind of unfavorable balance was attained by 1976. As I shall argue in reviewing other
kinds of indicators below, this portrait of public feeling about the political
parties is not simply an artifact of these particular questions or this particular population of respondents.

Confidence in the Parties Relative to Other Institutions

Evidence confirming this general finding can be found in the level of simple trust and confidence that people have in the political parties, relative to how much trust and confidence they have in other political institutions. The National Election Studies of 1972, 1974, and 1976 provide at least short-term comparisons of confidence in four different institutions, including the parties. The National Election Studies asked:

> Which part of the government on this list do you most often trust to do what's right? (Congress, Supreme Court, President, Political Parties)? Which of the others do you most often trust to do what's right? Which do you least often trust to do what's right?

Table 2-2 shows, in answer to the first question, that only 1 percent

Table 2-2
Confidence in the Political Parties in Relation to Confidence in the Presidency, Supreme Court, and Congress, United States 1972-1976

	1972	*1974*	*1976*
Institution most trusted			
Congress	32%	26%	28%
Supreme Court	26	50	40
President	41	22	30
Political parties	1	3	2
Total	100%	101%	100%
Base *N*	952	2170	1977
Total *N*	2705	2523	2872
Institution *next* most trusted			
Congress	41%	46%	36%
Supreme Court	24	22	26
Pesident	30	27	32
Political parties	5	5	5
Total	100%	100%	99%
Base *N*	882	2069	1873
Total *N*	2705	2523	2872
Institution least trusted			
Congress	4%	5%	11%
Supreme Court	18	7	11
President	11	14	8
Political parties	67	74	70
Total	100%	100%	100%
Base *N*	889	2170	2030
Total *N*	2705	2523	2873

Source: Inter-University Consortium for Political and Social Research.

chose the parties in 1972. In 1974 this figure rose to 3 percent, but it sank again in 1976 to 2 percent. Almost *no one* trusts the parties more than they do the three major branches of national government. On the negative side, in 1972 67 percent said they trusted the parties least. This figure was 74 percent in 1974 and 70 percent in 1976. The point here is a simple one. There has been no marked change over the past few years from a situation in which the parties fared very badly in such cross-institutional comparisons.

In my Wisconsin data, where more types of cross-institutional comparisons have been made—although over a shorter time period and for a more limited population—the parties also compare poorly in relative levels of institutional confidence. This low status is shown in table 2-3, in which we see that the parties are near the bottom in positive institutional ranking over a wide range of institutional comparisons. Thus the political parties fail to achieve or to maintain even an average standing among the various political institutions about which these Wisconsin respondents were asked. In general terms, therefore, comparative diffuse support has remained low—a pattern that conforms to the national evidence based on related questions.

Table 2-3
Confidence in the Political Parties Relative to Other Institutions, Wisconsin 1974 and 1976

	1974	1976
Percent confidence in parties		
1 No confidence at all	7%	5%
2	9	6
3	19	11
4	34	32
5	16	19
6	8	11
7 Complete confidence	3	9
Don't know	4	8
Total	100%	101%
N =	916	581
Means on institutional confidence		
Congress	4.6	4.8
Supreme Court	4.8	5.0
Presidency	4.3	5.3
Political parties	3.8	4.3
Elections	4.3	4.9
Interest groups	3.7	4.0
Federal administrative agencies	4.1	4.3

Performance of the Party System

One reason that people may have lower confidence in the parties is that the parties are seen as having failed to perform well. If the parties are unable to carry out the functions normally assigned to them, then people may have accordingly little confidence in them. Although it is difficult to sort out the causal sequences here—given that we have only these successive cross-section samples available—we can see that there is at least a prima facie case for suggesting such a relationship. Let us look at the evidence on perceived performance.

1. *In general*: One of the things I reported earlier, using the data through early 1974, was that the parties are not widely perceived to make much of a contribution to the individual's own sense of well being. In Wisconsin in 1972, about 32 percent of the respondents said that the parties didn't do them much good; 28 percent were neutral; and 33 percent said that the parties did do something worthwhile for them. In 1974 in Wisconsin, 42 percent denied any personally relevant performance of the parties; 26 percent were neutral; and only 28 percent affirmed a party contribution. While this question was not repeated in 1976, the available recent data suggest declining levels of support on this dimension of party-system evaluation.

2. *Partisan efficacy*: This perceived lack of performance related to individual needs may in part be an outgrowth of a sense that the parties do not genuinely reflect the concerns of individual Americans—that the individual is helpless to affect what the parties do in choosing candidates to run for office or in posing policy alternatives. It is also possible that even if the parties do try to represent the needs of ordinary members or identifiers, they do so ineffectively. Some evidence on each of these points follows.

Some national data collected in the National Election Studies from 1968 to 1976 show a noticeable trend toward feeling that the parties are unresponsive to people's wishes (table 2-4). These data indicate that while less than half agreed that the "parties are only interested in people's votes but not in their opinions" in 1968, by 1976 this proportion had become almost two-thirds—a 16 percent increase in negative sentiment over the eight years. The Wisconsin data reported earlier confirm this relatively low sense of institutional efficacy in cross-institutional context.[9]

On the question of the parties' relative effectiveness in getting the government to pay attention, I showed earlier—using U.S. data—a general decline from 1964 to 1974 in the belief that the parties help make the government pay attention to what the people want.[10] In 1964, 44 percent thought the parties helped a good deal; only 23 percent thought so by 1974. In 1976 this figure dropped to 18 percent, continuing the downward trend discernible across the whole period (table 2-5).

Table 2-4
Individual Efficacy in Relation to the Parties, United States 1968-1976

Question: "Parties are only interested in people's votes but not in their opinions."

	1968	1970	1972	1974	1976
Agree	48%	56%	59%	61%	64%
Disagree	52	44	41	39	36
Total	100%	100%	100%	100%	100%
Base *N*	1295	1450	2617	2380	2258
Total *N*	1557	1507	2705	2523	2870

Source: Inter-University Consortium for Political and Social Research.

Taken together, these various bits of evidence suggest that the parties are increasingly viewed by citizens as ineffective in presenting clearly defined opposing points of view that are influential in the making of public policy. This parallels the fact that people are increasingly disinclined to believe that the parties are responsive to their own needs.

3. *Policy differences*: Part of the implicit reasoning here may be that the parties fail to provide clearly defined alternatives for public choice. We have seen already in figure 2-1 that the preponderant feeling is probably in that direction. An additional bit of evidence in this connection comes from the National Election Studies. A fairly constant effect across the whole 1952-1976 period pertains to public perception of whether there is any difference between what each of the two major parties stands for.

Table 2-6 shows that 45 percent of those with an opinion in 1952 could perceive no difference between the two parties; in 1976 this figure was 47

Table 2-5
The Efficacy of the Parties, United States 1964-1976

Question: "How much do you feel that political parties help to make the government pay attention to what the people think?"

	1964	1968	1970	1972	1974	1976
A good deal	44%	39%	35%	31%	23%	18%
Some	42	43	45	48	57	55
Not much	14	18	20	20	20	27
Total	100%	100%	100%	100%	100%	100%
Base *N*	1340	1256	865	1274	2399	2296
Total *N*	1571	1557	915	2705	2523	2871

Source: Inter-University Consortium for Political and Social Research.

Table 2-6
Perception of a Difference Between the Two Major Parties, United States
1952-1976

Question: "Do you think there are any important differences in what the Republicans and Democrats stand for?"

	1952	1960	1968	1972	1976
Perceive a difference	55%	54%	45%	51%	53%
Perceive no difference	45	46	55	49	47
Total	100%	100%	100%	100%	100%
Base *N*	1600	1704	1557	998	2561
Total *N*	1899	1954	1557	2705	2871

Source: Inter-University Consortium for Political and Social Research.

percent. The fact that nearly half of the respondents are unable to discern a meaningful party difference suggests an important reason that people do not have much confidence in the efficacy of existing partisan institutions.[11] As Kagay and Caldeira showed in chapter 1, issue differences between the parties *are* important for voter decision; and such differences are increasing in relevance. Thus a failure to present clear policy differences becomes increasingly frustrating to the general public.

In general, therefore, an area of considerable weakness in the self-presentation of the party system is in the general area of performance. The parties appear to the average person to be unable to do much to affect the course of policy making in America, and therefore they are no longer seen as able to perform their important intermediary functions. Accompanying this perception is the idea that the individual is unable to have substantial input into party councils. Nor are the parties thought to offer clearly defined policy alternatives. The average citizen is therefore inclined to doubt her or his capacity to affect the course of government through the party mechanism. This probably serves to undermine whatever lingering trust and confidence citizens have carried into the present era from their earlier partisan experience and socialization.

Salience, Knowledge, Contact, and Contributions

If people feel that the parties are not especially responsive to their needs, and that they are ineffective in providing competing programs of public policy and in influencing the policy process, then the parties may be expected to become less personally relevant. As time passes, of course, the fact that parties become increasingly irrelevant to individuals' own lives may serve to reinforce a general lack of approval of the existence of the party system or of the way in which it operates. A pattern is likely to develop in which people pay less and less attention to partisan events, know less about party matters, involve themselves less frequently in party-related activities, and begin to lose any former willingness to contribute their own resources to party organizations.

1. *Salience*: Let us take party salience as our first expected concomitant. The National Election Studies (1952-1976) have consistently asked a question that probably taps in part the sense of salience of party to the respondent. While other variables no doubt operate to affect the distribution of response to this question—such as who is leading the respective party tickets in a given year—we may assume that these other sources of variation are probably random. The Center for Political Studies/Survey Research Center (CPS/SRC) at the University of Michigan has asked whether the respondent cares which party wins (except in 1970 and 1974, when the question was whether the respondent cared about the way the elections came out). Table 2-7 presents these data.

We find that a general decline in positive affect has occurred for the American population. A substantial 68 percent cared very much or pretty much about these outcomes in 1952. By 1976, with some variations over the years, this had dropped to 58 percent. Thus, based on this somewhat indirect measure, partisan outcomes and thus parties themselves appear to have become less salient. Obviously, the drop in voter turnout as a more general phenomenon is also related to this effect.[12]

2. *Partisan knowledge*: If party has become a less salient object of attention for the average American, then we should expect some drop in the degree to which people hold knowledge relevant to partisanship. Table 2-8 shows the distribution of partisan information from two series of American National Election Study questions. The first question in particular reveals a roughly similar level of ignorance across the whole period; approximately one-third of respondents knew nothing about which party controlled Congress, and another 8 percent were wrong, on the average about such control.

As for knowing which party did better in the congressional elections, there is an overall rise in the percentage admitting they do not know, although this shows considerable variation from election to election. Incorrect answers range from only 1 percent in 1958 and 1964 to 44 percent in 1966.[13] Thus, while partisan ignorance has not increased markedly in this period, it certainly has not declined, and there are at least marginal changes upwards.

3. *Partisan contact*: If people in general consider partisanship less relevant, then an aggregate byproduct should be a less intensely partisan campaign effort. Obviously, there is considerable room for ambiguity here, because the extent to which campaign efforts are easily identifiable with a party organization rather than merely being carried out by a candidate-centered organization (or indeed, by some other organization such as the League of Women Voters) is likely to remain obscure in the minds of many voters. Given this caveat, however, we can employ a time-series question from the American National Election Studies (table 2-9).

Table 2-7
The Salience of Party, United States 1952-1976

Question: "Generally speaking, would you say that you personnaly care a good deal which party wins the presidential election this fall, or that you don't care very much which party wins?"

	1952	1956	1958	1960	1964	1968	1970[a]	1972	1974[a]	1976
Very much	29% } 68	27% } 64	21% } 54	28% } 67	32% } 69	25% } 60	26% } 66	62%	24% } 58	58%
Pretty much	39	37	33	39	37	35	40	38	34	42
Not much	22 } 33	22 } 36	28 } 46	19 } 33	15 } 31	22 } 40	26 } 34		26 } 41	
Not at all	11	14	18	14	16	18	8		15	
Total	101%	100%	100%	100%	100%	100%	100%	100%	99%	100%
Base N	1733	1682	1750	1831	1491	1457	1471	2602	2456	2769
Total N	1899	1762	1812	1954	1571	1557	1507	2705	2523	2870

Source: Inter-University Consortium for Political and Social Research.
[a]Variation in question wording: "care about the way the elections come out."

Table 2-8
Partisan Knowledge, United States 1958-1976

Question: "Do you happen to know which party had the most numbers in the House of Representatives in Washington before the elections (this/last) month?"

	1958	1960	1964	1966	1968	1970	1972	1976
Democrats	47%	64%	64%	69%	70%	50%	64%	61%
Republicans	19	6	7	3	3	11	8	4
Don't know	34	31	28	28	27	39	28	35
Total	100%	101%	99%	100%	100%	100%	100%	100%
Base N	1810	1826	1443	1285	1342	1502	1109	2394
Total N	1822	1954	1571	1291	1557	1507	2705	2870

Question: "Do you happen to know which party elected the most members to the House of Representatives in the elections (this/last) month?"

	1958	1960	1964	1966	1968	1970	1972	1976
Democrats	77%	55%	79%	21%	49%	54%	56%	58%
Republicans	1	8	1	44	14	6	11	2
Don't know	21	37	20	35	36	39	33	40
Total	99%	100%	100%	100%	99%	99%	100%	100%
Base N	1810	1819	1442	1282	1342	1499	1110	2392
Total N	1822	1954	1571	1291	1557	1507	2705	2870

Source: Inter-University Consortium for Political and Social Research.

Table 2-9
Partisan Contact, United States 1952-1976

Question: "Did anybody from either one of the parties call you up or come around to talk to you during the campaign?"

	1952	1956	1960	1964	1966	1968	1972	1974	1976
Yes	12%	17	22	26	25	26	29	24	29%
No	88	83	78	74	75	74	71	76	71
Total	100%	100%	100%	100%	100%	100%	100%	100%	100%
Base *N*	1707	1741	1792	1448	1285	1344	1119	2523	2394
Total *N*	1899	1762	1954	1571	1291	1557	2705	2523	2870

Source: Inter-University Consortium for Political and Social Research.

We see that there has probably been an *increase* in the level of perceived electoral campaign contacts over these years. Only 12 percent of respondents perceived that they had had party contact in 1952, whereas from 1960 on there was about twice that level of perceived contact. This could indicate that with the decline of partisan organizations, party activists are driven to increasingly frantic efforts as they try to compensate for the larger pattern of party erosion. This finding might also mean that, as parties decline, the candidate organizations make a greater total effort to contact potential voters, since they are no longer able to depend on party-organizational efforts to mobilize supporters. This might also mean that activist support has actually increased while mass support has declined.[14]

Even if we accept that there is now a higher level of perceived partisan effort that was true in the 1950s, this does not necessarily mean greater mass involvement in contributory activities. There may still be no increase in the number of situations in which the respondent is an active participant rather than merely a passive receiver of partisan contact. Nor does it mean that the *personal* relevance of partisanship is high. Let us turn to these questions next.

4. *Contributor support*: As shown in my 1975 report, dues-paying party membership remained relatively stable from 1964 to 1974, according to Wisconsin data.[15] If we update that observation, we arrive at the distributions shown in figure 2-2. In 1976 there was essentially the same level of self-perceived contributions that characterized the earlier years. Thus, self-reported contributor support has not been greatly affected by recent experience. The small activitist fraction of the total population has remained fairly steady in the face of declining approval of the parties in general.

Considering the more general population's attitude toward contributing personal effort to partisan campaigns, however, we do find a decline. In putting together the 1964 set of observations with a previously unreported, late-1974 set of observations on the question, "People who work for political parties during political campaigns do our nation a great service," we see such a drop in favorable orientation.

As shown in table 2-10, the more general population seems distinctly less willing to regard partisan activity as a civic virtue in 1974 than was true in 1964. At an attitudinal level, contributor support appears to be declining, based on a rather limited set of time-series observations.

Partisan Affiliation

In the literature of political science, the most prominent mode of relating citizen political attitudes to the political parties has been political party identification—one's self-perceived affiliation with one of the political parties. As I have argued previously, this is not the most crucial aspect of

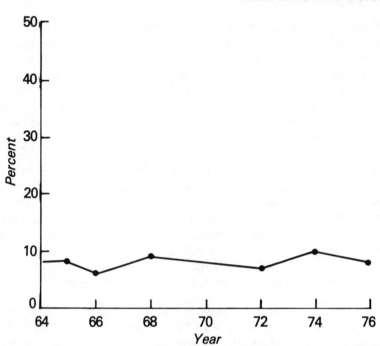

Figure 2-2. Wisconsin Data on Contributor Support: Dues-Paying Party
Membership, 1964-1976 (Percent Members)

positive feeling about the party system as a whole. Conceivably a person
could believe strongly in the necessity for organized party competition, or
indeed in a two-party form of such competition, and yet be disillusioned
with both of the present major parties. Nonetheless, as the party system is
increasingly regarded as unnecessary and as performing poorly, one should
expect that some part of this general negative sentiment will be reflected in a
decline in individual willingness to be associated with one of the existing
major parties. A probable effect of general delegitimation of the institution
should be to dislodge partisan self-images.

Is there evidence that this is a plausible hypothesis? One relatively
straightforward indicator of such an effect would be the trend in the aggregate level of overt identification with one of the two major parties.
Figure 2-3 presents some trend data on party identification from three sets
of surveys—Gallup, the University of Michigan's CPS/SRC, and the
Wisconsin Survey Research Laboratory.

We find that the general erosion of aggregate partisan self-images has
continued in the most recent data well beyond the point of decline last
reported.[16] There has been no marked improvement in the level of positive
affiliation with a party in the post-1974 data, although there has also been
no sharp drop. Rather, the trend of decomposition has continued.

Table 2-10

Contributor Support: Civic Virtue in Partisan Activity, Wisconsin 1964 and 1974

Question: "People who work for political parties during political campaigns do our nation a great service."

	1964	*1974*
Strongly agree	7% } 68%	4% } 53%
Agree	61	49
Agree/disagree	19	27
Disagree	10 } 10	15 } 16
Strongly disagree	—	1
Don't know	4	3
Not ascertained	—	1
Total	101%	100%
N =	702	548

A majority of respondents in all four series of measurements, even the most recent, still maintain a partisan self-image; party identification has not collapsed by any means. And as some recent studies have attempted to show, there may be greater *concealed* partisanship than these figures alone would suggest.[17] On the other hand, if people are losing interest in the whole idea of political parties, then the kind of gradual erosion of partisan self-images that we find here is probably what one ought to expect. Party identification is clearly going through some fundamental long-term aggregate change. While this decline may not yet be fully translated into action at the level of individual voting behavior for all offices and candidates, it is a phenomenon that will require close and continuous monitoring and causal investigation. Something important has been happening along this dimension of party-system orientation, and we ought to know more about it—especially how it is connected to wider sentiment about the role of the parties in American society.

Self-Perceived Partisan Consistency

A related and final dimension of partisan orientation that we will explore briefly is what might be called partisan consistency. If partisanship has strong salience for individuals, then they are more likely to exhibit consistent patterns of belief and action when partisan responses are called for. A variety of indicators can be used to test for these effects, including the self-perception of having voted for the same or for different parties for president over the years. The American National Election Studies provide evidence for this kind of question, and table 2-11 shows one of these trends.

We see that in relation to 1952 there has been a marked drop in self-perceived consistency in presidential voting—from 66 percent in 1952 to only 47 percent by 1976. Other data on partisan consistency and straight-

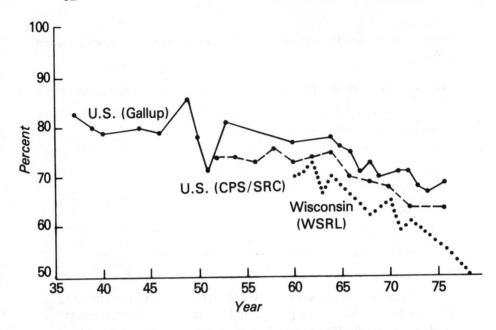

Figure 2-3. Gallup, Center for Political Studies/Social Research Center
(CPS/SRC), and University of Wisconsin Research Survey
Laboratory (WRSL) Data on Political Party Identification,
United States and Wisconsin, 1937-1978 (Percent Identifiers)

ticket voting confirm this trend.[18] We would expect that a declining sense of
partisan relevance would be accompanied by rising partisan inconsistency,
and in aggregate terms the two trends have covaried. As the party system
has lost some measure of what was formerly a more positive set of feelings
by the general public, there has also been a falloff both in partisan self-
images and inconsistent partisanship.

Summary

Up to this point, the major effort has been to carry forward earlier kinds of
analysis of trends in public regard for the party system. When we introduce
the more recent data—after early 1974—we find essentially the same
deligitimation phenomena as before. The earlier trends continue with little
interruption data from these later years give evidence of no sharp reversal in
any of the indicators. Neither the fact of a new administration nor the
phenomenon of a relatively peaceful recent period in U.S. politics—in con-

Table 2-11
Consistent Partisanship, United States 1952-1976

Question: "Have you always voted for the same party or have you voted for different parties for president?"

	1952	1956	1958	1960	1962	1964	1966	1968	1970	1972	1974	1976
Same	66%	57%	59%	54%	57%	58%	46%	52%	48%	46%	46%	47%
Different	34	43	41	46	43	42	54	48	52	54	54	53
Total	100%	100%	100%	100%	100%	100%	100%	100%	100%	100%	100%	100%
Base N	1369	1380	1491	1571	1072	1267	1085	1240	1235	2073	2037	2281
Total N	1899	1762	1822	1954	1297	1571	1291	1557	1507	2705	2523	2872

Source: Inter-University Consortium for Political and Social Research.

trast to the 1960s and early 1970s—has cured the ills of party malaise. Such lesions have continued to fester and to reconfirm the lack of recovery of this diseased organ of the body politic.

Alternatives to Party and the Possibilities of Reform

If the people in our society have continued to hold the party system in such low regard, as the evidence suggests, then to what kinds of alternatives to party do they subscribe? One lively possibility is an increase in the already strong tendency to *personalismo* in elections. A feature of the American political process that is widely remarked among political scientists is the capacity of self-starting individuals to enter contests for public office and to win despite what party leaders and activists do or say. In general, the extant party organizations are so weak that they have little control over candidacies or over what is represented as their own party's point of view. In Wisconsin, for example, a popular office holder such as William Proxmire is able, for all practical purposes, to ignore all official Democratic party activities, principles, and leaders. The 1978 Republican candidate for governor in Wisconsin, Lee Dreyfus, has shown how simple it is to overcome the candidate endorsed by the state Republic organization in the party primary. For some time now it has entailed little cost for candidates to step beyond party in our system. For present purposes, the question becomes: How well established and fast-growing is a general norm that emphasizes the rightness of candidates acting alone versus a norm of party control of candidacies?

One test of the competing norms of partisanship and personalismo is contained in a question that investigators have posed to mass publics over the years. The question concerns person versus party as a rule guilding voter choice; table 2-12 presents the relevant evidence from Wisconsin in 1964, 1974, and 1976. It shows that a noticeable shift has occurred in the relative proportion who endorse the idea of choosing candidates for public office without reference to party labels. About 83 percent endorsed this idea in Wisconsin in 1964; this figure rose to 91 percent in 1974 and to 93 percent by 1976. Gallup has asked a parallel question at least twice, and his data show essentially the same overwhelming and increasing endorsement of the idea of choosing person over party. In response to the question, "Generally speaking, do you think it is better to vote for the man or the party?" Gallup found that 74 percent chose "the man" in 1956, and 84 percent by 1968.[19]

At the level of competing general norms, therefore, "person power" easily overcomes "party power" in the minds of the mass public. An alternative to party in elections is, for the public, no party, or at least a more personal form of electoral competition. We have probably already entered an epoch in which this principle operates fully. Burns has critically observed

Table 2-12
Norms of Partisanship: Person versus Party, Wisconsin 1964, 1974 and 1976

Question: "The best rule in voting is to pick the best candidate, regardless of party label."

	1964	1974	1976
Agree very strongly	a	a	44%
Agree strongly	23%	34	19
Agree	59	56	26
Agree/disagree	6	4	2
Disagree	9	4	3
Disagree strongly	1	1	1
Disagree very strongly	a	a	2
Don't know	2	1	1
Not ascertained	b	b	3
Total	100%	100%	101%
N =	702	548	581

[a]Not asked.
[b]Less than 1 percent.

that party politics in America is more "a free-for-all among candidates and personal followings cutting across party lines" than it is a clear confrontation between Democrats and Republicans. Burns compares this to a continuing game of "king of the rock" with the emphasis placed on personalities rather than issues in campaigns.[20]

How about other kinds of general changes that people might prefer? We have already seen in figure 2-1 that a relatively high proportion of the public would endorse the idea of removing party labels from the ballot entirely. Well over half, at least in Wisconsin, favor nonpartisan elections altogether. This change, should it be instituted, would be fundamental.

Such a finding is supported by evidence from more general questions as to whether the parties ought to be reformed or even eliminated. Some 41 percent of my 1970 Wisconsin statewide sample agreed to the reform or elimination of the national parties. This sentiment was also strong in my 1972 and 1974 Wisconsin samples, with 28 percent wanting to change the parties in 1972 and 43 percent in 1974.[21] Yankelovich's data on college and noncollege young adults in 1969 and 1973, for example, show essentially the same high level of support for institutional change.[22] Thus, the general desire to do something substantial about the parties has probably increased in recent years.

As indicated in my 1975 report, one change that the mass public would enthusiastically endorse would be the elimination of what remains of the present activist capacity to choose the presidential and vice-presidential candidates at the national nominating conventions, and the return of the choice to the voters in some form of national primary election. In 1976, for example, about 60 percent favored such a shift.[23]

Another strong preference that Americans have shown over the years is for decentralized, ideologically diffuse parties. The package of proposals for party system reform usually referred to as "reponsible party government" was shown earlier to have little public appeal. Data absent from the earlier report tend to confirm the earlier findings, and even to suggest a reinforcing trend. Whereas in 1964 about 23 percent of Wisconsin respondents agreed that "A Senator or Representative should follow his party leaders, even if he doesn't want to," only 10 percent agreed by late 1974. Party discipline is hardly an idea whose time has come![24] And this fact probably applies to all the proposals usually included under the "responsible parties" rubric.

Ideological Realignment

One change suggested by many reformers is an ideological realignment of the parties so that one party is clearly the "liberals" and the other the "conservatives." Such an ideological reordering would make possible greater policy coherence, and thus more responsible parties, among the people elected to office. The general public does not favor such a change, however. In November 1974 Gallup asked the following: "Some people say that the time has come to have a new political party arrangement in the United States, with conservatives making up one party and liberals making up the other major party. Do you agree or disagree?" The distribution of response was: agree, 27 percent; disagree, 56 percent; and no opinion, 17 percent.[25] This idea appears to have only limited popular appeal, showing that

Table 2-13
Responsible Party Government, Wisconsin 1964-1974

Question: "A Senator or Representative should follow his party leaders, even if he doesn't want to."

	Late 1964	Late 1974
Strongly agree	1% } 23%	— } 10%
Agree	22	10
Agree/disagree	9	8
Disagree	56 } 63	57 } 79
Strongly disagree	7	22
Don't know	4	3
Not ascertained	1	—
Total	100%	100%
N =	702	548

ideological clarity is not one of the changes in the parties that most people are thinking about. Indeed, a recent national survey by Gallup suggests that 41 percent of the adult population would favor creation of a nonideological "center party" that would stand between the Republicans and Democrats on the left/right ideological continuum.[26]

Summary

People do want to see the parties reform, but probably in a way that would limit further their capacities to structure elections. The public does not really endorse either greater centralization and discipline or ideological realignment to give the parties more internal coherence and thus a more "responsible" mode of operating. Thus, the parties as an institution are not likely to find themselves in a more commanding position as a result of whatever changes are made.

Explanation of Support for the Party System

Up to this point we have attempted to describe the extent of public support or nonsupport for the political party system as it has evolved in recent years, against the background or earlier changes. We have not tried to give any account of differences among various subgroups of the population or to provide explanatory evidence. At this point let us turn briefly to the latter.

In my earlier reports, I showed the effects of such demographic variables as education, income, age, sex, and race. Only some of these, including aged and education (or more generally social class), seem to be significant as predictors of party system support. Essentially the same kinds of relationships pertain to the 1976 Wisconsin data. In the earlier work, I focused also on such political variables as strength of partian identification, sense of political efficacy, political involvement, and sentiment toward other institutions and toward the regime in general. I will want to repeat some of the latter analysis here in the context of a more general model. Third, in earlier work I tried to show the relationship of party-system support to such nonpolitical attitudes as sense of alienation and relative deprivation.[27] I will also want to incorporate some of these variables into the present approach.

If one thinks in terms of a flow of causality, and in particular of a simple recursive system, then one can readily sort out theoretically two stages of influences on party-system support. The earlier stage has to do with long-term attitudes and statuses that begin to take shape in childhood. These long-held attitudes would include, for example, existence and strength of political party identification as well as sense of political efficacy.[28] Social class, and therefore the influence of social class on behavior, also begins very early in life.

At a second stage, one could think of short- and medium-term experiences and feelings that might serve to shape one's attitudes toward the parties as an institution. One presumed influence would be the attitudes that one develops toward the variety of institutions surrounding the parties. While one suspects that the parties have suffered greater and longer-term erosion of favorable public sentiment than have these other institutions, one can see (for example, in table 2-3) that all the various institutions of American national government largely tend to rise and fall in public confidence together. This should also pertain to feelings about the regime as a whole. Thus, one needs to determine the contribution of confidence or lack of confidence in related institutions or in the regime in general to the standing of the parties.

Second, one's sense of participation in the political system should help to shape people's party-system orientations. People who are more involved politically are more likely to regard parties as having positive relevance for the operation of a democratic system, and thus they should exhibit higher general party-system support. Third, the kinds of general experiences people have with the system, especially how well they and others like them are perceived as being treated in the sharing of available benefits, should also come into play. These three kinds of antecedents are more immediately causal than early-socialization-based variables such as party identification or political efficacy.

Let us put these together in diagrammatic form in terms of a simple path model. Figure 2-4 presents a first approximation of such a model; the path diagram indicates, under the assumptions pertaining to such a model, that all six of the hypothesized antecedents have significant effects. The significant direct paths (β) are presented, so that one can readily see the relative sizes of these direct effects in the diagram.[29]

The largest direct effect is for "support for the regime"—a composite index measuring confidence in the structures and norms of the regime as such ($\beta = 0.41$).[30] Also significant are relative gratification (in relation to negatively valued reference groups), which has a path coefficient of 0.08, and political involvement, which adds together measures of political participation of various types ($\beta = 0.15$). Strength of party identification ($\beta = 0.14$) and sense of political efficacy ($\beta = 0.11$) also show significant direct effects. And socioeconomic status, which here is a linear combination of educational attainment, income, and occupational prestige (using an updated Duncan measure), has at least important indirect effects on party-system support.

There are thus a number of hypothesized direct and indirect effects that

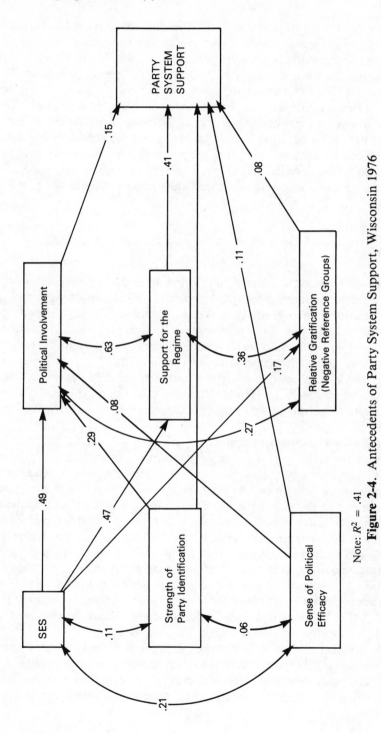

Note: $R^2 = .41$

Figure 2-4. Antecedents of Party System Support, Wisconsin 1976

receive at least some empirical support. These antecedents can be arrayed in terms of two preceding stages; if they are so portrayed, then one sees that there are important indirect effects of the earlier variables through the later ones. This influence is especially noteworthy for socioeconomic status. The people most likely to remain supportive of the party system during this period of deinstitutionalization are those who are higher in social status (indirect), have a stronger partisan self-image, have greater political efficacy, support the regime of democracy in general, are more politically involved, and feel less hostility toward other groups who share in the struggle for benefits available in American society. These are among the most important attributes of those who retain support while general support for political parties continues to decline.

Conclusion

The present analysis has attempted to bring up to date our account of the state of public opinion about the American political party system and to throw additional light on antecedents of such opinion. Despite the evidence suggesting an upsurge in the relevance of political-party identification to voting in 1976, one sees no corresponding improvement in how the general public views the partisan institution as a whole. The variety of indicators that are available suggests essentially a continuation of earlier trends when we add the more recent evidence. While the evidence on this point is not perfectly uniform, the weight of the data suggests continuing difficulties for the parties.

As the level of popular support for the party institution continues to decline, one would expect that party organization would continue to decay as well. As people lose their sense of partisan institutional relevance, they will doubtless also begin to lose what remains of their personal identification with one of the major parties. This, in turn, should affect negatively the strength of party organizations. Jeane Jordan Kirkpatrick has recently observed at least one of these links: "It is doubtless significant that party identification was diminishing, just as it was no accident that party organization developed and expanded alongside an expanding electorate. If there is a causal relation between strong organization and party identification, then policies which weaken the former should also tend to weaken the latter."[31] (For more extended discussion of the declining effectiveness of party organization, see Janda, chapter 9 in this book.)

The argument therefore is that the climate for rejuvenation of the parties is not necessarily favorable. Internal organizational reform—even if it is not counterproductive, as some recent critics of reform have argued—may not be enough to stem this strong public antipartisan tide.[32] Many long-term, broader institutional changes that have already been set in motion will inhibit institutional recovery. Kirkpatrick argues, with respect to the decline of party identification that the major causes "lie beyond policies and rules—in the emergence of new issues, the decreased confidence in social and political institutions, the increased use of television which enables candidates to establish a direct, personal relationship with voters unmediated by parties, and, perhaps especially, in the progressive ineffectiveness of the family and other agencies of vertical socialization."[33] This argument may well apply at a broader level as well.

Whether or not this is the precise list of significant causes that one should pursue—and some of the evidence presented in figure 2-4 would confirm that at least one of these potential causes is present—these are clearly priorities for investigation. Indeed, we need more intensive inquiry into this general phenomenon, especially since the phenomenon itself is increasingly verified in time-series observations such as those reported here. Partisan deinstitutionalization is one of the major phenomena of our time, and is thus one of the great empirical puzzles that political science in America must address in coming years. Partisan delegitimation is, moreover, a change of great potential consequence for the operation of the American political system. Given that these changes are relatively gradual, the wider American political system may already be making adjustments to a different kind of system.

The outlines of this emerging system are still unclear. The evidence presented on public attitudes toward the party system suggests a possible public receptivity to some type of institutional reform. But what the public is most likely to respond in positive fashion to are changes that enhance the capacity of the parties to play a more effective set of intermediary functions. Whether such reform, to be effective, can only be carried out *within* each of the two major parties—which several chapters in this volume address in some detail—or whether *external* reforms are also important, remains to be seen. While getting the two party houses in order is probably an important prerequisite of wider institutional reform, we should not neglect the need for changing the institutional standing of the parties with respect to other institutions and major forces of American politics. At this point, the legitimacy of party as institution is low. Thus, actual and possible inroads by competing organizations seem to be increasing each year.

For example, the campaign funding reforms of recent years have not proved significant as the salvation of the national party organizations, although these reforms have made available to the parties a small amount of public funding. (See chapter 7 by Jacobson for a discussion of the funding reforms.) Instead, the rules regulating the funding of election campaigns mainly continue to benefit candidate organizations, political action committees (and thus special interests), and a variety of other nonparty forces.

Without a broader effort toward external institutional improvement, the internal reforms of the past decade may only postpone the evil day of total collapse. Without a more basic realignment of the parties' institutional standing, the political future may be even more sharply characterized by the recent tendencies toward electoral instability. These trends, only partially visible at present, are usually thought to include such phenomena as an increasingly volatile and sometimes wildly oscillating electorate, an electorate that tends toward including only a minority of eligible persons in the voting population, a lower aggregate sense of political involvement and political efficacy among those who do participate, a growing perceptual distance between leaders and average citizens, and indeed a strong element of mistrust and alienation. These tendencies also include an enhanced role for "image politics," which accompanies the intensely candidate-centered forms of electoral competition and gives new electoral scope to the mass media of communication, to professional campaign managers, and to nonparty fund raisers—who further drain available resources from the parties in addition to taking over their functions. There is also likely to be an enhancement of the already tightening grip of incumbency on many offices, now seen so strongly in the U.S. Congress. In addition, there may well be a growth in the role of "single-issue" publics, special interest groups, "public-interest" organizations such as the League of Women Voters and Common Cause, and the like. All these forces not only step in to fill the vacuum left by the retreating parties, but also at times put pressure on the institutional structure of American government to hasten the parties' withdrawal.

While we should not discount the more general sense of institutional malaise that infects the American political system in this decade (and for additional evidence on this point, see, for example, chapter 8 by Davidson), in some ways the parties face a unique situation. The available evidence suggests a broader pattern of delegitimation of partisanship in American political culture. Only relatively strong and comprehensive reforms will be able to address successfully the problem of rebuilding a place for party institutions, as well as the deeper problem of regaining public support for the maintenance of the parties' organizing role in elections and in other sectors of the structure of government. This will prove to be a challenging task for reform in the 1980s.

Notes

1. Dennis (1966) and Dennis (1975).

2. Walter Dean Burnham, *Critical Elections and the Mainsprings of American Politics* (New York: Norton, 1970); David S. Broder, *The Party's Over: The Failure of Politics in America* (New York: Harper, 1971); and Norman H. Nie, Sidney Verba, and John R. Petrocik, *The Changing American Voter* (Cambridge, Mass.: Harvard University Press, 1976).

3. Bruce Keith et al., "The Myth of the Independent Voter" (Paper presented at the Annual Meeting of the American Political Science Association, Washington, D.C., September 1-4, 1977).

4. Richard A. Brody, "Stability and Change in Party Identification: Presidential to Off-Years" (Paper presented at the Annual Meeting of the American Political Science Association, Washington, D.C., September 1-4, 1977).

5. Warren E. Miller and Teresa E. Levitan, *Leadership and Change: Presidential Elections from 1952 to 1976* (Cambridge, Mass.: Winthrop Publishing, 1976), pp. 250-255; and Arthur H. Miller, "The Majority Party Reunited? A Summary Comparison of the 1972 and 1976 Elections," in *Parties and Elections in an Anti-Party Age*, ed. Jeffrey Fishell (Bloomington: Indiana University Press, 1978).

6. See, for example, Herbert F. Weisberg, "Towards a Reconceptualization of Party Identification" (Paper presented at the Annual Meeting of the Midwest Political Science Association, Chicago, Ill., April 20-22, 1978.

7. Dennis (1966) and Dennis (1975).

8. I had asked a similar question in 1970: "Democracy works best where the principle of competing political parties is well established." About 73 percent (80 percent adjusted) agreed with this statement at that time—again, a high level of approval of partisan pluralism. The Center for Political Studies asked their 1964 national sample: "Over the years, do you think that control of the government should pass from one party to the other every so often, or do you think that it's all right for one party to have control for a long time?" About 75 percent believed that control should change. (Data from Inter-University Consortium for Political and Social Research, *Codebook of the 1964 ANE Study*, vol. 394.)

9. Dennis (1975), p. 208.

10. Ibid, pp. 204-205.

11. For a more extended treatment of the implications of what kind of differences, if any, people see in what the parties stand for, see, for example, Trilling (1976). We might also note that Gallup recently found, when asking which party can best handle America's problems, that nearly half either said "no difference" or had no opinion, and only 54 percent chose either the Republicans or the Democrats. In 1976, the comparable figures had been 34 percent saying no difference or no opinion, and 66 percent preferring either Republicans or Democrats (*Gallup Opinion Index*, Report No. 157 [August, 1978], cover page). Also see Devine (1972), p. 250.

12. See the evidence in Dennis (1975), p. 191.

13. The distribution of seats by party in Congress over time is given, for example, in Congressional Quarterly, *Congress and the Nation*, vol. 4.

14. Dennis (1975), p. 211.

15. Ibid., p. 209.

16. Ibid., p. 193.

17. Keith et al., "Myth of the Independent Voter."

18. For examples of such evidence, see Dennis (1975).

19. Ibid., p. 202.

20. James MacGregor Burns, "Coming to the Aid of the Parties," *Newsweek*, 2 December 1974, p. 15.

21. Dennis (1975), p. 213.

22. Daniel Yankelovich, *The New Morality: A Profile of American Youth in the 70's* (New York: McGraw-Hill, 1974), p. 52.

23. *Current Opinion*, vol. 4 (October, 1976), p. 109. Also see *Gallup Opinion Index* no. 82 (April 1972), p. 26.

24. For related evidence that supports the idea that Americans are relatively hostile to centralized (and responsible) parties, see Devine (1972), pp. 175-176.

25. *Current Opinion*, vol. 3 (February 1975), p. 20.

26. "Gallup Poll: Many Like 'Center Party' Idea," *Milwaukee Journal*, 13 November 1978, p. 5.

27. Dennis (1975), p. 222.

28. See, for example, David Easton and Jack Dennis, "The Child's Acquisition of Regime Norms: Political Efficacy," *American Political Science Review* 61 (March 1967):25-38; and Jack Dennis and Donald McCrone, "Preadult Development of Political Party Identification in Western Democracies," *Comparative Political Studies* 3 (July 1970):243-262.

29. For an explanation of the procedures used in decomposing effects, see Duane F. Alwin and Robert M. Hauser, "The Decomposition of Effects in Path Analysis," *American Sociological Review* 49 (February, 1975):37-47. Also see John M. Finney, "Indirect Effects in Path Analysis," *Sociological Methods and Research* 1 (November 1972):175-186; and Otis Dudley Duncan, *Introduction to Structural Equation Models* (New York: Academic Press, 1975).

30. The index of support for the regime combines in linear fashion the responses to the following items:

a.   "It's important to protect the rights of persons accused of a crime, even if it makes it harder for the police to catch and convict law-breakers." (Responses range, for purposes of the index, from: 1. "disagree very strongly" . . . 7. "agree very strongly.")

b.   "Black people have a right to live where they want to just like white people." (Responses were scored: 1. "disagree very strongly" . . . 7. "agree very strongly.")

c.   "One of the things I am most proud of about America is its system of government." (Responses were scored: 1. "disagree very strongly" . . . 7. "agree very strongly.")

d.   "Many basic changes should be made in the way this country is organized if we are ever to achieve liberty and justice for all."

(Responses were scored: 1. "agree very strongly" . . . 7. "disagree very strongly.")

e. "Democracy is the best form of government." (Responses were scored: 1. "strongly disagree" . . . 5. "strongly agree.")

31. Jeane Jordan Kirkpatrick, *Dismantling the Parties: Reflections on Party Reform and Party Decomposition* (Washington, D.C.: American Enterprise Institute, 1978).

32. Ibid., p. 18ff.

33. Ibid., p. 17.

References

Books

Barber, James David. *The Presidential Character*. Englewood Cliffs, N.J.: Prentice-Hall, 1972.

Dennis, Jack, ed. *Socialization to Politics: A Reader*. New York: John Wiley and Sons, 1973.

Devine, Donald J. *The Political Culture of the United States*. Boston: Little, Brown and Company, 1973.

Greenstein, Fred I. *Personality and Politics: Problems of Evidence, Inference and Conceptualization*. Chicago: Markham, 1969.

Jennings, M. Kent, and Niemi, Richard G. *The Political Character of Adolescence*. Princeton, N.J.: Princeton University Press, 1974.

Niemi, Richard G., ed. *The Politics of Future Citizens*. San Francisco: Jossey-Bass, 1974.

Sniderman, Paul M. *Personality and Democratic Politics*. Berkeley: University of California Press, 1974.

Trilling, Richard J. *Party Image and Electoral Behavior*. New York: Wiley-Interscience, 1976.

Weissberg, Robert. *Political Learning, Political Choice and Democratic Citizenship*. Englewood Cliffs, N.J.: Prentice-Hall, 1974.

Wolfenstein, E. Victor. *Personality and Politics*. Belmont, Calif.: Dickenson, 1969.

Easton, David. *The Political System*. New York: Alfred A. Knopf, 1964.

Articles, Reports, and Papers

Abramson, Paul R. and Inglehart, Ronald E. "The Development of Systemic Support in Four Western Democracies." *Comparative Political Studies* 2 (January 1970): 419-442.

Citrin, Jack. "Comment: The Political Relevance of Trust in Government.'' *American Political Science Review* 68 (September 1974):973-988.

Dennis, Jack. "Support for the Party System by the Mass Public." *American Political Science Review* 60 (September 1966):600-615.

_____ . "Trends in Public Support for the American Party Party System." *British Journal of Political Science* 5 (April 1975):187-230.

Dennis, Jack; Lindberg, Leon; McCrone, Donald J.; and Stiebold, Rodney. "Political Socialization to Democratic Orientations in Four Western Systems." *Comparative Political Studies* 1 (April 1968):71-100.

Greenstein, Fred I. "What the President Means to Americans: Presidential 'Choice' Between Elections." In *Choosing the President*, edited by James David Barber, pp. 121-147. Englewood Cliffs, N.J.: Prentice-Hall, 1974.

_____ . "Personality and Politics." In *Handbook of Political Science*, edited by Fred I. Greenstein and Nelson W. Polsby, pp. 1-92. Reading, Mass.: Addison-Wesley, 1975.

Jaros, Dean; Hirsch, Herbert; and Fleron, Frederic, Jr. "The Malevolent Leader: Political Socialization in an American Subculture." *American Political Science Review* 62 (June 1968):564-575.

Miller, Arthur H. "Political Issues and Trust in Government: 1964-1970." *American Political Science Review* 68 (September 1974):951-972.

Sniderman, Paul M., and Citrin, Jack. "Psychological Sources of Political Belief: Self-Esteem and Isolationist Attitudes." *American Political Science Review* 65 (June 1971):401-417.

3 The Franchise: Registration Changes and Voter Representation

William J. Crotty

The Problem

Voter turnout, and the impact of formal registration requirements on it, is receiving renewed attention—and with good reason. The level of political involvement in American elections has decreased consistently to the point that voting—the most fundamental of all political acts—is becoming (and in the vast majority of elections has already become) a minority habit. Ninety million people did not vote in the off-year election of 1978. The importance of such abstentions for the continued vitality of the American political system is beginning to receive a modest but significant amount of attention. The columnist David S. Broder, for one, has attempted to put the matter in perspective. His assessment is well put, if stark. Writing on the eve of the nation's birthday celebration in 1978, Broder noted:

> The real story of American politics this year does not make a good Fourth of July speech. It is an invisible story. It is the play that was never performed because the audience never showed up. It is, in short, the story of the non-voting, the decision of millions of American citizens not to participate in the most basic and fundamental of the rites of democracy; the choice of elected officials. . . .
>
> It is a grim story to be telling on the 202nd birthday of the country, for, more than any other warning sign, it signals that the foundations of the experiment in self-government are crumbling.[1]

The foundations of the American government do appear in some jeopardy. People are participating less in the most basic form of political involvement, voting. This development cannot be a healthy sign for a governing system that depends on the support of its citizenry.

Broder's insights have been confirmed by a number of studies of the American electorate. Among the most significant of the recent investigations concerned with the decline in political participation has been the work of the Committee for the Study of the American Electorate, a group established to analyze and report on the changing patterns of turnout in

67

American elections. The committee's views, as expressed by its director, Curtis Gans, are much the same as Broder's. Gans puts the matter thus:

> The crucial difference between democracy and other forms of government . . . is that in a democracy the leadership of the nation derives its legitimacy and support from the consent of the governed. Perhaps the principal problem facing the United States today is the degree to which that consent is being withdrawn—the degree to which fewer and fewer Americans believe it necessary, important, or even worth their while to cast their ballots.[2]

The Committee for the Study of the American Electorate backs its concern with figures. It reported:

> During the last decade more than fifteen million eligible Americans, many of whom were regular voters, have stopped voting altogether.
>
> In the last four presidential elections, the percentage of eligible Americans who voted decreased from 63.8 in 1960 to 54.4 in 1976. There has been a similar trend in local, state, and congressional elections—and at a substantially lower level of participation than in presidential elections.
>
> Nearly seventy million Americans failed to cast their ballots in the 1976 presidential election; nearly one hundred million did not vote in the congressional elections in 1974.
>
> Fewer than 28 percent of Jimmy Carter's fellow citizens voted for him for president in 1976. Brendan Byrne of New Jersey received a "mandate" of less than 15 percent of the eligible vote in his successful 1977 reelection bid. Mayor Ed Koch was the "choice" of less than 12 percent of New York's voters. Senator Henry Jackson "won" the 1976 New York presidential primary by garnering less than 6 percent of the potential vote.
>
> The 1978 primary turnout has been down in almost every state except Arkansas and California.
>
> Even in California, only about 40 percent of California's eligible voters turned out for the heralded Proposition 13 initiative, nearly 10 percent lower than the number of eligible voters who cast their ballots in the 1976 presidential election and nearly 20 percent fewer than 1972 totals.
>
> Not only is turnout—the percentage of eligible voters who actually vote—decreasing, but a smaller percentage of Americans are even bothering to register to vote each year.[3]

The essay that follows addresses the problems with the franchise in contemporary America. In the process of examining the trends in voter turnout and assessing their impact, it will make a number of points. First, voting participation is down. This can be shown. It has been decreasing consistently for two decades. The chances are that it will get worse. The problem is a serious one, as Broder and the Committee for the Study of the American Electorate have indicated, and it should not be ignored.[4]

The decline in voting is a product of many forces. Gans, for example, has argued that it involves such problems as the ". . . the decay of political and social institutions, most notably the political party; the growing impotence felt by the citizen in the face of large public and private institutions and increasingly complex problems; the role that mass media, especially television, has in creating confusion in the minds of some; and the degree to which our public dialogue reflects none of the central public questions of the day."[5] Undoubtedly he is right. Politics has fallen on bad times. Two decades of turmoil, civil rights revolutions and busing, Vietnam and Watergate, inflation and economic bad times have left their mark.[6] But there is something that can be done that would facilitate rather than obstruct the vote, and that could encourage larger rates of participation. The immediate results might be incrementally better or they might show substantial improvement over previous levels of turnout. At a minimum, the government would not be a partner in making voting in America the most difficult and demanding exercise of the franchise in the free world.

Registration can, and does, directly affect voter turnout. It does so in two ways. First, registration qualifications define the eligible electorate: those who are permitted to qualify to vote.[7] Second, registration laws detail the obstacles that citizens must meet before they can exercise the franchise. Such procedures have an impact on the voter and on turnout.[8] This will be shown through several examples and one experiment with change.

The United States is unique in the burden it places on its citizenry. The individual is asked to make more electoral decisions in relation to the vote than citizens in any other nation. The demands on the citizen in terms of time, knowledge, interest, motivation, and physical energy are extensive. Before they can vote, Americans must face, and master, the most cumbersome and restrictive registration practices of any country. Furthermore, efforts to overcome these must be self-initiated; unlike the governments of most other major democracies, the U.S. government does not take the responsibility for certifying the eligibility of its electorate.

Registration provisions are often arcane carryovers from the politics and social concerns of another age. Prospective voters are not educated to deal with these; their attention, like that of the media and of the nation at large, focuses on the election and its outcome. The lack of attention given to the necessity of meeting the formal requirements that qualify one to participate in the election is a sign of the traditional public—and, more specifically, governmental—indifference to the problems the system raises. As a consequence, individuals have little knowledge of the two-tiered election process and little sensitivity to the types of demands it will make on them. Ironically, the first stage, meeting the registration demands—the one about which they have least information or concern—may be the most important in deciding who will turn out on election day.[9] It could be argued that outdated registration procedures trivialize the voting decision by misdirecting the attention and energy of those who are forced to meet them away from the more significant concerns of the election. In sum, they poorly serve the broader purposes of a democratic and representative government.

Registration practices have emerged as candidates for reform in the 1980s. The concern began in the 1960s with the civil-rights revolution, and it has continued. Notable gains have been made, especially through the Voting Rights Acts of 1965, 1970, and 1975. These in turn, as well as the new and more critical approaches to registration limitations, have encouraged a relaxation of many regulations governing federal election practices in particular. Concomitant with these developments has been the evolution of new court doctrines less sympathetic to voting restrictions. There is an increasing unwillingness on the part of courts at all levels to sanction procedures that serve to curtail participation unless they can be shown to fulfill "a compelling state purpose."[10] This is a difficult standard to meet.

Nonetheless, much remains to be done. In this context, the major proposals for reform will be introduced and their potential ramifications evaluated. Registration reform, by itself, would not induce a turnout in the United States comparable to the best of other democratic nations. But it could make a potentially significant contribution to a more representative turnout and to a greater citizen participation in elections and in government. It would do this by removing the more arbitrary barriers to an eased involvement in a critical political act, voting. It would constitute a noteworthy beginning; attention then could turn to some of the other factors—from the failures of political leadership to the economic and social burdens that have plagued the last generation of American politics—that have contributed to the stagnation and loss of faith that characterize the current American malaise.

Voter Participation

Turnout over Time

There is general agreement on several points in the debate over expanding the electorate. One such point is that voting participation has declined in recent years. Since the introduction of female suffrage in 1920, voter participation appeared to be on a modest but consistent climb toward respectability. Turnout in presidential elections was low in the 1920s (averaging 43.7 percent) as the newly enfranchised familiarized themselves with their duties (table 3-1). Turnout increased significantly in the presidential election of 1928, marking the beginning of the New Deal coalition and (in the 1930s) the Democratic party's dominance in American politics. The New Deal era witnessed a generally consistent increase in voting; an average of 55 percent of those eligible voted in the 1930s and 1940s, 60 percent in the 1950s, and 62 percent in the 1960s. Slowly but surely turnout consistently edged upwards. As it happened, the participation figures for the 1960 presidential race (62.8 percent) would stand as the high voter-turnout mark for the next

Table 3-1
Turnout in Presidential and Congressional Elections, 1920-1978

| Year | Election Contest | |
	President	U.S. House
1920	43.5%	40.8%
1922	—	32.1
1924	43.9	40.6
1926	—	29.8
1928	51.9	47.8
1930	—	33.7
1932	52.4	49.7
1934	—	41.4
1936	56.9	53.5
1938	—	44.0
1940	58.9	55.4
1942	—	32.5
1944	56.0	52.7
1946	—	37.1
1948	51.1	48.1
1950	—	41.1
1952	61.6	57.6
1954	—	41.7
1956	59.3	55.9
1958	—	43.0
1960	62.8	58.5
1962	—	45.4
1964	61.9	57.8
1966	—	45.4
1968	60.9	55.1
1970	—	43.5
1972	55.5	50.9
1974	—	36.1
1976	54.4	—
1978	—	37.9

Source: Statistical Abstract of the United States.

two decades. Turnout fell slightly in 1964 and again in 1968. By the 1970s, and with the enactment of the eighteen-year-old vote for the election of 1972, turnout was averaging in the mid-50 percentiles.

Traditionally, voter participation at the presidential level is higher than at any other level of electoral contest. A look at the congressional elections since 1922 (table 3-1), when universal suffrage was in effect, shows a pattern similar to that at the presidential level, but at a much lower level of participation. Poor rates of turnout is the 1920s (averaging just over 30 percent of the eligible electorate) gave way to consistently higher (but still modest) turnouts, peaking in the congressional elections of 1958-1966 with rates between 43 and 46 percent. By the 1970s, the figures had dropped to about one-third of eligible voters taking part in these contests.

Turnout figures for states electing statewide (as against federal-level) officeholders for the years 1962-1978 parallel the trends in presidential and congressional voting. Comparative data for states holding statewide elections in 1962, 1974, and 1978 (table 3-2), show a decrease from an average of 48.1 percent participating in 1962 to 37.7 percent in 1978. The turnout in 24 states fell an average of 8 percentage points between 1974 and 1978 alone. Comparing 1978 with 1962, the latter being the high-water mark for participation in statewide races, the number of eligible voters registered was down in twenty-four of the thirty-one states for which comparable data were available, despite the loosening of registration requirements; the percentage of registered voters who actually voted was down in twenty-three of the twenty-nine states for which data were available; and the percentage of eligible voters participating was down in 78 percent of the forty-five states for which comparisons could be made (table 3-2).

Most of the states showing increases in these categories were southern states: five of the seven that had improved registration between 1962 and 1978; all (of the meager four) with an increase in the proportion of registered voters actually turning out; and seven of the eight with increases in the proportion of eligible voters participating were southern. Even among the southern states, however, the picture is discouraging. The election of 1970—five years after the first and most significant of the Voting Rights Acts—witnessed the highest level of turnout for the southern states. Since that point, voter participation has declined. Between 1970 and 1978, in statewide contests, the percentage of eligible voters registered decreased or stayed the same in six of the seven states for which data are available; the number of registered voters actually participating in elections increased in four states and went down or remained the same in four others; and, most importantly, the percentage of eligible voters actually voting went up in one state, went down in ten others, and stayed the same in two (table 3-3).

Figures for specific states accentuate the trend (table 3-4). New Jersey gubernatorial races show a decline in turnout, particularly marked for the

Table 3-2
Turnout in Statewide Elections, 1962 and 1978

I. Percentage of eligible voters registered in 1978 as compared to 1962

Increase (7)

Arkansas (12.8)
Florida (5.3)
Hawaii (5.3)
Louisiana (9.1)
Michigan (2.2)
South Carolina (2.8)
Virginia (1.9)

Decrease (24)

Arizona (1.9)
California (7.8)
Colorado (7.4)
Connecticut (6.6)
Delaware (11.4)
Idaho (8.5)
Illinois (6.6)
Kentucky (8.9)
Maryland (3.0)
Massachusetts (9.1)
Montana (5.9)
Nevada (1.3)
New Hampshire (8.8)
New Jersey (5.8)
New Mexico (6.0)
New York (8.2)
Oklahoma (15.0)
Pennsylvania (12.2)
Rhode Island (5.3)
Utah (1.6)
Vermont (2.3)
Washington (11.5)
West Virginia (21.5)
Wyoming (8.4)

II. Percentage of registered voters who actually voted in 1978 as compared to 1962

Increase (4)

Florida (14.2)
South Carolina (10.8)
Virginia (6.6)
Louisiana (7.6)

Decrease (23)

Arizona (16.2)
Arkansas (3.5)
California (10.2)
Colorado (8.9)
Connecticut (15.3)
Delaware (11.9)
Hawaii (17.4)
Idaho (14.8)
Illinois (18.5)
Kentucky (20.3)
Maryland (11.6)
Massachusetts (13.0)
Michigan (19.9)
Montana (8.5)
New Hampshire (11.4)
New Jersey (15.4)
New Mexico (3.1)
New York (17.8)
Oklahoma (1.8)
Pennsylvania (15.0)
Rhode Island (12.3)
Vermont (17.6)
Wyoming (17.4)

Stayed the Same (2)

Nevada (− 0.4)
West Virginia (+ 0.2)

Table 3-2 *(cont.)*

III. Percentage of Eligible Voters Voting in 1978 as compared to 1962

Increase (8)	*Decrease* (35)	*Stayed the Same* (2)
Alabama (7.2)	Arizona (11.0)	Tennessee (−0.2)
Alaska (7.0)	California (12.5)	Texas (−1.0)
Arkansas (4.3)	Colorado (11.5)	
Florida (11.6)	Connecticut (16.0)	
Louisiana (8.7)	Delaware (15.9)	
Mississippi (3.7)	Georgia (17.2)	
South Carolina (7.2)	Hawaii (6.1)	
Virginia (4.6)	Idaho (18.8)	
	Illinois (18.2)	
	Iowa (9.0)	
	Kansas (3.0)	
	Kentucky (18.2)	
	Maine (6.7)	
	Maryland (6.4)	
	Massachusetts (16.4)	
	Michigan (14.7)	
	Minnesota (5.3)	
	Montana (11.1)	
	Nebraska (9.7)	
	Nevada (1.3)	
	New Hampshire (14.9)	
	New Jersey (10.4)	
	New Mexico (5.5)	
	New York (16.9)	
	North Carolina (2.0)	
	Ohio (14.6)	
	Oklahoma (9.9)	
	Oregon (5.7)	
	Pennsylvania (19.5)	
	Rhode Island (13.4)	
	South Dakota (9.5)	
	Vermont (16.1)	
	West Virginia (11.1)	
	Wisconsin (7.0)	
	Wyoming (19.3)	

Source: Committee for the Study of the American Electorate, Washington, D.C.

elections after 1969. The Virginia gubernatorial contests, with turnouts as low as 16 percent in 1961, could rise to only 35 percent even with an increase in two-party competition. The mayoral races in some of the nation's major cities exhibited similarly depressed participation scores. During the 1960s and 1970s, these ranged from a low (in contested races) of 25 percent in Atlanta (1965) to a high of 53 percent in Detroit (1969). In almost all cases, the turnout rates for the 1970s declined. For the seven cities in table 3-4, turnout averaged about 38 percent for the seventeen contested races held in the 1970s. An examination of the figures in table 3-4 for both gubernatorial and mayoral races shows that the turnout rate for registered voters is significantly higher

Table 3-3
Turnout in Statewide Elections in Southern States, 1970 and 1978

I. Percentage of southern states' eligible voters registered in 1978 as compared to 1970

Increase (1)	*Decrease* (6)	*Stayed the Same* (1)
Louisiana (3.4)	Alabama (6.6)	Kentucky (+0.5)
	Arkansas (1.4)	
	Florida (3.9)	
	South Carolina (5.4)	
	Virginia (8.3)	
	West Virginia (10.6)	

II. Percentage of southern states' registered voters who actually voted in 1978 as compared to 1970

Increase (4)	*Decrease* (3)	*Stayed the Same* (1)
Florida (2.6)	Alabama (12.7)	West Virginia (+0.4)
South Carolina (3.2)	Arkansas (26.7)	
Virginia (6.8)	Kentucky (25.0)	
Louisiana (20.9)		

III. Percentage of southern states' eligible voters who voted in 1978 as compared to 1970

Increase (1)	*Decrease* (10)	*Stayed the Same* (2)
Louisiana (9.0)	Alabama (13.5)	Florida (0.0)
	Arkansas (18.5)	Virginia (−0.8)
	Georgia (16.4)	
	Kentucky (23.5)	
	Mississippi (21.9)	
	North Carolina (3.5)	
	South Carolina (1.2)	
	Tennessee (7.2)	
	Texas (8.6)	
	West Virginia (4.7)	

Source: Committee for the Study of the American Electorate, Washington, D.C.

than for the electorate as a whole, usually averaging between 15 and 20 percent. In a number of cases (Virginia, 1977; Cleveland, 1975, 1977; Louisville, 1973; New York City, 1977) the discrepancy between the two groups increases to between 26 and 30 percentage points.

Given these figures, there should be no illusions as to how the United States compares to other nations. Data for national-level turnouts (those most comparable to the presidential contests in this nation) for twenty-four countries in elections held between 1969 and 1973 make the point. Nine countries (Australia, Italy, Malta, Belgium, Austria, West Germany, and New Zealand) had turnouts of 90 percent or better; seven (Iceland, Sweden, Denmark, Luxembourg, the Netherlands, Finland, and Norway) had turnouts between 80 and 90 percent; and six more (Israel, France, Ireland, Canada, Japan, and Great Britain) had turnouts between 70 and 80 percent.

Table 3-4
Voter Turnout of Registered Voters and the Voting Age Population in Selected Gubernatorial and Mayoral Elections, 1961-1977

Year	Voting Age Population	Registered	Registered (%)	Total Turnout	Registered Voting (%)	Voting Age Population Voting (%)
New Jersey governor						
1977	5,194,000	3,662,499+	70.5	2,038,502	55.7	39.2
1973	5,030,000	3,541,809	70.4	2,122,099	59.9	42.2
1969	4,432,500	3,239,374	73.1	2,366,606	73.1	53.4
1965	4,187,000	3,151,599	75.3	2,229,583	70.7	53.3
1961	4,004,000	3,013,718	75.3	2,152,662	71.4	53.8
Virginia governor						
1977	3,617,000	2,020,623	56.1	1,265,535	62.6	35.0
1973	3,243,000	2,039,630	62.9	1,035,495	50.8	31.5
1969	2,770,000	1,750,201	63.2	915,764	52.3	33.1
1965	2,573,500	1,304,653	50.7	562,789	43.1	21.9
1961	2,402,500	1,046,973	43.6	394,490	37.7	16.4
Atlanta mayor						
1977	296,407	202,697	68.4	85,990	42.4	29.0
1973	312,777	206,257	65.9	125,641	60.9	40.2
1969	305,446	215,026	70.4	113,921	53.0	37.3
1965	304,230	—	—	77,053	—	25.3
1961	303,014	—	—	100,318	—	33.1
Cleveland mayor						
1977	428,441	273,342	63.8	182,473	66.8	42.6
1975	445,879	259,735	58.3	184,775	71.1	41.4
1973	467,296	304,480	65.2	135,617	44.5	29.0
1971	479,851	315,163	65.7	230,095	73.0	48.0
1969	470,609	316,340	67.2	238,843	75.5	50.8
1967	490,039	326,003	66.5	257,153	78.9	52.5
1965	509,469	—	—	236,736	—	46.5
1963	528,899	—	—	154,257	—	29.2
1961	548,329	—	—	199,293	—	36.3
Detroit mayor						
1977	893,779	659,495	73.8	369,230	56.0	41.3
1973	1,003,901	820,248	81.7	449,265	54.8	44.8
1969	953,725	740,619	77.7	510,283	68.9	53.5
1965	1,003,426	800,341	79.8	440,261	55.0	43.9
1961	1,053,127	880,064	83.6	359,191	40.8	34.1
Louisville mayor						
1977	232,947	174,961	75.1	81,791	46.7	35.1
1973	248,389	139,605	56.2	103,270	74.0	41.6
1969	228,968	112,441	49.1	91,225	81.1	39.8
1965	235,368	151,683	64.4	113,192	74.6	48.1
1961	241,768	—	—	117,019	—	48.4

Table 3-4 *(cont.)*

Year	Voting Age Population	Registered	Registered (%)	Total Turnout	Registered Voting (%)	Voting Age Population Voting (%)
Minneapolis mayor						
1977	280,428	242,762	86.6	103,648	42.7	37.0
1975	293,793	247,159	84.1	98,122	39.7	33.4
1973	317,966	254,501	80.0	126,139	49.6	39.7
1971	317,783	226,068	71.1	112,847	49.9	35.5
1969	289,716	224,120	77.4	122,660	54.7	42.3
1967	296,156	232,732	78.6	110,485	47.5	37.3
1965	302,596	243,977	80.6	96,909	39.7	32.0
1963	309,036	250,739	81.1	120,235	48.0	38.9
1961	315,476	262,239	83.1	120,379	45.9	38.2
New York City mayor						
1977	5,561,280	2,887,000	51.9	1,419,330	49.2	25.5
1973	5,633,744	3,758,267	66.7	1,790,053	47.6	31.8
1969	5,283,466	3,026,745	57.3	2,458,203	81.2	46.5
1965	5,311,358	3,281,689	61.8	2,652,451	80.8	49.9
1961	5,339,250	3,239,879	60.7	2,467,546	76.2	46.2
Pittsburgh mayor						
1977	333,503	232,576	69.7	144,289	62.0	43.3
1973	354,816	263,808	74.4	67,033	25.4	18.9[a]
1969	347,993	261,490	75.1	181,197	69.3	52.1
1965	369,257	219,517	59.4	175,743	80.1	47.6
1961	390,521	304,098	77.9	185,748	61.1	47.6

Source: Committee for the Study of the American Electorate, Washington, D.C.
[a]Uncontested election.

Four nations—Switzerland with 56 percent, the United States with 55 percent, and Botswana with 34 percent—fell well below the others, making up the tail end of the participation curve. According to these calculations (and since India was not considered a democracy during the period examined) the United States ranks above only Botswana in the level of voting participation of its eligible electorate.[11]

A number of factors motivate people to register and vote. But those who registered during the 1970s in the elections reviewed did vote in greater proportions and often at significantly higher levels than did the electorate as a whole. If a nation really wanted a higher voter involvement in its affairs, it would appear that a reasonable first step would be to ensure that as many people as possible were registered.

Nonvoting

The Nonvoters

Another major point generally agreed on by those studying political participation is the nature of those who do not vote. In effect, those left out of the active electorate are the ones least able to afford it. They tend to be disproportionately drawn from those with a grade-school education or less; those whose earnings are at the lowest end of the income scale; the young; and minorities (table 3-5).[12]

The problem is even more pressing than these data indicate. Those not voting at the presidential level are among the least likely to vote, or to participate in any politically effective way, in politics or community activities at any level. For example, in a study of 2,006 voters and nonvoters during the 1976 presidential election, Hadley (1978) attempted to assess the broader patterns of political involvement of nonparticipants.[13] Forty percent of the nonvoters either had not been registered to vote in other elections or did not know if they were registered or not, and 77 percent of the nonvoters (compared to 66 percent of the voters in 1976) reported that they either had not voted in the previous congressional election (1974) or had never been registered. The majority of voters admit that they never vote in local elections; that they discuss political or community affairs with others less often than once a week; and that they have never worked with others in the community to solve common problems. The majority of the nonparticipants appear to be very much outside the normal bounds of political activity.

Finally, it is worth noting—because it is the key to whether substantial registration reform is enacted—the political and ideological dispositions of the nonvoters. Those who oppose registration changes fear that the new voters in the electorate, should they materialize in any numbers, could provide a potent threat to the values and politics they hold dear. In particular, the Republican party's leadership (aided by many Democratic legislators comfortable with present electoral arrangements) favor maintaining a restricted electorate. They fear change, and they oppose it.

Most nonvoters are too apolitical to swell the ranks of liberals or Democrats, as many contend they would. If they had any motivating political interests of consequence (and the foregoing would suggest that most of the nonvoters do not), they would presently affiliate with a party and would vote. The majority of nonvoters are open to persuasion by either party; they are tied to neither. Hadley's data would indicate that this assessment is accurate. The modal group of nonvoters were independent in party affiliation. The proportion of nonparticipants associating with either political party was below that for voters, although the dropoff was slightly greater among Republican identifiers.

In relation to political ideology, twice as many nonvoters as voters declared none. The modal group for both was moderate and the proportions of liberals and conservatives among the nonparticipants fell 3 to 7 percentage points below those for the voters. Nonvoters are a politically unmoored group. They have no political or ideological anchoring, and they are open to conversion by either of the major parties.

This depiction of the nonvoter is, for the most part, not new. What is beginning to be realized, however, is that the "hardcore nonvoter" seg-

Table 3-5
Voting and Nonvoting in the 1976 Presidential Election
(percentage)

	Vote	*Not Vote*
Demographic characteristics		
Region		
New England	78.8	21.2
Middle Atlantic	70.8	29.2
East North Central	81.2	18.8
West North Central	78.7	21.3
Solid South	64.1	35.9
Border states	68.6	31.4
Mountain states	81.7	18.3
Pacific states	72.6	27.4
Size of place		
Twelve largest cities	74.8	25.2
Other large cities	73.3	26.7
Suburbs of twelve largest cities	74.7	25.3
Other suburbs	72.5	27.5
Adjacent areas	74.3	25.7
Outlying areas	67.5	32.5
Age		
18-24	55.7	44.3
25-35	68.2	31.8
36-50	81.6	18.4
51-65	80.3	19.7
66 and up	71.7	28.3
Education		
Eighth grade or less	60.7	39.3
Some high school	59.8	41.2
High school	69.4	30.6
High school plus noncollege schooling	75.8	24.2
Some college	83.8	16.2
College graduate	86.4	13.6
Advanced degree	92.2	7.8
Occupation		
Professional	88.9	11.1
Managerial	82.3	17.7
Clerical or sales	78.4	21.6
Craftsman-foreman	74.1	25.9
Operatives	65.7	34.3
Services	60.9	39.1
Laborers	59.6	40.4
Farming	71.7	28.3
Union membership		
Member	78.6	21.4
Not member	71.2	28.8
Class identification		
Lower class	40.0	60.0[a]
Average working class	65.7	34.3

Table 3-5 *(cont.)*

	Vote	*Not Vote*
Working class	60.0	40.0
Upper working class	74.6	25.4
Average middle class	79.9	20.1
Middle class	63.0	37.0
Upper middle class	83.4	16.6
Income level		
Under $2,000	41.0	59.0
$2,000-4,999	61.0	39.0
$5,000-9,999	68.1	31.9
$10,000-14,999	72.8	27.2
$15,000-19,999	76.4	23.6
20,000 and above	87.6	12.4
Religion		
Protestant	73.8	26.2
Catholic	74.9	25.1
Jewish	83.7	16.3
Sex		
Male	78.3	21.7
Female	69.1	30.9
Race		
White	73.9	26.1
Black	65.5	34.5
Party identification		
Strong Democrat	82.0	18.0
Weak Democrat	68.9	31.7
Independent Democrat	72.7	27.3
Independent	57.3	42.7
Independent Republican	76.3	23.7
Weak Republican	75.4	24.6
Strong Republican	92.3	7.7
Information on politics		
Follow public affairs		
Most of the time	86.5	13.5
Some of the time	78.9	21.1
Only now and then	56.2	43.8
Hardly at all	38.9	61.1
Watch evening national news broadcasts on television		
Frequently	77.9	22.1
Sometimes	67.7	32.3
Rarely	66.9	33.1
Never	65.1	34.9
Read a daily newspaper		
Yes	78.7	21.3
No	58.0	42.0

Source: Center for Political Studies.

[a]Only five people self-identified themselves as lower class.

ment—consisting of almost one-half of the electorate—is becoming increasingly easy to distinguish from the more affluent, better-educated professional and business people who make up most of the active electorate. The numbers of the hardcore nonvoters are on the rise, and the group as a whole appears to be increasingly less susceptible to political involvement. The electorate is becoming progressively more polarized, but recognition of this phenomenon is recent.

There is some evidence for these speculations. Thomas Cavanagh, working on a grant from the Committee for the Study of the American Electorate, has suggested that periodic increases and decreases in turnout are a function almost entirely of trends among voters of higher socioeconomic status. Cavanagh writes: "The aggregate decline in turnout has been far from neutral in class terms. It has tended to exaggerate the already pronounced bias in participation patterns."[14]

Cavanagh goes on to point out that an incredible eighteen million former voters have stopped voting. These declines are in the face of increased turnout in the South, due to the effective enfranchisement of blacks since the 1960s and to increasing party competition as well as the fact that ". . . the increase in education levels, independent of other factors, should have been sufficient to increase turnout by approximately 6.5 percent since 1964."[15] Not unexpectedly, the decisive drop in participation for the 1964-1976 period has been concentrated among "the young, the poor and the least educated."[16] The groups most marginal to the society, and most in need of representation, are the most likely to fall from the electorate. The dropoff in participation is most heavily concentrated among those groups. In increasing numbers they are operating effectively outside the contemporary political system.

The Reasons for Nonparticipation

The reasons given for nonvoting are complex (table 3-6). First, 59 percent of the eligible population claims to have voted in the 1976 presidential election, an overreporting of involvement on the order of 4 percent. This is not uncommon in studies of this nature. Of those not voting, the percentages are decisively higher for blacks (51.3 percent) and those of Hispanic origin (68.2 percent) than for whites (39.1 percent). When the respondents were asked why they did not vote, 4 percent or less, on the average, cited illness, travel, problems with work, long voting lines, or the inability to get to the polls. Another group of less than 2 percent of the electorate mentioned basically political and attitudinal factors: they did not support either of the candidates; they believed their votes made no difference in the election; they thought politicians were not concerned about their problems; they were not interested in the election; or they simply refused to become involved in politics. It is likely that such attitudes have more of an impact than they

Table 3-6

Reasons for Not Voting or Registering, November 1976 (Civilian Noninstitutional Population) *(in thousands)*

Voter Participation and Reason for Not Voting and Registering	Total	White	Black	Spanish Origin	Percent Distribution			
					Total	White	Black	Spanish Origin
Total, 18 yr. and over	146,548	129,316	14,922	6,594	100.0	100.0	100.0	100.0
Voted	86,698	78,808	7,273	2,093	59.2	60.9	48.7	31.8
Did not vote	59,850	50,508	7,655	4,495	40.8	39.1	51.3	68.2
Registered and did not vote	11,063	9,521	1,453	396	7.5	7.4	9.7	6.0
Unable to vote	5,887	5,088	755	187	4.0	3.9	5.1	2.8
Had no way to get to polls	438	330	104	14	.3	.3	.7	.2
Illness or emergency	2,157	1,860	293	63	1.5	1.4	1.9	1.0
Couldn't take time off from work	767	623	135	28	.5	.5	.9	.4
Lines too long, machines not working	248	239	5	5	.2	.2	[1]	.1
Out of town or away from home	1,561	1,441	114	33	1.1	1.1	.8	.5
Other reason	716	595	114	44	.5	.5	.8	.7
Did not want to vote or not interested	2,498	2,238	233	81	1.7	1.7	1.6	1.2
Did not prefer any of the candidates	1,265	1,173	82	41	.9	.9	.5	.6
Politicians are not interested in my problems	65	56	7	0	[1]	[1]	[1]	0
My vote would not make a difference in the election	133	115	17	2	.1	.1	.1	[1]
Just don't want to get involved in politics	122	103	13	8	.1	.1	.1	.1
Not interested in election this year	795	683	100	21	.5	.5	.7	.3
Other reason	118	103	14	9	.1	.1	.1	.1
Other reason	1,846	1,579	256	90	1.3	1.2	1.7	1.4
Reason not reported	832	617	210	37	.6	.5	1.4	.6
Not registered	48,787	40,987	6,202	4,100	33.3	31.7	41.5	62.2

Unable to register:								
Not a citizen	4,383	3,245	217	1,670	3.0	2.5	1.5	25.3
Residence requirement not satisfied	1,077	984	81	57	.7	.8	.5	.9
Recently moved, never got to register	1,514	1,349	146	65	1.0	1.0	1.0	1.0
Permanent illness or disability	1,383	1,084	283	53	.9	.8	1.9	.8
No transportation, hours or place of registration inconvenient	1,484	1,236	235	86	1.0	1.0	1.6	1.3
Did not know how or where to register	959	793	143	143	.7	.6	1.0	2.2
Can't read English	291	212	47	126	.2	.2	.3	1.9
Other reason	1,702	1,313	351	88	1.2	1.0	2.4	1.3
Did not want to register or not interested:								
Did not prefer any of the candidates	2,718	2,535	142	109	1.9	2.0	1.0	1.7
Politicians are not interested in my problems	412	346	56	23	.3	.3	.4	.3
My vote would not make a difference in the election	758	675	76	48	.5	.5	.5	.7
Just don't want to get involved in politics	2,320	2,014	259	113	1.6	1.6	1.7	1.7
Not interested in election this year	4,241	3,714	460	246	2.9	2.9	3.1	3.7
Other reason	970	818	139	52	.7	.6	.9	.8
Other reason	14,043	11,930	1,949	713	9.6	9.2	13.1	10.8
Reason not reported	1,720	1,308	368	104	1.2	1.0	2.5	1.6

Source: U.S. Bureau of the Census, *Current Population Reports*, series P20, no. 304, "Voter Participation in November 1976" (Washington, D.C.: U.S. Government Printing Office," 1976).

[a]Less than 0.05.

seem to. It is reasonable to expect that they would have more profound consequences on the registration process—normally more difficult than actual
voting—than they would on voting. Table 3-6 appears to bear this out.
Once people have taken the trouble to register, most will vote.

By far, the reason given by the greatest number in explaining their non-
voting was registration. Taking the population of nonvoters as a whole, 82
percent said the reason that they did not vote was that they were not
registered. The proportion failing to register, and thus unable to vote, was
particularly high for those of Hispanic origin. The comparative figures are
(for nonvoters): whites, 81 percent; blacks, 81 percent; and Hispanics, 91
percent.

Hispanics present a particular problem, one with increasing significance
for much of the southwestern United States and for most of the major
cities, areas that are becoming, at least in part, bilingual. One-fourth of
those not registered of Hispanic origin are not citizens. There is also a hint
in table 3-6 of problems with English and with the system (not knowing
where to register, for example). Not surprisingly, such factors can combine
to produce a low interest in politics and a low registration rate.

Among nonregistered whites and blacks, various institutional factors
(inability to register, failure to meet residency requirements, lack of
transportation) combined with attitudinal and political factors (lack of interest in election, refusal to become involved in politics, dislike of the candidates) begin to explain the lack of involvement. Political disinterest, of
course, can be fueled by legal barriers (such as registration) that are little
understood and, for many, are too much trouble to cope with.

The figures supplied by the U.S. Bureau of the Census delineate the
outlines of the problem. They do not suggest the depth of the political
dissatisfaction nor the corresponding malaise it breeds. They also do not indicate the complexity of the registration process and the psychological and
physical demands it makes on the individual. It is to these concerns that we
now turn.

Attitudinal Concerns

There are basically two sets of underlying reasons for nonvoting. The first
deals with attitudinal problems of faith and trust in the system that affect
the individual's response to such things as voting. Americans have
undergone a profound period of disillusionment that began, roughly, with
the assassination of John Kennedy.[17] The first signs were evident in the
presidential election of 1964. Since that point there has been a steady decline
in trust and support for government officials and the political system. Vietnam, Watergate, and a sick economy have done little to reassure voters.

The result has been a crisis in confidence and a political depression with continuing consequences for the vote.[18] Academic research, commercial polls and government-sponsored research have made the point with monotonous regularity: Americans are "turned off"; they are angry and disappointed in their government and its leaders; their faith in the United States and its future has been shaken; and their changing attitudes have adversely affected their tolerance for politics.

A sample survey of 1,486 nonvoters was conducted in 1976 by Peter D. Hart Research Associates, a Washington polling firm, for the University of Denver and the Committee for the Study of the American Electorate. The research was advised and supported by a number of concerned Americans and organizations, such as the president of Common Cause, the United Auto Workers, the National Committee for an Effective Congress, the International Association of Machinists, businessmen, and former Republican and Democratic national and state-level office holders. Funding was provided by corporations, unions, and foundations, including the Atlantic Richfield Corporation, the American Federation of State, County, and Municipal Employees, the CBS Foundation, and Ashland Oil. The result was one of the few intensive studies of the problem of nonparticipation.[19] The research findings, and the publicity they received, did much to focus informed attention on the problem of nonvoting. Tables 3-7 and 3-8 are developed from data collected in the study.

The authors of the study were concerned with the reasons nonvoters gave for their failure to participate (table 3-7). Roughly one-half of the responses dealt with perceptions of the political system and what the individual felt was his role in it. It does not present an encouraging picture. When asked to choose what was important and what was not important in their decision not to participate, those interviewed placed first what they perceived as the hypocrisy of candidates for political office. In addition, 50 percent or more of the nonvoters mentioned such reasons as the unimportance of which candidate is elected, Watergate and its effects, the essential sameness of all candidates, and a personal refusal to bother with politics. Between 20 and 40 percent volunteered such reasons as government secrecy or their own perceived inadequacy (lack of information; "I don't feel qualified") to judge the candidates and issues in an election. Citizens that feel alienated from their government, for whatever reason, cannot represent a happy omen for a democratic system. The authors of the study concluded that the attributes of the nonvoter ". . . are a distrust of and disaffection from, major political and economic institutions, political leadership, and the media."[20]

In a follow-up to the summary questions about noninvolvement, the same study attempted to explore several underlying dimensions of voters' attitudes. The measures employed have been used in voting studies since

Table 3-7
Reasons for Not Voting, 1976 Presidential Election
(percent)

	Important[a]	Not Important	Not Sure
Candidates say one thing and then do another	68	27	5
It doesn't make any difference who is elected because things never seem to work right	55	38	7
Watergate proved that elected officials are only out for themselves	52	41	7
All candidates seem pretty much the same	50	43	7
I just don't bother with politics	50	45	5
It is hard to find reliable and unbiased information on the candidates	49	42	9
The government seems to act too secretly	47	46	7
One person's vote really won't make any difference	46	49	5
I don't feel qualified to vote	31	64	5
Most elections are already decided in advance	31	58	11
The choice of candidates is just limited to Democrats and Republicans	23	69	8
The registration rules make it difficult for people to register	21	69	10
I couldn't get to the polls during voting hours	18	76	6
They make it hard for people who don't speak English	16	75	9
The location of the polling place is inconvenient	15	77	8
Need help or transportation to get to the polls	15	78	7
No place to leave children while at polls	12	82	6
It takes too long to vote	11	81	8
Most of the people in charge of the polls are not of my race	8	86	6
I am too old to vote	8	86	6
Someone might try to hurt me or my family if I voted	7	87	6

Source: Committee for the Study of the American Electorate, Washington, D.C.

Note: Based on responses to the following question: "Here are a number of reasons why people have said they have not gotten involved or voted in the past few years. For each reason, tell me if this has been a very important, somewhat important or not a very important reason to you for not voting."

[a]Includes all those designating a reason as either very important or somewhat important.

the 1950s (table 3-8).[21] These attitudinal measures show a broad pattern of distrust and feelings of political ineffectiveness. More than 60 percent of the respondents believe that "quite a few" of the people running the government in Washington are crooked; that the government can be trusted to do what is right only some, or none, of the time; and that the government is run by a few big interests. On the latter question, only 22 percent felt the government was run for the benefit of all. Between 66 and 82 percent agreed with two items stressing the inability of citizens to influence government decisions. To round out a depressingly negative picture, a majority of respondents (52 percent) said that they felt there was no group or individual in the United States that could accomplish what needed to be done.

The Hadley survey of nonvoters, conducted by Market Opinion Research (a predominantly Republican polling firm) in November 1976, supplies more evidence of the problem. Hadley included the standard indices of political cynicism and feelings of impotence (similar to those reported), and the results were much the same. Nonparticipants felt both more cynical and less able to do something about politics (low political efficacy) than did voters. What makes Hadley's investigation different, however, is the inclusion of an item measuring the individual's control over his own life. Hadley wanted to ascertain whether those who felt life experiences could be planned and those who trusted to luck differed in ways helpful to explaining nonparticipation. He believes the answers to this item are the keys to the psychological attitudes underlying nonvoting:

> Voters and refrainers [nonvoters] divided from each other over whether life was largely a matter of planning or of luck as they did nothing else. Of the voters, 57 percent believed life was a matter of planning, only 38 percent found life more a matter of luck. For the refrainers these statistics dramatically reverse. Fifty-four percent of the refrainers believed life to be largely a matter of luck, and only 37 percent believed in planning ahead. Such wide, strong relationships on questions of attitude are highly unusual.[22]

Hadley believes these findings add an important new dimension to an understanding of the psychological roots of noninvolvement.

The results of the studies to date indicate that nonvoters have a depressing image of American politics and of their role in and influence over it. They see government as remote from the individual, run for the benefit of a few, and exploitive of the citizenry. Their own relationship to it is passive. They see it as complicated, insensitive to their concerns, and beyond their control. It is little wonder that with such an outlook these respondents would not contemplate voting. In this context, the act seems futile.

The cochairmen of the Republican National Committee, in testifying before the Congress on one of the many proposals to expand the electorate by reducing registration barriers, referred to voting as "a moral issue."[23] There are political and personal consequences for the individual in the deci-

Table 3-8

Responses to Measures of Political Trust and Effectiveness by Nonvoters, Presidential Election of 1976

(percent)

"Do you think quite a few of the people running the government in Washington are a little crooked, not very many are, or do you think that hardly any of them are crooked at all?"

Quite a few	61
Not many	24
Hardly any	6
Don't know	9

"How much of the time do you think you can trust the government in Washington to do what is right—just about always, most of the time, or only some of the time?"

Just about always	5
Most of the time	27
Only some of the time	57
None of the time (VOL)[a]	6
Don't know	5

"Would you say that the government in Washington is pretty much run by a few big interests or that it is pretty much run for the benefit of all people?"

By a few big interests	62
For all people	22
Other/depends (VOL)	6
Don't know	10

"Sometimes government and politics seem so complicated that a person like me can't really understand what's going on."

Strongly agree	52
Partially agree	30
Partially disagree	8
Strongly disagree	7
Not sure	3

"People like me don't have any say about what the government does."

Strongly agree	33
Partially agree	33
Partially disagree	18
Strongly disagree	12
Not sure	4

"There don't seem to be any people or groups in American politics that can accomplish what I think needs to be done."

Strongly agree	30
Partially agree	32
Partially disagree	17
Strongly disagree	9
Not sure	12

Source: Committee for the Study of the American Electorate.

[a]VOL = answer volunteered by respondent.

sion to vote or not to vote. But in many respects, voting may be a moral issue. It would appear that a government would want to keep faith with its citizenry and that it would want as many as humanly possible to participate. The more representative it is of the concerns of its electors, the greater its vitality and the better the long-run prognosis for its continued health. There is a moral dimension to such a concern with the operation of democratic government. A disillusioned citizenry, not participating in the most basic of democratic rituals, would not appear to augur well for a representative political system. Put in starker terms, with seventy to seventy-five million Americans not participating in presidential elections and ninety million or more not participating in congressional or lower-level elections, something is wrong. It is a problem for the American political system that should demand priority attention.

Registration and Voting

Institutional Limits on the Voter

The figures in table 3-3 appear to indicate that failure to register is the major block to voting. The evidence, while scarce (political scientists have not devoted many of their resources to the problem), is cumulative. A pioneering study by two early political scientists, Charles E. Merriam and Harold F. Gosnell, *Non-Voting* (1924), concluded that "there were three times as many adult citizens who could not vote because they had failed to register as there were registered voters who had failed to vote in the particular election."[24] Merriam and Gosnell were reiterating what politicians already knew: registration qualifications can substantially reduce an electorate. Government officials can define the electorate as including those they want to participate. Blacks, ethnics, and the poor learned this bitter lesson, but political scientists were slow to develop an appreciation of the registration process and its implications.[25]

The insights of Merriam and Gosnell were not followed up in depth. More than three decades were to pass before another equally influential study appeared. In 1967 Stanley Kelley, Jr., Richard E. Ayres, and William G. Bowen published their analysis of voter turnout in 104 of the nation's largest cities.[26] The focus was on the 1960 presidential vote. The authors correlated three sets of variables—socioeconomic (age, sex, race, education, income, and geographical mobility); competitive patterns; and registration practices (literacy tests, closing dates for registration, accessibility of registration places, whether the enrollment system was permanent or periodic, and qualifications such as residency requirements)—with turnout.

The analysis showed that "78 percent of the variation in the percentage of the population of voting age that voted could be accounted for by variations in the percentage of the population of voting age that was registered to vote."[27] The methodology of the study may seem flawed in retrospect, but its sentiments hold up: speaking of presidential elections, the authors conclude: ". . . registration requirements are a more effective deterrent to voting than anything that normally operates to deter citizens from voting once they have registered."[28] Registration, *not* voting, say the authors, is the first and the major hurdle to an inclusive electorate. Their study and its implications, important at a time when renewed political attention was being focused on the disenfranchised, helped spur a modest revival of interest in the problem.

Among the analyses concerned with registration over the last decade, several deserve particular attention. A study by Jae-On Kim, John R. Petrocik, and Stephen N. Enoksen (1975) measured the relationship of registration as well as electoral competition and individual socioeconomic data to voter turnout in the states.[29] The election chosen for analysis was 1960, the one with the highest turnout in recent times. The analysis illustrates the difficulty inherent in singling out legal factors and measuring their impact on individual behavior—in this case, voting. Statutes are enforced in restrictive or lenient ways that researchers cannot control; and the regulations governing an election, as well as their application, are a mixture of the social and political factors that have conditioned a state's political environment. Nonetheless, with these caveats in mind, the results do appear to be in the direction expected: the more facilitative the registration system, the greater the likelihood of increased voter turnout.[30]

An analysis by Douglas D. Rose (1975) supplementing that of Kim et al. focused on the 1972 state registration practices and their impact on the vote. The author explains his research and its implications as follows:

> The largest and most striking coefficient represents the unknown sources of registration. Age and state help relatively little in explaining why individuals do or do not register. The inability to explain registration is particularly important because . . . registration is regularly translated into voting turnout, and, aside from this relation, most of the causes of turnout are unknown. *Explaining registration is thus the single most important task of turnout research.*[31] [Italics added]

An analysis of the impact of registration practices on the 1972 presidential vote by Rosenstone and Wolfinger (1978) emphasizes the crucial role of registration in restricting the vote.[32] The authors looked at such things as residency requirements; registration closing dates; the use of deputy registrars; the location, accessibility, and hours of registration offices; and absentee registration provisions. They analyzed state differences in turnout in relation to these factors and the impact of each factor on different groups of potential voters. They concluded that if the states adopted such provisions for registration as regular office hours, evening and/or Saturday registration, local or neighborhood registration, selective absentee registration, a closing date seven days before the election, and an eight-year wait before purging the rolls, voter turnout could be increased by millions. Specifically, they predicted that "if all the states adopted the provisions . . . , turnout would increase by approximately 10.5 percent."[33] This would have meant an additional 14.1 million voters in 1972 and a turnout rate well in excess of that of any recent election.

A study by Daniel Yankelovitch, Inc. for the National Movement for the Student Vote agrees with the figures put forth by Rosenstone and Wolfinger. Based on its survey of the adult electorate, the Yankelovitch organization estimated that 11 percent of the citizens of the United States wanted to vote in the election of 1972 but could not.[34]

Registration Practices

There are two aspects of registration procedures: the rules themselves and the way in which the rules are applied. The Voters Education Fund of the League of Women Voters has been one of the most active groups in assessing the implications of these practices. In 1972, the League published an analysis of registration practices in a sample of 251 communities nationwide, encompassing large cities, suburbs, small towns, and rural areas and, in toto, including areas where forty million people (one-fifth of the population of the United States) lived.[35]

The results were disheartening. The League found that many of the proposals that would help to increase the pool of registrants, and therefore the number of voters, were not used in many places. Of the communities that could employ deputy registrars, 29 percent did not; only ten states expressly forbid evening or Saturday hours for registration, but 75 percent of the sample had no evening registration and 77 percent no Saturday registration in nonelection months. Even in the thirty days prior to the closing of the registration period, 38 percent of the communities studied allowed for no extra hours for registration. Fifty-two percent of the registration places were poorly marked and, therefore, difficult to find; one-fourth of the people associated with civic groups who attempted to be deputized as registrars were refused by election officials; one-half of the groups using registration lists to enroll voters found them inaccurate (and in one-half of these cases the inaccuracies exceeded 10 percent); and so on. "These examples," the League concluded, "once again illustrate an attitude on the part of many election officials which tends to obstruct rather than encourage the efforts of citizen groups to expand the electorate."[36]

The League believed that the following served as major depressants to the vote:

residency requirements;

difficult registration procedures;

confusing absentee voting provisions;

inconvenient registration hours;

distant and poorly accessible places of registration;

restricted times for registering;

limited public information concerning registration;

little personal contact with unregistered voters;

long lines;

personal appearances required to enroll.[37]

The League found such practices to be widespread. It also found local registrars to be basically unconcerned with the difficulties, to exercise a great deal of discretion over what they could (or would) do, and to be under no centralized supervision. In effect, local registrars were not held accountable for their actions. To make matters worse, most registrars considered voter enrollment to be a relatively unimportant function of their office. Given their other day-to-day administrative responsibilities, this attitude should not be surprising. Registration is often a part-time activity by officials ill-prepared for their duties and unsympathetic to the end results:

> Only eleven percent of the local officials . . . published a voter information guide; 28 percent provided no training for poll workers; and in approximately thirty percent of the registration places where bilingual assistance was needed, local officials failed to provide this service. Election officials clearly have the power to make registration and voting procedures easier for citizens but this study has found that, by and large, they don't use it.[38]

In its assessment of the helpfulness of registration officials, the League discovered that, in effect, the more it was needed and the more dependent the prospective registrant was on such help, the worse the situation was. Working-class or mixed-class areas could expect the least help from officials. People in racially mixed districts could expect little assistance, and in general the less well off were lucky to receive even courteous treatment. The figures on voter turnout reflect, in part, the breakdown of the system at this point. The League of Women Voters put the matter this way:

Considering the all too frequent occurrence of complex forms, unhelpful and poorly trained staff, machine breakdowns, and inconveniently located registration and polling places, it is surprising that so many citizens do vote. That the system functions at all is a tribute to the sheer determination of citizens to overcome these inconveniences and obstacles.[39]

Registration Makes a Difference: A Case Study

One of the most successful, and impressive, experiments in expanding the electorate in U.S. history was the Voting Rights Act of 1965.[40] The impact of this piece of legislation in increasing turnout in the southern states, in particular, to which it was applied argues forcefully for what can be done both in eliminating legal barriers to the vote and in facilitating a higher turnout. Future changes in registration laws and practices are unlikely to produce results as dramatic as those that followed the enactment of the 1965 act. What the experience with the Voting Rights Act (and its successors in 1970 and 1975) did show was the effect legal restraints and official attitudes can have on participation. If these are fundamentally changed, a new, more inclusive electorate is possible.

The Voting Rights Act was enacted in 1965 as the end product of a series of civil-rights disturbances in the South. It was intended to break down the officially supported barriers to political participation in the southern states and, unlike many of its predecessors, the legislation was both strict and enforceable. It called for a number of changes to provide for the full representation of minorities (predominantly blacks) in politics. The act banned literacy tests; it gave the federal government power to litigate in matters of electoral discrimination based on race; and, in its most significant departure, it allowed federal officials to supersede local officials in the registration of voters.

The federal government was given the power to send registrars into states or communities in which less than one-half of the eligible electorate voted, on the presumption that in such localities there was discrimination. This "triggering clause" was new—nothing like it had been contained in the previous civil-rights acts—and it allowed for immediate remedial action by the federal government. The legislation was to have profound consequences in the states to which it applied and, in a very short time, in the region and the entire nation. It is fair to say that the South's politics were changed and, with them, the role of the South in national politics.

The bill called for many improvements in registration qualifications and procedures and in the administration of elections well beyond the scope of this report. As noted, it did allow for direct federal intervention in the registration procedures of eleven southern states. The changes were marked. The pre-act registration of blacks and whites was estimated at 35.5

percent and 73.4 percent respectively. Two years after the act was passed, black registration had jumped to 57.2 percent. White enrollment had increased during the same period to 76.5 percent.[41] By 1972, in the seven southern states still covered by the act, black registration was 56.6 percent and white registration 67.7 percent. Only three (Louisiana, North Carolina, and South Carolina) of the seven states still covered by the act in 1975 actually collected registration figures by race. The results from these states can be used to illustrate the progression in the region as a whole (table 3-9).[42]

Between 1965 and 1974, Louisiana's black enrollment doubled and South Carolina's increased by 23 percentage points. North Carolina showed relatively modest increases in black enrollment (up 8 percent but a significant decline in white enrollment (down 25 percent). The white dropoff resulted from a more equitable application of registration requirements to all and an updating of unpruned enrollment lists. The result was not only that more blacks registered but also that in North Carolina and the other states they make up a bigger and politically more powerful voting bloc vis-à-vis whites in the electorate. It is difficult for politicians seeking elective office to ignore this many potential votes. One consequence has been that the redneck politics of race baiting becomes self-defeating and outdated in an electorate in which a majority of the blacks are registered.

As blacks have registered, they have begun to vote in large numbers. The results are changing the politics of the south.[43] Table 3-10 shows the participation figures for the seven states most influenced by the Voting

Table 3-9
Voter Registration Changes for Three Southern States, Pre- and Post-Voting Rights Act

State	Voting Age Population (1960) White	Black	Registration Number White	Black	Percent White	Black
Pre-act (prior to 1965)						
Louisiana	1,289,216	514,589	1,037,184	164,601	80.5	31.6
North Carolina	2,005,955	550,929	1,942,000	258,000	96.8	46.8
South Carolina	895,147	371,104	677,914	138,544	75.7	37.3
Post-act (1974)						
Louisiana	1,644,732	600,425	1,335,027	391,666	81.2	65.2
North Carolina	2,647,812	644,511	1,911,448	350,560	72.2	54.4
South Carolina	1,200,907	429,598	736,302	261,110	61.3	60.8

Source: For pre-act figures, United States Commission on Civil Rights, *Political Participation* (Washington, D.C.: U.S. Government Printing Office, 1968), pp. 222-223; for post-act information, United States Commission on Civil Rights, *The Voting Rights Act: Ten Years After* (Washington, D.C.: U.S. Commission on Civil Rights, 1975), pp. 53-54.

Table 3-10

Voter Turnout in the Presidential Elections of 1964, 1968, 1972, and 1976 in Southern States Covered by the Voting Rights Act

(percent)

State	Presidential Year Turnout				Percentage-Point Difference in Turnout 1964-1968	Percentage-Point Difference in Turnout 1964-1976
	1964	*1968*	*1972*	*1976*		
Alabama	35.9	52.7	44.2	47.7	+ 16.8	+ 11.8
Georgia	43.3	43.4	37.8	43.8	+ 0.1	− 0.5
Louisiana	47.3	54.8	45.0	50.8	+ 7.5	+ 3.5
Mississippi	33.9	53.2	46.0	49.9	+ 19.3	+ 16.0
North Carolina	52.3	54.3	43.9	43.8	+ 2.0	− 8.5
South Carolina	39.4	46.7	39.5	41.7	+ 7.3	+ 2.3
Virginia	41.1	50.1	45.6	48.5	+ 9.0	+ 7.4
Average for 7 states	41.9	50.7	43.1	46.6	+ 8.9	+ 4.7
United States	61.8	60.7	55.7	54.4	− 1.1	− 7.4

Source: United States Commission on Civil Rights, *The Voting Rights Act: Ten Years After* (Washington, D.C.: U.S. Commission on Civil Rights, 1975), p. 45; for 1976, Congressional Research Service, "States Ranking in 1976 in Registration and Participation Rates," (Washington, D.C.: The Library of Congress, n.a.).

Rights Act. Turnout jumped an average of 9 percentage points just in the period between 1964, the last election before the act's adoption, and 1968, the first election after its enactment. The gains for several of the states—Mississippi and Alabama are exemplars—that began with particularly low levels of voter involvement were especially dramatic. By 1976, the average turnout for the seven states was running about 5 percent over the pre-act figure. These increases came during a period when voter turnout for the nation as a whole was decreasing.

The improvements in these states are, of course, relative. They began from a low base point—the lowest in the nation. These states still have a long way to go. In 1976, five of the states ranked at the bottom of all the states in voter turnout and the seven states cited all ranked within the bottom twelve.

Black registration and increased black voter turnout has shifted the power distribution within the southern electorate. The early results are impressive. The number of black officials elected in the seven southern states increased almost 2,000 percent between 1964 and 1974, from 51 (counting liberally) to 963. South Carolina had no elected black officials prior to the Voting Rights Act. In 1974, it had 116, serving in positions at the city, county, and state levels. Mississippi and Alabama had 191 and 149, respectively, in 1974, up from 6 and 16. The number of black elected officials is not proportionate to the black population in the states or to their importance to the Democratic party's coalition. But it is increasing.

Many barriers to black participation remain to be overcome. Nonetheless, the 1965 Voting Rights Act did change the face of southern politics. Blacks are now a significant part of the electorate, and any candidate with serious aspirations for public office must pay them heed. The race-baiting, redneck politics of less than two decades ago are now past. The pace of the transformation and its impact on those caught in its web can be surprising. One election race can illustrate how fundamental the change has been.

Tom Wicker of the *New York Times* went down to South Carolina for an early assessment of Senator Strom Thurmond's 1978 race for reelection. He reported as follows on what he found:

> To watch Strom Thurmond these days, you might think he'd been the lifelong ally of black voters in South Carolina.
>
> Already campaigning for a fifth term in the Senate, still apparently vigorous at 76, Mr. Thurmond is publicly identifying himself with Senator Edward Kennedy, with whom he has co-sponsored a bill to provide free medicines and drugs for the elderly. He helped engineer the appointment of Matthew Perry, a South Carolina black leader, to the United States Court of Military Appeals and has made it clear that he favors Mr. Perry for the first Federal District Court opening in the state. And when John Lewis, the former civil rights leader and director of the Voter Education Project, was appointed this year to Federal office, Mr. Thurmond made him a well-publicized congratulatory phone call.
>
> It would be hard to tell from any of that that Strom Thurmond was one of the bitterest foes of any and all civil rights bills, including the Voting Rights Act, or that he ran for President in 1948 on the States' Rights ticket, or that he was one of the architects of Richard Nixon's Southern strategy which did not count on black voters.[44]

The Strom Thurmond that Wicker is reporting on epitomized the white, racist campaigner of the 1940s, 1950s, and 1960s. But with the passage of the Voting Rights Act and its implementation, Thurmond changed. He had to in order to survive politically. Of the one million registered South Carolina voters in 1978, 29 percent were black. One-half of these were expected to vote—more than enough to decide a competitive race. South Carolina is not unique. To greater and lesser degrees, the same drama is being played out at all electoral levels in the South.

The Voting Rights Act has had an enormous impact. Facilitative registration procedures can increase the turnout and, not incidentally, reshape the electorate. It is unlikely that anything approaching the gains from the Voting Rights Act could be realized again. Under the proper conditions, however, registration procedures could be changed and voter turnout increased.

The Proposed Solutions

A number of proposals are now before the nation for debate. These range from relatively modest, piecemeal approaches—the traditional manner of handling the problem—to more ambitious and inclusive programs to remodel the entire process of registration (table 3-11). The variety of plans can be divided into two major categories: the incrementalist solutions and the "big-bang" proposals. Incremental plans include the vast majority of proposals made over the last two decades. It is difficult to mobilize public support for modest, and generally arcane, proposals to change essentially technical aspects—the number of days registration remains open prior to an election, the conditions under which mobile registration units are permitted—of current registration laws. These are not issues that inflame public passions or dominate public discourse.

A second problem with this approach is its eventual impact. Many of these proposals, while improvements over previous practices, would result in a limited—in many cases possibly unmeasurable—impact on voter turnout.

Most of the incrementalist plans are voluntary. They represent suggestions to the states on ways to incorporate relatively minor changes into procedures that might improve the efficiency of electoral operations. There is no particular rationale tying the bundle of proposals into any coherent whole and no simple unifying theme that can help "sell" the plans to other states or to the public. Adoption then depends on the good will and self-motivation of the state or other electoral unit. The approach guarantees minimum impact. With no pressure, even assuming the logic and appeal of the suggestions (although this is not always evident), reform is unlikely. Apathy prevails. There has to be a strong incentive to change familiar ways, usually occasioned by pressure forced by a public concern and supplemented in federal legislation by monetary rewards. Without external pressure, it is easier to continue in the established pattern, whatever its deficiencies.

There is a plan—postcard representation—that does not completely fit these characterizations. It is not far removed from present practices (many

Table 3-11
Approaches to Changing Voter Registration System

Categories	Proposals
Incremental	Piecemeal—selected plans
	Postcard registration
"Big bang"	Universal Voter Enrollment
	Election Day Registration

localities and states now employ postcard registration) and the plan does have a logic and cohesion that escape the other incrementalist proposals. Although the increases in turnout are not likely to parallel those in the big-bang category, a national postcard-registration system could lead, nonetheless, to small but measurable improvements in participation.

The big-bang plan would fundamentally alter traditional practices. The two sets of proposals in this category include Universal Voter Enrollment and Election Day Registration. The assumptions underlying the proposals are quite different, as are both the machinery needed to put them into effect and the arguments used by critics against them. These are discussed below. What the plans have in common is that on a national scale they would introduce a new, more modern approach to registration into American politics—one that for most localities would constitute a fundamental departure from previous practices. Either plan could be expected to increase voter participation significantly by minimizing the obstacles encountered in registering to vote.

The following section introduces and analyzes the major proposals under the two categories.

The Incrementalist Plans

Piecemeal Reform. Possibly the most famous of the piecemeal plans for registration reform were those proposed by the President's Commission on Registration and Voter Participation established by President John Kennedy in early 1963. The commission was chaired by election analyst Richard M. Scammon and was intended to focus attention on—and do much to resolve—a continuing problem for the American democratic enterprise: the restraining effect of registration on voter participation. It was created with a great deal of publicity and its recommendations were eagerly anticipated. Unfortunately, they were to have little impact. The commission reported in November 1963, a few days after Kennedy's assassination. Its report lacked coherence, putting forth twenty-one standards against which to measure state and local enrollment practices. The recommendations were hardly new or revolutionary; most were, in fact, moderate and familiar proposals related to, for example, the length of registration periods and the use of mobile registration units that had been used in many localities and had often been proposed as reforms previously.

The commission's "standards," or recommendations, included the following:

> that each state examine its own registration practices through a body similar to the presidential commission (or through some other agency);

that voter registration should be easily accessible to all, through such devices as door-to-door registration, deputy registrars, and precinct and mobile registration;

that state residency requirements should not exceed six months and local residency requirements thirty days;

that new state residents should be allowed to vote for president;

that voter registration should extend as close to election day as possible and should not end more than three or four weeks before the election;

that voter registration lists should be kept current;

that registration should not be cancelled for failure to vote in any period less than four years;

that voter registration lists should be used only for electoral purposes;

that states should provide for absentee registration;

that literacy tests should not be a prerequisite for voting (a proposal that brought some dissent);

that long lines at polling places should be avoided;

that election day should be proclaimed a national holiday (the commission's boldest recommendation); and so on.[45]

The sentiments underlying the proposals were laudable. How the states would be forced to enact them—the practical problem of consequence and the biggest impediment to change—was left vague. The commission's last recommendation was that "each state should keep informed of other states' practices and innovations"[46] indicated how unprepared the group was to deal with the political problem of greatest importance. The commission's indecision on this point is best conveyed by their own words. In introducing its proposals, the report stated: "These recommendations are made for the consideration of all concerned with our electoral process. Some will affect certain authorities more than others, but the Commission would be gratified if all citizens would consider the suggestions which follow."[47] Such a mild change is not likely to excite much interest. Predictably, it did not.

The report left it up to the different electoral units to implement whatever recommendations they considered relevant, an approach that guaranteed that no fundamental change would occur. To further dilute its impact, commissioners appended a series of dissenting opinions to the official announcement. The overall results were disappointing. The report on a major problem of democratic governance, backed by the political muscle of a sympathetic administration, had little impact. It remains primarily as a testimonial to the nonproductiveness of this type of approach.

The incremental approach, nonetheless, continues to be the most popular. It appeals to the pragmatic nature of politicians. The obscure nature of most proposals, while uninteresting to the media and the public, is well adapted to the technical expertise of legislators; to the legal mind, which dominates in legislative settings; and to the legislative process, which favors incremental, as opposed to broad-scale, reforms. Also, such an approach offers hope of enacting some changes. Presently, incremental reforms before the Congress include such things as federal bonuses for computerizing registration processes and modernizing equipment and procedures; bonuses and federal assumption of costs in some cases for adopting deputy registrars; keeping enrollment offices open longer; adopting more inclusive federal election rules; federal help to update election machinery on such things as distribution practices for enrollment lists; relaxing absentee registration requirements; bonuses for states or election districts that attain certain levels of registration (75 to 90 percent of the eligible electorate), employing whatever means the electoral unit chooses; and general grants to the states with few strings or objectives other than to improve registration levels. Such proposals are constantly before the Congress, and periodically some are adopted. In the aftermath of the Voting Rights Act of 1965, the Congress has used the periodic debates over renewals to expand the act's comprehensiveness (for example, to minorities of Hispanic origin in northern urban areas) and to restyle, either through the act or in separate legislation, absentee registration and election procedures.

The courts have also been increasingly active since the mid-1960s and the cumulative impact of the judicial decisions has been to make it increasingly difficult for electoral units to initiate or sustain arbitrary or discriminatory registration practices. The process is slow, but the results, nonetheless, are important.

Two court decisions have had a particular impact and have set the standard for future decisions. In *Oregon* v. *Mitchell* (1971), the Supreme Court upheld the provisions of the Voting Rights Act of 1970, including the act's voiding of all state residency requirements for presidential elections that exceeded thirty days on the grounds that these did not serve a "compelling state interest."[48] In *Dunn* v. *Blumstein* (1972), the Supreme Court upheld the move to extend these criteria to state local residency requirements. As a consequence, the need for registration requirements to be justified in terms of "a compelling state interest" is the new standard by which such practices are to be judged.[49] It is a difficult standard to meet and over time should result in the lessening of registration barriers.

Incremental approaches to registration reform are popular. They fit the legislative mood and do not disrupt political patterns. They are, on occasion, enacted, although their ultimate impact is difficult to trace and their influence in increasing registration levels is usually unpredictable.

Postcard Registration. One incrementalist plan to change registration practices, proposals for postcard registration, does go beyond the usual short-run suggestions. It has a cohesiveness the other proposals lack; it would change practices nationwide, making them more uniform and simplifying them; and it could have an immediate and measurable impact on voter registration (although not as dramatic as the proposals discussed in the next section). It is included in the incrementalist category because the plan has been used in many localities; it is not revolutionary; its conceptualization is modest and its consequences likely to be equally so in comparison with the big-bang plans; and it would serve mainly as a supplemental device to enrollment procedures already in operation.

Postcard registration is not new. It has been used in a number of countries and cities and, in federal elections, for members of the armed services since the early 1940s. In many places, while on the books, it has not been actively promoted as an alternative avenue for registration. When it has been emphasized (Allegheny County [Pittsburgh] in Pennsylvania) it appears to work well.

Its chief assets are that it relieves the voter of the need to familiarize himself with the registration rules and enrollment deadlines and to appear personally at some predetermined place to register. These burdens are transferred to the governmental unit. The plan is fairly simple, depending on the registration authorities to mail the necessary forms to the prospective voter who can then complete and return them. The plan could be comparatively inexpensive.[50]

Under various legislative proposals, a national postcard-registration system would be administered by various federal agencies such as the Bureau of the Census, the U.S. Postal Service (a quasi-governmental agency), the General Accounting Office, or a special commission established for that purpose. Another proposal is to have the states implement their own mail registration systems backed by federal financial assistance.

The arguments against mail registration are much the same as those mobilized against any prospective change in enrollment practices. Some argue that it would be costly (from $30 million for the simpler proposals to over $500 million to establish a new federal agency). Others argue that it would involve the federal government more directly in an area normally reserved for the states; that it would encourage (or, at least, not protect as well as current systems against) election travel; that it would be inefficient; or that it would relieve the citizen of a duty he should be compelled to perform. In this scheme of things, voting (and hence registration) is both a moral and a personal act, and anyone not willing to make the effort to register should not be allowed to vote.

The most powerful argument against a national system of mail registration, and the one underlying most of the other objections, is the fear that it might work sufficiently well to bring new and untested voters into the electorate. This is a disturbing prospect for most politicians and one that could, although it is a long-shot possibility, tilt the balance of power in politics. An increasingly active and involved electorate would create new political demands and could undercut the influence of established interest groups and, consequently, disrupt traditional patterns of political decision making. As a result, postcard registration—and other forms of registration reform—can claim little interest-group or broad political support.

Congressional enactment of a national system of mail registration has failed to materialize. Yet partly as a result of the publicity the plan received in the Congress, a number of states have adopted mail registration during the 1970s. According to Smolka (1977), eighteen states enacted some form of mail registration between 1973 and 1976, and by the presidential election of 1976, 47 percent of the population lived in states in which all voters could register by mail.[51] The mail registration alternatives were not emphasized by the states and in most states registration forms were not mailed to all prospective voters as they would be under the federal proposals. Mail registration was used to supplement registration systems already in effect and, as a consequence, it appeared to have little effect.

The Big-Bang Proposals

The big-bang proposals call for major changes in thinking and in the operations of the current registration systems. Each, in different ways, would dramatically change registration practices; and each could be expected to increase substantially the number of people eligible to vote in elections. To be enacted, each plan would require a major commitment by the Congress, the administration in power, key interest groups (the AFL-CIO and some civic and business groups, for example) and at least some visible support from the public and the media. Each plan would modernize registration procedures, although in quite different ways. The Universal Voter Enrollment proposal is an elaborate and potentially expensive exercise that is patterned generally after the enrollment plans that have proved successful in other democratic nations (variations have also been used in some American localities). The second proposal, Election Day Registration, is far simpler and potentially much less expensive. It also would not depend on a national bureaucracy for execution. Both plans would constitute significant departures from current practices.

Universal Voter Enrollment. The United States has led in the development of many democratic practices. Unfortunately, for a variety of political and social reasons, for the century from 1865 to 1965 the principal emphasis was on creating, and then on protecting, means of limiting the vote. As a result, late in the twentieth century, the American democracy had a hodgepodge, antiquated system of registration practices—each tied into its own local traditions and most noted for their repressiveness—that continued to exist with little rationale. One consequence of the system has been a reduced voter turnout.[52]

As the civil-rights movement gained momentum in the 1960s, concern was increasingly directed toward the outdated registration procedures and the low voter turnouts in comparison with other democratic nations. In searching for ways to correct these failings, attention was drawn to the (primarily) European systems of voter enrollment in which the government assumed the responsibility for actively seeking out and registering the voter. The United States was the only major democracy without such a plan.

In reviewing the operations of the various national systems, one in particular seemed to hold promise for the unique difficulties faced by the United States. This was the Canadian system. Canada had to contend with many of the same problems of geographical dispersion and heterogeneity of the population as well as a federal system of government also found in the United States.

In Canada, a chief electoral officer is appointed, responsible to the parliament. He then appoints electoral officers for each of the 264 parliamentary districts to supervise the registration for that district. The electoral districts are subdivided into "polling districts" of approximately 250 people and two canvassers, one each appointed by the two candidates receiving the highest vote in the previous election, to go door to door to register voters. These canvassers receive a small salary plus a fee (eleven cents per registrant) for each person enrolled. The canvassing begins at a predetermined time (eight weeks) prior to the election, and individuals (or political parties or anyone else) are given the opportunity to challenge publicly the registration lists or to amend them (under proper administrative procedures) to remedy any errors. The system works well and it served as a model for the Universal Voter Enrollment plan introduced into the Congress.[53]

As with all the registration proposals, there are variations in the central theme of a national door-to-door canvass to enroll voters prior to federal elections. Some of the proposals would create a national voter commission to centralize the supervision of the enrollment, serve as a clearing house for information on elections and election administration, help the states and localities update and streamline their election practices, and collect and disseminate accurate information on election results (something this country does not have). Such a commission would be, in itself, a welcome addition. Other plans would give these functions to existing agencies, such as the Federal Election Commission, the Bureau of the Census, and other government agencies.

Under one set of proposals, the national election administration would appoint an election officer for each congressional district. This officer would recruit volunteers from the political parties, labor and business interest groups, civic associations, and such groups as the League of Women Voters to conduct the door-to-door canvassing. A national publicity campaign would be launched in conjunction with the enrollment drive.

Other plans would follow much the same pattern in establishing a national commission (or some type of substitute) and an "Administrator of Voter Registration" (or the equivalent) to supervise voter enrollment. Under these proposals, however, a good deal of discretion would be left to the states, which would appoint their own voter registration administrator. The federal commission would attempt to coordinate registration activities and help the states with their problems. Financial grants given by the national government to participating states would provide the incentive for the states to join in the federal enrollment canvass.

The funding schemes differ. Under most of the Universal Voter Enrollment plans, some type of financial award is given to the states to help them defray the costs involved in modifying their procedures and as an incentive to support the proposal. The grants could be awarded outright according to some type of allocation procedure, or, more popularly, a base grant would be given to all states and then supplemented by a fixed sum (thirty-five cents in one version) for each person registered and/or voting in the state. The emphasis in these proposals is on what the plan hopes to achieve: a significantly higher level of voter registration and turnout. States would also be encouraged, through financial incentives, to employ the federal voting lists in their own elections and to adapt their procedures for state and local elections to something close to the federal model.

The Congress has given a good deal of consideration to the Universal Voter Enrollment proposals.[54] The plans devised by the congressional committees seem workable. Under one proposal, for example, the states would receive basic grants of $15.5 million plus bonuses that would double or triple the initial amounts for qualifying states. Overall, based on turnout figures from the 1976 election, the total cost of the plan would be slightly less than $50 million.[55] Presumably, the cost would increase as the turnout in the individual states climbed.

Universal Voter Enrollment is a new idea for the United States. Predictably, it has many critics. It does represent a major departure from present practice, and it would mean a financial and administrative investment in voter registration and voter turnout that this country has never been willing to make. The plans advanced appear reasonable and practical. Given the general apathy that surrounds election management in the United States, however, the adoption of such an approach seems, at present, remote.

Election-Day Registration. A simpler, yet potentially effective, alternative has been proposed by the Carter administration. It is based on practices current in a handful of states. Under this plan, a prospective voter would be allowed to register at the polls on election day by signing some type of official document or affidavit, by filling out a standardized registration form, or by showing some type of official identification. Once registered, he would be permitted to vote, although if questions arose his registration and his vote would be challenged.

This plan increases the administrative work necessary on election day and therefore the cost of this aspect of election operations. It would require more personnel and facilities to insure that backlogs did not develop, and it does put more pressure on local election officials to perform additional duties at election time—one reason they would be likely to oppose it. The plan would be supplemental for many states; it would be allowed in addition to normal registration procedures. Also, most proposals of this nature do not include the concept of a national voter commission, which would provide additional services of consequence, as a clearinghouse for election information and election administration and as a spur to the modernization of election management.

In addition to cost (a perennial objection) and the potential confusion created at the polls, election-day registration has been opposed out of fear of increasing the likelihood of fraudulent voting. The safeguards against fraud appear as strong as in the more traditional enrollment systems, and the concern does not appear to have merit. Nonetheless, for a nation weaned on a negative approach to qualifying for election participation, a system as open and simple as election-day registration can create apprehension.

The Carter administration did manage, through a series of parliamentary maneuvers, to get their election-day registration plan to the floor of the House. The obstacles to passage appeared to be major, however, and it was withdrawn from consideration before being submitted to a vote.

There has been a limited experience in the United States, with election-day registration. North Dakota has no registration requirements and allows voters to identify themselves and vote with no particular difficulty on election day. Maine and Oregon allow election-day registration, but not at the polls. Voters are directed to register at specified central locations before proceeding to their polling places. Minnesota and Wisconsin instituted election-day registration as part of their permanent registration systems after the 1972 election.

The Minnesota and Wisconsin election-day systems are similar to the Carter administration's proposal. There were problems in the first application of the procedures. Richard Smolka, who has studied both states' experiences with election day registration, writes:

. . . election day registration probably contributed to a marginal increase in voter turnout, about 1 to 2 percentage points both in Minnesota and Wisconsin, but it also encouraged many voters to wait until election day to register. It caused confusion and long lines at the polls, and errors were made that permitted hundreds of voters to vote in the wrong precincts or wards.

Although there appears to be little evidence of vote fraud, there has been little investigation to determine whether there was vote fraud. The integrity of the system depends almost entirely on a single registrar at the polling place and the honesty of the voters themselves. There are almost no poll watchers, and the mail verification of election day registrants takes place too long after the election to affect the results or to produce evidence of vote fraud. The forms and procedures offer investigators little information about the identity of possible fraudulent voters.[56]

Smolka's evaluation is cautious. The problems with election-day registration do not seem major, and may well be less than could have been expected for a first-time application in a presidential contest. These should be manageable. The increased turnout is very modest, perhaps also a first-time phenomenon. Alternatively, there may be a level beyond which voter turnout in a given year does not rise or beyond which turnout is more affected by factors other than registration. Both Minnesota (72 percent) and Wisconsin (66 percent) were well above the national average (55.6 percent) in turnout; in fact, Minnesota led the nation. Wisconsin was fourth. North Dakota, a state with no registration requirements, ranked third (68.9 percent).[57]

Conclusion

Registration systems have a significant impact on voter turnout. They are not the only influence on voting, but they represent the one most amenable to immediate correction. Registration barriers do discourage people from voting. The need is for a facilitative approach that would minimize the procedural hurdles posed by registration processes and encourage voters to participate in elections.

There has been movement along these lines over the last two decades. The federal government has expressed a concern with the problem that has continued beyond the civil-rights crises of the 1960s. A number of states and localities have modified their approaches to permit a higher level of registration. Some of the approaches are imaginative. For example, Michigan adopted a law in 1979 that would allow high-school principals to serve as registrars and to enroll eligible high-school students. The law is patterned after a similar statute enacted by Georgia in 1971. Related legislation is pending in seventeen other states.[58]

The problem such laws attempt to deal with is the low turnout among eighteen- to twenty-four-yearolds. According to the NAACP, only 38 percent of the blacks in this age group were registered in 1976, and only 26 percent voted. The corresponding figure for whites in the same age category are 53 and 45 percent.[59] Obviously, some improvement would be welcome.

The difficulty with this and other such laws is that they are often ignored, as has been the experience in Georgia. It would seem to be the case with many of the incrementalist reforms that state and local registrars choose not to exploit them to the greatest possible extent. As a result, their impact is often less than could reasonably be expected.

Registration procedures in the United States could profit from a thorough overhaul. Two plans that would fundamentally (although in quite different ways) change enrollment practices—the universal voter enrollment and election-day registration proposals—have been before the Congress. Each has its benefits and each would constitute an improvement over current practices. The plans are not mutually exclusive, and ideally each might be enacted in some form.

At present, congressional approval is not likely. There has been a reaction in the Congress to the crises, and the consequent reforms, of the period from the mid-1960s to the mid-1970s. A post-Watergate weariness has set in, and legislators—never enthusiastic proponents of reform—appear unusually wary of any new ventures. The mood of the Congress appears clear in the statement of the chairman of the House Administration Committee, a body charged with considering the election-day registration proposal and other reform measures: "A lot of members feel we're about to reform ourselves out of business."[60] Elected officials are comfortable with the status quo. They fear change and they fear innovation. It takes considerable pressure to force them to adopt new departures in political practices, no matter how attractive these might seem in the abstract.

Yet it would appear that facilitative enrollment procedures and a higher voter turnout would be objectives worthy of intensive concern. The problem, and its ramifications, has been well stated by E.E. Schattschneider, one of the more eminent students of American politics: "The success or failure of the political system in involving a substantial fraction of the tens of millions of nonvoters is likely to determine the future of the country. This proposition goes to the heart of the struggle of the American people for democratic self-realization."[61] Schattschneider wrote in 1960. The problem would appear to be far more acute today.

Notes

1. David S. Broder, "Decline in Voting Appalling," *Boston Sunday Globe*, 2 July 1978, p. A7. Reprinted with permission.

2. Curtis Bans, "The Politics of Selfishness—The Cause: The Empty Voting Booths," *Washington Monthly*, October 1978, p. 27. Reprinted with permission.

3. Ibid., pp. 27-28.

4. See Kagay and Caldeira, chap. 1 in this volume; Richard W. Boyd, "Electoral Trends in Postwar Politics," in *Choosing the President*, ed. James David Barber (Englewood Cliffs, N.J.: Prentice-Hall, 1974), pp. 175-201; and Merle Black and George B. Rabinowitz, "American Electoral Change: 1952-1972 (With a Note on 1976)," in *The Party Symbol*, ed. W. Crotty (San Francisco: W.H. Freeman, 1980).

5. Curtis Gans, "Voter Turnout Declines for Fourth Straight Off-Year Election; Percentages Hit 36 Year Low" (Report of the Committee for the Study of the American Electorate, released December 8, 1978), p. 3. Reprinted with permission.

6. See Dennis, chap. 2 in this volume.

7. Andrews (1966); Freedom To Vote Task Force (1970); and Harris (1929).

8. Rosenstone and Wolfinger (1978); idem, "Who Votes?" (Paper presented at the Annual Meeting of the American Political Science Association, New York, 1977); Kelley, Ayres, and Bowen (1967); Karnig and Walter (1974); Orley Ashenfelter and Stanley Kelley, "Determinants of Participation in Presidential Elections," *Journal of Law and Economics* 18 (December 1975):695-731; and Kousser (1974).

9. Rosenstone and Wolfinger (1978); Kelley et al. (1967); and Paul Kleppner and Stephen C. Baker, "The Impact of Voter Registration Requirements on Electoral Turnout, 1900-16" (Paper presented at the Annual Meeting of the American Political Science Association, Washington, D.C., 1979).

10. Crotty (1977), p. 35.

11. U.S., Congress, Senate, Committee on Rules and Administration, *Federal Election Reform Proposals of 1977* (Washington, D.C.: U.S. Government Printing Office, 1977), p. 1094 [hereafter cited as *Federal Election Reform*]; and Kevin P. Phillips and Paul H. Blackman, *Electoral Reform and Voter Participation* (Washington, D.C.: American Enterprise Institute, 1975).

12. Crotty (1977), pp. 46-71; Verba and Nie (1972); Verba, Nie, and Kim (1978); Wolfinger and Rosenstone (1977); Milbrath and Goel (1977), pp. 86-122; and Kimball (1972).

13. Hadley (1978).

14. Thomas E. Cavanagh, "Changes in American Electoral Turnout, 1964-1976" (Paper presented at the Annual Meeting of the Midwest Political Science Association, Chicago, 1979), p. 14. Reprinted with permission.

15. Ibid., p. 2.

16. Ibid., p. 3.

17. Arthur H. Miller, "Political Issues and Trust in Government: 1964-1970," *American Political Science Review* 68 (September 1974):951-972.

18. Dennis, chap. 2 in this volume.

19. Among the major overviews of voting participation would be Verba and Nie (1972); Milbrath and Goel (1977); Nie and Verba, "Political Participation," in *Handbook of Political Science: Nongovernmental Politics*, vol. 4, ed. Fred I. Greenstein and Nelson W. Polsby (Reading, Mass.: Addison-Wesley, 1975), pp. 1-74; and Cavanagh, "Changes in American Electoral Turnout."

20. *Federal Election Reform*, p. 1085.

21. The basic study in this regard would be Angus Campbell et al., *The American Voter* (New York: Wiley, 1960). See also Miller, "Political Issues."

22. Hadley (1978), p. 31.

23. *Federal Election Reform*, p. 357.

24. Quoted in Kelley et al. (1967), as reproduced in Senate, Committee on Rules, *Federal Election Reform*, p. 1126. The study is by Merriam and Gosnell (1924).

25. Kousser (1974); Kleppner and Baker, "Impact of Voter Registration Requirements"; Crotty (1977); Milbrath and Goel (1977); and Matthews and Prothro (1963).

26. Kelley, Ayres, and Bowen (1967).

27. Ibid., as reproduced in *Federal Election Reform*, p. 1129.

28. Ibid.

29. Kim, Petrocik, and Enoksen (1975).

30. Ibid., as reproduced in *Federal Election Reform*, p. 1160.

31. Douglas D. Rose, "Comment on Kim, Petrocik, and Enoksen: The American States' Impact on Voter Turnout," *American Political Science Review* 69 (March 1975):128. Reprinted with permission.

32. Rosenstone and Wolfinger (1978).

33. Ibid., as reproduced in *Federal Election Reform*, p. 1119.

34. Daniel Yankelovitch, Inc., "A Study of the Registration Process in the United States—The Registered and the Nonregistered," in *Federal Election Reform*, p. 1096.

35. League of Women Voters Education Fund, *Administrative Obstacles to Voting* (Washington, D.C.: League of Women Voters, 1972).

36. Ibid., p. 15.

37. Ibid., p. 11.

38. Ibid., p. 8.

39. Ibid., p. 16.

40. Crotty (1977), pp. 61-69; and U.S. Commission on Civil Rights, *Political Participation* (Washington, D.C.: U.S. Government Printing Office, 1968).

41. U.S. Commission on Civil Rights, *Political Participation*, pp. 222-223.

42. U.S. Commission on Civil Rights, *The Voting Rights Act: Ten Years After* (Washington, D.C.: U.S. Commission on Civil Rights, 1975), p. 54.

43. William C. Havard, ed., *The Changing Politics of the South* (Baton Rouge: Louisiana State University Press, 1972); and Jack Bass and Walter DeVries, *The Transformation of Southern Politics* (New York: New American Library, 1977).

44. Tom Wicker, "The 'New' Thurmond," *New York Times*, 23 October 1977, p. 17. © 1977 by the New York Times Company. Reprinted by permission.

45. President's Commission on Registration and Voting Participation, *Report of the President's Commission on Registration and Voting Participation* (Washington, D.C.: U.S. Government Printing Office, 1963), pp. 31-48.

46. Ibid., p. 47.

47. Ibid., p. 30.

48. See discussion in Crotty (1977), pp. 34-35.

49. Ibid.

50. See the discussion in Crotty (1977), p. 93; and U.S. Senate, Committee on Post Office and Civil Service, *Voter Registration by Postcard* (Washington, D.C.: U.S. Government Printing Office, 1974). Richard Smolka has analyzed the experience of two states, Maryland and New Jersey, with mail registration and based on his research estimates that the cost is between fifty cents and one dollar per registered voter. The higher figure includes many of the hidden costs in processing and verifying registration forms. Richard G. Smolka, *Registering Voters by Mail* (Washington: American Enterprise Institute, 1975), pp. 68-69.

51. Richard G. Smolka, *Election Day Registration* (Washington, D.C.: American Enterprise Institute, 1977), p. i.

52. For discussions of this, see Kleppner and Baker, "Impact of Voter Registration Requirements"; Walter Dean Burnham (1965); and idem, *Critical Elections and the Mainsprings of American Politics* (New York: W.W. Norton, 1970).

53. Freedom To Vote Task Force, *That All May Vote* (Washington, D.C.: Democratic National Committee, 1970).

54. Senate, Committee on Rules, Federal Election Reform; and U.S., Congress, House of Representatives, Committee on House Administration, *Universal Voter Registration Act of 1977* (Washington, D.C.: U.S. Government Printing Office, 1977).

55. *Federal Election Reform*, p. 1071.

56. Smolka, *Election Day Registration*, p. 68. Reprinted with permission.

57. These figures are from the Congressional Quarterly's recording of the vote and are reported in *Federal Election Reform*, p. 1084.

58. Iver Peterson, "Michigan Gets Law to Aid Young Voters," *New York Times*, 15 August 1979, p. 15.

59. Ibid.

60. Terence Smith, "Congress is Balking on Election Revision," *New York Times*, 19 December 1977, p. 10.

61. Schattschneider (1960), p. 103.

References

Books

Crotty, William. *Political Reform and the American Experiment*. New York: Thomas Y. Crowell, 1977.

Gosnell, Harold F. *Getting Out the Vote*. Chicago: University of Chicago Press, 1927.

Hadley, Arthur T. *The Empty Polling Booth*. Englewood Cliffs, N.J.: Prentice-Hall, 1978.

Harris, Joseph P. *Registration of Voters in the United States*. Washington, D.C.: The Brookings Institution, 1929.

Kimball, Penn. *The Disconnected*. New York: Columbia University Press, 1972.

Kousser, J. Morgan. *The Shaping of Southern Politics: Suffrage Restrictions and the Establishment of the One-Party South, 1880-1910*. New Haven, Conn.: Yale University Press, 1974.

Ladd, Everett Carll, Jr. *Where Have All the Voters Gone?* New York: Norton, 1978.

Merriam, Charles E., and Gosnell, Harold. *Non-Voting*. Chicago: University of Chicago Press, 1924.

Milbrath, Lester W., and Goel, M.L. *Political Participation*. 2d ed. Chicago: Rand McNally, 1977.

Schattschneider, E.E. *The Semi-Sovereign People*. New York: Holt, Rinehart and Winston, 1960.

Seagull, Louis M. *Youth and Change in American Politics*. New York: New Viewpoints, 1977.

Thompson, Dennis F. *The Democratic Citizen*. Cambridge: Cambridge University Press, 1970.

Verba, Sidney, and Nie, Norman H. *Participation in America*. New York: Harper and Row, 1972.

Verba, Sidney; Nie, Norman H.; and Kim, Jae-On. *Participation and Political Equality*. Cambridge: Cambridge University Press, 1978.
_____ . *The Modes of Democratic Participation*. Beverly Hills, Calif.: Sage Publications, 1971.

Articles, Reports, and Papers

Andrews, William G. "American Voting Participation." *Western Political Quarterly* 19 (December 1966):639-652.
Burnham, Walter Dean. "The Changing Shape of the American Political Universe." *American Political Science Review* 59 (March 1965):7-28.
Burnham, Walter Dean. "Theory and Voting Research: Some Reflections on Converse's 'Change in the American Electorate'". *American Political Science Review* 68 (September 1974):1002-1023.
Converse, Philip E., with Niemi, Richard G. "Non-Voting Among Young Adults in the United States." *Political Parties and Political Behavior*. 2d ed. Edited by W. Crotty, D.M. Freeman, and D.S. Gatlin. Boston: Allyn and Bacon, 1971.
Ferejohn, John A., and Fiorina, Morris P. "The Paradox of Not Voting: A Decision Theoretic Analysis." *American Political Science Review* 67 (June 1974):525-536.
Freedom to Vote Task Force. *Registration and Voting in the States*. Washington, D.C.: Democratic National Committee, 1970.
Karnig, Albert B. and Walter, B. Oliver. "Registration and Voting: Putting First Things Second." *Social Science Quarterly* 55 (June 1974):159-166.
Kelley, Stanley, Jr.; Ayres, Richard E.; and Bowen, William G. "Registration and Voting: Putting First Things First." *American Political Science Review* 61 (June 1967):359-377.
Kim, Jae-On; Petrocik, John R.; and Enoksen, Stephen N. "Voter Turnout Among the American States: Systemic and Individual Components." *American Political Science Review* 69 (March 1975):107-131.
Matthews, Donald R., and Prothro, James W. "Political Factors and Negro Voter Registration in the South." *American Political Science Review* 57 (June 1963):355-367.
_____ . "Social and Economic Factors and Negro Voter Registration in the South." *American Political Science Review* 57 (March 1963):24-44.
Nie, Norman H.; Powell, G. Bingham; and Prewitt, Kenneth. "Social Structure and Political Participation: Developmental Relationships." *American Political Science Review* 63 (June 1969):361-378.
Nie, Norman H., and Verba, Sidney. "Political Participation." *Handbook of Poltical Science*, vol. 4. Edited by Fred I. Greenstein and Nelson W. Polsby, pp. 1-74. Reading, Mass.: Addison-Wesley, 1975.

Rosenstone, Steven J., and Wolfinger, Raymond E. "The Effect of Registration Laws on Voter Turnout." *American Political Science Review* 72
(March 1978):22-45.

4 Electoral-College Reform: Problems, Politics, and Prospects

Lawrence D. Longley

The contemporary electoral college is a curious political institution.[1] Obscure and even unknown to the average citizen,[2] it serves as a crucial mechanism for transforming popular votes cast for president into electoral votes which actually elect the president. If the electoral college were only a neutral and sure means for counting and aggregating votes, it would likely be the subject of little controversy. The electoral college does not, however, just tabulate popular votes in the form of electoral votes. Instead, it is an institution that operates with noteworthy inequality—it favors some interests and hurts others. In addition, its operations are by no means certain or smooth. The electoral college can—and has—deadlocked, forcing a resort to extraordinarily awkward contingency procedures. Other flaws and difficulties with the system can also develop under various electoral situations. In short, the electoral-college system has important political consequences, multiple flaws, possible grave consequences, and inherent gross inequalities. Yet it continues to exist as a central part of our presidential electoral machinery.

In the following discussion, five central questions concerning this institution and its reform are posed: (1) How did the electoral college come to be part of our Constitution? (2) How does this electoral institution operate today? (3) What have been the major reform plans and proposals that have been advanced—and what might be their consequences? (4) What happened to electoral reform on the way to adoption by the Senate in 1970 and in 1978? (5) What are the politics and prospects for electoral reform in the 1980s? Throughout, the focus of this discussion will be on the adequacy and desirability of the electoral college as a democratic electoral institution.

How It Came to Be

The electoral-college system was accepted and written into the Constitution at the Constitutional Convention in 1787 not because it was seen as a particularly desirable means of electing the president, but rather because it was an acceptable compromise—"the second choice of many delegates though . . . the first choice of few."[3] Torn and divided, but finally in agreement on the monumental issues of national-stage powers, presidential-congressional relationships, and most of all the issue of equal state representation versus population representation in the new national legislature, the Founding Fathers were not about to let the convention split anew over the means of presidential election. Some delegates favored election of the president by Congress; others strongly favored a direct popular election by the people. Even more important, each proposal had adamant opponents; adoption of either might mean a breakdown of emerging convention consensus on the draft Constitution. The result was a compromise plan providing for an intermediate electoral body called an electoral college. This proposal, as awkward as it might appear, had several virtues: it resolved the need to decide something by being widely acceptable, it seemed unlikely to give rise to any immediate problem (it was clear to all that George Washington was going to be president, whatever the electoral system), and it seemed—incorrectly, it turned out—to incorporate a balance between state and popular interests. Most of all, however, it got the Constitutional Convention over yet another hurdle in its immensely difficult process of Constitution making. The result, however, was a complex and unwieldy multistage mechanism for electing the president. A camel has been said to be the product of a committee; so was the electoral college the result of immediate political necessity at the Constitutional Convention. As one noted commentator on this period, John Roche, has put it:

> The electoral college was neither an exercise in applied Platonism nor an experiment in indirect government based on elitist distrust of the masses. It was merely a jerry-rigged improvisation which has subsequently been endowed with a high theoretical content. . . . The vital aspect of the electoral college was that it got the Convention over the hurdle and protected everybody's interests. The future was left to cope with the problem of what to do with this Rube Goldberg mechanism.[4]

To the extent that the Founding Fathers attempted to anticipate how the electoral college would work, they were wrong. The assumption of the creators of the electoral college was that the electors chosen would, in effect, *nominate* a number of prominent individuals, with no one man, because of diverse state and regional interests, usually receiving the specified absolute *majority* of electoral votes. At times a George Washington might be the unanimous electoral-college choice, but, as George Mason of Virginia argued at Philadelphia, nineteen times out of twenty, the final choice of president among the three top contenders would be made not by the electoral college itself, but by the House of Representatives voting as states, with one vote per state.

Inherent in this system, then, was a mechanism for electing our president which has not, in fact, operated as the founders assumed. What was not foreseen was the rise of national political parties able to aggregate and focus national support on two, or occasionally three, candidates. Only in 1800 and 1824 has no contender received an electoral-vote majority, and the House contingency system as the usual means of presidential election has been replaced by election by the electors themselves—or, more accurately, by each state's voters electing electors. The structure of the original process remains, however, potentially chaotic if necessity forces its utilization.

Another aspect of the system as envisioned by its creators should also be noted. Under the assumption of the founders, the electoral college—reflecting roughly the population of the states—would favor the large states at the cost of the small states (or, more accurately, populations rather than individual states). When the House contingency procedure went into effect—as it usually would—the voting would be one vote per state delegation, thus representing individual states regardless of population. This system, then, was a compromise between the principles of *population* and of *state interest*—but a balance that rested on the assumpton that the House contingency election procedure would normally be used. Since 1824, however, this has not been the case, and the original balance of interests foreseen by the founders has been destroyed in favor of a representation of population—albeit a distorted representation.

The historical facts, then, are that the original electoral college system has not, for over one hundred fifty years, worked as intended by its creators; that it was replaced as a nominating mechanism by national political parties; and that it has not provided a balance between state interests interests and population interests. In addition, the electoral-college system has had a number of crucial changes introduced into its operations since its conception. Among these are the Twelfth Amendment to the Constitution, ratified in 1804, which served to ensure the electoral college's election of a president and vice-president of the same party; the development of universal popular election of electors early in the nineteenth century;[5] the occurrence of the curious phenomenon of the faithless elector (which itself could only happen with the development of the political-party-pledged elector);[6] and the emergence of the winner-take-all system for determining each state's electoral votes.[7] Together, these changes constitute major modifications of the system created and contemplated by the Philadelphia delegates. From the assembly of independently thinking statesmen usually serving to nominate three top contenders for House final decision, there has developed an electoral college made up of unknown individuals whose only virtue is a reflexive voting for their party's nominee, while the electoral college's only function is to confirm a popular electoral verdict handed down six weeks earlier.

How It Operates—and Threatens to Misbehave—Today

Up to this point I have been examining some of the original features of the electoral-college system and have been showing how its functions have changed over the years. Let me now elaborate on this in terms of the functions the electoral-college system serves today, and approach this question in terms of various features of the contemporary electoral-college system. Among these features are the possibility of one or more "faithless electors," the impact on presidential campaign strategy of voting distortions introduced by the electoral college—particularly the focusing on very large states and the loss of interest in "predictable" states; the opportunities for mischief—and even national chaos—in the "absolute electoral college majority or House contingency election" procedure (which has the result of encouraging *regionally based third parties* while the state-wide, "winner-take-all" custom effectively suppresses nonregionally based *nationally oriented third parties*); and the fact that under the present electoral-college system, there is no guarantee—and in some recent elections not even a better than even chance—that the winner of a presidential election in popular votes will be the winner of the election in electoral votes.

These features of the electoral-college system can be summarized in terms of five basic characteristics:

1. the faithless elector;
2. the winner-take-all system concerning a state's electoral vote;
3. the constant two electoral votes per state;
4. the contingency-election procedure;
5. the uncertainty that the winner will win.

The Faithless Elector

The first characteristic arises out of the fact that the electoral college today is not the assembly of wise and learned elders assumed by its creators, but is rather a state-by-state assembly of political hacks and fat cats.[8] Neither in the quality of the electors nor in law is there any assurance that the electors will vote as expected. Pledges, apparently unenforceable by law, and party and personal loyalty seem to be the only guarantee of electoral voting consistent with the will of a state's electorate.[9]

The problem of the faithless elector is neither theoretical nor unimportant. Republican elector Dr. Lloyd W. Bailey of North Carolina, who decided to vote for Wallace after the 1968 election rather than for his pledged candidate, Nixon, and Republican elector Roger MacBride of

Virginia who likewise deserted Nixon in 1972 to vote for Libertarian Party candidate John Hospers, are two examples of faithless electors. In the 1976 election, we once again had a faithless elector—once again a deviant Republican. Washington Republican Mike Padden decided, six weeks after the November election, that he preferred not to support Republican nominee Ford but to cast his electoral vote for Ronald Reagan. Similar defections from voter expectations also occurred in 1948, 1956, and 1960—in other words, in six of the eight most recent presidential elections. Even more important is that the likelihood of this occurring on a multiple basis would be greatly heightened in the case of an electoral-vote majority resting on one or two votes—a very real possibility in 1976, as in other recent elections.

In fact, when one looks at the election returns for the 1976 election, one observes that if about 5,560 votes had switched from Carter to Ford in Ohio, Carter would have lost that state and had only 272 electoral votes, two more than the absolute minimum of 270 needed. In that case, two or three individual electors seeking personal recognition or attention to a pet cause could withhold their electoral votes, thus making the election outcome very uncertain.

A startling reminder of the possibilities inherent in such a close electoral-vote election as 1976 was provided recently by Republican vice-presidential nominee Robert Dole. Testifying before the Senate Judiciary Committee on January 27, 1977 in *favor* of abolishing the electoral college, Senator Dole remarked that during the election count:

> We were looking around on the theory that maybe Ohio might turn around because they had an automatic recount.
>
> We were shopping—not shopping, excuse me. Looking around for electors. Some took a look at Missouri, some were looking at Louisiana, some in Mississippi, because their laws are a little bit different. And we might have picked up one or two in Louisiana. There were allegations of fraud maybe in Mississippi, and something else in Missouri.
>
> We need to pick up three or four after Ohio. So that may happen in any event.
>
> But it just seems to me that the temptation is there for that elector in a very tight race to really negotiate quite a bunch.[10]

The Winner-Take-All System

The second problem of the contemporary electoral-college system lies in the almost universal custom of granting all of a state's electoral votes to the winner of a state's popular vote plurality—not even a majority.[11] This can lead to interesting results, as in Arkansas in 1968 where Humphrey and Nixon together split slightly over 61 percent of the popular vote, while Wallace, with 38 percent, received 100 percent of the state's electoral votes. Even more significant, however, is the fact that the unit voting of state electors tends to magnify tremendously the relative voting power of residents of the larger states, since each of their voters may, by his vote, decide not just one vote, but how 41 or 45 electoral votes are cast—if electors are faithful.

As a result, the electoral college has a major impact on candidate strategy—as shown by the obsession of Carter and Ford strategists, in the closing weeks of the 1976 campaign, with the nine big electoral-vote states with 245 of the 270 electoral votes necessary to win. Seven of these nine states were, in fact, exceedingly close, with both candidates receiving at least 48 percent of the state vote.

The electoral college does not treat voters alike; a thousand voters in Scranton, Pennsylvania are far more strategically important than a similar number of voters in Wilmington, Delaware. This also places a premium on the support of key political leaders in large-electoral-vote states. This could be observed in the 1976 election in the desperate wooing of Mayors Rizzo of Philadelphia and Daley of Chicago by Carter because of the major roles these political leaders might have in determining the outcome in Pennsylvania and Illinois. The electoral collge treats political leaders as well as voters unequally—those in large marginal states are vigorously courted.[12]

The electoral college also encourages fraud—or at least fear and rumor of fraud. New York, with more than enough electoral votes to elect Ford, went to Carter by 290,000 popular votes. Claims of voting irregularities and calls for a recount were made on election night but later withdrawn because of Carter's clear national popular vote win. *If* fraud was present in New York, only 290,000 votes determined the election; under direct election, at least 1,700,000 votes would have to have been irregular to determine the outcome.

The electoral college also provides opportunity for third-party candidates to exercise magnified political influence in the election of the president when they can gather votes in large, closely balanced states. In 1976, third-party candidate Eugene McCarthy, with less than 1 percent of the popular vote, came close to tilting the election through his strength in close pivotal states. In four states (Iowa, Maine, Oklahoma, and Oregon) totaling 26 electoral votes, McCarthy's vote exceeded the margin by which Ford defeated Carter. In those states, McCarthy's candidacy *may* have swung those states to Ford.[13] Even more significantly, had McCarthy been on the New York ballot, it is likely Ford would have carried that state with its 41 electoral votes, and with it the election—despite Carter's national vote majority.

The Constant Two Electoral Votes

A third feature of the electoral-college system lies in the apportionment of electoral votes among the states. The constitutional formula is simple: one vote per state per senator and representative. A significant distortion from equality appears here because of "the constant two" electoral votes, regardless of population, which correspond to the senators. Because of this, inhabitants of the very small states are advantaged to the extent that they "control" three electoral votes (one for each senator and one for the representative), while their population might otherwise entitle them to only one or two votes. This is weighting by states, not by population; however, the importance of this feature, as shown below, is greatly outweighed by the previously mentioned winner-take-all system.

The Contingency-Election Procedure

The fourth feature of the contemporary electoral-college system is probably the most complex—and probably also the most dangerous in terms of the stability of the political system. This is the requirement that if no candidate receives an absolute majority of the electoral vote—in recent years 270—the election is thrown into the House of Representatives for voting among the top three candidates. Two questions need to be asked: is such an electoral-college deadlock likely to occur in terms of contemporary politics, and would the consequences likely be disastrous? A simple answer to both questions is yes.

   Taking some recent examples, it has been shown that in 1960 a switch of less than 9,000 popular votes from Kennedy to Nixon in Illinois and Missouri would have prevented either man from receiving an electoral-college majority.[14] Similarly, in 1968 a 53,000-vote shift in New Jersey, Missouri, and New Hampshire would have resulted in an electoral-college deadlock, with Nixon receiving 269 votes—one short of majority. Finally, in the 1976 election, if slightly less than 11,950 popular votes in Delaware and Ohio had shifted from Carter to Ford, Ford would have carried these two states. The result of the 1976 election would then have been an exact tie in electoral votes—269-269. The presidency would have been decided *not* on election night, but through deals or switches at the electoral-college meetings on December 13, or the latter uncertainties of the House of Representatives.

   What specifically might happen in the case of an apparent electoral college nonmajority or deadlock? A first possibility, of course, is that a faithless elector or two, pledged to one candidate or another, might switch at the time of the actual meetings of the electoral college so as to create a majority for one of the candidates. This might resolve the crisis, although it is sad to think of the presidency as depending on such a thin reed of legitimacy.

If, however, no deals or actions at the time of the December 13 meetings of the electoral college were successful in forming a majority, then the action would shift to the House of Representatives, meeting at noon on January 6, 1977, only fourteen days before the constitutionally scheduled inauguration day for the new president.

The House of Representatives contingency procedure which would now be followed is an unfortunate relic of the compromises of the writing of the Constitution as discussed earlier. Serious problems of equity exist, certainly, in following the constitutionally prescribed one-vote-per-state procedure. Beyond this problem of voter fairness lurks an even more serious problem—what if the House itself should deadlock and be unable to agree on a president?

In a two-candidate race, this is unlikely to be a real problem; however, in a three-candidate contest, as in 1968, there might well be enormous difficulties in getting a majority of states behind one candidate, as House members agonized over choosing between partisan labels and support for the candidate (especially Wallace) who carried their district. The result, in 1968, might well have been no immediate majority forthcoming for twenty-six states and political uncertainty and chaos as the nation approached inauguration day.[15]

The Uncertainty of the Winner Winning

Besides the four aspects of the electoral-college system so far discussed—the faithless elector, the winner-take-all system, the constant two votes per state, and the contingency-election procedure—one last aspect should be described. Under the present system, there is no assurance that the winner of the popular vote will win the election. This problem is a fundamental one—can an American president operate effectively in our democracy if he has received *fewer* votes than the loser? I suggest that the effect on the legitimacy of a contemporary presidency would be disastrous if a president were elected by the electoral college after losing in the popular vote—yet this *can* and *has* happened two or three times, the most recent undisputable case being the election of 1888, when the 100,000 popular vote plurality of Grover Cleveland was turned into a losing 42 percent of the electoral vote.[16]

Was there a real possibility of such a divided verdict in 1976? An analysis of the election shows that if 9,245 votes had shifted to Ford in Ohio and Hawaii, Ford would have become president with 270 electoral votes, the absolute minimum, despite Carter's 51 percent of the popular vote and his margin of 1.7 million votes.[17]

One hesitates to contemplate the consequences of a nonelected president being inaugurated for four more years despite having been rejected by a majority of the American voters in his only presidential election.

The Multiple Roads to Electoral College Reform

Having considered the major features of the present system, let us now turn to an examination of the various plans for reform of the electoral college. Although over five hundred different reform proposals have at one time or another been introduced in the U.S. Congress,[18] four major types of reform plans can be identified: the automatic plan, the proportional plan, the district plan, and the direct-vote plan. The first of these, the *automatic plan*, is a limited reform proposal focusing on the problem of the faithless elector, while otherwise retaining the essentials of the existing electoral college.[19] The automatic plan would abolish the office of elector and provide for the automatic casting of the blocs of electoral votes as determined by the various states' popular votes. The unit rule would be kept—in fact, would be written into the Constitution for the first time. The present apportionment of electoral votes also would be maintained, along with the chance that the winner in popular votes might not win in the electoral college. Most versions also provide for a change in the contingency procedure through congressional voting by all Members—representatives and senators—as individuals in a Joint Session of Congress. The uncertainty lasting into January would, of course, remain, as would the possibility of congressional deadlock.

Perhaps the most important consequence of this plan is that distortions inherent in the present electoral-college system would be retained in the "reformed" electoral system. Therefore, in order to evaluate the automatic reform plan, it is necessary also to evaluate the distortions of the existing electoral college.

The Biases of the Electoral College
and the Automatic Plan

These biases have a number of different causes, among them the constant two electoral votes given each state regardless of population, the unit rule by which all of a state's electoral votes are determined by a plurality of the state's voters, the constitutional basing of electoral votes on population figures independent of actual voter turnout, and the fact that these population figures are themselves based on census figures that freeze the electoral-vote apportionments among the states for ten to fourteen years.[20] The result of these various structural features of the electoral college (as well as of the automatic plan's retention of a non-people-based electoral college) is to ensure that the electoral college can never be a neutral counting device, but must inherently contain varieties of biases dependent solely on the state in which a voter casts his vote for president. The contemporary electoral college is not just an archaic mechanism for counting the votes for president; rather, it is an institution that aggregates popular votes in an inherently imperfect manner.

Measuring State Biases of the Electoral College and the Automatic Plan. Major efforts have been made in recent years to measure the biases of the electoral college in terms of the ability of a voter to affect decisions through the process of voting. Methodologies based on the mathematical theory of games and utilizing computer simulations of thousands of elections have been developed to estimate the relative differences in voting power of citizen-voters in the different states.[21] Additionally, some studies have sought to determine the voting power of various categories of voters, including residency, regional, ethnic, and occupational groups.[22]

The purpose of this research is the same in every case—to discover the advantage or disadvantage the electoral college, as well as the automatic plan, gives to citizen-voters *solely according to where they chance to reside and vote*. Essentially, the "voting-power" approach to the evaluation of the electoral college involves three distinct steps.

1. A determination is made of the chance that each state has in a "fifty-one-person" game (actually fifty states plus the District of Columbia) of casting a pivotal vote in the electoral college.
2. The proportion of voting combinations to the number of all possible voting combinations in which a given citizen-voter can, by changing his vote, alter the way in which his state's electoral votes will be cast, is evaluated.
3. The results of the first step are combined with the results of the second to determine the chance that any voter has of affecting the election of the president through the medium of his state's electoral votes.

These calculations are normalized with the power index of the state whose citizens have the least voting power set at one; all other states have voting powers greater than one, and the result is an index of *relative voting power* of each citizen, vis-à-vis voters residing in other states.

Table 4-1 reports the relative voting-power figures under the electoral college for the electoral-college apportionments of the 1960s for citizens of the fifty states and the District of Columbia. The voting-power figures are normalized on the power index of the "state" with the least voting power

Table 4-1

Voting Power under the Electoral College in the 1960s Based on State Populations, Arranged by Size of State

State Name[a]	(1) Electoral Vote: 1964/1968	(2) Population: 1960 Census	(3) Relative Voting Power[b]	(4) Percent Deviation From Per Citizen-Voter Average Voting Power[c]
Alaska	3	226,167	1.838	9.9
Nevada	3	285,278	1.636	−2.2
Wyoming	3	330,066	1.521	−9.1
Vermont	3	389,881	1.400	−16.3
Delaware	3	446,292	1.308	−21.8
New Hampshire	4	606,921	1.384	−17.2
North Dakota	4	632,446	1.356	−18.9
Hawaii	4	632,772	1.356	−18.9
Idaho	4	667,191	1.320	−21.1
Montana	4	674,767	1.313	−21.5
South Dakota	4	680,514	1.307	−21.8
Dist. of Columbia	3	763,956	1.000	−40.2
Rhode Island	4	859,488	1.163	−30.5
Utah	4	890,627	1.143	−31.7
New Mexico	4	951,023	1.106	−33.9
Maine	4	969,265	1.096	−34.5
Arizona	5	1,302,161	1.069	−36.1
Nebraska	5	1,411,330	1.026	−38.6
Colorado	6	1,753,947	1.120	−33.1
Oregon	6	1.768,687	1.115	−33.3
Arkansas	6	1,786,272	1.110	−33.7
West Virginia	7	1,860,421	1.224	−26.8
Mississippi	7	2,178,141	1.131	−32.4
Kansas	7	2,178,611	1.131	−32.4
Oklahoma	8	2,328,284	1.213	−27.5
South Carolina	8	2,382,594	1.199	−28.3
Connecticut	8	2,535,234	1.163	−30.5
Iowa	9	2,757,537	1.292	−22.8
Washington	9	2,853,214	1.270	−24.1
Kentucky	9	3,038,156	1.230	−26.5
Maryland	10	3,100,689	1.327	−20.7
Louisiana	10	3,257,022	1.295	−22.6
Alabama	10	3,266,740	1.293	−22.7
Minnesota	10	3,413,864	1.265	−24.4
Tennessee	11	3,567,089	1.382	−17.4
Georgia	12	3,943,116	1.352	−19.2
Wisconsin	12	3,951,777	1.351	−19.3
Virginia	12	3,966,949	1.348	−19.4
Missouri	12	4,319,813	1.292	−22.8
North Carolina	13	4,556,155	1.392	−16.8
Indiana	13	4,662,498	1.376	−17.7
Florida	14	4,951,560	1.506	−10.0
Massachusetts	14	5,148,578	1.476	−11.8
New Jersey	17	6,066,782	1.628	−2.7
Michigan	21	7,823,194	1.679	0.4

Table 4-1 *(cont.)*

State Name[a]	(1) Electoral Vote: 1964/1968	(2) Population: 1960 Census	(3) Relative Voting Power[b]	(4) Percent Deviation From Per Citizen-Voter Average Voting Power[c]
Texas	25	9,579,677	1.844	10.3
Ohio	26	9,706,397	1.916	14.5
Illinois	26	10,081,158	1.880	12.4
Pennsylvania	29	11,319,366	2.011	20.2
California	40	15,717,204	2.421	44.7
New York	43	16,782,304	2.478	48.1

Source: John H. Yunker and Lawrence D. Longley, *The Electoral College: Its Biases Newly Measured for the 1960s and 1970s,* American Politics Series, vol. 3, copyright 1976 (Beverly Hills, Calif.: Sage Publications, 1976), pp. 10-11.

[a]Includes the District of Columbia.

[b]Ratio of voting power of citizens of state compared with voters of the most deprived state.

[c]Percent by which voting power deviated from the average per citizen-voter of the figures in column 3. Minus signs indicate less than average voting power. Average voting power per citizen-voter = 1.673.

(in this case, the District of Columbia). Citizens of the three most populous states have at least twice the relative voting power of the inhabitants of the least avantaged state—Pennsylvania with 2.011, California with 2.421; and New York with 2.478. Column 4 of this table reports the percentages by which the relative voting power (column 3) of citizens in each state deviates from the average (mean) relative voting power per citizen-voter. Thus, forty-three of the fifty-one states have *less* than the average relative voting power (in this case, 1.673); eight (seven of which are the seven most populous states) have *greater* than average relative voting power. The advantage that citizens in the very large states enjoy *solely because of their place of residence* is as great as 48.1 pecent.

Figure 4-1 presents the results from table 4-1, columns 2 and 4, in graphic form. The populations of the various states are measured along the horizontal axis, and the percentage deviation from average voting power (from column 4 in table 4-1) of citizens residing in each state is represented on the vertical axis. A free-hand line illustrates the general trend of the points in figure 4-1. With the exception of the seventeen smallest states at the extreme left-hand side of the graph, the plotting of states is almost linear, with the relative voting power of citizens increasing steadily with the size of the state population. The linearly increasing advantage of citizen-voters in the thirty-four most populous states is a result of the rule feature of the contemporary electoral college. The relative voting power of citizens in specific states departs from an exact linear relationship because electoral votes only approximate state populations. The citizens of the small states at the extreme left-hand side of the graph also have a relative voting power that is disproportionately large in comparison with the population of these

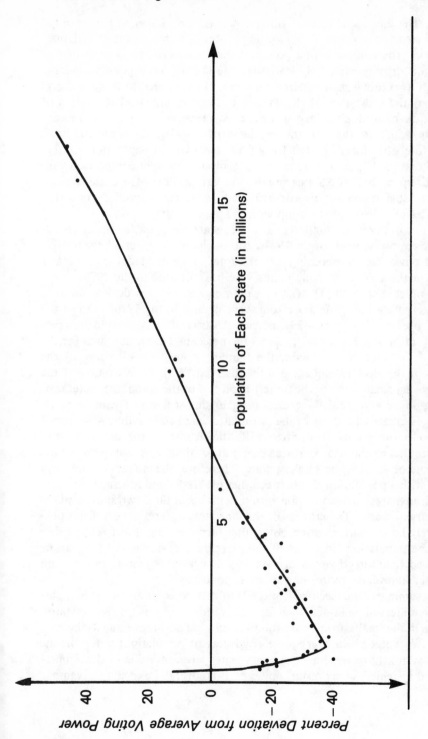

Source: John H. Yunker and Lawrence D. Longley, *The Electoral College: Its Biases Newly Measured for the 1960s and 1970s* American Politics Series, vol. 3, copyright 1976 (Beverly Hills, Calif.: Sage Publications, 1976), pp. 10-11. Reprinted with permission.

Figure 4-1. Percent Deviation from Average Voting Power of States under the Electoral College, Population Basis 1960s

states. The increased relative voting power of the residents of these small states stems from the two electoral votes not based on population. However, the relative voting power of the citizens of the District of Columbia is disproportionately low, since the District has a population large enough to entitle it to four electoral votes, but is limited to three electoral votes by the provisions of the Twenty-third Amendment. The citizens of Texas, the nation's sixth largest state, have a relative voting power approximately equal to that of the residents of Alaska, the smallest state. Therefore, the citizens of the forty-four states with a population size between that of Alaska and Texas are at a disadvantage in comparison with the citizens of these two states and the five largest states. The citizens of the five largest states have a disproportionately large relative voting power that increases in a direct relationship with the population.

Table 4-2 presents similarly calculated state bias data for the electoral-college apportionment for the 1970s. Although only two states have relative voting-power ratios exceeding 2.0, the total range of inequities is greater than for the 1960s, with one man's vote in California in the 1970s worth 2.546 times that in the District of Columbia. Percentage deviations from average voting power also are somewhat greater in the 1970s than in the 1960s, now ranging from —39.7 percent (District of Columbia) to 53.6 percent (California). Figure 4-2 presents the percentage-deviation data for the 1970s in graphic form. Again, the familiar "check-mark" curve of the biases of the electoral college can be observed. With the exception of the twenty very small states at the far left-hand side of the graph, the increase of voting power as state size increases is again almost linear. The most disadvantaged citizens are those of the medium-to-small-sized states, with from 4 to 14 electoral votes. The citizens of Massachusetts, the nation's tenth largest state, have a relative voting power approximately equal to that of the residents of Alaska, the smallest state. Therefore, the citizens of the forty states with a population size between that of Alaska and Massachusetts are at a disadvantage in comparison with the citizens of these two states and the nine largest states. The citizens of the nine largest states have a disproportionately large relative voting power that increases in a direct relationship with the population. In terms of the percentage-deviation data, it can be observed that forty-five states have less than average voting power, and only six states have more—the six most populous!

In summary, the electoral college is formed to contain two major, partially countervailing biases, each favoring residents of quite different states. Voters in the smallest states are found to have an advantage due to the constant two votes given every state regardless of population; voters in the larger states, however, have an even greater advantage due to the winner-take-all system. The *net* result, however, is an overall large-state advantage

Table 4-2

Voting Power under the Electoral College in the 1970s Based on State Populations, Arranged by Size of State

State Name[a]	(1) Electoral Vote: 1972, 1976, 1980	(2) Population: 1970 Census	(3) Relative Voting Power[b]	(4) Percent Deviation From Per Citizen-Voter Average Voting Power[c]
Alaska	3	300,382	1.587	−4.3
Wyoming	3	332,416	1.509	−9.0
Vermont	3	444,330	1.305	−21.3
Nevada	3	488,738	1.244	−25.0
Delaware	3	548,104	1.175	−29.1
North Dakota	3	617,761	1.107	−33.3
South Dakota	4	665,507	1.366	−17.6
Montana	4	694,409	1.337	−19.3
Idaho	4	712,567	1.320	−20.4
New Hampshire	4	737,681	1.297	−21.7
Dist. of Columbia	3	756,510	1.000	−39.7
Hawaii	4	768,561	1.271	−23.3
Rhode Island	4	946,725	1.145	−30.9
Maine	4	992,048	1.119	−32.5
New Mexico	4	1,016,000	1.106	−33.3
Utah	4	1,059,273	1.083	−34.7
Nebraska	5	1,483,493	1.035	−37.6
West Virginia	6	1,744,237	1.131	−31.8
Arizona	6	1,770,900	1.123	−32.3
Arkansas	6	1,923,295	1.077	−35.0
Oregon	6	2,091,385	1.033	−37.7
Colorado	7	2,207,259	1.137	−31.4
Mississippi	7	2,216,912	1.134	−31.6
Kansas	7	2,246,578	1.126	−32.0
Oklahoma	8	2,559,229	1.219	−26.5
South Carolina	8	2,590,516	1.212	−26.9
Iowa	8	2,824,376	1.160	−30.0
Connecticut	8	3,031,709	1.120	−32.4
Kentucky	9	3,218,706	1.244	−25.0
Washington	9	3,409,169	1.209	−27.1
Alabama	9	3,444,165	1.203	−27.5
Louisiana	10	3,641,306	1.281	−22.7
Minnesota	10	3,804,971	1.253	−24.4
Maryland	10	3,922,399	1.234	−25.6
Tennessee	10	3,923,687	1.234	−25.6
Wisconsin	11	4,417,731	1.291	−22.2
Georgia	12	4,589,575	1.324	−20.1
Virginia	12	4,648,494	1.316	−20.6
Missouri	12	4,676,501	1.312	−20.8
North Carolina	13	5,082,059	1.462	−11.8
Indiana	13	5,193,669	1.446	−12.8
Massachusetts	14	5,689,170	1.459	−12.0
Florida	17	6,789,443	1.611	−2.8
New Jersey	17	7,168,164	1.568	−5.4
Michigan	21	8,875,083	1.648	−0.6
Ohio	25	10,652,017	1.815	9.5

Table 4-2 *(cont.)*

State Name[a]	(1) Electoral Vote: 1972, 1976, 1980	(2) Population: 1970 Census	(3) Relative Voting Power[b]	(4) Percent Deviation From Per Citizen-Voter Average Voting Power[c]
Illinois	26	11,113,976	1.888	13.9
Texas	26	11,196,730	1.881	13.5
Pennsylvania	27	11,793,909	1.913	15.4
New York	41	18,236,967	2.360	42.4
California	45	19,953,134	2.546	53.6

Source: John H. Yunker and Lawrence D. Longley, *The Electoral College: Its Biases Newly Measured for the 1960s and 1970s*, American Politics Series, vol. 3, copyright 1976 (Beverly Hills, Calif.: Sage Publications, 1976), pp. 14-15. Reprinted with permission.

[a]Includes the District of Columbia.

[b]Ratio of voting power of citizens of state compared with voters of the most deprived state.

[c]Percent by which voting power deviated from the average per citizen-voter of the figures in column 3. Minus signs indicate less than average voting power. Average voting power per citizen-voter = 1.658.

under the electoral college, with the most disadvantaged citizen-voters being residents of the medium to small states with from 4 to 14 electoral votes.[23] Specifically, a citizen voting in California in the present electoral college (or under the automatic plan) as apportioned in the 1970s, is found to have 2.546 times the potential for determining the outcome of the presidential election of a citizen voting in the most disadvantaged area—the District of Columbia.[24]

Measuring Regional and Group Biases of the Electoral College and the Automatic Plan. The biases inherent in the present electoral college and various reform plans for inhabitants of different sized *states* have been shown. The data as presented up to now have not, however, dealt with the question of whether various *groups* of voters may be similarly favored or disadvantaged because of their residency in various states. In order to examine this important question, the relative-voting-power data were used to determine the average voting power of various population categories under the electoral-college and other plans as compared to the average voting power of the total population.

The groups chosen were placed in two categories: regions and population groups. Regions chosen were East, South, Midwest, Mountain, and Far West groupings of states. Population groups were blacks; and residents of urban areas, central cities, and rural areas (including rural non-farm and rural farm areas).

The average voting power of urban residents for the present electoral college, for example, was calculated by multiplying each state's relative voting-power index (table 4-2, column 3) by its number of urban residents. The sum of these products divided by the total number of urban residents in

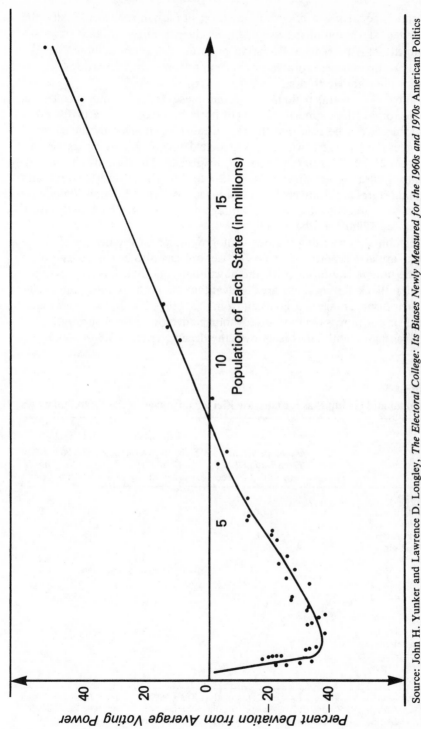

Source: John H. Yunker and Lawrence D. Longley, *The Electoral College: Its Biases Newly Measured for the 1960s and 1970s* American Politics Series, vol. 3, copyright 1976 (Beverly Hills, Calif.: Sage Publications, 1976), pp. 14-15. Reprinted with permission.

Figure 4-2. Percent Deviation from Average Voting Power of States under the Electoral College, Population Basis 1970s

the nation equals the average voting power per urban resident. Finally, the percentage deviation of this average from the per-citizen-voter average was obtained. This percentage deviation gives an indication of how this particular group in the electorate fares in comparison with other groups, as well as with the total electorate.

Table 4-3 presents regional and group biases for the electoral college in the electoral college apportionments of both the 1960s and the 1970s. From this table, it can be seen that the region most advantaged by the electoral college is the Far West, with its percentage deviation from average increasing from 26.7 to 33.1 in the course of the decade. The East also has an advantage, but a decreasing one, from 13.8 to 8.9. The Midwest, South, and Montain states are relatively less advantaged, with the Mountain states having a percentage-deviation disadvantage increasing insignificantly from −28.8 to −29.0 over the decade.

Estimates concerning various demographic groups under the electoral college are also reported in table 4-3. Central-city and urban citizen-voters are the most advantaged (with the advantage slightly decreasing over the decade). Black citizen-voters are disadvantaged in both the 1960s and 1970s, yet their disadvantage is decreasing from −5.2 to −2.4. Rural voters maintain their position as the most disadvantaged demographic group, with their disadvantage slightly increasing over the decade, from −8.8 to −9.5

Table 4-3
Regional and Group Biases under the Electoral College in the 1960s and 1970s

	(1) *1960s* *Percent Deviation* *From National* *Average Voting Power*	(2) *1970s* *Percent Deviation* *From National* *Average Voting Power*	(3) *1960s-1970s* *Net Change* *Over Decade*
Regions			
Eastern states	13.8	8.9	−4.9
Southern states	−15.0	−13.4	1.6
Midwestern states	−5.6	−6.2	−0.6
Mountain states	−28.8	−29.0	−0.2
Far Western states	26.7	33.1	6.4
Groups			
Rural citizen- voters	−8.8	−9.5	−0.7
Urban citizen- voters	3.8	3.4	−0.4
Central-city citizen-voters	6.3	5.7	−0.6
Black citizen- voters	−5.2	−2.4	2.8

Source: John H. Yunker and Lawrence D. Longley, *The Electoral College: Its Biases Newly Measured for the 1960s and 1970s*, American Politics Series, vol. 3, copyright 1976 (Beverly Hills, Calif.: Sage Publications, 1976), p. 36. Reprinted with permission.

Earlier it was found that the electoral college has countervailing biases that result in a net large-state advantage and a disadvantage to states with 4 to 14 electoral votes. To this, we can now add the additional information that the electoral college also advantages central-city and urban citizen-voters as well as inhabitants of the Far West and East. On the other hand, the present electoral arrangement discriminates against blacks and rural residents, as well as inhabitants of the Mountain, Southern, and Midwestern states.

As suggested by conventional wisdom, the South appears to be disadvantaged by the electoral college and would stand to gain from the direct proposal. However, it should be noted that this bias has nothing to do with the low turnout in southern states or with the supposed bloc voting of Southerners for the Democratic party. It merely measures the disadvantage stemming from the effect of the unit rule and the constant two.

These data seem in most respects to confirm the often stated hypothesis that the electoral college favors urban and ethnic interests. Urbanized areas and central cities are above the national average voting power for the electoral college. Rural voters, on the other hand, are found to be relatively disadvantaged by the present electoral college.

Further analysis finds one group that stands out as profoundly *advantaged* by the existing electoral college. This group is suburban residents.[25] For the electoral college in the 1970s, suburban residents are found to have an average voting power of 1.779 and a percentage deviation from national average voting power of +7.3 percent, making this category of voters the most advantaged (nonregional) group studied.[26]

The Voting Power of Blacks in the Electoral College and the Automatic Plan. The findings for one group contradict conventional wisdom concerning the biases of the electoral college.[27] Table 4-3 reports that black citizen voters are *disadvantaged* by the electoral college, both in the 1960s and 1970s data sets. Other findings—that urban and central-city voters are advantaged and rural voters are disadvantaged under the present system—seem to confirm widely held assumptions about the biases of the electoral college. However, the findings concerning black voters differ from those reached by many analysts (a review of the conclusions of a number of scholars concerning the comparative voting power of black voters in presidential elections under the electoral-college and direct-vote systems can be found in "Comparative Voting Power of Black Voters Memorandum," reprinted in appendix B of Longley (1977), especially in the section on recent empirical analyses of black voter strength in the electoral college versus direct popular election).

Actually, one cannot say that *all* blacks are advantaged or *all* blacks are disadvantaged by the electoral college. A black voter in California has approximately two and one-half times the chance of affecting the election outcome that a black voter in the District of Columbia has (see table 4-2 above). The differences in voting power arise because people live in different states, not because of any differences in race.

The measurement of the bias affecting black voters as a group involves *averaging* the voting power of blacks in all fifty states and D.C. If blacks gain from the electoral college (that is, have above average voting power), then they must be concentrated more heavily in the six most populous states than is the general population. However, that is indeed *not* the case. Tables 4-4 through 4-6 document that *urban* and *central-city residents* are more concentrated in Ohio, Texas, Illinois, Pennsylvania, New York, and California than is the entire U.S. population. On the other hand, *blacks* and *rural residents* are less concentrated in these six states than the U.S. population as a whole.

Table 4-4 lists the highest-voting-power state, California, at the top of the list with voting power decreasing as one goes down the list. The percentage deviation from average voting power under the electoral college for each state is listed in column 1. Columns 2 and 3 display the percentage of the U.S. population and the percentage of the black population that lives in each state. Table 4-5 shows the percentages of the central-city population, urban population, and rural population that live in each state.

Table 4-6 summarizes the two previous tables by showing all these various percentages for groups of states, ranked by voting power. For example, table 4-6 shows that while 40.8 percent of the United States population (1970 census) lives in the six most powerful and populous states, only 37.1 percent of the black population lives in these states.

In which states is the black population significantly more concentrated than the general population? If we examine states in which the percentage of blacks is 1 percent or more above the percentage of the U.S. population located in that state, we find from table 4-4 that generally these are southern states that are *disadvantagd* by the electoral college. Florida, North Carolina, Georgia, Virginia, Louisiana, Maryland, South Carolina, Alabama, Mississippi, and the District of Columbia are in this category; all have below average voting power. Floridians' voting power is 2.8 percent below average; North Carolina residents are 11.8 percent below average; and the rest have voting power ranging from 20.1 percent to 39.7 percent below average.

Likewise, we should examine those states in which blacks are significantly *less* concentrated than the general population. The states for which the percentage of the U.S. population is 1 percent or more above the percentage of blacks are: California, Pennsylvania, Massachusetts, Indiana, Wisconsin, Minnesota, Washington, and Iowa. This group includes two of the largest states that benefit from the electoral college: California and Pennsylvania. In fact, California has 9.8 percent of the U.S. population but only 6.2 percent of the blacks in the United States. Furthermore, California is the most advantaged state, with voting power 53.6 percent

Table 4-4
Voting Power under the Electoral College in the 1970s, and Black Populations, Ranked by State Voting Power

State	(1) Percent Deviation From Average Voting Power	(2) Percentage of United States Population	(3) Percentage of U.S. Black Population
California	+53.6	9.8	6.2
New York	+42.4	9.0	9.6
Pennsylvania	+15.4	5.8	4.5
Illinois	+13.9	5.5	6.3
Texas	+13.5	5.5	6.2
Ohio	+9.5	5.2	4.3
Michigan	-0.6	4.4	4.4
Florida	-2.8	3.3	4.6
Alaska	-4.3	0.1	0.0
New Jersey	-5.4	3.5	3.4
Wyoming	-9.0	0.2	0.0
North Carolina	-11.8	2.5	5.0
Massachusetts	-12.0	2.8	0.8
Indiana	-12.8	2.6	1.6
South Dakota	-17.6	0.3	0.0
Montana	-19.3	0.3	0.0
Georgia	-20.1	2.3	5.3
Idaho	-20.4	0.4	0.0
Virginia	-20.6	2.3	3.8
Missouri	-20.8	2.3	2.1
Vermont	-21.3	0.2	0.0
New Hampshire	-21.7	0.4	0.0
Wisconsin	-22.2	2.2	0.6
Louisiana	-22.7	1.8	4.8
Hawaii	-23.3	0.4	0.0
Minnesota	-24.4	1.9	0.2
Nevada	-25.0	0.2	0.1
Kentucky	-25.0	1.6	1.0
Maryland	-25.6	1.9	3.1
Tennessee	-25.6	1.9	2.8
Oklahoma	-26.5	1.3	0.8
South Carolina	-26.9	1.3	3.5
Washington	-27.1	1.7	0.3
Alabama	-27.5	1.7	4.0
Delaware	-29.1	0.3	0.3
Iowa	-30.0	1.4	0.1
Rhode Island	-30.9	0.5	0.1
Colorado	-31.4	1.1	0.3
Mississippi	-31.6	1.1	3.6
West Virginia	-31.8	0.9	0.3
Kansas	-32.0	1.1	0.5
Arizona	-32.3	0.9	0.2
Connecticut	-32.4	1.5	0.8
Maine	-32.5	0.5	0.0
North Dakota	-33.3	0.3	0.0
New Mexico	-33.3	0.5	0.1
Utah	-34.7	0.5	0.0
Arkansas	-35.0	0.9	1.6
Nebraska	-37.6	0.7	0.2
Oregon	-37.7	1.0	0.1
District of Columbia	-39.7	0.4	2.4

Table 4-5
Group Populations within States, Arranged by State Voting Power under the Electoral College in the 1970s

State	(1) Percentage of Central City Population	(2) Percentage of U.S. Urban Population	(3) Percentage of U.S. Urban Population
California	11.4	12.1	3.4
New York	14.6	10.4	4.9
Pennsylvania	5.2	5.6	6.2
Illinois	6.7	6.2	3.5
Texas	8.4	6.0	4.2
Ohio	5.3	5.4	4.9
Michigan	3.9	4.4	4.3
Florida	3.0	3.7	2.5
Alaska	0.0	0.1	0.3
New Jersey	1.8	4.3	1.5
Wyoming	0.0	0.1	0.2
North Carolina	1.5	1.5	5.2
Massachusetts	2.7	3.2	1.6
Indiana	2.8	2.3	3.4
South Dakota	0.1	0.2	0.7
Montana	0.2	0.2	0.6
Georgia	1.6	1.9	3.4
Idaho	0.1	0.3	0.6
Virginia	1.8	2.0	3.2
Missouri	2.2	2.2	2.6
Vermont	0.0	0.1	0.6
New Hampshire	0.2	0.3	0.6
Wisconsin	2.1	1.9	2.8
Louisiana	1.8	1.6	2.3
Hawaii	0.5	0.4	0.2
Minnesota	1.5	1.7	2.4
Nevada	0.3	0.3	0.2
Kentucky	0.9	1.1	2.8
Maryland	1.4	2.0	1.7
Tennessee	2.1	1.5	3.0
Oklahoma	1.2	1.2	1.5
South Carolina	0.4	0.8	2.5
Washington	1.4	1.7	1.7
Alabama	1.4	1.3	2.7
Delaware	0.1	0.3	0.3
Iowa	1.0	1.1	2.2
Rhode Island	0.5	0.6	0.2
Colorado	1.3	1.2	0.9
Mississippi	0.4	0.7	2.3
West Virginia	0.3	0.5	2.0
Kansas	0.6	1.0	1.4
Arizona	1.3	0.9	0.7
Connecticut	1.6	1.6	1.3
Maine	0.2	0.3	0.9
North Dakota	0.1	0.2	0.6
New Mexico	0.4	0.5	0.6
Utah	0.5	0.6	0.4
Arkansas	0.5	0.6	1.8
Nebraska	0.8	0.6	1.1
Oregon	0.8	0.9	1.3
District of Columbia	1.2	0.5	0.0

Table 4-6

State Percentages of U.S. Population and Various Group Populations, Grouped and Ranked According to State Voting Power under the Electoral College in the 1970s

(1) Voting Power Ranks of Grouped States	(2) Percentage of U.S. Population	(3) Percentage of Black Population	(4) Percentage of Central City Population	(5) Percentage of Urban Population	(6) Percentage of Rural Population
States 1-6	40.8	37.1	51.6	45.7	27.1
States 7-11	11.5	12.4	8.7	12.6	8.8
States 12-16	8.5	7.4	7.3	7.4	11.5
States 17-21	7.5	11.2	5.7	6.5	10.4
States 22-26	6.7	5.6	6.1	5.9	8.3
States 27-31	6.9	7.8	5.9	6.1	9.2
States 32-36	6.4	8.2	4.3	5.2	9.4
States 37-41	4.7	4.8	3.1	4.0	6.8
States 42-46	3.7	1.1	3.6	3.5	4.1
States 47-51	3.5	4.3	3.8	3.2	4.6

States 1-6 have voting power ranging from +53.6 percent to +9.5 percent *above* average. States 7-11 range from −0.6 percent to −9.0 percent *below* average voting power. States 12-16: −11.8 percent to −19.3 percent; states 17-21: −20.1 percent to −21.3 percent; states 22-26: −21.7 percent to −24.4 percent; states 27-31: −25.0 percent to −26.5 percent; states 32-36: −26.9 percent to −30.0 percent; states 37-41: −30.9 percent to −32.0 percent; states 42-46: −32.3 percent to −33.3 percent; states 47-51: −34.7 percent to −39.7 percent.

above average! Thus, blacks are not any more heavily concentrated in the large states than is the general population.

Table 4-3 reports that the average black voter has voting power 2.4 percent below the average U.S. voter. The average voting power of blacks was calculated by multiplying each state's relative voting power (table 4-2, column 3) by the state's number of black residents. These products for the fifty states and the District of Columbia were then added and finally divided by the total number of blacks in the United States. The result is average black voting power (1.618). Average voting power for other groups is calculated in similar fashion.

The average U.S. voter's power is calculated by multiplying each state's relative voting power by the state's population. The sum of these fifty-one products is then divided by the total U.S. population. The result is average U.S. voting power under the electoral college (1.658), which is greater than average black voting power. To be precise, black voting power is 2.4 percent below the U.S. average.

Similar calculations showed that urban and central-city residents are 3.4 percent and 5.7 percent respectively, above average. Rural citizens have voting power 9.5 percent below average.

Table 4-6 also explains the advantage accruing to urban and central city residents and the disadvantage to rural residents. While 40.8 percent of the population lives in the six most powerful (and populous) states, a greater percentage of the urban population (45.7 percent) and of the central-city

population (51.6 percent) lives there. Only 27.1 percent of the rural population lives in the six states that benefit from the electoral college. Percentages
of these electoral groups residing in each of the other states are listed in
table 4-5. Table 4-6 lists the remaining states by groups of five, ranked by
their voting power under the electoral college, and the percentage of these
electoral groups that are located in each of these five-state groupings.

These tables, especially table 4-6, establish that urban and central-city
residents *are*, and rural residents and blacks *are not* more concentrated in
the large states, which the electoral college favors, than the general U.S.
population. Because of these distributional characteristics, *urban and central city residents are advantaged, and black voters are disadvantaged by the
electoral college* (as well as by the automatic-reform plan).

The Proportional Plan

The second and third major reform plans are somewhat similar in that they
have far different sets of biases. Under the *proportional plan*, not only
would the office of elector be abolished, but so would the statewide,
winner-take-all unit system.[28] Each state's electoral vote—apportioned,
however, as at present with the small-state advantage in the "constant
two"—would be divided in proportion to the popular vote. This would
eliminate the inequities favoring the populous states arising from the unit
vote, while retaining the inequities favoring the smallest states arising from
the constant two. The result would be a *large systematic bias* favoring the
smallest states—in fact, the relative voting power under this "reform" of a
resident of Alaska in the 1970s would be 4.442 times that of a resident of
New York. In effect, the proportional plan transforms the complex and
partially opposing biases of the electoral college into a system containing
substantially greater biases, sharply favoring the smallest states. In terms of
regional and group biases, it also greatly favors inhabitants of the Mountain
states and rural citizen-voters. Inhabitants of the South, Midwest, East, and
Far West, as well as urban, black, and central-city citizen-voters, are
discriminated against by the proportional plan.[29]

Interestingly, the proportional plan also increases the uncertainty of electoral outcomes by removing the electoral college's multiplier effect, which
usually—but not in 1976—transforms relatively thin popular vote margins
(and sometimes nonmargins) into large electoral-vote majorities. Recent
calculations by the Library of Congress have led to the conclusion that in the
1976 election, the proportional plan would have resulted in an electoral vote
of: Carter, 269.6645; Ford, 258.0255; and "other," 10.2371.[30] A proportional plan with a majority electoral-vote requirement (270 votes) would

have given us a 1976 deadlock; a 40 percent electoral-vote requirement would have produced a Carter win—by 11 electoral votes rather than the actual margin of 57 votes.

The District Plan

The third plan, the *district plan*, would keep the pledged elector, but abolish the statewide unit rule *except* for the two votes corresponding to the senators.[31] The other votes would be decided on a district-by-district vote—a sort of miniature winner-take-all. The inequities arising from the constant two votes would be retained, while the populous-state advantage arising from the unit vote would be eliminated. The result, predictably, is a set of biases similar to the marked small-state advantage found for the proportional plan. Under this plan, a resident of Alaska in the 1970s would have 2.857 times the relative voting power of a resident of California—assuming that the voting districts were equal in population and that no thought of political gerrymandering had occurred to the draftees.

The district plan has similar yet somewhat less marked regional and group biases than the proportional plan. It sharply advantages inhabitants of the Mountain states and the South as well as rural citizen-voters. Inhabitants of the states of the Midwest, East, and Far West, and black, urban, and central-city citizen-voters are disadvantaged by the district plan.[32]

The Direct-Vote Plan

The fourth system has the virtues of being simple and—unlike the three preceding plans—of dealing with all five problems of the present system. The *direct vote plan* would totally abolish the electoral college, winner-take-all voting, the constant two, and the House-based contingency-election procedure.[33] Under this plan, a vote for president, whether cast in Pennsylvania or Wisconsin, would count equally in the election of the president. If no candidate received 40 percent of the vote, a runoff election would be held between the top two contenders. The winner in terms of the greatest number of votes would in fact always be the winner of the election. In terms of voting power, a vote cast anywhere would count equally in determining the presidency. If data on state as well as regional and group biases were presented, the percentage deviations for any categoric group from the citizen-voter average would be zero. In other words, under this reform plan, all citizens have, by definition, equal voting power.

The direct-vote plan contains many virtues, among them being simplicity and comprehensiveness, a basic equality of votes for president no matter where cast, and an assurance that the winner in popular votes will always be the winner of the election.[34] This reform plan has been, in fact, the major reform alternative advocated in recent years. What happened, however, to account for its ultimate failures in 1969-1970 and in 1978, and what are the politics and prospects for electoral reform in the 1980s?

How Did Electoral Reform Fail in 1969-1970?

The story of what happened to electoral reform in 1969 and 1970 has been told elsewhere and can be quickly summarized.[35] A constitutional amendment incorporating the direct-vote plan was favorably reported by the House Judiciary Committee early in 1969 by a strong 29-6 vote. On September 18, 1969, the House of Representatives passed this proposal by a margin of 338-70 (coincidentally, the percentage of those voting for the measure in the committee and on the floor was identical: 83 percent).[36] Passed by the House by a huge margin; supported by an unprecedented lobbying coalition made up of the American Bar Association, the Chamber of Commerce of the United States, the AFL-CIO, and the League of Women Voters; endorsed by President Nixon; and favored, according to the Gallup Poll, by 81 percent of the American people, the direct-vote plan finally looked like a reform about to be accomplished. The Senate, however, was to intervene.

The direct-vote constitutional amendment had severe difficulties in even emerging from the Senate Judiciary Committee, as conservative Republicans and southern Democrats joined in efforts to bottle it up at that stage. Finally reported to the Senate floor late in 1970—almost one year after House passage—the direct-vote plan was subject to an undeclared yet extremely effective Southern filibuster during September. Motions calling for cloture of debate failed to obtain a two-thirds vote on September 17 and September 20, and the constitutional amendment was finally indefinitely postponed (or killed) on October 6, 1970.

What were the charges made against the direct-vote plan that contributed to its defeat? In ascending order of importance, they were that direct election of the president would encourage electoral fraud, damage federalism, fundamentally undermine the two-party system, and create major problems because of its 40 percent or runoff contingency plan. These arguments have been assessed in depth elsewhere,[37] and space here will allow only for a brief comment on them.

The charge that the direct-vote plan would encourage *fraud* was based on the belief that the present electoral college insulates the results of electoral fraud in separate state compartments. On the other hand, it can be easiy shown that the electoral college enormously magnifies the possible results of fraud when it occurs in a swingable state, while the direct-vote plan tends to dilute the impact of any fraud in a national pool of votes. In 1968, for example, a shift of a minimum of 53,034 popular votes in three states could have resulted in an electoral-college deadlock; in the same election, a comparable national shift of a minimum of 4,491,395 popular votes would have been necessary in order to have resulted in a runoff election, had the direct-vote plan been in effect.[38]

In 1976, a shift of a minimum of 9,245 popular votes in two states could have changed the outcome of the election, while the direct-vote plan, if in effect in 1976, would have required a fraudulent national shift of over 890,000 votes to have shifted the popular-vote lead to Ford. As can be seen, the closeness of the 1976 election was in the electoral college, not in the popular vote. Putting it another way, the usual multiplier effect of the electoral-college margin far exceeding the popular-vote margin was reversed in 1976 so as to create an artificially close cliff-hanging election.

Federalism was also seen as likely to be eroded by an abandonment of the electoral-college system. This argument seemed to be based more on the similarity of the structure of the electoral college to the structure of federalism than on any real evidence that the electoral-college method of electing the president actually is a central feature of contemporary federalism. Rather, federalism would appear to be based on and maintained by the existence of strong state and local levels of government actively engaged in significant decision making and policy administration, rather than on some mechanism for electing the president.

The third belief is similar and complementary. This is that the present electoral college is a vital support for our *two-party system*. The proponents of the direct-vote plan responded to this by pointing out that in actuality what the direct-vote reform would acomplish would be to remove the loopholes through which third-party candidates can sometimes exercise inordinate power either by being pivotal in swinging large-electoral-vote states, or by deadlocking the electoral college, as George Wallace came so close to doing in 1968.

One additional benefit of the direct-vote plan in relation to the two parties is that under it a vote anywhere would be equally desirable. Parties would have to seek votes throughout the country, albeit at greater cost and with possible increased use of mass media. As a consequence of the search for votes, political parties would have to be concerned with party structure and get-out-the-vote campaigns even in states where they are in the minority. Two-party competition would be strengthened—especially where it is weak today.

The *runoff contingency plan* was a final source of criticism of the direct-vote plan in 1970. Charges of cost, delay, and uncertainty, should a runoff election be necessary, were raised by direct-vote opponents. Nevertheless, it seems unlikely that this contingency plan would be used frequently—not as long as the 40 percent popular-vote threshold level is retained;[39] should a resort to it be necessary, the runoff plan also appears far superior to any conceivable Joint Session of Congress or other non-popular-vote-based contingency plan. These four major arguments were the politically most decisive ones during 1969-1970. Other concerns about the direct-vote plan, however, were also expressed during congressional considerations: abolishing the electoral college would take away some special advantage that urban, minority, or black voters enjoy; it is not really necessary to reform the electoral-college system since we have not had recent actual electoral problems; and we generally should be reluctant to tamper with a Constitution that has served us well.[40] Whatever the reason, the results were clear: support for reform of the electoral college that had been building for five years was ultimately stymied in 1970. The electoral college continues unreformed today.

Politics and Prospects for Electoral Reform: The 1980s and Beyond

What, then, are the prospects for reform of the electoral college in the immediate future?[41] Prior to the 1976 election, much of the impetus for electoral reform appeared to have dissipated.[42] But as discussed earlier, the 1976 election provided dramatic evidence of the potentially disastrous shortcomings of the electoral-college system. A number of pre- and postelection newspaper and magazine artcles on the electoral college—both pro and con—paved the way to renewed electoral-reform activity in the U.S. Senate in 1977 and 1978.[43]

In late January 1977, the Senate Judiciary Committee[44] launched the most extensive Senate hearings on electoral reform since earlier exhaustive 1967-1968 hearings.[45] In five days of hearings, thirty-eight witnesses testified, compiling a printed record (along with various exhibits and statements) totalling 600 pages. This activity itself generated additional press and editorial commentary concerning electoral reform.

The single most dramatic event during this period was the unexpected and strong endorsement of the direct-vote plan by President Carter on March 22, despite widely reported assumptions that he would take a much weaker or limited reform position.[46] Thus, for the first time in the twentieth century, a president had personally committed himself to the abolition of the electoral college.

It has been suggested by some that President Carter's conversion to direct election may have been due to the persuasive efforts of Vice-President Mondale, long a direct-election supporter. It is also possible that missionary work by a coalition of interest-group leaders may have been significant. Certainly, President Carter was not disposed to ignore a letter soliciting his support jointly signed by the presidents of the American Bar Association, the United Auto Workers, Common Cause, the AFL-CIO, the Chamber of Commerce of the United States, and the League of Women Voters.[47] Politics, indeed, does make for strange bedfellows.

The significance of the Carter endorsement, however, would prove to be less than initially expected. The direct-vote plan was part of a package of presidential electoral-reform proposals, such as election-day voter registration and public financing of congressional elections. All the other proposals in the package proved to be politically weak, and all were dead within six months. Direct election would suffer throughout 1977 from association with these political losers. In addition, the endorsement by the president also made abolition of the electoral college a partisan issue, putting Republican traditional electoral-reform supporters such as Senators Baker, Bellman, and Dole somewhat on the spot. Finally, presidential support was not actively forthcoming throughout 1977 and 1978 because of President Carter's deep and necessary preoccupation with crucial issues such as the Panama Canal treaty, energy legislation, and the Middle East.

After the Carter announcement, little immediate Senate activity was evident. Rather, what was underway was quiet vote counting, both in the Senate committee and on the floor. In mid-march, letters went out from Senator Birch Bayh (D-Ind.), leader of the direct-vote advocates, to thirty-one uncommitted senators, pointing out that recent studies by political scientists had shown that their states were disadvantaged by the electoral college.[48] Besides noting the disadvantages specifically suffered by the voters of each state, Senator Bayh went on to observe:

> Contrary to the thinking that prevailed a few years ago, residents of small to medium sized states are the most disadvantaged group of voters under the electoral college system. I am sure you will share my concern over this latest evidence of the unfairness of the electoral college.

Meanwhile, the staff of the Subcommittee on Constitutional Amendments was preparing ammunition to deal with the charge that a vote to abolish the electoral college was a vote to deprive black voters of a special voting advantage they enjoyed because of the electoral college.[49]

Despite this low-level activity, the direct-vote constitutional amendment appeared by late spring to be losing momentum and to be running into formidable committee difficulties and sticky floor-scheduling problems should it even be able to get out of committee. Southern Democrats on the committee—Senator James V. Eastland (D-Miss.), the chairman; James B. Allen (D-Ala.); and John L. McClellan (D-Ark.) joined with all but one Republican on the committee in an eight-vote opposition. Only if Senator

Bayh could hold every other Democrat and Republican Charles Mc.
Mathias (R-Md.), could the bill hope to get reported by the Senate Judiciary
Committee.[50] Adding to the difficulties were the uncertainties as to the
views of the Black Congressional Caucus, and the outright opposition to
electoral-college abolition on the part of some black leaders such as
Clarence Mitchell, revered (and retiring) head of the NAACP. Meanwhile,
the floor calendar for Senate business in July and September-October was
filling up, largely with energy legislation.[51]

On June 22, however, meaningful activity in the Senate Judiciary Committee finally occurred. A test vote to refer the constitutional amendment
back to subcommittee to kill it was defeated by a 9-8 vote, indicating that
the full-committee votes were possibly there to pass the direct-vote plan—if
the committee were allowed to come to a vote on passage.[52]

This is not always easy, especially when a bill is strongly opposed by the
committee chairman, as well as by both the ranking majority and minority
members of the committee. Speculation grew that the bill floor manager,
Senator Bayh, might be forced to try to bypass the committee totally by
having the bill put directly on the Senate calendar.[53] This expedient, as difficult and even desperate as it might be, appeared to be possibly the only option left to electoral-reform supporters in light of a committee filibuster
begun and led by Senator William L. Scott (R-Va.).

For five committee meetings following the June 22 test vote, Senator
Scott held fast to his filibuster, preventing the committee from taking up the
direct-vote bill. Suddenly, on July 13, an agreement was struck allowing for
a committee vote on passage of the direct-vote plan "on or before
September 16." In return, committee hearings on electoral-college reform
were reopened, with Senator Scott selecting a number of the new
witnesses.[54]

These renewed hearings were held on four days between July 20 and
August 2, 1977, and included testimony supporting retention of the electoral
college by political scientists Judith Best, Aaron Wildavsky, Herbert Storing,
and Martin Diamond (who tragically died in the Committee room shortly
after completing his testimony). Despite the compilation of an extensive additional hearing record during these reopened hearings totaling over 500
pages,[55] these July hearings seem not to have had any effect on either the
perceptions or the votes of the members of the Senate Judiciary Committee.
The arrangement of July between Senators Scott and Bayh proved to be
somewhat one-sided. Senator Bayh got what he needed, a firm agreement for
a committee vote, while Senator Scott got only the less tangible reward of additional opposing testimony. In doing so, Senator Scott gave up what had
been proving to be a most effective weapon—his committee filibuster.
Whatever the reason, however, the die was cast: the full Judiciary Committee
would vote on the direct election plan "on or before September 16."

The final stage of committee consideration of S.J. Res. 1—the direct-vote plan—occurred on September 15, one day before the deadline. Direct-election opponent Senator James B. Allen (D-Ala.) started by offering seven nongermane (not on the same topic) amendments to the direct-election plan. These dealt with busing, popular election of judges, school prayer, abortion, balanced federal budgets, former presidents to be senators, and the metric system. All were voted down.[56] Senator Allen was not acting without intent—he seldom did. Rather, the effort being made here was to entice some direct-vote supporters into voting for abortion or busing prohibitions, thus creating a composite constitutional amendment that Senator Bayh would be reluctant to bring to the Senate floor. These efforts failed, however, although only on a 9-7 vote in the case of busing.

Next, three germane substitute amendments were offered—to replace the direct-election plan with, respectively: the automatic plan (defeated 10-8), the proportional plan (defeated—but only just—by a 8-7 vote), and the district plan (defeated 8-6).[57] One more motion was finally made by the opponents: Senator Allen proposed that the runoff election be replaced by a joint-session-of-Congress contingency arrangement. This also lost, but only by an 8-7 decision. Finally, S.J. Res. 1 came to a final vote, and by the thinnest of margins (8-7) was approved by the Senate Judiciary Committee. The vote proved to be identical to that of the test vote nearly two months earlier, prior to the reopened hearings.[58]

As of September 1977, direct election had triumphed by emerging from committee. By being approved by the Senate Judiciary Committee, electoral reform appeared to some to be a proposal now ready to sweep through the Senate, subsequently to pass the House, and then to be ratified by the states. Once again, however, the Senate itself was to intervene—as in 1970—to stymie electoral-college reform. What happened to electoral reform in the Senate in 1977 and 1978 can be summarized in two words: *agendas* and *procedures*.

Despite the favorable Judiciary Committee vote in September, the business of the Senate—and especially the massive logjam resulting from the deadlocked energy conference committee—kept S.J. Res. 1 from being scheduled for floor consideration during the remaining months of 1977. Further, Senate Majority Leader Robert C. Byrd, (D-W.Va.), proved to be extremely reluctant to schedule the bill for *any* floor consideration throughout 1977 and 1978 until direct-vote supporters could show him that they had 60 firm votes, sufficient to impose cloture on the almost inevitable Senate filibuster.

Electoral-reform strategists were, in fact, faced with a double task: to prove to the leadership that they had the 60 cloture votes, and to convince the leadership to schedule time for what would be in any case lengthy debate on the direct-vote plan. This latter was difficult in light of urgent demands for similarly lengthy floor consideration of other matters on the legislative agenda such as the Panama Canal Treaty, government reorganization, energy legislation, and the like.

Throughout late 1977 and into 1978, the struggle for cloture commitments and floor time went on. By the summer of 1978, however, an additional problem was proving an overwhelming obstacle—the end-of-session crunch of legislative business. It should be noted that as the legislative calendar slips toward the end of any Congress, a controversial bill, such as the direct-vote plan, becomes highly susceptible to filibuster and other delaying tactics—as was the fate of electoral-college reform in 1970.

Such tactics also caused the demise of electoral-reform efforts in 1978, as other legislation gained priority over direct election in their claim for precious floor time in the hectic closing weeks. The result was that S.J. Res. 1 died with the adjournment of Congress in October 1978 without having been taken up on the floor of the Senate. The most direct-vote supporters were able to salvage was a commitment on the part of the Senate leadership to bring electoral-college reform to the floor early in the new Congress in 1979. Once again electoral reform, which had blossomed forth as a reform about to be accomplished, was to be put on the shelf to be considered at a later time.

Two things did occur during 1978 that have the potential of affecting the electoral college as well as the politics of electoral-college reform. In late August 1978, the Senate approved and sent to the states a previously House-passed constitutional amendment providing for congressional representation for the District of Columbia. Among the provisions of the amendment is language that would repeal the Twenty-third Amendment to the Constitution, which limited the District to electoral votes equal to the least number allotted to any state—in other words, three. Instead, under the proposed amendment, the District would receive the same electoral votes it would be entitled to if it were a state—in all likelihood four.[59]

Also in 1978, the Twentieth Century Fund Task Force on Reform of the Presidential Election Process issued its final report, entitled *Winner Take All*. In this report, the task force pointed out that initially it had been deeply divided on the merits of the existing electoral college and the direct-vote alternative, but had finally reached agreement in supporting a *new* alternative electoral-reform plan called "The National Bonus Plan." Such unanimity was especially noteworthy in light of the considerable breadth of perspective of the members of the task force, which included political scientists and historians Heinz Eulau, Jeane Kirkpatrick (who served as cochairman of the group), Tom Cronin, Paul Puryear, William Keech, and Arthur M. Schlesinger; political journalists and writers Neal Peirce, Jules Witcover, Richard Rovere, and Stephen Hess (the other cochairman); and political strategists John Sears, Jill Ruckelshaus and Patrick Caudell. This highly diverse group included not only political partisans, but also noteworthy political analysts. It also brought strong critics of the direct-election plan, such as Arthur M. Schlesinger, together with committed supporters of direct election such as Neal Peirce. Despite this variety of membership, the task force found itself in agreement on the National Bonus Plan as a desirable form of electoral-college reform.

The National Bonus Plan would add to the existing 538 electoral votes 102 additional votes (two corresponding to each of the fifty states and the District of Columbia). These "bonus votes" would be awarded as a bloc to the candidate who received the most popular votes nationally. The effect of this plan—jointly authored by journalist and writer Neal Peirce and historian Arthur M. Schlesinger—would be virtually to ensure the election in the reformed electoral college of the popular-vote winner, while retaining the alleged strengths of the historic electoral college.[60] The National Bonus Plan was introduced as a constitutional amendment by Senator Birch Bayh shortly after the task force's report was made public, but no further legislative action occurred on it—or on the direct-vote plan—during 1978.

Time will determine whether the National Bonus Plan turns out to be what it was conceived as by its creators—a reasonable compromise between those who wish to retain the traditional electoral college because of its perceived virtues in such areas as supporting federalism and maintaining the two-party system, and those who have called for the direct-vote plan so as to ensure that the winner of the popular vote will always be elected president. At least 1978 produced a fascinating *new* proposal for electoral-college reform—one on which initially leading critics and supporters of the electoral college agreed.

Electoral-college reform is a perennial issue that waxes and wanes but never disappears. Reform of the electoral college in some form will undoubtedly be before the Senate again in 1979. One problem that will somewhat inhibit electoral-reform efforts in 1979 and 1980 is the realization that any reform efforts will be irrelevant to the presidential election of 1980. There may well be a feeling that it is better to wait and see what happens in late 1980—an attitude that so often hinders electoral-reform efforts in the last two years of each presidential term.

Enhancing electoral-reform chances in 1980, however, will be fundamental changes in the composition of the Senate Judiciary Committee. As of January 1979, Senator Edward Kennedy will assume the chairmanship from retiring Senator James Eastland (D-Miss.). With the retirement of reform opponents Eastland and William Scott (R-Va.), together with the 1978 deaths of Senators McClellan (D-Ark.) and Allen (D-Ala.), the Senate Judiciary Committee will be a vastly more receptive forum for electoral-reform efforts in the 1980s than in the past.

Further, should a constitutional amendment arrive on the Senate floor, it is now possible to invoke cloture of debate with the affirmative votes of "only" sixty senators. This is considerably easier than obtaining the sixty-seven votes necessary in 1970, especially if legislative action occurs in the first sesson of a Congress (as in 1979) when the press of competing business is somewhat less. Action then allows the inevitable filibuster to run its course prior to seeking a cloture vote, making that task easier. Should direct election have the opportunity for full Senate debate in 1979 or a subsequent year, with cloture eventually terminating the filibuster, then *all* that will be necessary to abolish the electoral college would be a final two-thirds vote in the Senate for passage, favorable committee action in the House, a two-thirds vote there for passage, and ratification by both houses of three-fourths of the state legislatures. The road to reform of the electoral college is rocky and the prospects quite uncertain, yet it is to the credit of the direct-vote supporters that they are willing again and again to travel down that difficult road to reform.

A Brief Conclusion and Final Word

At its best, the electoral college operates in an inherently distorted manner in transforming popular votes into electoral votes. In addition, it has enormous potential as a dangerous institution threatening the certainty of our elections and the legitimacy of our presidents. These defects of the contemporary electoral college cannot be dealt with by patchwork reforms such as abolishing the office of elector. This distorted and unwieldy counting device must be abolished, and the votes of the American people—wherever cast—must be counted directly and equally in determining who shall be president of the United States.

Notes

1. An earlier version of this chapter was delivered as a paper at the Annu al Meeting of the American Political Science Association, Washington, D.C., September 1, 1977. Some of this material was also presented earlier in 1977 as the "Statement of Lawrence D. Longley Before the Committee on the Judiciary, United States Senate," Hearings on the Electoral College and Direct Election, 95th Cong., 1st sess., January 27, February 1, 2, 7, and 10, 1977 [hereafter cited as *February 1977 Senate Hearings*]. Earlier research drawn on includes: Longley and Braun (1975); Longley (1974); Yunder and Longley (1976).

2. In another publication, the following man-on-the-street interviews are cited: "Every boy and girl should go to college, if they can't afford Yale or Harvard, why, Electoral is just as good if you work." "The group at the bar poor-mouth Electoral somethin' awful. Wasn't they mixed up in a basketball scandal or somethin'?" (quoted in Longley and Braun [1975], p. 1).

3. Neal R. Peirce, *The People's President: The Electoral College in American History and the Direct Vote Alternative* (New York: Simon and Schuster, 1968), p. 43. See also American Enterprise Institute, *Direct Election of the President* (Washington, D.C.: American Enterprise Institute, 1977), especially "Historical Development of the Present System"; Longley and Braun (1975), chap. 2, "The Creation and Operation of the Electoral College," and Diamond (1977).

4. John P. Roche, "The Founding Fathers: A Reform Caucus in Action," *American Political Science Review* 55 (December 1961):811. Reprinted with permission.

5. The last state to resist the movement to the popular selection of presidential electors was South Carolina, which adopted election of electors only after the Civil War. The previous method, generally abandoned early in the nineteenth century, was the state legislative election of presidential electors. See Peirce, *The People's President*, pp. 74, 76, and Longley and Braun (1975), pp. 30-31.

6. The first faithless elector was Samuel Miles, a 1796 Federalist elector in Pennsylvania, who declined to vote for Adams, the Federalist candidate, and instead cast his vote for Jefferson. See Peirce, *The People's President*, p. 64, and Longley and Braun (1975), pp. 29-30.

7. The district division of electoral votes had been common early in the nineteenth century, but completely disappeared by 1826. It momentarily reappeared in Michigan for one election late in the nineteenth century for particular partisan reasons. In 1969, Maine resurrected the district division of electoral votes through adoption of a plan, which went into effect with the presidential election of 1972, allowing for determination of two of its four votes on the basis of its two congressional districts. See Peirce, *The People's President*, pp. 74-78, and Longley and Braun (1975), p. 31. As of the 1976 election, however, an actual division of Maine's electoral votes 3-1 (the only division possible) had not yet occurred.

8. See Lawrence C. Longley, "Why the Electoral College Should be Abolished" (Speech to the 1976 Electoral College, Madison, Wisconsin, December 13, 1976). Despite being referred to as "political hacks and fat cats," the Wisconsin electors there assembled proceeded to go on record supporting the abolition of their office.

9. Only sixteen states have laws requiring electors to vote according to their pledge, and these laws themselves are of doubtful constitutionality. See James C. Kirby, Jr., "Limitations on the Power of State Legislatures over Presidential Elections," *Law and Contemporary Problems* 27 (Spring 1962):495-509.

10. "Testimony of Honorable Robert Dole, U.S. Senator from the State of Kansas," *February 1977 Senate Hearings*, pp. 36-37. A *Washington Post* editorial commenting on this Dole statement can be found reprinted in these same hearings, pp. 114-115.

The 1976 election gave rise to another fascinating event. Following the election, a letter was sent to all members of the 1976 electoral college by Robert L. Brewster (of Albuquerque, New Mexico), urging them to elect him as president in order to save the country from earthquakes and tidal waves. Nevertheless, Mr. Brewster received no electoral votes for president. There are no data available reporting unusual earthquakes and tidal waves. See *February 1977 Senate Hearings*, p. 115.

11. See note 7.

12. For a discussion of campaign-resource-allocation biases, see Colantoni, Levesque, and Ordeshook (1975), and the discussion concerning this article in the same issue; Brams and Davis (1974); Brams (1975), esp. chap. 3, "Testimony of the Honorable Herbert H. Humphrey, U.S. Senator from the State of Minnesota," January 27, 1977, in *February 1977 Senate Hearings*, p. 25; "Testimony of Douglas Bailey," media manager of the Ford-Dole campaign, August 2, 1977, in U.S., Congress, Senate Judiciary Committee, Subcommittee on the Constitution, *Hearings on Electoral College and Direct Election*, 95th Cong., 1st sess., July 20, 22, 28 and August 2, 1977 [hereafter cited as *July 1977 Senate Hearings*], pp. 258-273, as well as the testimony at the same Hearings by Senator Robert Dole, who also stressed the campaign distortions created by the electoral college (pp. 26-40). See also "Impact of Direct Election on the Smaller States," in U.S., Congress, Senate, Judiciary Committee, *Direct Popular Election of the President and Vice President of the United States* (Washington, D.C.: U.S. Government Printing Office, 1977) [hereafter cited as *December 1977 Senate Report*], pp. 14-16.

13. Testimony of Neal Peirce, journalist and author, *February 1977 Senate Hearings*, p. 248.

14. *The People's President*, pp. 317-321. The concept of hairbreadth election is also discussed in Longley and Braun (1975), pp. 37-41.

15. For a detailed analysis of the 1968 presidential election in terms of the electoral college, see Longley and Braun (1975), pp. 7-17.

16. For a consideration of the elections of 1876 and 1960 as elections in which the popular leader lost in the electoral college, see Longley and Braun (1975), pp. 1-7, 33-35. See also, concerning the election of 1876, the discussion in William R. Keech "Background Paper," in *Winner Take All: Report of the Twentieth Century Fund Task Force on Reform of the Presidential Election Process* (New York: Holmes and Meier Publishers, 1978), chap. 3, "Comparing the Alternatives: Does the 'Right' Candidate Win?"

17. This analysis assumes, of course, the nondefection of Republican elector Mike Padden of Washington. If he had nevertheless declined to vote for Ford, then the election would have been inconclusive and would have gone to the House in January 1977.

18. One count found at least 513 different purposes for change introduced in the U.S. Congress through 1966. See Longley and Braun (1975), p. 43.

19. The automatic plan is subject to detailed analysis and assessment, with a summary of arguments pro and con, in Longley and Braun (1975), pp. 43-49, 76-78.

20. John H. Yunker and Lawrence D. Longley, "The Biases of the Electoral College: Who is Really Advantaged?" in *Perspectives on Presidential Selection*, ed. Donald R. Matthews (Washington, D.C.: The Brookings Institution, 1973), pp. 173-74; and Longley and Braun (1975), pp. 95-96.

21. See Longley and Braun (1975), pp. 103-128; Yunker and Longley, "The Biases of the Electoral College," pp. 174-203; Longley and Yunker (1973); and Yunker and Longley (1976). The latter work contains the most complete and current statement of the methodology followed.

22. See also the works cited in the last section of this chapter, on recent empirical research on the electoral college. See Longley and Braun (1975), pp. 121-128; Yunker and Longley, "Biases of the Electoral College," pp. 190-195; Longley and Yunker (1973), pp. 207-210; and Yunker and Longley (1976), pp. 31-44. This literature is subject to a very thoughtful and complete critique in Keech, "Background Paper," chap. 2, "Comparing the Alternatives: The Effect on Voter Equality."

23. Longley and Braun (1975), p. 115. Yunker and Longley, "Biases of the Electoral College," p. 182; Longley and Yunker (1973), pp. 189-200; Yunker and Longley (1976), pp. 9-21.

24. Longley and Yunker (1973), p. 193; Yunker and Longley (1976), p. 13.

25. Suburban residents are defined as residents of urban areas contained within SMSA regions, minus central-city areas inside SMSAs. In effect, we are looking at the urban fringe within SMSAs. Appreciation is expressed to John H. Yunker of the University of Minnesota for this analysis.

26. The voting advantage of suburban residents in the electoral college is due to the fact that 49.5 percent of the nation's suburban population is contained in the six largest (and greatly advantaged) states, while only 40.8 percent of the nation's population as a whole is located in these six states.

27. Much of the following discussion was originally prepared by John H. Yunker of the University of Minnesota for the Senate Judiciary Committee, and can be found on pp. 498-500 of the *February 1977 Senate Hearings*. Appreciation is expressed to John H. Yunker for permission to use this analysis in this paper. For a discussion of the current literature and controversy concerning the voting power of blacks under the electoral-college and direct-election systems, see Longley (1977), appendix B, "Comparative Voting Power of Black Voters Memorandum," esp. section IIIB, "Recent Empirical Analysis of Black Voter Strength in the Electoral College Versus Direct Popular Election." See also *December 1977 Senate Report*, esp. "Racial and Minority Group Voting Power Under Electoral College and Direct Election Systems," pp. 20-23.

28. The dangers of the contingency-election procedure generally are not dealt with by this plan—except that, in all probability, an electoral-college

deadlock is made greater since the multiplier effect of the electoral college would be absent. The proportional plan is subject to detailed analysis and assessment, with a summary of arguments pro and con, in Longley and Braun (1975), pp. 49-57, 78-79.

29. Longley and Yunker (1973), pp. 201, 209; Yunker and Longley (1976), pp. 30, 39.

30. Joseph B. Gorman, "1976 Presidential Election: Comparative Results Under the Present System and the Proposed Proportional Method of Assigning Electoral Votes," unpublished memorandum, Library of Congress.

31. The district plan is subject to detailed analysis and assessment, with a summary of arguments pro and con, in Longley and Braun (1975), pp. 57-64, 79-81.

32. Longley and Yunker (1973), pp. 204, 209; Yunker and Longley (1976), pp. 30, 40.

33. The direct-vote plan is subject to detailed analysis and assessment, with a summary of arguments pro and con, in Longley and Braun (1975), pp. 64-69, 82-128.

34. In another publication, more elaborate criteria for evaluation of our presidential election system are presented, in terms of which the direct-vote plan is favorably weighed. The criteria there discussed are that an electoral-reform plan should further three broad goals:

1. It should contribute to democracy, specifically:
   a. provide a basic equality of votes, and
   b. ensure that the winning candidate is the one who received the most votes.
2. It should ensure the effectiveness of the presidency, specifically:
   a. contribute to its legitimacy through providing a broad mandate,
   b. provide a clear, easily comprehended, and distinctive source for the president's mandate,
   c. ensure a quick and decisive verdict not subject to conflicting claims, and
   d. avoid a constitutional crisis that might arise either through an extended election deadlock or through questionable proceedings and deals in the course of a contingent procedure
3. It should both preserve and invigorate the political system, specifically:
   a. maintain the existing two-party system and encourage effective two-party competition while recognizing the legitimate right of potential third and fourth parties to electoral influence,
   b. encourage popular political participation—especially voter turnout—while minimizing campaign expenditures,

c. preserve federalism while securing an equitable electoral influence for all sections of the country in terms of campaign time and political attention,

d. provide no systematic and inherent political biases favoring or hurting partisan, ideological, or categoric groups in American society, and

e. avoid any incentive for electoral fraud and minimize the consequences of accidental circumstances.

Longley and Braun (1975), pp. 75-76. For a different set of criteria, see *Winner Take All*, where the Task Force reports its agreement that "a fair and democratic system should maximize the likelihood that the candidate with the most popular votes would win, should encourage healthy competition through a strong two-party system (without unduly restricting the development of third parties), should promote greater voter participation, and should sustain the vitality of the federal system" (p. 4). The way different criteria influence reform preferences is analyzed in Keech, "Background Paper," esp. chap. 7, "The Nature of the Choice."

35. The legislative politics surrounding the defeat of electoral reform in 1969 and 1970 is the subject of Longley and Braun (1975), chap. 5.

36. Curiously enough, the 1969 House vote has been frequently and erroneously reported as *339*-70. The mistake has been traced by this author to an error in wire-service reports as well as in the *daily* edition of the Congressional Record, which credited absent Congressman de la Garza (D-Tex.) as voting for the constitutional amendment. His absence has been confirmed through personal correspondence. The later bound *Congressional Record*, and the *Congressional Quarterly*, correctly reported the vote as *338*-70.

37. Longley and Braun (1975), pp. 82-94.

38. Ibid., p. 85. See also *December 1977 Senate Report*, pp. 16-18.

39. In only one election among the thirty-seven for which popular-vote totals are available did no candidate receive 40 percent of the popular vote. In the 1860 election the leading candidate, Lincoln, received 39.76 percent of the national popular vote, although he was not on the ballot in several states and thus could receive no popular votes at all in those states. See also *December 1977 Senate Report*, pp. 18-19.

40. See Longley and Braun (1975), chap. 5. These arguments are addressed once again in the *December 1977 Senate Report*, pp. 1-23, especially "the opponents' arguments and some counterpoints," p. 10; and in the minority report of the same committee, pp. 24-32. The conclusions of the minority concerning the dangers resulting from direct election of the president are presented in the last section of this chapter. See also Keech, "Background Paper," chaps. 4 and 5.

41. The interpretive summary that follows, of 1977 and 1978 Senate activities concerning electoral-college reform, is drawn from numerous personal and confidential conversations, correspondence, and interviews of the author with senators and senatorial staff personnel during 1977 and 1978. The author would deeply appreciate being challenged and/or corrected on any statement of fact or interpretation.

42. See, for example, the general lack of attenton paid to the 1973 *Hearings on Electoral Reform* of the Senate Constitutional Amendments Subcommittee, and to the limited Committee activities during 1974 and 1975.

43. A sampling of recent magazine and newspaper articles evaluating the electoral college can be found in the last section of this chapter.

44. The hearings were only formally by the entire committee since subcommittee members had not yet been officially determined. The hearings were actually organized by the staff of the Subcommittee on Constitutional Amendments, and chaired by its long-time chairman, Senator Birch Bayh (D-Ind.).

45. See *February 1977 Senate Hearings*. All 1977 and 1978 congressional activity was in the Senate since the House seemed disinclined to expend any energy on the issue until the Senate had shown it could act—a different situation from that of 1970.

46. See, for example, "Carter Proposes End of Electoral College in Presidential Vote," *New York Times*, 23 March 1977, where Warren Weaver, Jr. reports: "The President's full endorsement of direct popular election came as a modest surprise. His recent public and private statements indicated that he would support elimination of the electors, and retain in some modified form the electoral vote machinery that distorts the one man—one vote principle in all national elections." The text of President Carter's statement concerning the electoral college can be found in the *July 1977 Senate Hearings*, p. 2.

47. The text of this famous (and possibly unique) letter can be found in the *July 1977 Senate Hearings*, p. 10.

48. Letters were not sent to senators from the six states shown to be advantaged by the retention of the electoral college. See also, in the *December 1977 Senate Report*, "Impact of Direct Election on the Smaller States," pp. 14-16.

49. See Longley (1977), appendix B on comparative voting power of black voters.

50. There was some concern at this time over how solid Democratic senators Joseph R. Biden (D-Del.), and John C. Culver (D-Iowa) were in support of abolishing the electoral college. As noted below, both, however, supported abolition on the committee test vote of June 22, as well as on the final committee vote of September 15.

51. Direct-vote supporters found encouragement in evidence of con-

tinued public support for abolishing the electoral college. A Harris survey released in late May reported that 74 percent of the respondents favored (and 13 percent opposed) "passing a constitutional amendment to abolish the electoral college and have the President and Vice-President elected by popular vote." Similarly, a Common Cause membership poll found 82 percent favored abolishing the electoral college (12 percent opposed, the rest uncertain). See *In Common*, Spring 1977, p. 17. A slightly earlier Gallup Poll, in February, had found 75 percent of the respondents approved of "an amendment to the Constitution which would do away with the electoral college and base the election of a President on the total vote cast throughout the nation." Louis Harris concluded in his release of May 30, "As far as public opinion is concerned, the opponents of the electoral college system have won their battle." The February 10, 1977 Gallup Poll and May 30 Harris survey releases can be found in the *July 1977 Senate Hearings*, pp. 6-9.

52. For keeping the direct-vote plan alive: Senators Kennedy (D-Mass.), Bayh (D-Ind.), Byrd (D-Va.)—at only the last moment, Abourezk (D-S.D.), Biden (D-Del.), Culver (D-Iowa), Metzenbaum (D-Ohio), De Concini (D-Ariz.), and one Republican, Senator McC. Mathias, (R-Md.). Opposed to the direct-vote plan were: Senator Eastland (D-Miss.), Mc-Clelland (D-Ark.), Allen (D-Ala.), Thurmond (R-S.C.), Scott (R-Va.), Laxalt (R-Nev.), Hatch (R-Utah), and Wallop (R-Wy.).

53. See Rhodes Cook, "Bayh May Bypass Committee on Electoral College Bill," *Congressional Quarterly*, 25 June 1977.

54. These reopened Senate hearings were technically held by the Subcommittee on the Constitution, but they were in effect, a direct continuation of the *February 1977 Senate Hearings* by the entire Senate Judiciary Committee. See note 44. For a discussion of the July arrangements between Senators Scott and Bayh, see *July 1977 Senate Hearings*, pp. 1-2.

55. These hearings are cited as *July 1977 Senate Hearings*. Very little press coverage was given these hearings, which did not seem to upset electoral-reform supporters. The printed hearing was itself not available until January 1978, five months after the hearings and four months after the final committee vote.

56. The votes by which these Allen nongermane amendments were tabled (defeated) were 9-7, 10-5, 9-6, 10-6, 8-6, 9-6, and voice vote.

57. The automatic-plan substitute was moved by Senator Scott (R-Va.), the proportional plan by Senator Thurmond (R-S.C.) and the district plan by Senator Allen (D-Ala.).

58. There had been some hope, in August, that Republican Senators Hatch (R-Utah) or Wallop (R-Wy.) might be persuaded to support the direct-vote plan on final committee passage in September. This did not occur, however. The individual votes for both the test vote in July and the final vote in September are given in note 52.

59. It was understood that the demands for ratification would preclude any possibility of the change taking place in time to effect the 1980 election.

The proposed constitutional amendment would also treat the District of Columbia as a state for purpose of ratifying future amendments to the Constitution. By thus creating fifty-one ratifying units, the amendment would also raise the three-fourths ratifying margin necessary for future amendments from thirty-eight "states" to thirty-nine "states."

The amendment, if ratified, would also have the effect of temporarily increasing the size of the electoral college from 538 to 539 because of the likely fourth electoral vote for the District of Columbia. This temporary increase would only exist until the next congressional reapportionment of seats among the states (in 1981 or 1991) which would return the size of the House from 437 to its usual 435. As a result, the "permanent" size of the electoral college would then be 537 (against the current 538)—corresponding to 435 House members and 102 Senators. This assumes, of course, that the electoral college has not meanwhile, through some stroke of wisdom, been abolished.

60. The National Bonus Plan would also do away with electors, with the electoral votes being automatically determined. The Task Force plan also provides for a run-off election in the unlikely instance that no one candidate has received a majority of electoral votes. This run-off would be between the top two candidates in electoral votes, and would once again be in terms of the traditional electoral votes plus a winner-take-all pool of 102 bonus votes. Task Force member Neal Peirce dissented from the report in this respect, calling instead for a simple direct election run-off, should one be necessary. All were in agreement that *any* run-off was unlikely ever to be necessary because of the effect of the bonus 102 electoral votes. Even more importantly, all agreed that this plan would virtually ensure the electoral college's election of the popular vote leader. See *Winner Take All*; Neal Perice, "A Plan to Break Electoral College Logjam," *Minneapolis Tribune*, 19 March 1978, and in many other newspapers nationally as a syndicated column; *Congressional Quarterly Weekly Report*, 25 March 1978, p. 753; and Thomas F. Cronin, "Instead, 640 Electors," *New York Times*, 1 May 1978, idem, "The Direct Vote and the Electoral College: The Case for Meshing Things Up" (Paper prepared for delivery at the Center for the Study of Democratic Institutions, Santa Barbara, California, June 26, 1978); and idem, "Choosing a President," *Center Magazine*, September/October 1978, pp. 5-15.

References

Books

Best, Judith. *The Case Against Direct Election of the President*. Ithaca, N.Y.: Cornell University Press, 1975. Chapters 1 and 7 of this book can also be found in U.S. Congress, Senate Judiciary Committee, Subcommittee on the Constitution, *Hearings on the Electoral College and Direct Election*, 95th Cong., 1st sess., July 20, 22, 28 and August 2, 1977, pp. 65-113. [Hereafter cited as *July 1977 Senate Hearings*.]

Brams, Steven J. *Game Theory and Politics*, esp. pp. 191-192 and 243-278. New York: The Free Press, 1975.

———. *The Presidential Election Game*. New Haven, Conn.: Yale University Press, 1978.

Longley, Lawrence D., and Braun, Alan G. *The Politics of Electoral College Reform*. 2d ed. New Haven, Conn.: Yale University Press, 1975.

Sayre, Wallace S., and Parris, Judith H. *Voting for President: The Electoral College and the American Political System*. Washington, D.C.: The Brookings Institution, 1970.

Zeidenstein, Harvey. *Direct Election of the President*. Lexington, Mass.: Lexington Books, D.C. Heath and Company, 1973.

Articles, Reports, and Papers

Best, Judith. "The Case For the Electoral College." Paper prepared for delivery at the Annual Meeting of the American Political Science Association, Washington, D.C., September 1-4, 1977; also in *July 1977 Senate Hearings*, pp. 56-64.

Blair, Douglas H. "Electoral College Reform and the Distribution of Voting Power." Discussion Paper no. 362, Wharton School Department of Economics. Reprinted in U.S., Congress, Senate, Judiciary Committee, *Hearings on the Electoral College and Direct Election*, 95th Cong., 1st sess., January 27, February 1, 2, 7, and 10, 1977, pp. 503-514. [Hereafter cited as *February 1977 Senate Hearings*.]

Brams, Steven J. "How the Presidential Candidates Run the Final Stretch." In *February 1977 Senate Hearings*, pp. 538-540.

———. "Bias in the Electoral College." *February 1977 Senate Hearings*, pp. 540-542.

Brams, Steven J., and Affuso, Paul J. "Power and Size: A New Paradox." *Theory and Decision* 7 (1976):29-56.

Brams, Steven J., and Davis, Morton D. "The 3/2 Rule in Presidential Campaigning." *American Political Science Review* 68 (March 1974):113-134. Reprinted in *February 1977 Senate Hearings*, pp. 515-537.

Brams, Steven J., and Fishburn, Peter C. "Approval Voting." Paper prepared for delivery at the Annual Meeting of the American Political Science Association, Washington, D.C., September 1-4, 1977.

Brams, Steven J., and Lake, Mark. "Power and Satisfaction in a Representative Democracy." Paper prepared for delivery at the Conference on Game Theory and Political Science, Hyannis, Mass., July 10-17, 1977.

Colantoni, Claude S.; Levesque, Terrance J.; and Ordeshook, Peter C. "Campaign Resource Allocations Under the Electoral College." *American Political Science Review* 69 (March 1975):141-154. Brams, Steven J., and Davis, Morton D. "Comments," pp. 155-156. Colantoni, Levesque, and Ordeshook. "Rejoinder," pp. 157-161.

Diamond, Martin. *The Electoral College and the American Idea of Democracy*. Washington, D.C.: American Enterprise Institute, 1977. Reprinted in *July 1977 Senate Hearings*, pp. 161-185.

Goetz, Charles J. "Further Thoughts on the Measurement of Power in the Electoral College." Paper presented at the Annual Meeting of the Public Choice Society, May 4, 1972.

_____ . "An Equilibrium-Displacement Measurement of Voting Power in the Electoral College." Paper delivered at the Annual Meeting of the American Political Science Association, New Orleans, La., September 4-8, 1973.

Hinich, Melvin J., and Ordeschook, Peter C. "The Electoral College: A Spatial Analysis." Paper delivered at the Annual Meeting of the Midwest Political Science Association, May 1973.

Hinich, Melvin J.; Michelsen, Richard; and Ordeshook, Peter. "The Electoral College vs. a Direct Vote: Policy Bias, Indeterminate Outcomes and Reversals." *Journal on Mathematical Sociology*, in press.

Keech, William R. "The Electoral College Controversy." In *Winner Take All: Report of the Twentieth Century Fund Task Force on Reform of the Presidential Election Process*. New York: Holmes and Meier Publishers, 1978.

Longley, Lawrence D. "The Electoral College." *Current History* 67 (August 1974):64-69ff.

_____ . "Prepared Statement of Lawrence D. Longley." *February 1977 Senate Hearings*, pp. 88-105.

_____ . "The Case Against the Electoral College." Paper prepared for delivery at the 1977 Annual Meeting of the American Political Science Association, Washington, D.C., September 1-4, 1977.

Longley, Lawrence D., and Yunker, John H. "Who Is Really Advantaged by the Electoral College—and Who Just Thinks He Is?" Paper delivered at the Annual Meeting of the American Political Science Association, Chicago, September 7-11, 1971.

_____ . "The Changing Biases of the Electoral College." Paper delivered at the Annual Meeting of the American Political Science Association, New Orleans, La., September 4-8, 1973. Also in U.S., Congress, Senate, Judiciary Committee, Subcommittee on Constitutional Amendments, *Hearings on Electoral Reform*. 93rd Cong., 1st sess., September 26 and 27, 1973, pp. 187-212.

Michelsen, R., and Ordeshook, P.C. "The Electoral College and the Probability of Reversals." In *Modeling and Simulations*, vol. 5. Pittsburgh, Pa.: University of Pittsburgh Press, forthcoming.

Nelson, Michael C. "Partisan Bias in the Electoral College." *Journal of Politics* 27 (November 1974):1033-1048.

Niemi, Richard, and Riker, William H. "The Choice of Voting Systems." *Scientific American* 234 (June 1976):21-27.

Owen, Guillermo. "Multilinear Extensions and the Banzhaf Value." *Naval Research Logistics Quarterly* 22 (December 1975):741-750.

_____ . "Evaluation of a Presidential Election Game." *American Political Science Review* 69 (September 1975):947-953. Chester Spatt. "Communication: Evaluation of a Presidential Election Game." *American Political Science Review* 70 (December 1976):1221-1223. Guillermo Owen. "Rejoinder." *American Political Science Review* 70 (December 1976):1223-1224. The Spatt and Owen exchange is reprinted in the *February 1977 Senate Hearings*, pp. 549-553.

Power, Max S. "A Theoretical Analysis of the Electoral College and Proposed Reforms." Ph.D. dissertation, Yale University, 1971.

_____ . "The Logic and Illogic of the Case for Direct Popular Election of the President." Paper deliverd at the Western Political Science Association Meeting, Albuquerque, N.M., April 8-10, 1971.

_____ . "Logic and Legitimacy: On Understanding the Electoral College Controversy." In *Perspectives on Presidential Selection*, edited by Donald R. Matthews. Washington, D.C.: The Brookings Institution, 1973.

Sindler, Allan. "Basic Change Aborted: The Failure to Secure Direct Popular Election of the President, 1969-70." In *Policy and Politics in America*, edited by Allan Sindler. Boston: Little, Brown and Company, 1973.

Spilerman, Seymour and Dickens, David. "Who Will Gain and Who Will Lose Influence Under Different Electoral Rules." Discussion paper, Institute for Research on Poverty, University of Wisconsin-Madison, December 1972. Also, *American Journal of Sociology* 80, no. 2 (1975): 443-477. Reprinted in *February 1977 Senate Hearings*, pp. 554-591.

Sterling, Carleton W. "The Political Implications of Alternative Systems of Electing the President of the United States." Ph.D. dissertation, University of Chicago, 1970.

_____ . "The Failure of Bloc Voting in the Electoral College to Benefit Urban Liberal and Ethnic Groups." Paper delivered at the Annual Meeting of the American Political Science Association, Los Angeles, September 1970.

_____ . "The Electoral College and the Impact of Popular Vote Distribution." *American Politics Quarterly* 12 (April 1974):179-204.

_____ . "A Geometric Analysis of Electoral College Misrepresentation." In *July 1977 Senate Hearings*, pp. 409-432.

_____ . "The Electoral College Biases Revealed, The Conventional Wisdom and Game Theory Models Notwithstanding." In *July 1977 Senate Hearings*, pp. 432-454.

_____ . "Biases of the Electoral College Evaluated Through Mathematical Models." Manuscript, n.d.

_____ . "The Electoral College: The Representation of Non-Voters." Manuscript, n.d.

Uslaner, Eric M. "Pivotal States in the Electoral College: An Empirical Investigation." In *Annals of New York Academy of Science*, edited by Lee F. Papayanopovlos, *Proceedings of the Conference on Quantitative Methods, Measures and Criteria*, vol. 219, pp. 61-76. New York: New York Academy of Science, 1973.

_____ . "Spatial Models of the Electoral College: Distribution Assumptions and Biases of the System." Paper delivered at the Annual Meeting of the American Political Science Association, Chicago, August 29-September 2, 1974.

Yunker, John H. "Prepared Statement of John Yunker." Senate Judiciary Committee, *Hearings on the Electoral College and Direct Elections*, 95th Cong., 1st sess., February 1977, pp. 498-500.

Yunker, John H., and Longley, Lawrence D. "The Biases of the Electoral College: Who Is Really Advantaged?" In *Perspectives on Presidential Selection*, edited by Donald R. Matthews. Washington, D.C.: The Brookings Institution, 1973.

_____ . *The Electoral College: Its Biases Newly Measured for the 1960s and 1970s*. Beverly Hills, Calif.: Sage Publications, 1976.

Selected Recent Magazine and Newspaper Articles Evaluating the Electoral College

Works Generally Supporting the Abolition of the Electoral College

"Demolish the College." Editorial, *Washington Post*, 1 February 1977. Also in *February 1977 Senate Hearings*, p. 114, and in *July 1977 Senate Hearings*, pp. 493-494.

Feerick, John D. "The Electoral College and the Election of 1976." *Journal of the American Bar Association* 63 (June 1977):757-775. Also in *July 1977 Senate Hearings*, pp. 360-363.

_____ . "Electoral College Archaic, Dangerous: Democracy Demands Popular Vote." Syndicated column, 21 January 1977. Also in *July 1977 Senate Hearings*, pp. 490-492.

Lewis, Anthony. "Again: Why Keep the Electoral College?" *New York Times*, 7 November 1976.

Longley, Lawrence D. "Electoral College Should Be Abolished." *The Minneapolis Tribune*, 12 December 1976.

Peirce, Neal R. "Electoral College: Its Time Has Run Out." *Washington Post*, 3 December 1976. Also in *July 1977 Senate Hearings*, pp. 485-486.

Wicker, Tom. "An Old Idea Still Needed." *New York Times*, 16 November 1976. Also in *July 1977 Senate Hearings*, p. 480.

―――― . "One Person, One Vote." *New York Times*, 27 March 1977.

―――― . "Black Voting Power." *New York Times*, 16 September 1977.

See also the various statements contained in Senate Judiciary Committee, *Hearings on The Electoral College and Direct Election*, 95th Congress, 1st session, January 27, February 1, 2, 7, and 10, 1977 [hereafter cited as *February 1977 Senate Hearings*], especially by Senators Humphrey and Dole; Longley, Yunker, and Braun; Justin Stanley and John Feerick of the American Bar Association; Gus Tyler of the ILGWU; and Clark Mac Gregor of the U.S. Chamber of Commerce. Additional statements supporting the abolition of the Electoral College can also be found in the reopened hearings, Senate Judiciary Committee, Subcommittee on the Constitution, *Hearings on the Electoral College and Direct Election*, 95th Congress, 1st session, July 20, 22, 28, and August 2, 1977 [hereafter cited as *July 1977 Senate Hearings*], especially by Prof. Paul A. Freund, Richard M. Scammon, Lance Tarrance, Douglas L. Bailey, and Senator Robert Dole. The *July 1977 Senate Hearings* contains an extensive selection of newspaper and magazine editorials and articles favoring electoral-college reform; see pp. 471-503.

An excellent summary of the case *for* the abolition of the electoral college will be found in the December 1977 Report of the Senate Judiciary Committee, *Direct Popular Election of the President and Vice President of the United States* (Washington, D.C.: U.S. Government Printing Office, 1977), pp. 1-23. [Hereafter cited as the December, 1977 Senate Report.] This report includes discussions of the defects and deficiencies of the present electoral college system; the opponents' arguments and some counterpoints; the effects of direct election on the two-party system, federalism, and direct election; the impact of direct election on the smaller states; its consequences in terms of voter fraud, vote recounts, and possible run offs; and social and minority group voting power under electoral college and direct electoral systems.

Works Generally Supporting the Retention
of the Electoral College

"A Bad Idea Whose Time Has Come." Editorial, *New Republic*, 7 May 1977, pp. 5-8. Also in *July 1977 Senate Hearings*, pp. 525-528.

American Enterprise Institute. *Direct Election of the President*. Washington, D.C.: American Enterprise Institute, 1977. Reprinted in *July 1977 Senate Hearings*, pp. 384-397.

"Busybody 'Reform.'" Editorial, *Wall Street Journal*, 28 March 1977. Also in *July 1977 Senate Hearings*, pp. 511-512.

Diamond, Martin. "Testimony in Support of the Electoral College." Reprint no. 76, American Enterprise Institute, 1977.

"Election Reform." Editorial, *New Republic*, 25 June 1977. Also in *July 1977 Senate Hearings*, pp. 534-535.

"Electoral College Reform." Editorial, *New York Times*, 16 November 1976.

Kilpatrick, James J. "Yes, an 18th Century Idea." Syndicated column, *Washington Star*, 11 August 1977. Also in *July 1977 Senate Hearings*, pp. 536-537.

"Making the Vote and Voting More Popular." Editorial, *New York Times*, 23 March 1977. Also in *July 1977 Senate Hearings*, pp. 510-511.

"Old Reform, New risks." Editorial, *New York Times*, 6 February 1977. Also in *February 1977 Senate Hearings*, p. 357, and *July 1977 Senate Hearings*, pp. 506-507.

Perkins, Paul M. "What's Good About the Electoral College." *Washington Monthly*, April 1977, pp. 40-41.

"'Reforming' the Electoral College." Editorial, *Wall Street Journal*, 6 January 1977. Also in *July 1977 Senate Hearings*, pp. 505-506.

Schlesinger, Arthur M. "The Electoral College Conundrum." *Wall Street Journal*, 4 April 1977. Also in *July 1977 Senate Hearings*, pp. 514-516.

"Senator Bayh's Nightmare." Editorial, *Washington Star*, 18 November 1976.

Will, George F. "Don't Fool With the Electoral College." *Newsweek*, 4 April 1977. Also in *July 1977 Senate Hearings*, pp. 509-510.

_____ . "Constitutional Numbers Games." *Washington Post*, 18 August 1975. Also in *July 1977 Senate Hearings*, pp. 519-520.

Williams, Eddie N. "Would Popular Election Dilute the Black Vote?" *Washington Post*, 14 April 1977. Also in *July 1977 Senate Hearings*, pp. 518-519.

See also the various statements contained in the *February 1977 Senate Hearings*, and in the reopened *July 1977 Senate Hearings*, especially by Austin Ranney, Aaron Wildavsky, Martin Diamond, Herbert Storing, Judith Best, and Eddie Williams. The *July 1977 Senate Hearings* contains an extensive selection of newspaper and magazine editorials opposing electoral-college reform; see pages 505-537.

A comprehensive summary of the case *against* the abolition of the electoral college will be found in the December 1977 Minority Report of the

Senate Judiciary Committee, pp. 24-32. These "Minority Views of Messrs. Eastland, Allen, Thurmond, Scott, Laxalt, Hatch, and Wallop on S.J. Res. 1" conclude:

In summary, we believe that the proposal should be rejected for the following reasons:

It would cripple the party system and encourage splinter parties;

It would undermine the federal system;

It would alter the delicate balance underlying separation of powers;

It would encourage electoral fraud;

It could lead to interminable recounts and challenges;

It would necessitate national control of every aspect of the electoral process;

It would give undue weight to numbers, thereby reducing the influence of small states;

It would encourage candidates for President to represent narrow geographical, ideological, and ethnic bases of support;

It would encourage simplistic media-oriented campaigns and bring about drastic changes in the strategy and tactics used in campaigns for the Presidency; and,

It would increase the power of the big city political bosses [p. 32].

Part II
Institutional Perspectives: Political Parties, Campaign Finance, and the Congress

5 Party Nationalization in America

Charles Longley

Many of the recent works on American political parties repeat a familiar litany with respect to party organization. In the context of federalism and separation of powers,

> . . . the national parties have little power vested in them and possess no real authority over state and local party organizations or elected officials . . . [they are] little more than paper organizations during the years between presidential campaigns.[1]

Or,

> The national party organization can best be described as a loose coalition of local and state parties which agree to work together when it is in the mutual interest of state and local parties to do so.[2]

And when speaking of national party committees, Cotter and Hennessy suggest they are

> large groups of people variously selected who come together now and then to vote on matters of undifferentiated triviality or importance, about which they are largely uninformed and in which they are often uninterested.[3]

Two terms in particular are employed to characterize American party organization: decentralization and local autonomy.[4] The national party organization is at best regarded as an ephemeral and episodic adjunct. That parties are currently buffeted by decreased party identification among voters, increased ticket splitting, competing sources of political information and campaign organizations, and an overall decline in electoral participation only further the parties' plight.

And yet reports of the demise of parties may be premature. Indeed, some commentators have expressed the opinion that the national party

This is a revision of a paper originally titled, "Party Reform and Party Nationalization: The Case of the Democrats," delivered at the Annual Meeting of the Midwest Political Science Association, April 29-May 1, 1976. Ellen Goldstein, Susan Smith, and Sheila Hixson of the Democratic National Committee and Donald Allen of the Republican National Committee provided helpful background information. Professor Patricia Longley provided thoughtful criticism and Alexa Longley assisted with numerical computations.

organization is alive and well, even prospering. For example, Austin Ranney speaks of the 1972 delegate selection reforms as constituting an "unprecedented national intrusion . . . [into the] historic rights of state parties to make their own rules."[5] William Keefe, while emphasizing the overall decentralization of American parties, sees "a growth in importance of national party organization: over state and local party organizations."[6] And Gerald Pomper also writes that the Democratic party is evolving into a "truly national association."[7]

This inquiry will assess the extent to which the traditional autonomy of state parties has been circumscribed by more recent events. Of particular concern is the degree to which the Democratic and Republican national party organizations have assumed more prominent and varied roles with respect to state party organizations. Four general dimensions will be examined here: (1) party rules and, for the Democrats, the party charter; (2) party "law"; (3) party finance; and (4) party elites. In this fashion it will be possible to comment on the emergence of party nationalization in America. And while it may not be time to declare the arrival of responsible party government, it is surely time to assay the conventional wisdom and probe the contemporary boundaries of state-national party relationships.

Party Rules

The Democrats

An extensive body of literature chronicles the history of party politics in America and affords specific attention to party reform.[8] Increasingly, the focal point for recent inquiry is the national convention and the delegate-selection process. Indeed, some authors would suggest that the selection and seating of convention delegates is the most significant springboard for Democratic party nationalization.[9]

In 1964 the Democratic National Convention passed a resolution which barred discrimination in any state party affairs on the basis of race, color, creed, or national origin, and established a Special Equal Rights Committee. In 1966 this committee adopted six antidiscrimination criteria, and in January 1968 these "six basic elements" became party policy through action of the Democratic National Committee (DNC).[10] It is at this juncture that national standards were meaningfully imposed on state and local parties. Failure to comply adequately resulted in Mississippi's entire delegation to the 1968 convention being unseated. More importantly, recognition as the official agent of the national Democratic party was withdrawn from the established "regular" party apparatus and extended to the so-called loyalist faction, whose actions were largely responsible for the introduction of the 1964 resolution.

While the 1964 convention initiated the practice of national non-discrimination standards, the 1968 convention mandated state parties to afford "all Democratic voters . . . a fully, meaningful and timely opportunity to participate" in the entire delegate selection process.[11] The Democratic National Committee subsequently established a Commission on Party Structure and Delegate Selection in February 1969, chaired first by Senator George McGovern and later by Representative Donald Fraser. Following nationwide hearings, the commission adopted a series of eighteen guidelines in November 1969.

In a "Summary of the Guidelines" the McGovern-Fraser commission noted:

> The guidelines are divided into two broad classifications, one in which the Commission *requires* certain action by state parties and one in which the Commission *urges* action by the parties.[12]

The wisdom or practicality of the guidelines notwithstanding, the importance of the commission's determinations for party nationalization is obvious. A national-convention-mandated party body laid claim to the legitimate authority to tell state and local party units what to do. Noncompliance could result in the unseating of state convention delegates or, ultimately, nonrecognition of the traditional state party organization by the national Democratic party.

Consider what was required of state parties:

1. adoption of "explicit" party rules for delegate selection;
2. adoption of "procedural rules and safeguards," such as no proxy voting, unit rule, mandatory party-imposed delegate assessments, adequate public notice, and uniform meeting times in public places;
3. reasonable representation of minority groups, women, and youth in delegations based on "presence in the population in the State";
4. procedural changes that included prohibitions on ex officio membership in a delegation and closed slatemaking or preferential treatment by party units, calendar year selection, comparable selection procedures for delegates and alternates, and intrastate allocation guidelines.[13]

In addition, the commission urged that state parties ease or remove financial burdens associated with becoming a delegate, work toward the elimination of procedural barriers to participation, terminate arbitrary delegate selection by party committees, and seek to insure "fair representation" of candidate preference. In the event state law controlled either the required or recommended reforms, state parties were to "make all feasible efforts to repeal, amend or otherwise modify such laws to achieve the state purpose."

The results of the McGovern-Fraser guidelines were substantial. It has been suggested that the new rules led to an unparalleled number of challenges before the 1972 Credentials Committee, spawned numerous lawsuits, contributed to a convention characterized as a "hodge-podge of representative inconsistencies," caused no little acrimony between party regulars and reformers, were essential for McGovern's nomination, and complemented his disaster in the general election.[14] The guidelines also focused considerable attention on the once obscure delegate-selection process. The present concern is neither to praise nor condemn the rules.[15] It is more important here to note that

> . . . forty-five of the fifty-five state and territorial parties were in full compliance with the guidelines by convention time and the other ten were in substantial compliance.[16]

In other words, the McGovern-Fraser commission defined and implemented new party rules—many of which directly and substantially impinged on the traditional prerogatives of state and local parties. In contrast to the customary deference found in a decentralized and largely autonomous party structure, an unprecedented degree of procedural conformance ensued on the part of subnational party units. To say that the rules were misguided, costly, antidemocratic or the like—either in part or in whole—simply misses the point. Or, as Austin Ranney forcefully states concerning the guidelines:

> But the point to be emphasized here is what they have done to revive *national* party agencies' power over state affiliates. The commission was mandated by a *national* convention, appointed and encouraged by a *national* chairman and given real clout by a *national* committee. The guidelines required state parties to make radical changes in many of their accustomed ways of doing things, and the state parties all got into line.[17][Emphasis added.]

And, however unwittingly, it was the state and local representatives to the turbulent 1968 convention who originally provided the mandate for the 1972 reforms.

Reform of the delegate-selection process did not end with the McGovern-Fraser guidelines. The 1972 convention continued to make sweeping assertions of the superiority of national party rules over *state party rules and state laws*.[18] A second party commission was prescribed to formulate delegate-selection rules for 1976. Under the leadership of Baltimore city councilwoman Barbara Mikulski, the commission adopted a series of guidelines in October 1973, and these were subsequently approved by the Democratic National Committee in February 1974.[19] In many ways the Mikulski guidelines perpetuated the 1972 rules, but the 1976 criteria afford another basis for assessing the extent to which party rules can contribute to party nationalization. It is again important to bear in mind that regardless of the language employed the rules flow from a national party commission and bear directly on state and local party operations.

Noteworthy of the Mikulski commission's innovations are those concerning fair reflection of presidential preference, restriction of participation in the delegate-selection process to Democrats, and the establishment of a Compliance Review Commission to review and approve state-party affirmative-action and delegate-selection plans. In concert these revisions carry the nationalizing process beyond the frontiers charted in 1972.

The "fair-reflection" guideline meant that statewide winner-take-all primaries would not be allowed in 1976. In so doing, the guideline sought to insure that participants in the delegate-selection process would not confront a situation where a plurality vote for one candidate would result in a 100 percent delegate gain, as California had for McGovern in 1972. The "open primary" also ran afoul of the new rules. Particularly affected was Wisconsin, which in 1972 had seen extensive cross-over voting by Republicans in the Democratic primary.[20] Thus, in these two instances, the Mikulski commission directly assaulted existing state law controlling delegate selection and thereby asserted the primacy of national-party standards.

The Mikulski commission renovated the 1972 rules by allowing state and local parties to engage in slate-making activities (but not subsequent preferential treatment), thus removing one basis of the 1972 Chicago delegate challenge. State Democratic committees, where appropriate, were also empowered to name up to 25 percent of a state's delegates, rather than 10 percent as in 1972. In addition, the controversial "quota" guidelines were replaced by affirmative-action programs, but delegation composition alone was precluded as the basis for challenges before the 1976 Credentials Committee. Even so, the new guidelines reaffirmed the 1972 reform effort, and Senator McGovern himself voiced the opinion that the old rules should not be regarded as "engraved in stone."[21]

The Compliance Review Commission (CRC), appointed at the national level, had the authority to review and approve state proposals—intimately embroiling the CRC in state and local affairs. Where noncompliance was adjudged to exist, the CRC was mandated to work with state parties, retaining the authority to *require* corrective action where necessary. Should state parties ultimately fail to comply, the DNC Executive Committee could establish a delegate-selection procedure for a state. In effect, the national committee could determine the entire delegate-selection process within a state! Moreover, the CRC was empowered to monitor state-party progress and (as originally constituted) serve as a pre-Credentials Committee screening agency.[22]

The language and deliberations that led to the adoption of the 1976 reforms stressed the need for accommodation and cooperation between the national and state parties. These objectives were reflected in the proceedings of the CRC, although one CRC member (himself a state chairman) expressed the opinion that many state chairpersons believed that the primary purpose of the CRC was the "harrassment and disruption of state party processes."[23] More generally, however, the CRC voted to accord state parties a degree of flexibility in meeting the 1976 rules.[24]

Even so, the rules were drafted by a national-level panel and approved by the national committee, and state-party compliance was assessed by a national-level commission. For 1976, as for 1972, the simple lesson is that party change does not operate in a vacuum. But for both years it is beyond question that nationally adopted standards continued to define the rules of the game. And the same is true for the 1980 delegate-selection process, as the Democrats' third reform commission, chaired by Morley Winograd, has demonstrated its intent to assert further the role of the national party.[25]

The Party Charter

Meeting in 1974, Democrats adopted the party's first written charter, the culmination of more than two years of deliberations. The charter, in effect a party constitution, was the first such document ever adopted by a major American political party and represented the labors of a variety of party commissions and personalities. The early proponents of the charter—most notably Representative Donald Fraser—sought to draft a document that would strengthen the Democratic party by more clearly defining membership, creating a mechanism for regular policy conferences, and codifying traditional party practices. One critic observed that the charter as initially conceived would "Europeanize" the Democratic party to the detriment of state and local components.[26]

A draft charter was adopted by the 1972 Democratic Rules Committee, chaired by Representative James O'Hara, and thus became a part of the agenda for that year's national convention. The proposed charter contained stipulations unprecedented in American political parties. For example, to support his Europeanization charge, Ben Wattenberg suggested that the 1972 language would have:

1. restricted participation in party affairs to card carrying members;
2. required midterm national conventions to adopt uniform positions on policy issues;
3. introduced a degree of discipline over party candidates and elected officials not exercised previously;

4. reduced the power of local party bodies, transforming them into mere satellites of the Washington-based national party.[27]

One need not agree with all of Wattenberg's conclusions, but it is nonetheless evident that the original draft charter would move the Democratic party closer to what Duverger termed "mass parties." Austin Ranney also notes that the Fraser-O'Hara document would be a further step in the direction of the party model set forth by the American Political Science Association's 1950 Committee on Political Parties.[28] The 1972 convention, however, deferred action on the proposed charter. Instead, it adopted a compromise resolution to establish a new charter commission, and it authorized a 1974 midterm conference to review the work of the commission and to adopt a charter, as well as to discuss other policy issues.[29]

The Charter Commission, chaired by former North Carolina Governor Terry Sanford, met across the country in six public sessions prior to the December 1974 convention. En route to the Kansas City conference the charter was buffeted by contests between party regulars and reformers, women's and minority caucuses, labor unions, governors, and Democratic Members of Congress. Many of the preconference disputes centered on specific charter provisions, rather than on the significance of a charter per se.[30]

It is not the present concern to recount the controversies surrounding the adoption of the charter. It is, instead, the substance of the final language and its significance for party nationalization that will be appraised. Writing just prior to the conference, one long-time observer noted:

> The stilted phrases spelling out the trade-offs between centralized guarantees of free access to party decision-making and a reaffirmed commitment to a federalized party structure mark the terms of agreement which the diverse elements of the nation's oldest party will accept as the ground rules for their own cooperation and fraternal combat.[31]

The twelve-article charter finally adopted largely conformed to this observation.

Article 1 reaffirms the traditional role of the party in nominating and working toward the election of presidential candidates, but also provides for the standardization of rules for party members engaging in this process. Article 2 details the national committee's formulation and procedures, making explicit that contrary state laws and party rules are summarily preempted absent "provable position steps" to rectify the offending provisions. The national convention is reaffirmed as the "highest authority of the Democratic Party," and delegate-selection guidelines largely drawn from the McGovern-Fraser and Mikulski commissions are elaborated. Article 3 sets forth the responsibility of the DNC and denominates both membership and apportionment. Articles 4 and 5, respectively, provide for an executive committee and a full-time national chairperson to be elected after the national convention and again following the succeeding presidential election.

Article 6 makes optional a between-convention party policy conference. Article 7 establishes a national-committee-appointed Judicial Council, whose task is to review and approve state delegate-selection plans. The national convention and committee, however, retain the final say on credentials challenges to their respective members. In article 8, a National Finance Council is prescribed, and article 9 establishes a National Education and Training Council to further the objectives of the Democratic party.

Article 10 asserts that the party shall be "open to all," setting forth criteria to that end. Included within article 10 are antidiscrimination provisions on the basis of "sex, race, age (if of voting age), religion, economic status of ethnic origin . . . at all levels." Also required are affirmative-action programs at all levels of party organization absent the mandatory imposition of quota systems. Articles 11 and 12 address "general provisions" and "Amendments by-laws and rules." Article 2 and articles 4 through 7 became operational after the 1976 national convention; the others took effect on adoption in 1974.

The extent to which the party charter contributes to the further nationalization of the Democratic party can be assayed on two levels. It is evident that the charter affirmed the need for a uniform delegate-selection process and open access to party affairs on all levels. State and local party organizations are now under explicit national guidelines with respect to participation. Moreover, the charter codified the mechanisms for determining the party's presidential-level nominees. Newly established were additional national-level components such as the judicial, finance, and education and training councils.

At the same time, the charter did not require an interim policy conference and consequently maintained the relative issue autonomy of Democatic candidates for public office. Nor did reformers succeed in gaining approval for a fixed-term national chairperson, an objective intended to insulate further the DNC's head from the vagaries of presidential-election returns. Moreover, the initial goal of a "card carrying, dues paying" membership was in fact never brought to the convention floor for a vote. Strong party advocate Donald Fraser subsequently commented that almost nothing of his original conception was left in the Kansas City document, leading one observer to write that,

> The prevailing federalism of American politics persists in the new charter, leaving the Democrats . . . a confederation of state and local organizations, subject to common rules but playing politics and choosing candidates with great autonomy.[32]

Even so, the charter should be appraised in light of a second dimen-sion—its symbolic importance for Democratic party politics. A constitution was, after all, adopted. The relationships between national and state organizations were made formal, and in the context of American party history this is not an insignificant gain. As Austin Ranney, long concerned and involved with the party reform effort, suggests:

> there is little doubt that if the proposed charter or anything like it is adopted, it will no longer be accurate to describe the national party, as most scholars have in the past, in terms like "a ghost party" or "a loose alliance of [state and local parties] to win . . . the presidency."[33]

And while the tangible nationalization of the Democratic party may have fallen short of the proponents' original design, the charter might be re-garded for what it symbolizes and portends as well as for what it codifies.[34]

The Republicans

Concern for party reform has been evidenced also within the Republican party; both the 1968 and 1972 national conventions voted to establish reform panels. At the 1976 convention, the delegates mandated a perma-nent rules-review commission within the Republican National Committee (RNC). The GOP's efforts thus far contrast markedly with the Democratic experience, and the reasons for this reveal much about the prospects for na-tionalization within the Republican party. The evidence to date suggests that the GOP is firmly committed to the principle that the national organization not supplant the preeminent role of state-party rule or state statute in the conduct of delegate selection.

In early 1969 a sixteen-member Delegates and Organizations (DO) Committee, appointed by RNC Chairman Rogers C.B. Morton, began its labors. Chaired by Missouri National Committeewoman Rosemary Ginn, this panel presented a series of recommendations to the RNC in January and July of 1971. In some respects the DO Committee's suggestions paralleled the McGovern-Fraser guidelines. For example, convention alter-nates were to be elected in the same manner as delegates. Proxy voting was to be banned, and ex officio delegates were proscribed at all levels of the selection process. Conditional assessments imposed on delegates or alter-nates were also to be eliminated. Also, in addition to recommending a broad public-information program, the DO Committee urged that where delegates were selected through conventions, the meetings be open, and that district and state conventions not be held on the same date in the same place.[35]

Of particular concern to the DO Committee was the 1968 convention's mandate to study the implementation of party rule 32, which barred discrimination on the basis of race, religion, color, or national origin in the delegate-selection process. Of the ten recommendations offered by the DO Committee, three dealt specifically with rule 32; all three generated controversy. It was proposed that each state appoint one man, one woman, one young person, and one member of an ethnic minority to each of four national-convention standing committees. Each state was also to "endeavor" to have an equal number of men and women in their delegations, and it was further suggested that delegates under the age of twenty-five be represented in proportion to their voting strength within the state. In effect, then, the DO Committee had sought to impose a minimum level of demographic representation on state delegations. But the committee avoided establishing formal criteria whereby its recommendations were to be achieved. It was noted instead that:

> There are legitimate reasons for states to use the procedures they follow, so it is not that we praise or criticize one over the other but recognize that reasons of geography, population, economy and politics determine the methods used.[36]

As an adjunct of the national committee, the DO Committee's guidelines were subject to review by both the RNC's Rules Committee and then by the RNC itself. Following these steps, the reforms had also to be approved by the national convention's Rules Committee prior to a final vote by the convention delegates. In contrast to those of the McGovern-Fraser commission, the DO Committee's recommendations were, at best, tentative. Perhaps because of this, the 1972 convention voted approval of the less controversial guidelines.[37] Hence, the DO Committee could lay claim to having raised the visibility of the national party organization, although its assertion of authority did not directly impinge on the traditional operations of the state party organizations. The RNC largely remains partisan polyglot.

Those DO Committee recommendations dealing with broadening participation were either rejected outright or considerably watered down by the RNC. As finally adopted, convention rule 32 provided that the RNC and state parties would take "positive action" to maximize participation by women, young people, minority and heritage groups, and senior citizens. To pursue the matter, the 1972 convention mandated the establishment of a second reform group. As a result, GOP Chairman George Bush appointed a fifty-seven member Rule 29 Committee (that convention rule which authorized the committee) in April 1973. Named to chair the committee was Wisconsin Representative William Steiger.

The Rule 29 Committee, composed of party officials as well as RNC members, began meeting in September 1973. At its first session five subcommittees were set up, although Subcommittee Four (headed by former RNC and Ohio State Party Chairman Ray Bliss) was charged to deal with delegate selection and quickly became the most visible. There was, as might have been expected, no little dispute over the meaning of "positive action" and "endeavor" as well as the role of the national party in this context.

At the subcommittee stage, those favoring a more stringent set of guidelines concerning party responsibility to "open the door" were successful. Evidence for this is seen in the language that set forth a series of steps to be taken by state parties in meeting positive-action requirements. There was, however, no final agreement in light of the expressed concern that failure to comply with the proposed action lists might subject state delegations to credentials challenges.[38] Subcommittee Four, in its last session, was able to agree on compromise language whereby state parties were to engage in a variety of informational and promotional efforts. Quotas of any form were explicitly prohibited. The full Rule 29 Committee, however, eliminated all language which could be interpreted as mandating specific state action; "'shalls' turned to 'shoulds'."[39] Thus, state parties were to submit positive action plans to the RNC for "review and comment," but submission was voluntary.

The Rule 29 Committee also proposed a series of reforms dealing with other facets of party operations; taken together, they constitute a move toward strengthening the national party organization—not, however, at the expense of the party's subnational units. For example, the RNC would be expanded by affording committee membership to the heads of six party auxiliary organizations as well as providing seats for six elected party officials. Eight vice-chairs of the RNC would be elected by regional caucuses. The RNC chairman would be elected to a two-year term (subject to removal only by a two-thirds RNC vote) to provide greater continuity in operations as well as a degree of security. RNC members would be directly elected by the states, in contrast to the prevailing practice of state nomination and national convention election. All RNC meetings would be open to the public unless a majority of the members objected. Also recommended by the Rule 29 Committee was the establishment of a Select Committee on Presidential Affairs, to be chaired by the head of the RNC. This seven-person body would review the campaign expenditures of the party's presidential candidate, and one member would periodically also serve as one of the three "designated agents" required by law to review and approve campaign expenditures. In addition, the RNC chairman would have to approve all campaign expenditures in excess of $1,000, although this provision was subsequently deleted. The proposal, although coming in the wake of the 1972 financial scandals, would nonetheless provide for an unparalleled role for the RNC but, again, not at the expense of state party organizations.

The RNC reviewed the reform committee's recommendations in early 1975, and the results—as in 1972—are indicative of the GOP's disposition with respect to party reform as it affects a redefinition of national-state authority relationships. Consider, for example, the debate surrounding the positive-action requirements of rule 32. The proposed submission of state plans was characterized as an infringement on the right of state parties to conduct their internal affairs. Review and comment by the RNC, it was argued, could become acceptance or rejection; positive action smacked of quotas.[40] The RNC thus adopted language that provided that states should submit examples of the plans (not the plans themselves), after which the RNC could review and comment in an effort to assist state parties. The accompanying interpretation of rule 32 noted that "reasonable implementation of a state effort substantially in compliance" with the requirements and recommendations of rule 32 would constitute *prima facie* evidence of a "good faith effort by the state organization."[41] At the same time, however, the failure of a state party to conform to any of the rule 32 language was not to be deemed evidence of a failure to comply, or to make a good faith effort to comply, with the positive-action provisions. The requirements of rule 32, themselves couched in terms of recommendations, obviously posed little immediate threat to state parties as the national party organization refused to impose uniform standards or dictate implementation criteria.

Final action on the Rule 29 Committee's proposals came at the 1976 national convention. But as in 1972, when the DO Committee's effort was overshadowed by debate on a delegate allocation formula for 1976, this second attempt at party reform was largely lost in the tight Ford-Reagan nomination contest. The convention's Rules Committee was the scene of heated debate, but the controversy dealt with last-minute attempts by the respective candidates' organizations to win the nomination. The questions of "When should vice-presidential nominations be announced?" and "How binding are primary results?" not only bore little relation to the work of the Rule 29 Committee, but also indicated how little weight the party-reform effort carried. With minimal debate, the convention adopted the Rule 29 Committee's report as amended by the RNC. The delegates chose, however, to reject national committee membership for party auxiliaries and also voted to establish a permanent standing RNC Rules Review Committee restricted to members of the RNC, rather than a "broadly representative" one proposed by the RNC. This latter move, commented one Republican reformer, represented a clear victory for party conservatives.[42]

What, then, of future reform efforts within the Republican Party? As seen in the work of the DO and Rule 29 Committees, the party has in fact altered its rules, but these changes are largely cosmetic. Moreover, attempts to redefine the traditional authority relationships between the national and state parties have been unsuccessful. In no small way, this outcome is understandable given the sentiment expressed by one conservative member of the Rule 29 Committee during debate on RNC membership for party auxiliaries. "There simply is no such thing as a national Republican Party. It is simply a federation of states."[43] With membership predicated on places rather than population (complemented by a four-tier reform-review process) there is little reason to suspect that the GOP will in the near future witness a nationalization of party rules comparable to that of their Democratic counterparts.

Party Nationalization and "Party Law"

Writing in the *Georgetown Law Journal* (1974), John Quinn suggests that the national-political-party convention system has engendered:

> two interrelated sets of constitutional conflicts. . . . The first set of conflicts involve the relationship of *state* election laws governing delegate selection to national political party delegate selection rules such as those promulgated by the Democratic Party under mandate of the 1968 and 1972 presidential nominating conventions . . . [The second set of conflicts] arise between the parties' interests in delegate selection and the individual voter's interests in representation protected by the due process and equal protection clauses of the Constitution.[44]

Stated more poignantly, Donald Fowler—chairman of the South Carolina Democratic party, member of the Compliance Review Commission, and then chairman of the Association of Democratic State Chairmen—observed:

> Now a state party puts itself in one hell of a difficult political situation when it pays attention to party rules and not the state law. Now if you want to run in a bad atmosphere, you run where your party has apparently with deliberate intent ignored or violated a state law in order to adhere to a party rule. You will find in most of the states in this country you are going to just catch hell.[45]

It is, as some politicians might say, like being caught between a rock and a hard place.

That the judiciary has been involved in attempting to resolve electoral disputes in general and partisan conflicts in particular need not be recounted here. What does merit initial comment, however, is more recent court consideration that has been specifically directed toward the question of who wins when national party rules are alleged to contravene state electoral law. The answer to this question obviously carries substantial importance for the relationship between state and national party organizations. Should the courts repeatedly and consistently give cognizance to national-party-rule supremacy, state parties may be dissuaded from lingering non-compliance through prolonged litigation. Moreover, an atmosphere will be engendered which further affirms a pronounced and judicially confirmed national-party supremacy.

Political parties seek refuge under the First Amendment right of association accorded their members. States, on the other hand, take solace in article 2, section 1 of the Constitution, which provides for state control over the selection of presidential electors. As Bain and Parris have noted, however, the last decade in particular bears witness to increasing party-rule primacy over state delegate-selection laws.[46] Of more importance is the fact that since 1972 the federal judiciary has acted to legitimize the national party's de facto determinations. Notable of these rulings directly concern the conflict between state law and party rule governing the national convention's delegate-selection and allocation processes.

The Democrats

The action of the 1972 Democratic Credentials Committee was responsible for the filing of two lawsuits contesting the unseating of delegates from Chicago and California (*Keene et al.* v. *National Democratic Party* and *O'Brien et al.* v. *Brown et al.*, respectively). In both instances, delegates selected in accord with state law were unseated. The Federal District Court in Washington initially dismissed both actions, stating that the cases presented nonjustifiable questions. The Court of Appeals denied relief to the Chicago delegates, upholding the action of the Credentials Committee. At the same time that court found in favor of the unseated California delegates and thereby reversed the party committee. The Supreme Court, through a *per curiam* opinion issued less than seventy-two hours before the 1972 convention was to convene, stayed both actions of the Court of Appeals. The end result of this judicial imbroglio was to leave the ultimate seating decision for both the Chicago and California contest with the national convention delegates. Why did the Supreme Court so act, and what are the ramifications for party nationalization?

Two factors appear of primary importance in the court's decision: the novelty of the controversy and the proximity of the convention. The Court noted the lack of precedent for judicial intervention and the traditional prerogative of a party to resolve its own disputes, saying:

> No case is cited to us in which any federal court has undertaken to interject itself into the deliberative processes of a national political convention; no holding of this Court up to now gives support for judicial intervention in the circumstances presented here, involving as they do relationships of great delicacy that are essentially political in nature.[47]

Furthermore,

> It has been understood since our national parties came into being as volun-
> tary associations of individuals that the convention itself is the proper
> forum for determining intraparty disputes as to which delegates shall be
> seated.[48]

And, after reiterating the party's historic role in resolving credentials
challenges, the Court concluded:

> If this system is to be altered by the federal courts in the exercise of their ex-
> traordinary equity powers, it should not be done under the circumstances
> and time pressures surrounding the actions brought in the District Court
> and the expedited review in the Court of Appeals and in this Court.[49]

Hence, even though recognizing that serious constitutional electoral
questions were posed by the action of the Credentials Committee, the
Supreme Court choose not to interfere in the party's deliberative processes.
In so ruling, the Court gave the national convention authority to uphold
party rule over state law. To observe that the convention might have opted
to reseat the Chicago delegates and thereby "affirm" state law misses the
point. It is the *party's* tribunal that makes the ultimate determination.

The Chicago primary contest also spawned a concurrent case, *Cousins*
v. *Wigoda*.[50] This litigation raised anew the question of resolving a conflict
between state law and party rule pertaining to delegate selection. The
unseated Chicago delegates sought and obtained an injunction barring the
successful challengers from taking their seats in Miami Beach. Nonetheless,
the challengers were recognized and participated as delegates at the convention. The challengers then sought relief from their eventual state-court contempt conviction, but the Illinois Court of Appeals unanimously upheld the
lower court's injunction, ruling in part:

> Initially it is necessary for this court to state that although the purposes and
> guidelines for reform adopted by the Democratic National Party in its call
> for the 1972 Democratic National Convention were issued, they in no way
> take precedence in the State of Illinois over the Illinois Election Code.[51]

And,

> Because election to the office of convention delegate in Illinois is governed
> by nondiscriminatory state legislation, the instant case is not merely an in-
> traparty factional dispute to be settled by party discipline. In this case the
> law of the State is supreme and party rules to the contrary are of no
> effect.[52]

And,

> The interest of the State in protecting the effective right to participate in primaries is superior to whatever other interests the party might wish to protect.[53]

And, finally,

> We think the convention, a voluntary association, was without power or authority to deny the elected delegates their seats in the Convention and most certainly could not force them upon the people of Illinois as their representatives contrary to their elective mandate. Such action is an absolute destruction of the democratic process of this nation and cannot be tolerated.[54]

For the Illinois appellate court, at least, the right to participate under non-discriminatory state law cannot be usurped by national party rules, lest there be a calamitous violation of the state electoral process.

The U.S. Supreme Court, however, reached a different conclusion in its January 1975 ruling on *Cousins* v. *Wigoda*. Mr. Justice Brennan stated for the majority:

> We granted certiorari to decide the important question presented whether the Appellate Court was correct in according primacy to state law over the National Political Party's rules in the determination of the qualifications and eligibility of delegates to the party's national convention. We reverse.[55]

The Court's rationale can be seen through its contrasting the right of free political association for the petitioners with the appellate court's holding that the "interest of the state in protecting the effective right to participate in primaries is superior to other interests the party itself might work to protect."[56] But, notes the Court, attention must be given to the fact that involved here is the election of delegates to a national party convention.

> Consideration of the special function of delegates to such a Convention militates persuasively against the conclusion that the asserted state interest constitutes a compelling state interest.[57]

Because state parties are affiliated with a national party to determine presidential and vice-presidential nominees (that is, the state party *accepts* a nationally issued call),

> The states themselves have no constitutionally mandated role in the great task of selection of Presidential and Vice-Presidential candidates.[58]

In point of fact,

> If the qualifications and eligibility of delegates to the National Political
> Party Conventions were left to state law . . . each of the 50 states could
> establish the qualifications of its delegates to the various party conventions
> without regard to party policy, an obviously intolerable result.[59]

Furthermore, the Court argues that because a nominating convention serves
the "persuasive national interest . . . this national interest is greater than
any interest of an individual state."[60] As a result, the interest Illinois has in
protecting its state electoral process must yield to the determination of the
national convention.

Some caution should perhaps be exercised in reading too much into the
Cousins decision. It is not altogether clear, for example, that the clarity with
which the Illinois appellate court posed the issues—state law versus party
rule—is wholly resolved by the Supreme Court. It would appear here that
the Court has decided only that the injunction against seating the
challengers was inappropriate; other possible constitutional issues (or, at
least for Mr. Justice Powell, other efforts to regulate conventions) being
neither intimated nor decided. Nevertheless it is clear that this assault on the
primacy of party rule and ultimate party determination was unsuccessful.

In adopting its 1976 delegate-selection rules, the Democratic party
sought to forestall cross-over voting such as had occurred in Wisconsin's
open primary. In response to the mandate of the 1972 convention, delegate-
selection rule 2(a) required that

> state parties must take all feasible efforts to restrict participation in the
> delegate selection process to Democratic voters only.[61]

Rather than comply with rule 2(a), the Wisconsin Democratic party sought
partial relief, arguing that controlling state laws "do not require that such
voters in the primary elections publicly declare their membership or affiliation with the political party in whose primary they vote."[62] Further alleging
violations of states' rights (article 2, section 1; the Tenth and Twelfth
Amendments) and individual rights (vote, association, and privacy),
Wisconsin asked that the offending rule be voided on its face. In an extensive reply, the defendants maintained that the court lacked jurisdiction,
Wisconsin lacked standing, and that

> Plaintiffs have attempted to avoid the unambiguous holding of the
> Supreme Court in *Cousins* by arriving in court early, with a different set of
> alleged constitutional rights and alleged infringements, but with the same
> claim to the same relief.[63]

The District Court dismissed the Wisconsin case, holding that judicial intervention would be premature.

The Republicans

Litigation has also embroiled the Republican party. In November 1971 the Ripon Society initiated a suit against the RNC challenging the constitutionality of the allocation formula for 1972 national convention delegates. At issue specifically was the Republican party's practice of awarding additional delegates to states after Republican electoral success.[64] The Ripon suit maintained that a uniform bonus system ran afoul of the Fourteenth Amendment and was, in effect, "territorial discrimination," violative of the one-person, one-vote standard set forth in the reapportionment cases. Although the U.S. District Court for the District of Columbia upheld the Ripon contention, Associate Supreme Court Justice William Rehnquist issued a stay prior to the 1972 convention and thereby negated the lower court's ruling. Following the convention, a U.S. Court of Appeals dismissed the suit as moot.

In December of 1972 the Ripon Society returned to court, challenging the delegate-allocation formula adopted for 1976. An initial court ruling satisfied neither party. The uniform bonus system was held unconstitutional, but the court deemed legitimate the proportional-bonus aspect of the formula.[65] Both the RNC and the Ripon Society appealed this determination, and in March 1975 a three-judge appeals-court panel sustained the Ripon position on both counts. The decision, however, was vacated until the entire Court of Appeals for the District of Columbia could review the issues involved. On reargument, the appeals court reversed the lower court's holdings and in so doing upheld the suzerainty of the national party organization, as it had in the *Cousins* decision.

Ripon had argued that national-convention representation should be based on the general rules that govern legislative apportionment, specifically the equal protection clause of the Fourteenth Amendment. While recognizing that conventions may be subject to the equal-protection clause, the court ruled that this does not *ipso facto* mandate application of one person, one vote. Consequently,

> . . . the public and private interests in making decisions through some other scheme of representation outweigh the interests served by numerically equal apportionment.[66]

While not denying that the right to vote is entwined in the nomination process, the court maintained

. . . that between that right and the right of free political association, the latter is more in need of protection in this case.[67]

According to the court, the First Amendment protects a political party in establishing an allocation formula. The extent to which such a formula either constricts or broadens the party's prospects for electoral success is not a matter for judicial consideration. Should a party choose to consolidate its strength, the court was not about to adjudge such an "irrational way to seek political success." A subsequent writ of certiorari filed by the Ripon Society was eventually denied by the Supreme Court.

The evolution of party law, arising from litigation involving both major parties, points to but one conclusion. While not totally foreclosing party operations to judicial intervention (for example, upon demonstration of racial discrimination), the judiciary appears unwilling to validate state law over national-party rules. Nor has the court been willing to interfere with the national parties' rights under the First Amendment to conduct internal affairs as they best see fit. Together, these holdings clearly establish a body of precedent and provide a constitutional framework for the supremacy of national-party authority.

Moreover, the courts' rulings give rise to an apparent partisan "catch-22." States (or individuals) seeking judicial relief can go to court, but not too early because to do so would be premature. At the same time, to wait until the convention takes formal action may be too late. Besides, the Supreme Court has found that the appropriate forum for resolution will probably be the national convention itself. In the face of judicial reluctance to deny national-party primacy, it is more than likely that state parties in particular will continue—in Chairman Fowler's words—to "just catch hell."

Party Nationalization and Party Finance

The general concern of literature discussing "money and politics" focuses largely on electoral matters. It is relatively easy, for example, to ascertain the amount of money spent on securing nominations and conducting general election campaigns.[68] The recent federal legislation on reporting and identifying sources of campaign contributors has also broadened substantially our knowledge of who gives financial support and of the overall costs of elections. On the other hand, considerably less attention is afforded the general subject of organizational revenues and expenditures.[69] And with particular reference to national activities, observers have reported on the activities of congressional and senatorial campaign committees more thoroughly than on the financial dealings of the national party organization itself.

That party financing constitutes an important dimension has not passed unnoticed. In discussing the application of public funding, Herbert Alexander observed:

> If the money is given to the national committee this could significantly change power balances within the parties. I do not say it is necessarily wrong to give it to the national committee if you recognize that you are thereby strengthening the national committee vis-à-vis state and local committees or even vis-à-vis senatorial and congressional committees. . . .[70]

And, in another context, Alexander suggests,

> Direct national fundraising weakens the power of state and local organizations to the degree that they cannot claim credit as the chief source of the party's wealth, or the federal candidates resources. . . . When national funds are ample, only the power of the ballot remains as the bastion of local power.[71]

The current concern is not to assess public funding or party organizations generally, nor to suggest that national funds are ample. Nonetheless, it will be suggested first that the national party organizations have become more financially secure, and second that the national party has become an increasingly important revenue source for state party organizations and individual candidates. These two developments further argue for a change in the traditional understanding of national-state party relations.

The Democrats

Consider, for example, the information in table 5-1 concerning the recent status of DNC finances. It is obvious that the size of the Democratic debt

Table 5-1
National Democratic Party Finances

1968 Presidential campaign deficit	$6,000,000
1968 Humphrey primary debt assumed	1,500,000
1968 Kennedy primary debt assumed	1,000,000
Operating losses, 1968-1971	800,000
Total deficit, 1968-1971	9,300,000
Deficit, 1972	5,000,000
Deficit, 1973	3,000,000
Deficit, 1974	2,600,000
Deficit, 1975	2,800,000
Deficit, 1976 (Carter campaign debt included)	3,600,000
Deficit, 1977	1,800,000

Source: Data obtained from Democratic National Committee.

has been substantially reduced. And while such data must be treated warily (debt reduction, for example, was in part accomplished by negotiating "so-many-cents-on-the-dollar" settlements with creditors), it is clear that the DNC is on a firmer—although by no means solid—financial footing.[72] The financial status of the DNC can also be examined in terms of its annual budget. In 1970 the estimated monthly expenditure was $150,000. Following a 1972 decline, monthly expenditures increased to $200,000 in 1975; by that year, the DNC reported a $4.1 million budget with average monthly expenditures of $340,000.[73] Even so, the party is encumbered with debts dating back as far as 1968. Payments to AT&T and American Airlines currently total nearly $50,000 a month, contributing substantially to the operating deficit.[74]

Revenues are generated from two primary sources. Direct mail and sustaining memberships constitute one financial leg, and major contributors represent the second. Prior to 1977, the DNC received nearly 80 percent of its revenues from smaller contributors. Following Carter's election, major donors accounted for a larger share, totaling approximately 60 percent of the DNC's funds. White House incumbency has obviously resulted in a revised funding pattern, albeit one that has not yet balanced the party's books. Additionally, the DNC will benefit from a series of 1978 fund raisers featuring the president; revenues from these should enable the party to rid itself of its deficit. Although there may be little reason to conclude that the DNC is now bullish on America, clearly the financial prospects are more promising than at any other time in the last decade.

The Democratic national party organization has also been innovative with respect to fund raising and has moved to enrich the coffers of state parties. To date, there have been three Democratic telethons in which state parties have shared monetarily. The total dollar amounts involved are presented in table 5-2, and need little general comment.

A detailed investigation of the telethon earnings, however, reveals that

Table 5-2
Telethon Financial Recap

	1973	1974	1975	Total
Income	$4,215,215	$5,403,672	$3,700,000[a]	$13,318,887
Expenses	2,273,237	2,555,839	2,751,336	7,580,412
Net	1,941,978	2,847,833	1,009,272	5,798,903
State share	1,100,000	1,815,086	504,636	3,419,722
Democratic National Committee share	841,987	1,032,747	504,636	2,379,370

Source: Data provided by Ms. Kitty Halpin, Democratic National Committee telethon coordinator.
[a]Estimated.

for the three-year period the California state party led the states with a net
of nearly $500,000 ($484,151), while the lowest net, $5,649, occurred in
Wyoming. The state-party median was almost $52,000, and the mean was
slightly more than $73,000. Taken alone these figures may not appear
awesome, but they represent *new* revenues. Additionally, one source of
state-party budgets indicates the telethon was specifically identified as a
revenue source in thirty-four states, with an ascribed percentage available
for twenty-seven states and the District of Columbia.[75] The state data further indicate that the telethon's dollar input ranged from a low of 2 percent
(New Jersey and Rhode Island) to a high of 75 percent (Oregon; the figure
for the District of Columbia was 80 percent) of the annual state-party
budget. The median percentage reported was 15 percent, and the mean was
22 percent. What stands out from these data is simply that the DNC's initia-
tion of the telethon resulted in a flow of hard dollars to state party
treasuries with no strings attached, the DNC thereby becoming an ally
rather than an antagonist.

Critics might contend, however, that the telethon was merely tapping
donors who would ordinarily support the state party directly and that the
DNC's intrusion actually cost the local organization money because of the
fee-splitting arrangement and the high costs associated with production. A
similar concern is voiced by Alexander in commenting on one of the
Democrats' chief fund raising devices of the early 1960s—the President's
Club.

> Some local democratic managers complained that the club drained off local
> funds to Washington, adding problems in soliciting money for state and
> local candidates.[76]

In point of fact, the telethon became a potential source of additional new
revenue for state parties in that an estimated two-thirds of the telethon contributors were first-time donors.[77] Thus, state parties were afforded a list of
contributors who could later be solicited for subsequent donations. Equally
important, state organizations were provided with a list of persons to be approached for other types of party service.

The Republicans

RNC finances offer a startling contrast to the Democratic picture. Consider, for example, the party's situation in 1977. For the first three-quarters
of the year, approximately $10 million had been received against anticipated
revenues of $17 million.[78] From this effort, the RNC projected a $10.5
million net, more than four times the comparable budget of the DNC. Of

the gross, 80 percent was expected from direct mail programs (including $15 annual sustaining memberships) aimed at a 2.6-million-name mailing list. For 1977, the average contribution was $23, which—at least on the surface—would suggest a financial core of over one-half million people. Also of significance is the RNC's Eagle Club which produces 20 percent of the gross in amounts of $10,000 or more.

The size of the RNC's budget is noteworthy for a variety of reasons. At the very least, the Republican national organization is capable of maintaining a 220-member staff, and also has contracted for the full-time service of a private polling firm with offices in the national headquarters. Of even greater importance, however, is the manner in which the RNC has become involved in areas with direct impact on state and local party operations. Two types of activities in particular illustrate the role of the national party.

First, on assuming the chairmanship of the RNC, former U.S. Senator William Brock created a new series of "field organizer" positions. Persons so employed would work full-time on the state level as adjuncts to the state party organization, with the bulk of their time to be spent on the road, linking more closely the local party units with the state offices and, indirectly, with the national level. As of early 1978, forty-seven field personnel had been hired. Particularly important, however, is that recruitment of the organizers was left to the state party, while funding was assumed by the national party. For most state parties this full-time position constitutes a bonus, and the position obviously provides for increased communication between the two levels of party organization. Additionally, the RNC established ten "field coordinator" positions whose focus is on nonfederal, nonstatewide electoral contests. These national staff members concentrate on providing campaign-related services, such as training seminars that detail direct-mail and media usage.

Second, the RNC has undertaken the direct financial support of state and local candidates in contests that are defined by the national party as "winnable." In 1977, the RNC distributed altogether more than $100,000 dollars to nonfederal candidates, including a $5,800 contribution to a county-level candidate in Kentucky.[79] For 1978, one estimate projects the expenditure of as much as 60 percent of the RNC's campaign funds on state and local elections, an unprecedented amount of national-committee support for such contests.[80] The RNC is thus working to establish as strong a base as possible in anticipation of the redistricting that will follow the 1980 census. In so doing, the national party is becoming more firmly enmeshed in the operations of the entire party organization.

The RNC is also involved in funding candidates for federal offices. In 1978, each of the Republican Senate incumbents will likely receive the maximum allowable national-committee contribution of $20,000, while House candidates are projected to share in an estimated $750,000. These figures are substantial in themselves, but they merely complement $3 million raised by the National Republican Congressional Committee by early 1978. According to one RNC staff member, campaign contributions for federal candidates will be "coordinated" between these two bodies; this too represents an opportunity for increased national-level organizational cooperation. The RNC has also made available to Republican incumbents its state mailing lists, compiled during the recent presidential election; this constitutes a previously untapped resource of the national organization, which can be brought into action by GOP members.[81]

Both national party organizations can play a further role under the reformed campaign-finance law. As Adamany and Agree noted when commenting on the 1974 Federal Elections Campaign Act, the state or national party committees were authorized

> to spend up to the greater of two cents times the voting age population of $20,000 to support senatorial candidates and their candidates for House in states with a single representative, and both national state and party committees to spend up to $10,000 to support each House candidate.[82]

Party committees can also undertake unlimited expenditures for such activities as voter education and registration. The importance of these programs may be less readily measured, but many of the usual campaign activities assumed by candidates may be curtailed as:

> the trend will be to shift these functions to party committees to allow the candidate to use his full quota for final appeals to the voter.[83]

This discussion of the extent to which party nationalization can be associated with party finances is admittedly speculative. It should be evident, however, that the DNC is better off financially, that the RNC appears financially viable, and that both national party organizations have undertaken the funding of state parties and candidates. Finally, the expanded range of activities initiated at the national level has enabled both parties to achieve an unparalleled degree of vertical organizational integration thereby contributing to the prospects for party nationalization.

Party Nationalization and Party Elites

An examination of national-committee membership affords a final basis on which to appraise party nationalization in America. Prior to 1972 each state (including the District of Columbia) held two seats on the DNC. At the 1972 convention, however, committee representation was pegged to a combination of population and Democratic presidential voting strength, raising the total membership to over three hundred.[84] At the same time, the reformed DNC was to be constituted under affirmative-action guidelines. The GOP, on the other hand, rejected even a minimal change in RNC membership proposed by the Rule 29 Committee and has continued its practice of seating one committeeman, one committeewoman and the state chairman from each of its subnational units.[85]

An analysis of national-committee membership provides two types of information. For the Democrats, we can assay the impact of party reform and for the Republicans we can note committee membership in the absence of any structural change. Second, the data also allow for interparty comparisons, shedding light on the makeup of contemporary party elites. The point is simply that the character of national-committee membership may well bear directly on the assertion of authority by the national party organization. Six descriptive indicators will be employed here: (1) age, (2) race-ethnicity, (3) education, (4) religion, (5) party background, and (6) public office holding.[86]

Age

The data in table 5-3 reflect the available age distribution. For Democrats, the postreform committee clearly comprises a younger clientel; nearly 20 percent being less than 40 years old compared with 12 percent of the prereform group. Proportionately, there are nearly twice as many committee members over age 60 in the earlier period, 25 percent versus 12 percent, but for both DNCs, the model category remains the 40-49 age group. The average age for the prereform DNC membership is 50 years compared with 48 years for the latter committee.

Table 5-3
National Committee Age Distribution

Age	Democrats[a]		Republicans[b]	
	Prereform	*Postreform*	*1968*	*1972*
29 or younger	0%	2%	0%	0%
30-39	12	18	7	9
40-49	37	37	44	39
50-59	26	31	30	32
60-69	17	10	16	16
70 or older	8	2	3	3
N	92	220	135	142

[a]Prereform—August 1970; postreform—November 1975.

[b]Republican National Committee members are elected to a four-year term at each national convention.

RNC membership evidences little change. The latter period reflects a slight increase in the 30-year-old category, but a comparable gain also for those in their 50s. In both instances, however, nearly three-quarters of the RNC members are between the ages of 40 and 60, and nearly 20 percent of the members are over 60. The average age of RNC members is 50 and 51 for the respective periods, inversely paralleling the Democratic averages. Thus, while some movement is seen in the Democratic ranks, age alone for both sets of the two committees does not reveal substantial variation. For both committees, a sizable majority of members is between 40 and 60 years old.

Race-Ethnicity

As already noted, the latter DNC was subject to affirmative-action guidelines. Consequently, we might expect to see a greater degree of racial diversity on the reformed DNC. The data in table 5-4 do in fact show that the latter DNC is marked with an increase in the presence of nonwhites. To be sure, both committees are predominantly white in makeup, but nonwhites constitute nearly 20 percent of the latter period's members. Black membership more than doubled over the two periods (from 6 percent to 13 percent) and even more substantial growth occurred for Hispanic delegates (from 1 percent to 5 percent). Along this dimension, then, the reconstituted DNC contrasts sharply with its predecessor. The same cannot be said for RNC membership. From the available data, there is no record of racial-minority membership for either committee under consideration.

Education

In *Politics Without Power*, Cotter and Hennessy (1964) compiled educational data for national-committee members for the period 1948-1963, and these are presented in table 5-5 along with the data for the more current

Table 5-4
Democratic National Committee Racial Diversity

Race-Ethnicity	Prereform	Postreform
White	92%	81%
Black	6	13
Hispanic	1	5
Other	1	1
N	102	323

Table 5-5
National Committee Education Levels

Education	Democrats			Republicans		
	1948-1963	*Prereform*	*Postreform*	*1948-1963*	*1968*	*1972*
High school or less	16%	10%	9%	9%	5%	5%
Some college	20	28	24	21	22	25
College	53	58	52	60	59	63
Unknown	11	4	15	10	14	6
N	306	102	323	376	152	153

members. It is readily evident that there is little significant difference between the two DNC committees. In contrast to the 1948-1963 data there is a comparable gain in the percentage of members with some college education. However, the pre- and postreform periods are in fact quite similar for those members whose levels of education had been determined. With the elimination of "unknowns" both groups fall at the 60 percent college-educated level.

RNC members for the two periods are also similar, with only a slight increase in the latter period of those with a college education. Of greater interest, however, is the comparability seen between the two party committees. Both are well educated, with RNC members slightly more likely to hold a college degree. But for both RNC and DNC members the overall level of education has remained generally static over the past twenty-five years, and both are considerably more highly educated than the general population.[87]

Religion

The known religious preference for national-committee members, presented in table 5-6, indicates some variation, but it is restricted to one party. Among DNC members, Protestant affiliation declines while the percentage of Jewish indentifiers increases slightly. In fact, the most noticeable point of comparison exists only when the data collected by Cotter and Hennessy are reintroduced. They reported only 2.3 percent Jewish identifiers in their earlier analysis of DNC members.[88] The restructured DNC would thus appear to be marginally more encompassing for only one religious preference, given available data, but for one that has traditionally been supportive of the party. The religious preference of RNC members is also generally consistent for both periods. Protestants account for nearly 80 percent of the total RNC, but this is down from the 86 percent reported by Cotter and

Table 5-6
National Committee Religious Preference

Religion	Democrats		Republicans	
	Prereform	Postreform	1968	1972
Protestant	54%	45%	73%	75%
Catholic	24	23	8	9
Jewish	8	10	2	2
Other	3	3	3	3
Unknown	12	19	14	10
N	102	323	152	153

Hennessy.[89] The percentage of Catholic and Jewish identifiers increases slightly on the latter RNC.[90] As was the case for the Democrats, however, the RNC data are generally comparable over time.

Party Background

Writing about national committees, Cotter and Hennessy noted that "many members are selected because they are already important in the state party."[91] Further,

> To them that have shall be given. The most common reason for selection as a national committee member is simply the fact that the individual is already a successful and visible party or governmental leader in the state. More than any other way, national committeemen and women get the job because they are governors or mayors or congressmen or state legislators or party committee chairmen (state or local) and vice-chairmen.[92]

To what extent (if any) do committee members differ in their party backgrounds? For example, we might expect that the reformed DNC would evidence a greater number of individuals who lack an extensive record of prior party service, given the reformers' allegation that the party's councils were largely the province of "regulars" committed to politics-as-usual. For the RNC, on the other hand, we might well anticipate that the party records of both sets of committee members would continue to be similar. The data in table 5-7 enable us to pursue this line of inquiry.

There is little difference between the entry-level patterns for pre- and postreform DNC members. The latter group is less likely to have entered on the local level, but this trait is offset by more extensive state-level entry. It appears, in fact that both groups of DNC members are party veterans, with nearly 75 percent of the committee previously having served at either the state or local level. "National" Democrats are less visible in each instance,

Table 5-7
National Committee Party Entry Level

Entry Level[a]	Democrats		Republicans	
	Prereform	*Postreform*	*1968*	*1972*
Local	57%	51%	50%	56%
State	17	20	25	23
National	19	20	13	17
None	0	2	0	0
Unknown	8	7	13	4
N	102	323	152	153

[a]First recorded party office held prior to national committee service.

but even so they surpass the percentage of DNC members in the latter period who held no previous party office. The data for the GOP reveal a gain among members elected in 1972 who initially entered the party at the local and national levels, although the overall figures for both committees are similar. And, as was true for DNC personnel, fully 75 percent of the RNC members began their service at the local and state levels. The point made by Cotter and Hennessy still appears valid: national committee members are well-practiced party politicians. Moreover, whatever increase among "amateur" Democrats may have occurred following the 1972 reforms was readily counterbalanced by increasing the total size of the DNC and affording ex officio membership to state party chairpersons.

Public Office Holding

One final descriptive indicator can be assessed in contrasting national-committee membership data. Cotter and Hennessy noted, for example, that national party service was occasionally enjoyed by virtue of holding public elective office.[93] In table 5-8 we can observe to what degree this continues to hold true for the time periods under current investigation. For the DNC, the reformed committee is characterized by somewhat less office holding. Whereas 30 percent of the earlier DNC members held office, only 23 percent so served after the committee was expanded. But local and state office is the more typical incubator for DNC service, and the relative percentages for these levels are similar for both committees. While the RNC had fewer local and state office holders in the latter period—a decrease of 7 percent—the GOP maintained a steady level of national office holders, all of whom were Members of the House. For both the DNC and RNC it appears that public office may complement party service but is by no means a prerequisite. In all instances, holding elective office is the exception rather than the rule.

Table 5-8
National Committee Office Holding

Public Office[a]	Democrats		Republicans	
	Prereform	Postreform	1968	1972
Local	7%	9%	11%	6%
State	18	15	15	13
National	6	2	3	3
None, Unknown	70	77	71	78
N	102	323	152	153

[a]Highest office held.

Party Elites

This examination of national-committee members' characteristics provides a collective portrait of contemporary party elites. The findings suggest that both Democratic and Republican National Committees, though different in some respects, share a number of common traits. The majority of members are white, likely to be between the ages of 40 and 60, and are more likely to be seasoned state and local organizational veterans than public office holders. While the DNC evidences more heterogeneity with respect to religious preferences and racial backgrounds, both committees reveal comparable degrees of educational background. To be sure, the postreform DNC is "most unlike" its counterparts, but the differences are of degree rather than kind.

The extent to which party-elite demographics can be—or even should be—associated with party nationalization remains, at best, problematic. Said one DNC reformer, "It used to be, with about 100 members, I felt I had some impact on what happened. But I don't now."[94] And for the RNC, the continuity in backgrounds offers little reason to expect any substantive role redefinition for the national party organization.

On Party Nationalization

This analysis of American parties has sought to probe the characterization of national parties as "politics without power." On the one hand, the Democratic party *has* undergone considerable change since 1968, with a resultant lessening of state-party autonomy. This is particularly true in the area of national-convention delegate selection. More generally, the Democrats have adopted a party charter and in so doing have codified a mélange of rule and ritual. The GOP, on the other hand, chose not to redefine its organizational balance. State party organizations retained considerable autonomy, a noteworthy example being the RNC's refusal to mandate uniform positive action programs. Both national parties, however, have successfully contested lawsuits challenging their authority to define the "rules of the game." The judiciary has by and large upheld national-party rule in the face of contrary state statute or rule.

At the same time, a more prominent role for national party organizations can be seen in the financial realm. The Democratic party has successfully reduced a sizable outstanding debt dating back to 1968. Moreover, the DNC has initiated novel fund-raising techniques designed to benefit state party treasuries as well as national coffers. The Republicans' considerably brighter financial picture has enabled their national organization to become deeply involved in supporting state and local candidates with services and contributions. Republican state parties have also been aided with additional staff funded by the national organization. Recent federal campaign-finance legislation has enhanced even further the prospects for an expanded role by the national parties.

Our study of party elites, however, suggests that national-committee membership has undergone less extensive change. Although the DNC was greatly expanded in 1972—more than trebling—the collective characteristics of its members were not substantially altered. Those changes that could be identified, such as notable increase in racial diversity, may well be of greater symbolic than tangible import in charting the DNC's future agenda. The RNC did not significantly change its representative structure, retaining a three-member-per-state formula, and the two committees examined here are markedly similar in demographic composition. Overall, members of both the DNC and RNC are predominantly white, Protestant, middle-aged, well-educated party veterans. These results may well have been expected, but the generally static portrait of party elites is another reminder of the persistence of recruitment patterns as well as the limitations of structural reform.

Party change, of course, does not operate in a vacuum and the extent to which national parties have in fact acquired a larger role should not lead us to confuse the trees with the forest. The development of strong national party organizations confronts a wide array of problems. Consider, for example, the traditional role of the president as "head of party." On assuming office, President Carter "took complete command of the national Democratic party machinery," noted one long-time observer, because Carter wanted "the party firmly in the hands of his supporters."[95] Less than a year later the DNC's head resigned, citing the burdens of office. Others, however, suggested that the chairperson was eased out at the instigation of the White House.[96] This leadership change clearly illustrates the problem of balancing an institutional role with the felt needs of a chief executive. Consider also the Democratic party's third encounter with party reform. Under mandate to review and revise delegate-selection procedures for 1980, the party's Commission on Presidential Nomination and Party Structure was thought by some to be more concerned with facilitating presidential renomination than with institutional reform.[97] In other words, short-term objectives represent substantial problems for longer-range organizational development.

The Republican national party must also contend with problems stemming from more immediate matters. Factional disputes arising over the RNC's role with respect to ratification of the Panama Canal treaty quickly isolated RNC Chairman William Brock from the party's more conservative members. Similar policy disagreements obviously carry implications for the eventual resolution of future questions dealing with the status of the national organization. The GOP is further confronted with competitive fund-raising campaigns by conservative elements within the party. While there may be little evidence that such monies would otherwise go to the RNC, these efforts hardly promote party unity and institutional coherence. Rather, they promise to perpetuate, if not further fracture, a national organization based on the premise of on party decentralization.

The conventional wisdom concerning national parties is no longer accurate—nor is it wholly inaccurate. Allied with the highly visible "practical" problems already noted, there remain the systemic constraints fostered by the separation of powers and federalism. In sum these considerations argue against a wholesale revision of our understanding of American party politics. Indeed, it may be more proper to suggest that there has been a "procedural nationalization" of the party system largely stemming from rules reform. So far, however, there simply is insufficient evidence to anticipate an American party system characterized by strict national-party control over membership, candidates, or policy determination. In so observing, we should not ignore those changes that have occurred. However tentative, they do in fact constitute a move toward the nationalization of American political parties.

Notes

1. Joyce Gelb and Marion Leif Palley, *Tradition and Change in American Party Politics* (New York: Thomas Y. Crowell, 1975), p. 211.

2. Frank. B. Feigert and M. Margaret Conway, *Parties and Politics in America* (Boston: Allyn and Bacon, 1976), p. 141.

3. Cotter and Hennessy (1964), p. 3.

4. See the extensive bibliography provided by Bernard Hennessy in "On the Study of Party Organization," in *Approaches to the Study of Party Organization* ed. William Crotty (Boston: Allyn and Bacon, 1968), pp. 34-44. For a succinct statement on the Democratic Party see Austin

Ranney, "The Evolution of the Democratic Party's National Organization: Characteristics, Causes, and Consequences" (Paper prepared for presentation at a joint meeting of the Commission on Party Structure and Delegate Selection and the Commission on Rules, Washington, D.C., November 19, 1971).

5. Ranney (1975), p. 2.

6. William J. Keefe, *Parties, Politics and Public Policy in America* (New York: Holt, Rinehart and Winston, 1976), p. 186.

7. Gerald Pomper et al., *The Election of 1976* (New York: David McKay, 1977), p. 7.

8. See, for example, Ranney (1975) and idem (1962); Stephan K. Bailey, *The Condition of Our National Parties* (New York: Fund for the Republic, 1959); David S. Broder, *The Party's Over: The Failure of Politics in America* (New York: Harper and Row, 1972); E.E. Schattschneider, *Party Government* (New York: Farrar & Rinehart, 1942); and American Political Science Association, "Toward a More Responsible Two-Party System, a Report of the Committee on Political Parties," *American Political Science Review* 44 (September 1950) supp.

9. Ranney (1975). See also Richard C. Bain and Judith H. Parris, *Convention Decisions and Voting Records* (Washington, D.C.: The Brookings Institution, 1973). Delegate selection is of course closely allied with candidate and policy preferences, both of which have contributed to the current debate. Although this chapter has concentrated on delegate-selection rules, the importance of candidates and of issues, both of which are of an increasingly national character, should in no way be denigrated.

10. The six criteria are reprinted in Commission on Party Structure and Delegate Selection, *Mandate for Reform* (Washington, D.C.: Democratic National Committee, 1970), p. 39. [Hereafter cited as *Mandate*.]

11. Ibid., p. 9. *Mandate* further contains an extensive listing of presumed shortcomings of the 1968 delegate-selection process.

12. Ibid., p. 34. The commission maintained that its authority came directly from the 1968 convention and hence was subject only to review by the 1972 convention—and not by the DNC or its executive committee. Successful assertion of this argument effectively insulated the guidelines from late-blooming attempts to curb its determinations and represents a little acknowledged coup. See *Mandate*, p. 36.

13. Ibid., p. 34.

14. The characterization is from Ranney (1975), p. 176.

15. See, for example, the exchange of views between Judith A. Center, "1972 Convention Reform and Party Democracy," *Political Science Quarterly* 89, no. 2 (June 1974):325-349, and Jeffrey L. Pressman and Denis G. Sullivan, "Convention Reform and Conventional Wisdom: An Empirical Assessment of Democratic Party Reform," *Political Science*

Quarterly 89, no. 3 (Fall 1974):539-562. Another perspective that takes issue with some of the reforms can be found in a report of the Task Force on Democratic Rules and Structure of the Coalition for a Democratic Majority, *Toward Fairness and Unity—for '76* (Washington, D.C.: Coalition for a Democratic Majority, 1974).

16. Ranney (1975), p. 184.

17. Ibid., p. 185.

18. Ibid.

19. Commission on Party Structure and Delegate Selection, *Democrats All* (Washington, D.C.: Democratic National Committee, 1973).

20. One estimate suggests that 20 percent of the total vote in the 1972 Wisconsin presidential primary was cast by cross-overs, accounting for about 300,000 voters. See "Outside Agitators in Democratic Primaries," *The Informed Delegate*, no. 4 (Washington, D.C.: Center for Political Reform, 1972), p. 2.

21. William Chapman, "McGovern Abandons 2 Reforms," *Washington Post*, 11 April 1973.

22. By action of the DNC on October 15, 1975, the Compliance Review Commission's jurisdiction was restricted to affirmative-action complaints.

23. Compliance Review Commission of the Democratic Party, Transcripts, June 20, 1975, p. 52.

24. See Charles Longley, "Party Reform and Party Organization: The Compliance Review Commission of the Democratic Party" (Paper delivered at the Annual Meeting of the Northeastern Political Science Association, November 10-12, 1977).

25. The Winograd commission, for example, has recommended that all 1980 Democratic presidential primaries be held within a three-month span.

26. Ben J. Wattenberg, "When you 'Quota' Somebody In, Somebody is Booted Out," *Los Angeles Times*, 1 December 1974.

27. Ibid.

28. Ranney (1975), p. 44.

29. See R.M. Koster, "Surprise Party," *Harper's*, March 1975, p. 24.

30. Most hotly disputed were the sections dealing with affirmative action and participation in all party affairs. See, for example, "We the Democrats of the United States . . . 'In Mini-Convention Assembled,' A Report on the Kansas City Charter Conference," *Democratic Review*, February/March 1975, pp. 37-43. One dissenting assessment of the conference, for its failure to take issue positions, is offered by Ronnie Dugger, "Fast Shuffle at Kansas City," *The Progressive*, February 1975, pp. 22-25. See also, Dennis G. Sullivan, Jeffrey L. Pressman, F. Christopher Arterton, *Explorations in Convention Decision Making* (San Francisco: W.H. Freeman, 1976).

31. David S. Broder, "Democrats Ready to Adopt Charter," *Washington Post*, 1 December 1974, p. A1. Reprinted with permission.

32. Ibid., p. A16.

33. Ranney (1975), p. 187.

34. By action of the 1976 national convention, DNC membership was accorded the president of the National Federation of Democratic Women. The delegates rejected amendment of the Judicial Council's functions which would have curtailed its scope of activities but voted to strengthen article 10 by requiring state parties to establish affirmative-action targets. The delegates also voted to hold a midterm conference in 1978.

35. See DO Committee, *The Delegate Selection Procedures for the Republican Party, Part II*, (Washington, D.C.: Republican National Committee, 23 July 1971).

36. Ibid. See also "DO Committee: Reform Without Teeth," *Ripon Forum* 7, no. 11 (September 1971):7.

37. See Crotty (1977), pp. 255-260.

38. Dick Behn, "Trusting Souls," *Ripon Forum* 10, no. 19 (October 1974):7-8.

39. "Commentary: Reform," *Ripon Forum* 10, no. 24 (December 1974):2.

40. See "Commentary: Rule 29," *Ripon Forum* 11, no. 5 (March 1975):1-2.

41. *The Rule 29 Committee* (Washington, D.C.: Republican National Committee, 5-6 March 1975), p. 20.

42. "Commentary: Rule 29," pp. 1-2.

43. Ibid., p. 1.

44. John Quinn, "Presidential Nominating Conventions: Party Rules, State Law, and the Constitution," *The Georgetown Law Journal* 62, no. 6 (July 1974):1621-1622. Reprinted with permission.

45. Compliance Review Commission, Transcript, May 31, 1975, p. 205A.

46. Bain and Parris *Convention Decisions and Voting Records*, p. 6.

47. 409 U.S. 4, 1972.

48. Ibid.

49. 409 U.S. 5, 1972.

50. 95 S. Ct. 541, 1975.

51. 14 Ill. App., 3d 460, 302, N.E. 2d, 625.

52. Ibid., 627.

53. Ibid., 629.

54. Ibid., 631.

55. 95 S. Ct. 545, 1975.

56. 95 S. Ct. 548, 1975.

57. Ibid.

58. 95 S. Ct. 549, 1975. But note, too, that Justices Burger, Stewart and Rehnquist do not concur with this.

59. Ibid.

60. Ibid.

61. Commission on Party Structure, *Democrats All*, p. 15.

62. The quote is from the Wisconsin brief, p. 5, filed in conjunction with *State of Wisconsin et al.* v. *Democratic Party of the United States of America et al.*, Civil Action No. 75-1457 (1974), U.S. District Court of Washington, D.C.

63. This quote is from the Democratic party's brief filed in the Wisconsin suit, p. 20.

64. This suit, in one form or another, spanned a period of five years and forms the basis for our discussion. It might also be noted that in *Graham* v. *March Fong Eu et al.* the Supreme Court dealt with national-party authority. Upholding California's winner-take-all Republican primary, the Court wrote, "Whether the voters will participate in the delegate selection process, and if so, at what stage, and whether their participation will be translated directly into delegate representation at the national convention are matters for the political parties themselves to determine, and, if the parties permit it, for the states."

65. *Ripon Society, Inc.* v. *National Republican Party*, nos. 74-1337 and 74-1338, 1975.

66. Cited in "Politics: The GOP," *Ripon Forum* 11, no. 19 (October 1975):1.

67. Ibid., p. 2.

68. See, for example, Congressional Quarterly, *Dollar Politics*, vols. 1 and 2 (Washington, D.C.: Congressional Quarterly, 1971 and 1974).

69. See the David Adamany, *Financing Politics: Recent Wisconsin Elections* (Madison: University of Wisconsin Press, 1969), and idem, *Campaign Funds as an Intra-Party Political Resource: Connecticut 1966-68* (Princeton, N.J.: Citizen's Research Foundation, 1972).

70. Quoted in Delmar Dunn, *Financing Presidential Campaigns* (Washington, D.C.: The Brookings Institution, 1972), p. 77.

71. Herbert Alexander, *Money in Politics* (Washington, D.C.: Public Affairs Press, 1972), p. 95.

72. Financial concerns obviously persist. In early 1978, the professional staff of the DNC was reduced from ninety to sixty and then pared again to approximately forty full-time employees.

73. These figures were provided by the DNC.

74. The DNC has also successfully petitioned the Federal Elections Commission for a waiver from current contribution limits to reduce debts incurred prior to the enactment of such legislation. Thus, the 1968 primary debts can more easily be retired without impairing a donor's status under the current legislation.

75. *Association of State Democratic Chairmen, State Chairman's Handbook* (Washington, D.C.: Association of State Democratic Chairmen, 1975).

76. Alexander, *Money in Politics*, p. 98.

77. Art Kosatka, "Behind the Scenes at the Democratic Telethon," *Democratic Review*, June/July 1975, p. 41.

78. See Walter Pincus, "Democrats Fall Way Behind Money-Making GOP," *Washington Post*, 12 December 1977, p. A1.

79. Ibid., p. A6.

80. Ibid., p. A1.

81. Walter Pincus, "'Dear Constituent': Hill Plugs into Computer Age," *Washington Post*, 10 December 1977, p. A2.

82. David W. Adamany and George E. Agree, *Political Money* (Baltimore, Md.: Johns Hopkins University Press, 1975), p. 58.

83. Ibid., p. 59.

84. DNC representation was also accorded various party and elected officials. Up to twenty-five additional members could be added to "balance" representation of Democratic voters. State representation ranged from four to eighteen members.

85. In addition, there is a fifteen-member executive committee as well as ex officio membership for various party and elected officials.

86. Sources employed here include *Who's Who in American Politics* (New York: R.R. Bowker), bibliographic files of the DNC, and a variety of additional biographical and secondary sources. Excluded from the DNC are ex officio members, with the exception of state chairpersons. The RNC data encompass only the members from each state. For both the DNC and the RNC, territorial representatives have been excluded.

87. Comparble data for the general population are: high school or less—75 percent, some college—12 percent, and four years of college or more—13 percent. U.S. Bureau of the Census, *Statistical Abstract of the United States: 1975*, (Washington, D.C.: U.S. Government Printing Office, 1975).

88. Cotter and Hennessy (1964), p. 49.

89. Ibid.

90. Catholic and Jewish membership on the RNC is accounted for in large part by the state-party chairpersons. For the two committees examined here, half of the Catholic identifiers are state chairs; for Jewish identifiers the figure is two-thirds.

91. Cotter and Hennessy (1964), p. 53.

92. Ibid., pp. 53-54.

93. Cotter and Hennessy (1964), p. 54.

94. Charles Roos, "Two Dems Doubt Party's Reform Working," *Denver Rocky Mounty Post*, 18 October 1975, p. 8.

95. David S. Broder, "Carter Takes Complete Control of Democratic Party Machinery," *Washington Post*, 22 January 1977, p. A3.

96. See Edward Walsh, "Curtis to Leave Chairmanship of Democratic Party," *Washington Post*, 8 December 1977, pp. A1, A2. We have not ex-

amined the role of the party chairperson. It might be noted, however, that the manner in which the party's national head defines his or her role may carry importance for the way in which the national committee operates. Even so, the events which have contributed to the growth of national-party authority are obviously not wholly dependent on a temporal role occupant.

97. The Winograd commission, for example, recommended a shortened primary season with increasingly stringent thresholds for delegate allocation. While cast in terms of promoting party consensus, attempts to curtail competition for the presidential nomination obviously promote the candidacy of a Democrat in the White House. Making it more difficult for rivals to challenge a sitting incumbent also decreases the likelihood of the preconvention period serving as a wide-ranging referendum on presidential policy.

References

Books

Burnham, Walter Dean. *Critical Elections and the Mainsprings of American Politics*. New York: Norton, 1970.

Cotter, Cornelius P., and Hennessey, Bernard C. *Politics Without Power*. New York: Atherton Press, 1964.

Crotty, William. *Decision for the Democrats*. Baltimore, Md.: Johns Hopkins University Press, 1978.

_____. *Political Reform and the American Experiment*. New York: Thomas Y. Crowell, 1977.

Kirkpatrick, Jeane J. *Dismantling the Parties*. Washington, D.C.: American Enterprise Institute, 1978.

_____. *The New Presidential Elite*. New York: Russell Sage Foundation and the Twentieth Century Fund, 1976.

Pomper, Gerald, ed. *Party Renewal in America*. New York: Praeger, 1980.

Ranney, Austin. *Curing the Mischiefs of Faction*. Berkeley: University of California Press, 1975.

_____. *The Doctrine of Responsible Party Government*. Urbana: University of Illinois Press, 1962.

Articles, Reports and Papers

Crotty, William. "Building a 'Philosophy' of Party Reform." Paper presented at the Annual Meeting of the American Political Science Association, New York, 1978.

_____ . "Assessing a Decade of Reform." Paper presented at the Annual Meeting of the American Political Science Association, Washington, D.C., 1979.

Kirkpatrick, Evron. "Toward A More Responsible Two Party System: Political Science, Policy Science or Pseudo Science." *American Political Science Review* 65 (December 1971):965-991.

Longley, Charles. "Party Reform and Party Nationalization: The Case of the Democrats." *The Party Symbol*. Edited by William Crotty. San Francisco: W.H. Freeman, 1980.

_____ . "Party Reform and the Republican Party." Paper presented at the Annual Meeting of the American Political Science Association, New York, 1978.

Nakamura, Robert T., and Sullivan, Denis G. "Party Democracy and Democratic Control." In *American Politics and Public Policy*, edited by Walter Dean Burnham and Martha Wagner Weinberg, pp. 26-40. Cambridge, Mass.: MIT Press, 1978.

Pressman, Jeffrey L., and Sullivan, Denis G. "Convention Reform and Conventional Wisdom: An Empirical Assessment of Democratic Party Reform." *Political Science Quarterly* 89 (Fall 1974):539-562.

Ranney, Austin. "Changing the Rules of the Nominating Game." In *Choosing the President*, edited by James David Barber, pp. 71-93. Englewood Cliffs, N.J.: Prentice-Hall, 1974.

_____ . "The Democratic Party's Delegate Selection Reforms, 1968-76." In America in the Seventies: Problems, Policies and Politics, edited by Allan P. Sindler, pp. 160-206. Boston: Little, Brown and Company, 1977.

_____ . "The Political Parties: Reform and Decline." In *The New American Political System*, edited by Anthony King, pp. 213-247. Washington: American Enterprise Institute, 1978.

6 Presidential-Nominee Selection: Primaries, Caucuses, and the National Conventions

Paul T. David

Since the election year of 1832, the selection of presidential nominees has been dominated by the national party conventions and the events that lead up to them. The first national conventions were held in secret by the Federalist party in 1808 and 1812. The first national convention held in public to nominate a presidential candidate was held by the Antimasons in Baltimore in 1831. The short-lived National Republican party also held a national nominating convention in 1831. Finally, in preparation for the elections of 1832, the Jacksonians, then known as the Democratic-Republicans, held a convention in May 1832 at which President Andrew Jackson was nominated for a second term. Vice-President John C. Calhoun was replaced as running mate by Secretary of State Martin Van Buren. What shortly thereafter became known as the Democratic party has nominated its presidential candidates in national conventions at quadrennial intervals ever since.[1]

The Whig party made nominations in national conventions for the elections of 1840, 1844, 1848, and 1852. Thereafter the party died rapidly and was replaced by the newly formed present-day Republican party. The Republicans held their first national convention in 1856 and have made their nominations for president in national conventions ever since.

Before the convention system was established, nominations for president had been made in a variety of ways. In George Washington's case, no formal nomination was necessary. He was the unanimous choice of the electoral college in 1789 and again in 1792. In preparation for the election of 1796, the Jeffersonians in Congress held a caucus in which they agreed to support Thomas Jefferson and Aaron Burr. This was the first congressional caucus to make an open presidential nomination. The Jeffersonians, then known as the Republicans (since they opposed monarchy), continued to nominate in congressional caucuses until 1816. No action was necessary to renominate President James Monroe in 1820. In 1824 what had become the Democratic-Republican caucus met to nominate for the last time in what was something of a rump session. They supported the unsuccessful William H. Crawford, then secretary of state.

The Federalists never arrived at any stabilized procedure for making presidential nominations. The caucus system was unnecessary while the party was in power with Presidents Washington and John Adams. Thereafter the party lost representation in Congress so rapidly that it had little basis for a representative congressional caucus. The experimentation with secret national conventions followed, but by 1816 the party was too weak for even this expedient. By 1824 it had disappeared.

The election of 1824 promised to be a wide-open affair, with no structured party system and with the congressional caucus largely discredited as a nominating body. Five candidates had emerged as serious possibilities. Proposals for a national convention came to nothing. Public support for the various candidates was generated mainly in the state legislatures. Four candidates won votes in the electoral college, with Senator Andrew Jackson leading with 99 votes in an electoral college of 261. The election was thrown into the House of Representatives, where Secretary of State John Quincy Adams was elected with the support of Speaker Henry Clay, who became his secretary of state.

This set the stage for a new party alignment of the Jackson men against the Adams men. Jackson was soon renominated for a second try by the Tennessee legislature. He resigned from the Senate to conduct his campaign and in 1828 defeated President Adams in an outpouring of the popular vote not previously seen. The movement to reform the nominating procedures came to a head during his first term and led to the three national conventions that prepared for the election of 1832. An early spokesman commented that

> . . . the democracy of the Union have been forced to look to a national convention, as the best means of concentrating the popular will, and giving it effect in the approaching election. It is in fact, the only defense against a minority president.[2]

Thereafter the convention procedures developed rapidly in both major parties, to remain largely unchanged until the end of the century.

A new series of institutional developments began in 1904 with the first election of delegates in an open presidential primary. The idea spread rapidly in 1912 under the pressure of the Teddy Roosevelt insurgents in the Republican party. Presidential primaries have been a factor in presidential nominating campaigns ever since, although they were not very important between 1920 and 1952. Since then they have been increasingly important and have tended to dominate the nominating scene, especially since the reforms that began after the conventions of 1968.

The system for making presidential nominations now seems to be in a state of uneasy balance. A majority of the states, including almost all the big states, have moved to some form of presidential primary. Will the other states join them, or will there again be a loss of interest in further extensions of the primaries to new states? On the Democratic side, about half of the states holding primaries have recently shifted from plurality election of delegates to some form of proportional representation. Other states were required to do the same by the Democratic National Convention of 1976. Will they accept this directive? As the result of these and other changes, the procedures for making presidential nominations in the Republican party have become significantly different from those in the Democratic party. Should the Republican party change its procedures to conform to the ideas of Democratic reformers? Should Congress take charge in order to restabilize the system on some basis that will be uniform in the two parties?

All these questions will be examined in this chapter, but first it is necessary to trace more fully the developments that have led to the present position.

Development of the National Party Conventions to 1968

The Antimasons of 1831 established a number of precedents in the organization and procedures of the national conventions that had continuing influence on the other parties. Delegations were chosen in a manner determined locally in each state. Each delegation was given as many votes as the state's representation in Congress and the electoral college—two votes for its senators and one vote for each of its representatives. A special majority was required for nomination—in the Antimason case, three-fourths.

The Democrats followed the same rules on local autonomy in delegate selection and in the apportionment of convention votes among the states. Each delegation was required to designate a spokesman to report the vote of his delegation, and the roll call for voting was taken by states. This feature gave the national conventions a more federal aspect even than Congress, and this is still true. The Democrats required a special majority of two-thirds for nominations at their first national convention. Attempts were made to change the rule at succeeding conventions, but it persisted even during the difficulties of the 1860 convention and for many years thereafter. In 1832 many delegations voted unanimously; in future years it was agreed that each delegation could decide whether or not to cast its vote as a unit, suppressing the vote of any internal minority. The unit rule became controversial, and in 1860 it was modified to provide that the convention would enforce the unit rule only in the case of delegations that had been instructed to follow it by action of a state party convention. No definite provision for party continuity between elections was made until 1848, when the Democrats elected a Democratic National Committee of one member from each state to serve until the next convention. Thereafter the call for each successive national convention was issued by the national committee, which determined the choice of time and place and made other arrangements.

The Whig conventions of 1839 to 1852 followed essentially the pattern set by the Antimasons and the Democrats. However, they never adopted the two-thirds rule, making their nominations by simple majority. They did adopt the unit rule at their first convention, and it was a factor in the defeat of Henry Clay for nomination on that occasion.

The Republicans followed on from the Whigs and were influenced by both the Whigs and the Democrats in establishing rules at their first national convention. They rejected the two-thirds rule in favor of nomination by simple majority and also rejected the unit rule in favor of the voting rights of the individual delegate. The unit rule was undoubtedly followed in practice by some Republican state delegations, and was a subject of controversy at the Republican conventions of 1860 and 1876. It was decisively rejected on both occasions, as it has been in subsequent Republican conventions to this day.

After the rules had become stabilized in both parties, they remained largely unchanged until after the turn of the century. The conventions did increase in size as more states were admitted to the Union and as some states insisted on sending oversize delegations in the Democratic party, a practice that led to fractional voting. The Democrats attempted to deal with this problem by authorizing twice as many delegates as votes in 1852, and then by doubling the number of votes accorded each state in 1872 while retaining the electoral-college proportions. The Republicans adopted a rule of double the electoral-college apportionment in 1860 and stayed with it until 1912, despite the fact that it grossly overrepresented the Republican strength in most of the southern states. After 1912 the Republicans moved to reduce the voting strength of states in which the party was excessively weak, and also to provide bonus votes for the states where party victories were gained. Bonus votes are still a major and controversial feature of Republican party rules.

After 1900, the coming of the presidential primaries brought new problems for both parties. Delegations elected in primaries were seated in most instances without controversy, but the separate election of delegates in congressional districts, as provided in most of the primaries, brought new emphasis to the position of the individual delegate. In 1912 in Ohio, the Democratic delegates elected in districts were split between Governor Judson Harmon and Governor Woodrow Wilson, with the Harmon delegates in the majority. A state party convention imposed a unit rule on the delegation. At the national convention, the rules committee would have allowed state party convention instructions to prevail, but a minority report signed by members from nineteen states asserted the supremacy of the voting rights of individual delegates elected in district primaries. The minority report was accepted by a substantial vote of the convention, thus favoring the Wilson candidacy.[3] After 1912, it was assumed in both parties until 1968 that the results of a state presidential primary in electing delegates were controlling where applicable. After 1912 and until 1968, there was no significant seating contest in either major party that involved a delegation elected in a primary.[4]

The two-thirds rule was a critical source of difficulties in the 1912 Democratic convention, where Speaker Champ Clark received a majority of the votes on the tenth ballot but Governor Woodrow Wilson was nominated with two-thirds of the votes on the forty-sixth ballot. This precedent encouraged minorities to hang on in subsequent conventions, leading to the 44 ballots of 1920 and the 103 ballots of 1924. Attempts to repeal the rule were repeatedly unsuccessful in the 1924 convention, were dropped in 1928, and were renewed in 1932 as a part of the strategy to nominate Governor Franklin D. Roosevelt. Roosevelt was finally forced to accept the two-thirds rule as a condition for his nomination, but a resolution was passed in 1932 recommending reconsideration of the rule at the next convention. In 1936, nearly 900 delegates appeared with instructions to oppose the rule, largely as the result of a campaign led by Senator Bennett Champ Clark, son of Speaker Champ Clark. Despite strong but minority opposition, the change to majority nominations was voted by 36 to 13 in the rules committee of 1936, and was approved by voice vote on the floor without a contest.

Repeal of the two-thirds rule in the Democratic party was undoubtedly one of the most important changes that has ever occurred in the unwritten constitution of the United States. The rule had been largely responsible for the weak executive leadership that prevailed for twenty years before the Civil War. Had it remained in effect after 1936, it might have endangered or prevented the third nomination of Franklin D. Roosevelt in 1940 and the nomination of Henry Wallace for vice-president in 1940. It would certainly have complicated the nominations of Adlai Stevenson for president in 1952 and 1956 and of John Kennedy for president in 1960. Attempts to restore the two-thirds rule continued for some years after its repeal but were all unsuccessful and were eventually abandoned. Majority rule is now taken for granted in the Democratic party, but its achievement was one of the most important reform actions ever taken.

The unit rule was linked with two-thirds rule throughout most of its history. Frequently it was asserted that both rules should be revoked at the same time if either was touched. Yet there was no significant move to restrict the unit rule in 1936, although by that time it probably was in use in less than half the states. By 1956 it had been abandoned as a practice by almost all the nonsouthern states and was important mainly for eight southern states, of which Texas was the largest. The rule became controversial at the 1968 convention, where it was opposed primarily by the supporters of Senator Eugene McCarthy. The rules committee recommended against any enforcement of the unit rule, over the opposition of Texas, and the action was sustained by a voice vote on the floor. Later in the 1968 convention, action was taken to forbid the unit rule at any stage in delegate selection in 1972.

Beginning in 1948, several Democratic national conventions were forced to deal with issues of party loyalty. Most of these issues stemmed originally from southern displeasure with national-party action on civil rights. In 1948, the Mississippi and Alabama delegations both arrived with instructions to walk out unless the platform took a strong states-rights stand in opposition to the position on civil rights that had been taken by President Harry S. Truman. The Mississippi delegation's credentials were challenged because of its instructions as contained in the credentials, but the delegation was seated nonetheless and later walked out with part of the Alabama delegation. Later that year, four southern states voted for the Thurmond-Wright ticket, partly because the Truman-Barkley ticket had been denied its place on the ballot as the regular Democratic ticket. This created a problem on rules and seating for the 1952 convention, where there was a strong and initially successful move to require pledges of party loyalty from any seated delegation. The positions of the Louisiana, South Carolina, and Virginia delegations were placed in question, but they were eventually allowed to remain and to vote. After the 1952 convention, however, a Special Advisory Committee on Rules of the 1956 Democratic National Convention, chaired by Stephen A. Mitchell, was created to deal with needed changes in the rules on seating and other matters.[5] Major recommendations on party loyalty as a condition for seating were incorporated in the Call for the 1956 convention, and almost all of the committee's recommendations were incorporated in the rules of the 1956 convention as adopted.[6] The authority of the national party convention in matters of party loyalty was generally accepted as a result of the patient efforts of the Mitchell committee, and as a result there were no notable seating contests in either 1956 or 1960.

In 1964 the regular delegations from both Alabama and Mississippi were challenged at the Democratic National Convention on grounds of party loyalty, partly because both states had elected electors in 1960 who defected from the Kennedy-Johnson ticket.[7] Members of both delegations were required to sign a pledge to support the national ticket as a condition for being seated. All but eleven of the Alabama delegation refused to sign the pledge and walked out, while all but four of the Mississippi delegates did likewise. The Mississippi delegation had also been challenged by an alternative delegation of Mississippi Freedom Democrats, largely black, who asserted that the all-white regular delegation had been selected through procedures in which black voters were intimidated and systematically discriminated against. Part of the Freedom delegation was seated, and the convention adopted a new rule against racial discrimination for promulgation and enforcement in 1968.

Issues of convention size and apportionment were important in the Democratic party during the 1950s and 1960s. The provision for bonus votes in the convention as a reward for party victory in the elections, made in 1944 as a concession to the southern states, was inflated in 1948 and again in 1956 with increasing departures from the electoral-college rule of apportionment. Half votes for everyone were authorized in 1956, with the result that the number of Democratic delegates rose to around 2500. For 1960, an attempt was made to reform the apportionment by ending the bonus system but providing two-and-one-half votes or five delegates for each member of Congress; but it was also provided that no state should suffer a reduction in the size of its delegation, which continued many of the bonus votes. The authorized voting strength of the convention rose to around three thousand persons and has remained at this level ever since. For 1964, however, the rules were shifted to reward the states that had supported the Kennedy-Johnson ticket in 1960. Three votes were given for each electoral vote plus one additional vote for every hundred thousand popular votes for the ticket in 1960, with every state given at least as many votes as it held at the 1960 convention. A similar set of rules prevailed in 1968, and the massive size of that convention was part of its problem in conducting its work under conditions of great disorder.

In the Republican party, convention size remained under much better control than with the Democrats, although apportionment problems were sometimes acute. Representation of the southern states at Republican conventions was reduced somewhat from 1916 on by the requirement of a minimum number of popular votes for a second congressional district delegate. Eventually this rule became ineffective as Republican voting strength moderately increased in the South. Bonus votes were provided for the first time at the convention of 1924. They were provided for party victory in the previous election without regard to size of state. At first they were provided only for victories in presidential voting, but later they were given for victories in senatorial and gubernatorial elections. By 1956, the Republicans were providing 252 bonus votes in a convention of 1,331 votes. No half votes were permitted, leaving the size of the convention the same as the number of votes.

Television coverage of the conventions first became important in 1952, and has since led both parties to make continuing efforts to improve the appearance of their conventions as deliberative and voting bodies. Rules limiting the number and length of nominating and seconding speeches have been introduced. The use of masses of outside demonstrators in floor demonstrations has been banned, and the length of demonstrations by the delegates in the hall has been restricted. Delegates have been urged to stay in their seats and to preserve decorum as fully as possible, admonitions that frequently have had little effect, perhaps least of all at the disorderly Democratic convention of 1968.

From their earliest days, the conventions have performed four major functions that still continue. They are preeminent in the function of nominating both president and vice-president, which has been performed uniformly in the conventions of both major parties since 1844. Platform drafting and adoption before making the nominations had been stabilized before 1852 and remains a convention activity of increasing importance. Currently in both parties a full draft of the proposed platform is generally available for study before the convention opens. Every convention since 1831 has been open to public view and has functioned to some extent as a campaign rally. With television coverage, this function tends to dominate convention planning and behavior. From the first, the conventions have had to set the terms on which the state parties could participate. This is the governing-body function of the conventions as the plenary bodies of the parties at the national level. In recent years, the governing-body function has been exercised with increasing vigor and has been an aspect of the increasing nationalization of the parties.

All these aspects of development had reached an advanced stage by 1968, but the conventions of that year and particularly the Democratic convention represented something of a turning point. The period of party reform that is still in process can be said to have begun in 1968. Events since that year will receive special treatment later in this chapter.

**Development of Delegate Selection
Systems to 1968**

By the time the national convention system was well established, delegates were generally elected at party meetings in the various states. Local meetings of party members in the precincts, wards, or towns usually elected delegates to county conventions, which in turn elected delegates to conventions at congressional-district and statewide levels. These elected the national convention delegates, frequently on the basis of slates nominated by party officials and often without a contest.

This system was first challenged after the turn of the century. The Progressive movement was bringing on a rapid shift to the direct primary for the nomination of governors and Members of Congress. In 1901 Florida passed general legislation to authorize primaries and included a provision to authorize the election of national convention delegates. This was used thereafter by the Democratic party in Florida. Wisconsin passed a law in 1905 that was a direct response to a seating contest in which a LaFollette delegation had been denied seating at the 1904 Republican National Convention. A LaFollette delegation elected under the new law was seated in 1908. In 1906 Pennsylvania authorized delegate elections in which each candidate for delegate could indicate his presidential preference on the ballot. The law was unused in 1908 but was put into practice in 1912.

In 1910 Oregon began the move toward clear voting on presidential preferences by providing both for the direct election of all delegates and for taking a presidential-preference vote for their guidance. This statute was acclaimed as part of the Progressive movement of the times. It provided a formula that could be seized on by the supporters of ex-President Theodore Roosevelt in their campaign to unseat President William Howard Taft. The result was a wave of legislation that made it possible to hold some form of presidential primary in fourteen states in 1912. By 1916 the number of states holding some form of primary had increased to at least twenty-two, but thereafter the number declined to around sixteen in the period from 1936 to 1948.

The declining interest in presidential primaries after 1916 was the result of several factors. For the most part the early primaries had failed to live up to the hopes of their sponsors. At the same time, the resistance of the party organizations to any primary they could not control had hardened. Usually the presidential primaries had to occur on a date different from that of the regular primary elections, which meant that they were a nuisance to administer and costly to hold. With declining interest and support, eight of the early primary-holding states repealed their presidential primary laws by 1936.[8]

The early presidential primaries were ineffective in part because most of the presidential candidates were reluctant to use them, or found them of little help if they did. In 1912 Theodore Roosevelt set a new precedent by campaigning locally in the presidential-primary states. He won spectacular victories in most of the primaries, only to go down to defeat in the convention. In 1916, the primaries were not much used in either party. In 1920, the candidacy of General Leonard Wood for the Republican nomination brought on active contests in a number of primaries, but General Wood was defeated at the convention along with other active candidates as the convention turned to a dark horse, Senator Warren G. Harding. In 1928, Herbert Hoover was entered in the primaries of ten states in his quest for the Republican nomination, but made no personal appearance in any of those states. On the Democratic side in 1928, Governor Alfred E. Smith was also entered in ten primaries and won impressive victories in California and Oregon without campaigning in those states. In 1932, Governor Franklin D. Roosevelt made active use of the New Hampshire primary, first in the nation, and was entered in a number of other primaries without leaving Albany to campaign in them. He was defeated decisively in the Massachusetts and California primaries, and these losses complicated considerably his position at the convention under the two-thirds rule.[9]

Despite these instances of use with varied results, most candidates stayed out of most of the primaries. In most of the primaries, candidates for delegate could not use the name of a presidential candidate on the ballot without his consent, and a presidential candidate was not entered in a preference poll unless he took the initiative. The decision to enter a state was therefore the candidate's choice, and usually that choice was not exercised until after a careful exploration of the situation with the state party organization. The organizations did not welcome divisive contests that might split the party organization and generally discouraged the entry of candidates with national standing, although frequently using the name of a local favorite son as a presidential candidate. New Hampshire and Oregon, the leading exceptions to these generalizations, were thus the frequent scene of contests and had a continuing influence on nominating politics that was unusual for any small state.

The situation began to change after World War II with a weakening of party-organization control and an increasing intensity of candidate activity. Governor Harold E. Stassen was the first of a series of independent candidates to challenge organization control by active use of the primaries in many states. In 1948, Stassen was challenging the Republican front runner and titular leader, Governor Thomas E. Dewey. Stassen defeated Dewey in Wisconsin and Nebraska, which brought on intensive local campaigning by both men in Oregon, where Dewey won and reestablished himself as front runner. In 1952, Senator Estes Kefauver defeated President Truman in New Hampshire and went on to success in most of the other primaries, only to lose the nomination to Governor Adlai E. Stevenson at the convention. The New Hampshire primary was also important in 1952 as the scene of a defeat for Senator Robert A. Taft by General Dwight David Eisenhower, although Eisenhower was still in Paris. Later the impressive write-in vote for Eisenhower in the Minnesota primary was a major factor in persuading him to return to the United States as an active candidate for the Republican nomination. Eisenhower was the first president whose nomination and election could be attributed to some substantial degree to vote-getting success in the presidential primaries. In 1956, Kefauver forced Stevenson into an active campaign in the primaries, and it was a series of defeats in the later primaries that brought the Kefauver candidacy to an end. In 1960, Senator John F. Kennedy was regarded initially as a hopeless choice because of his Roman Catholic religion. His successful campaign in the primaries and especially his victory over Senator Hubert H. Humphrey in the West Virginia primary was largely responsible for his nomination at the convention and his eventual election. In 1964, Senator Barry Goldwater had a lackluster record in most of the primaries; but his defeat of Governor Nelson A. Rockefeller at the end of the season in the California primary clinched the Republican nomination for Goldwater. In 1968, former Vice-President Richard M. Nixon assured his nomination in part by a long record of success in the primaries, although he was given a serious contest in almost none.

The resurgence of interest in the primaries from 1948 on was accompanied by interest in establishing new primaries in additional states. Three states that had earlier repealed their primary laws—Minnesota, Indiana, and Montana—passed new laws in 1949 and 1953, although Minnesota and Montana repealed their laws in 1959 because of dislike for the way they had operated. Other states began revising their laws. In 1955, Florida rewrote its statute completely to follow the recommendations of a group of political scientists.[10] Some years later, the law was revised to increase substantially the influence of the state party organizations. In 1959 Oregon developed what became known as the Oregon plan, under which the state secretary of state was directed to list for the preference poll the names of all presidential candidates whom he considered to be "generally advocated and recognized in the national news media." Thereafter, a candidate could remove his name from the ballot only by sending an affidavit stating that he did not intend to become a candidate for president in the forthcoming election. Nebraska followed the Oregon plan in 1965, and it has since become popular in a number of other states. Previously a candidate was likely to be on a ballot without his consent only in the states that allowed delegates to use his name without his consent, principally New Hampshire, Florida, and Wisconsin before 1948.

As of 1968, it remained rare for a candidate to find himself on a ballot in a state without his consent, and selective use of the primaries thus continued. But as the nominating campaigns became more active, with local campaigning by some candidates in many states (after the arrival of the jet age), all the candidates found themselves under increasing pressure to make a showing in at least a diversified selection of the primaries. Active contests in such states as New Hampshire, Massachusetts, Florida, Wisconsin, Michigan, Ohio, Nebraska, Oregon, and California became common, despite the widely differing provisions of their various state laws. By 1968, the election of delegates was occurring in presidential primaries in at least seventeen states and the District of Columbia; preference polls, usually only advisory, were being held in several other states. The presidential-primary system had not reached maturity, let alone any semblance of uniformity, but its importance in any nominating campaign had come to be taken for granted.

Problems Encountered and Recent Reforms

The 1968 Democratic National Convention at Chicago will be long remembered as a scene of unusual violence and disorder. Young people throughout the country were upset by the requirements of the unpopular Vietnam War. Organized youth groups had threatened for months to converge on President Lyndon Johnson's Chicago convention to visit their revenge. Several thousand young people did arrive, were harrassed by Mayor Richard J. Daley's police and the National Guard, and jointly with the police created scenes of violence that were widely viewed on national television. At times violence erupted even on the convention floor, as newsmen and delegates were roughed up by security guards and ushers.

Among the delegates, those most disturbed were the cohorts that had come pledged to the candidacies of Eugene McCarthy, the assassinated Robert Kennedy, and pinch-hitter George McGovern. Most of them had been outraged by earlier proceedings in which meetings had been called on short notice in obscure locations, parliamentary procedures had been widely disregarded, and organized majorities had trampled on the rights of minority groups and their presidential candidates. The disturbing events before the convention had led to the creation of an ad hoc voluntary commission headed by Governor Harold Hughes of Iowa, which rapidly produced a report just before the convention on the various abuses of democratic process that had occurred during the previous months.[11] The Hughes commission report was widely distributed among the delegates, the press, and others, and focused attention on a series of proposed reforms. Some of these reforms could be adopted immediately; others would take several years. The report was directly relevant to the work of two convention committees: the Credentials Committee and the Committee on Rules.

The Credentials Committee was charged with enforcing new rules on racial discrimination in delegate selection. These were the result of the conflict over seating the Mississippi delegation at the 1964 convention, and work meantime that had resulted in the new rules written into the Call for the 1968 convention. When the convention met, many delegations from the South and elsewhere were challenged as not being in accord with the new rules, or as having been created with gross disregard of fair procedures. On the racial issues, the Credentials Committee followed a tough line, seating the insurgents from Mississippi and half of those from Georgia, penalizing the Alabama delegation, and so on. But on the procedural challenges of northern delegations, brought mainly by the McCarthy people, the Credentials Committee denied most of the challenges, finding no basis in party law for dealing with them. Instead, the committee proposed a resolution providing for a new special committee or commission, preparatory to the 1972 convention, to investigate and report on all aspects of delegate selection and party structures. The basic principles that should be implemented were indicated. There was no opposing minority report and the resolution was adopted by the convention on a voice vote and without debate. It became the basis for what was later known as the McGovern-Fraser commission.

The Committee on Rules, generally a passive force at any convention, found itself the scene of active debate in 1968. Governor Harold Hughes appeared to advocate the reform program of his ad hoc commission, including specifically the immediate abolition of the unit rule in 1968 proceedings. Despite strenuous objections by the Texas delegation, the committee recommended and the convention approved a "freedom of conscience" proposal under which any delegate could vote as he saw fit, regardless of any prior action in a primary or state convention to impose binding instructions or a unit rule. The committee also recommended a resolution providing for the establishment of another special study commission to examine and codify the rules of the Democratic convention and to deal with any "other matters that may be appropriate."[12] This was approved by the convention without debate and became the basis for what was later known as the O'Hara commission. Finally, a minority report from the Committee on Rules went even further. It required that the Call for the 1972 convention include several specific provisions: that each state party assure that its delegates have been selected "through a process in which all Democratic voters have a full and timely opportunity to participate"; that "the unit rule not be used in any stage of the delegate selection process"; and that delegate selection take place only through processes open to public participation in the calendar year of the national convention.[13] These injunctions were directed more to the work of the eventual McGovern-Fraser commission than to that of the O'Hara commission, but the minority report was approved after limited debate by a vote of 1,350 to 1,206. It was obviously approved by many Humphrey supporters in the convention as well as by those who later voted for McCarthy.

The Commission on Party Structure and Delegate Selection, chaired by Senator George McGovern, was appointed and began active work early in 1969. It held an elaborate set of public hearings around the country at which the need for reforming the procedures of delegate selection was further documented. It published its famous report, *Mandate for Reform*, in April 1970.[14] This contained its eighteen guidelines for reforming the state party rules throughout the country, most of which guidelines the commission asserted were mandatory under the authority delegated to it by the 1968 convention, or under the actions that the convention itself had taken.

The first group of guidelines dealt with rules or practices that inhibited access to the delegate-selection process. The first of these required that "State Parties overcome the effects of past discrimination by affirmative steps to encourage minority group participation, including representation . . . in reasonable relationship to the group's presence in the population of the state." A footnote added, "It is the understanding of the Commission that this is not to be accomplished by the mandatory imposition of quotas."[15] The second guideline imposed similar requirements for women and young people. This was the beginning of the party-wide controversy over quotas, which led to the substantial enforcement of something like quotas in 1972 and to some relaxation later, although the controversy still continues. Other guidelines in the first group dealt with voter registration, costs and fees imposed on delegates, and an important requirement that every state party produce written rules for its procedures on delegate selection.

The second group of guidelines on rules or practices diluting the influence of the voter in delegate selection dealt with proxy voting (forbidden), mixing delegate selection with other party business, quorum requirements in meetings, selection of alternate delegates, the prohibition of unit-rule procedures, and two other matters of special importance. One was the representation accorded the voters who favored the less successful presidential candidates. On this it was recommended that the 1972 convention "adopt a rule requiring State Parties to provide for the representation of minority views to the highest level of the nominating process."[16] The commission said that this could be done in one of two ways: either by choosing delegates "from fairly apportioned districts no larger than congressional districts," or by dividing the delegate votes among presidential candidates "in proportion to their demonstrated strength" in large elections. The other matter was that of apportioning delegate strength among the districts within a state. On this it was required that "The apportionment is to be based on a formula giving equal weight to total population and to the Democratic vote in the previous presidential election."[17] It was also required that in states with convention systems at least 75 percent of the delegates be selected in the congressional districts or smaller units.

The third group of guidelines, a catch-all that combined aspects of the first two, was designed to clean up various procedures. It required adequate public notice of all meetings, confining the process to Democratic voters; timely processes within the presidential year; fair procedures in forming party committees; and orderly processes with public notice in making up slates of candidates for delegate. It also required that there be no automatic or ex officio members appointed to any state delegation—a direct attack on the national party rule by which national-committee members elected four years earlier were given delegate status, as well as on the widespread practices in states by which governors, senators, and ranking state party officials were automatically given positions as delegates-at-large. Public and party officialdom within the Democratic Party was outraged by this provision, and enforcement faltered, but it did bring on a considerable change in the composition of the 1972 convention.

The McGovern-Fraser commission remained in existence until the 1972 convention, although Senator McGovern left the chairmanship along the way and was replaced by Congressman Donald M. Fraser. The commission believed that its mandatory guidelines had the force of party law, and it was eventually upheld in this view by the legal counsel to the Democratic National Committee, Joseph Califano. Efforts to enforce the guidelines began while they were still in preliminary form and were continued assiduously up to the time of the convention. Every state was given an analysis of its existing status; these analyses revealed that every state was in need of several changes in its previous rules or practices. At the beginning of the effort, a count showed 465 violations of the guidelines, an average of more than 9 per state; when the convention met, only 13 of these violations remained.[18] The national committee had cooperated by including all of the eighteen guidelines in the Call for the convention without amendment.

At the 1972 convention, with challenges involving more than half the delegations, the Credentials Committee made changes in thirteen delegations, mainly to bring them more full into conformity with the requirements for fair representation of blacks, women, and young people. After these adjustments, women made up 40 percent of the convention, youth 21 percent, and blacks 15 percent.[19] In effect, quotas had been enforced. Also, the entire Daley delegation from Chicago had been unseated because of various violations of the guidelines, particularly on slate making, despite the fact that the delegation had been elected in a primary. The Daley delegates continued their vendetta in the Illinois state courts after the convention, where the anti-Daley delegates were found in contempt of court, but appeals were taken to the federal courts. The Supreme Court eventually ruled in *Cousins* v. *Wigoda* that the convention was supreme in this matter and could override state law where inconsistent with national party rules—a decision of the most far-reaching implications.[20]

The California delegation also received special attention at the 1972 convention. For many years California law had provided for a winner-take-all type of presidential primary at the statewide level. Representatives of the McGovern-Fraser commission repeatedly urged California party officials to secure change in the law; but in the face of Governor Ronald Reagan's opposition, nothing was done. In the 1972 election, Senator McGovern narrowly defeated Senator Humphrey and thereby became entitled to the entire state delegation under state law. Humphrey supporters contested the decision and sought a proportionate share of the delegation. For a time it appeared that they would win and their victory could be decisive in giving the nomination to Humphrey. The issue got into the federal courts and quickly reached the Supreme Court under emergency procedures, but the Court refused to act on the case and left the decision to the convention. In a roll-call vote, with the California delegation not voting, the McGovern forces were successful in seating their entire California delegation, and, of course, went on to win the nomination.

But with the issue on proportionate voting so sharply drawn, the rules committee of the 1972 convention recommended "that the delegates to the 1976 Convention shall be chosen in a manner which fairly reflects the division of preference expressed by those who participate in the presidential nominating process . . .''[21] The convention approved the recommendation as made, and also approved a recommendation for a new commission to review the guidelines in preparation for the 1976 convention.

The Commission on Rules that resulted from the 1968 convention was appointed in early 1969 under the chairmanship of Congressman James G. O'Hara. Its status was parallel to that of the McGovern-Fraser commission; but its task was less newsworthy, it functioned more slowly, and its results, although significant, were less important. It was charged essentially with revising and codifying the rules under which the conventions have historically operated. It took this to include all matters pertaining to convention arrangements and scrutinized all of them carefully in a long series of meetings.

Early in the process it recommended a revision of the rules for the apportionment of convention votes among the states. Eliminating all bonus votes, it proposed that about half of the votes in a convention of three thousand be distributed on the basis of state population and the other half on the basis of the Democratic vote for president in the most recent three elections. The Democratic National Committee argued the matter furiously and accepted the elimination of bonus votes but changed to a rule of half, on the basis of electoral votes and the other half, as proposed, on the average of recent presidential votes. This helped the representation of the numerous small states, then overrepresented in the national committee, but gave them no more than their share in the election results. The issue was argued in the federal courts, approved at the appellate level, and allowed to stand by the Supreme Court.

The O'Hara commission also brought on a change in the size, apportionment, and scheduling of the major convention committees. Historically there have been four of these committees. As the conventions have become larger and more unwieldy, it has become increasingly important to get as much of the work done as possible in the committees—and on a basis that the full convention will not feel impelled to revise in difficult floor debate and voting. But as of 1968 each state still had two members on each committee, regardless of state size. The rules commission successfully proposed an increase in committee size to about 150, with the smallest states given only one member and the remaining members distributed in proportion to state-delegation size. The long-standing but impotent Committee on Permanent Organization was abolished, and it was agreed that the other three committees—Platform, Credentials, and Rules—should all complete their work several days before the opening of the convention, with their reports available for study in advance.

Most of the O'Hara commission's work was intended to improve fairness, restrict arbitrary authority, and produce rules that could easily be understood and followed. It devised an entirely new and elaborate procedure for the early investigation of credentials disputes by hearing officers. This was an important contribution and did much to expedite credentials disputes at the 1972 convention.

Before the end of their tenure, the McGovern-Fraser and O'Hara commissions met jointly to propose the adoption by the Democratic party of a Democratic Party Charter—in effect, a written constitution for the party such as had never existed before. This brought together in one document the major structures and usages of the party, while revising and extending them with new bodies such as a proposed Judicial Council to deal with internal party disputes. Adoption of this document was proposed at the 1972 convention, but the decision was postponed for action at a specially called midterm party conference in 1974, at which a revised charter was finally adopted. But the 1972 convention acted immediately to revise the internal structure of the Democratic National Committee. The pattern used in reforming the convention committees was followed in part: equal representation of the states was replaced by representation based on state size for most of the committee, while adding a state party chairman and vice-chairman of the opposite sex for every state. The result is a much larger committee but also a much more representative committee to deal with party matters between conventions.

The McGovern defeat in the election of 1972 was attributed in part to the party-splitting effects of the new rules, which had been actively sought and defended by the McGovern supporters. A strong backlash was apparent after the election and during the winter of 1972-1973. But the authorized new commission to revise the guidelines was appointed with a representative membership. It functioned under the chairmanship of Barbara Mikulski of Baltimore and was generally known as the Mikulski commission. It rehashed the arguments over minority representation and agreed to outlaw quotas as long as states were aggressive in promoting affirmative action for blacks, women, and young people. It softened several of the other guidelines that had been most irksome, including the one on slate making that had tripped up the Daley delegation.

But the most far-reaching new action by the commission was on the proportionate representation of presidential candidate strength. In taking up the matter, Ms. Mikulski referred to their instructions as mandatory. The debate that followed was on the extent to which proportional representation was feasible and desirable, either statewide or at the congressional-district level. Reservations about the dangers of proportional representation were expressed. For example, Governor John J. Gilligan of Ohio commented that "the more you talk about giving proportional representation to losers, the more you guarantee that no one is ever going to be able to come into that Convention with enough votes to carry it on an early ballot."[22] But the commission went ahead and agreed that proportionality should be required at all stages of the delegate selection process in the caucus states, for candidates who received at least 10 percent of the votes at any level. (Previously the figure of 5 percent had been used in the commission's discussions, but it rose to 10 percent in its final action.) For the primary states, the commission also favored proportional representation both at district and at-large levels with a cutoff no higher than 10 percent, but it followed the McGovern-Fraser commission line in being willing to accept primaries where 75 percent or more of the delegates were elected on a plurality basis at the congressional-district level or lower. Such primaries became known as "loophole" primaries.

The Mikulski commission report was considered by the Democratic National Committee (the reformed committee) in January 1974. Most of the report was approved without change for inclusion in the Call to the 1976 convention. But the provisions for proportional representation were among those most hotly debated. Opponents claimed that they would lead to frivolous candidacies and to fractionalization of delegate strength. In the end, the recommendations were approved, but the cutoff provision was revised from 10 to 15 percent as a further safeguard against minor candidates. The provision for loophole primaries remained unchanged.[23]

The Democratic National Committee also established a Compliance Review Commission to monitor and advise the state parties on compliance with the revised rules for delegate selection. This body found itself involved in a long educational process as it explained to one state party body after another how to operate a proportional-representation system under caucus procedures or in a primary. Most of the states with long-established loophole primaries—including New York, New Jersey, Pennsylvania, Ohio, and Illinois—elected to retain them. California revised its primary law to permit each party to follow a system of its own choice: the Democrats opted for a combination of district and at-large elections, with proportional representation in both, while the Republicans opted to retain a statewide winner-take-all system, as favored by then Governor Ronald Reagan. Many states enacted new presidential-primary laws as a means of solving their problems without upsetting state party machinery. Most of the new laws provided for some form of proportional representation, either at party option for the Democrats or mandatorily for both parties. About thirty states prepared to hold primaries, and it was apparent that far more than a majority of the delegates in both parties would be elected in primaries in 1976.

During 1975 mass media commentators referred frequently to the probability of a "brokered convention" of Democrats in 1976. These expectations were based mainly on an estimate of the consequences of proportional representation in the approximately thirty-five states where it was to be used—coupled, of course, with the knowledge that there would be many candidates, none of whom seemed likely to develop outstanding appeal.

These expectations proved wrong, mainly because of Jimmy Carter's unexpected success as a campaigner. But the characteristics of the proportional-representation formula in use in most states were also important. The 15 percent cutoff rule, under which a candidate had to win 15 percent of the vote in order to get anything, did a great deal to limit the representation of minor candidates. The rule in caucus states under which every member of a party meeting either had to declare a candidate preference or else declare that he or she was uncommitted also tended to force early decisions, as probably did the increasing number of primary-holding states.

The emphasis on affirmative action for minority groups produced a convention in 1976 at which the representation of blacks, women, and young people was lower than in 1972 but still much higher than in any year prior to 1972. Blacks and women expressed discontent, but all moves to return to a quota system were defeated.

The results of proportional representation were reviewed and brought on one of the few controversies at the 1976 convention. With so many states already committed to the use of proportional representation in the Democratic party, liberal groups in the convention pressed to have the practice made universal. After a vigorous debate at a meeting of the convention's rules committee, the following resolution was proposed for convention action by a vote of 58½ to 58¼: "Resolved further that in reviewing and modifying the Delegate Selection Rules, the Commission on Presidential Primaries shall construe Article II, Section 4, clause (ii) of the Charter to bar the use of delegate selection systems in primary states which permit a plurality of the votes at any level to elect all of the delegates from that level."[24] Carter forces produced a softer proposal to leave the loophole primaries for consideration by the proposed commission without instructions, but in the end the majority report was approved on the convention floor without even a roll-call vote. What was to become the Winograd commission after the 1976 convention had a definite instruction to end loophole primaries, meaning that a number of the largest states in the country had to change their state laws under penalty of prospective action at the 1980 convention. The 1976 convention acted before it adjourned to provide for another midterm conference to be held in 1978, at which matters of party reform could be considered further.

Contemporary Reform Alternatives

As matters currently stand in this interval between national conventions, the impetus for reform has lessened from its peak between 1968 and 1972, but there is still an agenda of proposals for consideration. The most far reaching of these would call for the establishment of a national presidential primary.

A National Presidential Primary

Woodrow Wilson proposed a national presidential primary in his first State of the Union message. The proposal has been before Congress in one form or another ever since. The Gallup Poll has been reporting for at least twenty-five years that popular support for the idea exists among at least 75 percent of the population. It was long thought that a constitutional amendment would be required, but recent decisions of the federal courts support the view that Congress could provide successfully for a national presidential primary through simple legislation. Nevertheless, the prospects for a national presidential primary seem to be receding rather than coming closer.

As generally conceived, a national presidential primary would consist of an election held throughout the country in all states on the same day. All the admitted candidates would be on the ballot, which would be the same in every state. If no one received more than 40 or 45 percent of the votes, a likely outcome, a run-off election would be held between the two highest candidates. The primary might be held as late as September, with the general election following in November as at present. National conventions might still be held to write party platforms and perhaps to pick vice-presidential candidates, but they would no longer have any authority over the presidential nominations.

The basic merits of the scheme reside primarily in the virtues of a public election: simplicity of choice, clarity of decision, and unambiguous results. The process would be similar to the familiar primary elections in most states whereby nominees for governor and senator are chosen. It would provide a definite choice among the willing candidates, that is, those who were willing and able to put themselves on the ballot. The popular turnout in such an election would doubtless fall below that in the November general election, but in any serious contest it would surely be much larger than the turnout under present procedures. On its face the process seems assuredly democratic, and it would be relatively free of manipulation—at least after the candidate list on the ballot had been made final. Depending on filing requirements and timing, it might possibly bring on a somewhat shorter nominating campaign than has become customary under present procedures.

Doubts about the scheme begin with a major question: Would the best man win, or even be on the ballot? Potential candidates whose mood was like that of Dwight Eisenhower or Adlai Stevenson in 1952, or Edward Kennedy and Hubert Humphrey in 1976, would almost certainly not be on the ballot. The possibility of drafting a candidate or of finding a new alternative at the last minute—possibilities that have at times been important in American politics, especially during periods of party weakness—would cease to exist. Most of the time, most of the candidates would be the same as they would be under any other system, but as always, there would be no assurance that one candidate would become outstanding. A run-off between the two leading candidates would put forward the two with the most first-choice strength, while frequently omitting more generally popular candidates whose strength was largely as a second-choice alternative. These are often the centrist candidates in a field where more the visible polar candidates garner most of their first-choice strength from groups of supporters who strongly dislike each other. The centrist, second-choice position is illustrated by candidates like Franklin D. Roosevelt in the 1932 California primary or Thomas E. Dewey in the Wisconsin primary of 1948.

Campaign-finance requirements would be heavy in a national primary, although perhaps no heavier than they are already. But the timing of campaign finance requirements would be quite different. Under present conditions, candidates like George McGovern in 1972 or Jimmy Carter in 1976 could hope to raise most of their campaign funding after achieving initial successes in the early primaries. With a national primary, there would be no comparable opportunity for the relatively unknown candidates to make a showing in some early test. All those involved would need to have their funding substantially in hand by the time at which filing closed for the primary and the formal campaign began.

One of the greatest advantages of the present system of state primaries scattered between March and early June is that it provides a whole series of tests during which the electorate is given time to think and something to think about. Voter opinion on the candidates early in the season has repeatedly turned out to be weak, volatile, and easily changeable. In a national primary, it would remain that way up to the day of sudden-death decision. Under the present system, opinion gradually stabilizes as more and more evidence accumulates through repeated testing. This is a virtue of the present system that surely should be preserved.

A final potentially adverse effect on the party system would be the elimination of the most important function of the national party conventions. In a two-party system, the larger party in particular would undoubtedly find a national primary somewhat divisive. In state politics, bitter primary contests frequently weaken the position of what would otherwise be the majority party. Factional interests are strengthened and become more permanent, while general conceptions of party responsibility for the party as a whole are weakened. In the weaker party in a two-party system the considerations are somewhat different, but primary elections are not generally considered helpful in strengthening a weaker party, which may need most of all to draft a suitable candidate in order to build up its strength.

A mixture of considerations of this kind was undoubtedly responsible for the early and nearly unanimous decision of the McGovern-Fraser commission not to favor a national presidential primary. Indeed, that commission and its successors have opposed any increase in the number of existing state presidential primaries, although the increase that has occurred has been brought on by requirements that some of the states have found difficult to meet in any other way. The McGovern-Fraser commission was actively led by members of Congress who have been influential in Congress itself. They will undoubtedly continue to use their influence, like that of most congressional leaders, to oppose any change to a national presidential primary.

Proportional Primaries in Every State?

A second line of major reform would seek to promot existing tendencies to their ultimate limits. Presidential primaries under state auspices have been spreading to additional states, and they have been changing from primaries decided by plurality elections to primaries giving delegates to the major candidates on a proportional basis. The logical consummation of this process would be a primary in every state, all of them on a proportional basis.

The aspect of this change that is most controversial and most likely to be resisted is the switching of all the existing primaries to a proportional basis. As noted earlier, many states with long-established primaries have retained them on a plurality-election basis. In the Democratic party these are known as loophole primaries, and their shifting to a proportional basis was mandated at the 1976 Democratic convention. The mandate has been taken for granted in the work of the Winograd commission, which assumes that it will be accepted and carried out by the states concerned. But many of those states are large and powerful, with long-established party organizations that are still relatively strong. They also have active Republican parties, which will not necessarily cooperate in achieving a reform that is advocated primarily by liberal forces in the Democratic party.

There is more than inertia in defense of the status quo. Party organizations in such states as New York, New Jersey, Pennsylvania, Ohio, and Illinois prefer, if possible, to go to the conventions with unified delegations in order to exercise maximum influence. With district elections the rule, it is common in those states to have a few maverick dissenters; but in the past the great majority of the delegates usually have been prepared to follow their leaders in taking a unified line in each delegation. Proportional representation in a contest year would divide such delegations into two, three, or more identifiable groups with strong separate identities. Delegation unity would be shattered, and the power of the leaders and the influence of the party organizations would be replaced by directions from the candidates to whom the proportional groups were attached.

At least three arguments favor the change to proportionality in all primaries—aside from weakening the party organizations, which some may regard as a virtue. The proportional system has a strong element of fairness; in particular, it avoids situations in which a candidate who has captured only 40 percent of the vote in a state receives three-quarters or more of the delegates. The change would also eliminate an unfair advantage held by states that maintain the loophole primaries and that now maximize their power and influence at the expense of the states that have switched to proportional primaries. Finally, there are virtues in having the system standardized on one basis or the other. In the early days of the electoral-college system, there was uncertainty over whether every state should vote as a unit. The unit system prevailed and still does, although it is widely regarded as one of the deficiencies of the electoral-college system.

The present trend in the Democratic party toward proportionality in the presidential nominating process has gone so far that it would seem to have passed some kind of tipping point. It is likely that most of the remaining states will fall in line before the 1980 convention. Those that fail to do so will presumably be challenged by the delegates who would be seated on a proportional basis—which can easily be calculated from the election returns in such states—and probably the Credentials Committee and the convention will simply arrange seating for all on the proportional basis that has been mandated. In the Republican party, state law and state party rules will probably still control, but more states will be proportional even on the Republican side as the result of contemporary action in the Democratic party.

The situation of the remaining caucus states is quite different and much less of a problem from the point of view of the reformers. All these states have already been put on a proportional basis in the Democratic party, in party meetings from the precinct level to the state convention. Participants in all such meetings are required to declare either their candidate preference or that they are uncommitted. Party organizations and party leaders favored the uncommitted basis in many states in 1976, but had little success with that strategy. The result was that many of the caucus states were the scene of sharp contests among the candidates, with vote counts in the precincts and election results much like those of a primary, although with much lower turnout than would be likely in any primary. With these changes already in place in the Democratic party, the further change to a primary in such states can largely be left to arguments of convenience. Some party leaders will prefer a primary as a means of getting presidential politics out of the state party machinery, which they would prefer to retain solely for purposes of state and local politics. Others will oppose a primary in hopes of maintaining some organizational status and leadership even in matters of presidential politics. The public interest may not seem to be actively considered in this issue except with respect to the Republican party, which has not yet come to grips with the issue as it affects the caucus states, and has taken no national position on the issue in the primaries.

It might be argued that the remaining caucus states maintain an area of convention flexibility that is important for the vitality of the conventions and that should be maintained for that reason. Convention delegates who come out of a caucus system are more likely to be oriented toward the long-term interests of the party than those elected in a primary, who may be loyal only to the candidate of the moment. When a convention is heading toward deadlock and some group has to give way in order to achieve a nomination, the giving is more likely to occur among the delegates from the caucus states. That this is still true in the Republican party was virtually demonstrated in 1976. It may still be true for the caucus states even in the Democratic party, despite the candidate commitments that have become general in the caucus states. If this is so, it may be related to the reluctance of successive reform commissions to recommend the extension of the primaries to more states. Once they learn how to operate under the new rules, the caucus states may be content to stay as they are in the Democratic party. There might even be some rolling back in the number of states with presidential primaries if the considerations noted here are widely accepted.

Winograd Commission Recommendations?

After the 1976 election, the Commission on Presidential Nomination and Party Structure was formed by the Democratic party under the chairmanship of Morley Winograd of Michigan. A successor to the McGovern-Fraser and Mikulski commissions, it had essentially the same task of reviewing the delegate-selection rules for the party in the light of the most recent experience. It started with the rules as incorporated into the By-Laws of the Democratic Party Charter. It quickly decided that about half of the rules were satisfactory as they stood and identified eighteen specific provisions that were still causing trouble or that were controversial for one reason or another. On many of these it proposed little change. Its more important recommendations are considered here, starting with those on the scheduling of the process and the use of cutoff points in proportional primaries and meetings.

The timing of the delegate-selection process in the Democratic party in 1976 can be said to have started in precinct meetings in Iowa on January 19 and to have ended on June 13 in a party meeting picking at-large delegates in the state of Washington. As in former years, there were many complaints that the whole process was too prolonged, starting too early and ending too late in preparation for a convention scheduled to meet on July 12. There were also complaints about the undue influence of the early primaries, particularly that in New Hampshire, as the result of the impressive treatment they were accorded by television reporting and the other mass media. New Hampshire was self-selected for its earliest primary role and has strongly insisted on retaining it, despite the fact that it is a small and somewhat unrepresentative state.

The Winograd commission decided, at its final meeting on January 21-22, 1978, to recommend a new party rule under which no primary or first-tier caucus would be held before the second Tuesday in March and no such primary or meeting would be held after the second Tuesday in June, thus seeking to confine the formal steps in the delegate-selection process to a period of thirteen weeks.[25] Because of objections from New Hampshire and other early states, however, the commission also recommended exempting from this rule the states that had begun their delegate-selection process at earlier dates in 1976. The combined effect of the two recommendations is mainly to limit the freedom of states that may opt for a new presidential primary before 1980.

On the cutoff point in proportional primaries and meetings, states with proportional systems in 1976 were authorized to deny delegates to any candidate receiving less than 15 percent of the vote. Most of the proportional states used the 15-percent cutoff. California used 10 percent, Idaho and Nevada used 5 percent, and Massachusetts used approximately 5 percent. In Winograd commission discussions, some members favored reducing the cutoff for all states to 10 percent. At the urging of representatives of the Carter administration, a mixed system was finally accepted under which the 15-percent cutoff would be retained during the first third of the delegate-selection period but would rise to 20 percent during the second third and to 25 percent during the final third of the delegate-selection period. The object of the scheme is evidently to stiffen the pace of the elimination process and to hasten the dropping out of minor candidates as delegate-selection proceeds. It will probably help the front runner, but it may also help the candidates running in second or third place, while severely handicapping candidates who do not at least score among the top three.

The Winograd commission reconsidered the issues of affirmative action but did nothing to change existing rules against quotas and the rule that a delegation could not be challenged merely on grounds of composition after affirmative action had been pursued in the state. Some problems of affirmative action arising out of the rights of presidential candidates to approve delegates committed to them were noted. It was agreed that candidates had an obligation to handle approval consistently with affirmative action and that state plans on affirmative action could include provisions on the procedure for the exercise of candidate approval.

The problem of state laws incompatible with party rules was considered in the light of the intention to do away with loophole primaries and the implications of the Supreme Court decision in *Cousins* v. *Wigoda*.[26] The Winograd commission decided to retain the existing rule by which state parties are required to take "provable positive steps to achieve legislative changes" where necessary, but noted that delegates could be selected or seated outside of the provisions of inconsistent state law under the doctrines of *Cousins* v. *Wigoda*. The decision in that case provides both a weapon for securing changes in state law and a means for alternative action when state law is not changed.

The Republican Situation

Much of this chapter has dealt primarily with events and problems in the Democratic party, although the early history of rules changes in the Republican party has also been noted. The Republicans have never had the two-thirds rule and decisively rejected any convention enforcement of a unit rule at an early date. The 1912 Republican convention brought on a crisis over the apportionment of convention votes among the states which led to changes in the apportionment rules. Since then there have been few instances of major controversy over the rules in the Republican party. The party has had a set of written rules governing the convening and operations of the national convention, and these rules have been open to discussion and possible revision in the rules committees of successive conventions. After the 1968 convention and again after the 1972 convention special bodies were created, somewhat akin to the McGovern-Fraser commission of the Democrats, to consider revision of Republican rules.[27]

The Republicans have given active consideration to problems of affirmative action in these various bodies. State parties have been put under obligation to make strong efforts to increase the participation and representation of women and young people in Republican-party affairs. These efforts have had some effect on the composition of the last two national party conventions. Efforts to increase black representation have also been discussed, but they have not been pressed and have had little result.

The apportionment of convention votes among the states was the subject of a major controversy at the 1972 Republican National Convention. By that time there had been a considerable buildup of the system of bonus votes, which greatly favored the smaller states and the western region. The Ripon Society had taken the issue to the federal courts, and at the time of the 1972 convention it was anticipated that the federal courts might act to require a system of apportionment similar to the one then being adopted by the Democrats—one with no bonus votes and with apportionment partly following the electoral-college system and partly following the recent popular vote for the party's presidential candidates. Nevertheless, the 1972 convention voted on a sharply divided roll call to retain bonus votes in a complex formula that continued to reward the small and western states—a strategy favored at the time by supporters of Spiro Agnew, who hoped to see him as the party's candidate in 1976. Eventually the Supreme Court refused to hear the case and let stand an appellate-court decision favorable to the formula.[28] What seems to be a relatively clear case of malapportionment in the Republican party has thus been allowed to persist and may continue indefinitely.

The introduction of proportional representation in the Democratic party has brought on a series of state laws that provide for proportional representation in state presidential primaries. In eight or nine states, these laws have provided the same proportional system in both parties and have thus directly affected the Republicans. During the 1976 nominating campaigns, Governor Ronald Reagan asserted at least twice that his nomination would have been assured had the Republican party adopted proportional representation in all its processes. So far, however, there seems to have been no mobilization of sentiment in the party to follow the Democratic lead toward a complete system of proportional representation. This is probably the most important unresolved issue of party rules and practices with which the Republican party should currently be concerned. On other matters, with the exception of the apportionment question already discussed, there seems to be no important visible issue in that party.

Potential Action by Congress

In recent years, there has been increasing interest in some action by Congress to reform the presidential nominating process. Action by Congress would presumably be the same for both major political parties, and perhaps for minor parties as well.

Proposals currently pending in Congress take one of two main forms. One type would provide for some kind of national presidential primary; the other would provide for a series of regional primaries. In the first case, as of a recent date there were six proposals for a national presidential primary to be held on a single day. Some of these would simply elect all the national convention delegates on the same day; others conform more to the concept of a national presidential primary as discussed earlier in this chapter. In the second case, the regional-primary bills would divide the country into five or six regions and provide that all the primaries in each region would be held on the same day. The alleged advantage would be to simplify campaigning by the candidates and to clarify the results for the voters. A major difficulty lies in the complications of deciding which region should be allowed to go first.

None of these bills have had active committee consideration, nor do they seem likely to receive it. The Winograd commission considered them briefly and affirmed its strong opposition either to a national primary or to a set of regional primaries. It also followed the line of the 1976 convention in opposing any congressional intervention in these matters. At the 1976 convention, it was said that 65 percent of the delegates were opposed to a national primary, with only 22 percent in favor. That convention also adopted a strong resolution in which it urged the Congress "to refrain from intervening in these Party affairs unless and until the National Party requests legislative assistance, . . ."[29] Opposition to congressional intervention is undoubtedly as strong, if not even stronger, on the part of Republican-party activists and elites.

Should consensus emerge on some simple, sweeping, and internally consistent plan of reforming the presidential nominating process—for example, proportional primaries in every state—the prospects for congressional action would undoubtedly improve. It is probably the only means by which a nationwide standardization of the process could occur. Much of the present complexity of the process undoubtedly results from the idiosyncrasies of action by fifty different states and a hundred different major state parties. But the processes currently under way in both parties may lead through internal action to greater uniformity of action in the states, and this process probably must go further before congressional action will become feasible, even if it is desirable.

Conclusion

In conclusion, it seems clear that both national political parties will continue to study their rules for delegate selection and convention operation. Occasionally they will revise these rules as experience evolves. Currently the most important pending matter is the further extension of systems of proportional representation to additional states, especially the larger states with long-established party systems. This change would enhance the representative quality of the conventions and can probably be made without seriously impairing their ability to reach final decisions on the nominations. On other matters, we are still a long way from consensus on what changes would be improvements; and it may be necessary for the parties to experiment further before consensus emerges—if it ever does.

Notes

1. The introductory section of the chapter and much of the following pages are based almost entirely on the treatment found in David, Goldman, and Bain (1960), esp. chaps. 2, 9, and 10.

2. *Niles Weekly Register*, vol. 48, 23 May 1835.

3. David, Goldman, and Bain (1960), p. 201; and Bain and Parris (1973) pp. 186-187.

4. David, Goldman, and Bain (1960), pp. 264-265.

5. Ibid., p. 258.

6. Bain and Parris (1973), pp. 294-295.

7. Ibid., p. 315.

8. Davis (1967), p. 28.

9. These stories are told at greater length in ibid., chap. 3.

10. Ibid., p. 33; David, Goldman, and Bain (1960), p. 229; Manning J. Dauer et al., "Toward a Model State Presidential Primary Law," *American Political Science Review* 50 (March 1956):138-153.

11. Commission on the Democratic Selection of Presidential Nominees, *The Democratic Choice*, 1968.

12. Crotty (1978), chap. 1. Much of this part of the chapter is based primarily on this source, although the present writer was at the 1968 convention as a consultant to the Committee on Rules, and served later as a consultant to the O'Hara commission.

13. Ibid.

14. Commission on Party Structure and Delegate Selection (1970).

15. Ibid., p. 40.

16. Ibid., p. 44.

17. Ibid., p. 45.

18. Crotty (1978), chap. 4.

19. Ibid.

20. *Congressional Quarterly Weekly Report*, 15 February 1975, p. 334.

21. Democratic National Convention, Committee on Rules, Report (1972), article 18, section 4.

22. Transcript of Mikulski commission deliberations, 21 September 1973, p. 230.

23. Commission on Delegate Selection and Party Structure (1974). Much of this part of the chapter is based on a paper by Paul T. David and James W. Ceaser, "Operations and Consequences of Proportional Representation in National Convention Delegate Selection, 1976" (Presented in the alternative program at the Annual Meeting of the American Political Science Association, Washington, D.C., September 1976).

24. Democratic National Convention, Rules Committee, Report (1976).

25. For a report on the final commission meeting, see "White House Is a Winner on Rules Changes," *Congressional Quarterly Weekly Report*, 28 January 1978, pp. 199-200.

26. On *Cousins* v. *Wigoda*, see *Congressional Quarterly Weekly Report*, 15 February 1975, p. 334.

27. For a discussion of the work of these bodies, see Crotty (1977), pp. 255-260.

28. *Washington Post*, 24 February 1976; *Congressional Quarterly Weekly Report*, 28 February 1976, p. 468.

29. Quoted in Commission on Presidential Nomination and Party Structure (1977), part 1, p. 23.

References

Books

Bain, Richard C., and Parris, Judith H. *Convention Decisions and Voting Records*. 2d ed. Washington, D.C.: The Brookings Institution, 1973.

Ceaser, James W. *Presidential Selection: Theory and Development*. Princeton, N.J.: Princeton University Press, 1979.

Crotty, William. *Decision for the Democrats: Reforming the Party Structure*. Baltimore, Md.: The Johns Hopkins Press, 1978.

———. *Political Reform and the American Experiment*. New York: Thomas Y. Crowell, 1977.

David, Paul T., and Ceaser, James W. *Proportional Representation in Delegate Selection: Some Aspects of Presidential Nominating Politics in 1976*. Charlottesville: University Press of Virginia, 1979.

David, Paul T.; Goldman, Ralph M.; and Bain, Richard C. *The Politics of National Party Conventions*. Washington, D.C.: The Brookings Institution, 1960.

Davis, James W. *Presidential Primaries: Road to the White House*. New York: Thomas Y. Crowell, 1967.

Keech, William R., and Matthews, Donald R. *The Party's Choice*. Washington: The Brookings Institution, 1978.

Matthews, Donald R., ed. *Perspectives on Presidential Selection*. Washington: The Brookings Institution, 1973.

Ranney, Austin. *Curing the Mischiefs of Faction: Party Reform in America*. Berkeley: University of California Press, 1975.

Schier, Steven F. *The Rules of the Game: Democratic National Convention Delegate Selection in Iowa and Wisconsin*. Washington, D.C.: University Press of America, 1980.

Sullivan, Denis G.; Pressman, Jeffrey L.; and Arterton, F. Christopher. *Explorations in Convention Decision Making*. San Francisco: W.H. Freeman, 1976.

Sullivan, Denis G.; Pressman, Jeffrey L.; Rage, B.; and Lyons, John J. *The Politics of Representation*. New York: St. Martin's Press, 1974.

Watson, Richard A. *The Presidential Contest*. New York: John Wiley and Sons, 1980.

Wayne, Stephen J. *The Road to the White House*. New York: St. Martin's Press, 1980.

Articles, Reports, and Papers

Cavala, William. "Changing the Rules Changes the Game: Party Reform and the 1972 California Delegation to the Democratic National Convention." *American Political Science Review* 68 (March 1974):27-42.

Commission on Delegate Selection and Party Structure (Mikulski commission). *Report, as Amended*. Washington, D.C.: Democratic National Committee, 1974.

Commission on the Democratic Selection of Presidential Nominees (Hughes commission). *The Democratic Choice*. 1968.

Commission on Party Structure and Delegate Selection (McGovern commission). *Mandate for Reform*. Washington, D.C.: Democratic National Committee, 1970.

Commission on Presidential Nomination and Party Structure (Winograd commission). Preliminary Report, 2 parts, 1977.

_____. *Openness, Participation and Party Building: Reforms for a Stronger Democratic Party*. Washington, D.C.: Democratic National Committee, 1978.

Crotty, William. "Anatomy of a Challenge: The Chicago Delegation to the Democratic National Convention." In *Cases in American Politics* edited by Robert L. Peabody. New York: Praeger, 1976. Events leading to the decision in *Cousins* v. *Wigoda*.

_____. "Assessing a Decade of Reform." Paper presented to the Annual Meeting of the American Political Science Association, New York, September 1979.

Jackson, John S., III; Brown, Jesse C.; and Brown, Barbara L. "Recruitment, Representation and Political Values." *American Politics Quarterly* 6 (April 1978):187-212.

Jackson, John S., III, and Hitlin, R.A. "A Comparison of Party Elites: the Sanford Commission and the Delegates to the Democratic Mid-Term Conference." *American Politics Quarterly* 4 (October 1976):441-482.

Kirkpatrick, Jeane. "Representation in the American National Conventions: The Case of 1972." *British Journal of Political Science* 5 (July 1975):313-322.

Lengle, James, and Shafer, Byron. "Primary Rules, Political Power, and Social Change." *American Political Science Review* 70 (March 1976):25-40.

Ruback, Thomas H. "Amateurs and Professions: Delegates to the 1972 Republican National Convention." *Journal of Politics* 37 (May 1975):436-467.

_____. "Recruitment and Motives for National Convention Activism: Republican Delegates in 1972 and 1976." In *The Party Symbol*, edited by William Crotty. San Francisco: W.H. Freeman, 1980.

Rubin, Richard L. "Presidential Primaries: Continuities, Dimensions of Change, and Political Implications." In *The Party Symbol*, edited by William Crotty. San Francisco: W.H. Freeman, 1980.

Soule, John W., and Clarke, James W. "Amateurs and Professions: A Study of Delegates to the 1968 Democratic National Convention." *American Political Science Review* 64 (September 1970):888-898.

Soule, John W., and McGrath, W. "A Comparative Study of Presidential Nominating Conventions: the Democrats 1968 and 1972." *American Journal of Political Science* 19 (August 1975):501-518.

7 Campaign-Finance Regulation: Politics and Policy in the 1970s

Gary C. Jacobson

Introduction

"As it is now," Speaker of the House Thomas P. ("Tip") O'Neil once said, "there are four parts to any campaign. The candidate, the issues of the candidate, the campaign organization, and the money to run the campaign with. Without the money you can forget the other three."[1] Most academic students of the subject agree: money is by no means the only important component of political campaigns, but it is essential. Adequate funding is not a sufficient condition of electoral success because many other factors apart from campaigns (and, therefore, from campaign resources) affect election results: voters' partisan habits, national political tides, issues and events, candidates' personalities and skills, incumbency, and many others. But money is necessary because campaigns do affect election outcomes, and campaigns cost money.[2]

Competitive elections require adequate finances; democratic competition depends on the ability of opposing candidates to acquire the necessary funds to conduct serious campaigns. But the quality of democracy also depends on *how* the money is acquired, who supplies it and what they get in return. Privately financed elections—the rule in the United States until the 1976 presidential campaigns—inevitably raise a basic dilemma. Democratic ideology requires a rough political equality—one person, one vote. Money is distributed very unequally, however; insofar as it is used effectively as a political resource, political equality is violated. It is no coincidence that campaign finance has been a recurring political issue in the United States; it partakes of the inherent tension within our political tradition between the values of political equality and those of competitive economic individualism.

Our most recent national experience with campaign-finance reform at the federal level provides an object study of how this dilemma has been faced under current political conditions and practices. Fundamental alterations in the way political campaigns are financed have the capacity to restructure the political game decisively, if not always predictably. That, of course, is frequently their intention. The political stakes are high; the in-

---

Material in this chapter was previously published in Gary C. Jacobson, *Money in Congressional Elections* (New Haven, Conn.: Yale University Press, 1980). Reprinted by permission.

terests involved are numerous and conflicting; the issues raised reach to the core of democratic theory and practice; and the real consequences of policy changes are by no means easy to anticipate. The process of reform is therefore neither simple, smooth, nor necessarily consistent; and the effects of reform include some ironic surprises.

The first question requiring consideration is why campaign-finance reform was seriously pursued in the first place; politicians had, after all, managed to survive and prosper under an old system of regulation that had been thoroughly unworkable since its inception forty years earlier. Once this question is answered, the reform process itself is open to investigation: the actors, forces, events, practices, and ideas that shaped the system of campaign-finance regulation now in force. A further question then arises: what difference has campaign-finance reform made in the way the American political system operates? And once these things have been considered, the way is open to speculation about possibilities for further evolution of federal policy dealing with money in elections.

The Past: Nonregulation of Campaign Money

Although federal laws regulating campaign-finance practices have been on the books since the beginning of this century, serious efforts to control, or even to monitor, the flow of funds in election campaigns were not undertaken until the 1960s. For forty years previously the Federal Corrupt Practices Act of 1925, with some minor subsequent amendments (in the Hatch Act of 1940), was the major instrument of campaign-finance regulation. It was neither enforced nor enforceable. Its impossibly low ceilings on campaign spending ($10,000 to $25,000 for Senate candidates, $2,500 to $5,000 for House candidates) were easily circumvented by the fiction that candidates remained ignorant of, and thus not responsible for, most of the money spent on their behalf. The $5,000 individual-contribution limit was equally futile; it applied only to gifts to a single committee, so campaigns merely multiplied committees so that they could legally accept as much as anyone was willing to give. The law did not apply to primary elections at all. And in any case, its legal strictures were not enforced. No candidate was ever prosecuted for failing to report expenditures under the act, although many could have been.

The Corrupt Practices Act was uniformly regarded as a failure, and there were regular complaints about the questionable financial transactions it both required and permitted, but no strong support for reform developed until the 1960s. During that decade, however, the atmosphere changed dramatically; and in the early 1970s decisive and far-reaching changes in federal campaign-finance policy were enacted. It is not likely, moreover, that the cycle of campaign-finance reform is yet complete.

The underlying causes of this change are not hard to find; the most salient was the startling rise in the cost of major political campaigns. When the amount of money deemed adequate to finance a competitive campaign was relatively small, the obvious defects of regulation under the Corrupt Practices Act were tolerable, if bothersome and disquieting to some. Candidates who felt uncomfortable with the subterfuges necessary to finance their campaigns could still put up with them; it was easier to forgo questionable private contributions when the money did not seem so necessary. The possibly corrupting influence of campaign gifts was more easily perceived as petty when the amounts involved were comparatively small.

Once the cost of campaigning entered a period of rapid growth, however, the demand for ever larger campaign kitties exaggerated all the problems and the potential for abuse inherent in the system and brought campaign-finance reform issues forcefully to the attention of both "good-government" or "public-interest" groups and elected officials themselves. Once called into question, the old regulations found scarcely a defender; the issue was not whether campaign-finance policy should be changed, but *how* it should be changed.

The Growing Cost of Campaigning

A set of widely disseminated figures compiled by the Citizens' Research Foundation, a nonprofit organization specializing in campaign-finance research, gives a clear picture of the overall increase in campaign costs. Estimates of total campaign spending in presidential-election years between 1952 and 1972 were:

1952	$140 million
1956	155 million
1960	175 million
1964	200 million
1968	300 million
1972	425 million[3]

These aggregate figures hide some important differences among elections, however; the overall real-dollar increase of more than 200 percent between 1952 and 1972 did not occur equally across all types of contests. Presidential-election costs rose much faster than those for other offices. General-election expenditures for presidential candidates grew an estimated 400 percent (in constant dollars) over these years;[4] total presidential-election costs, including those of primaries, rose more than 360 percent. By comparison, expenditures for other offices increased by less than 50 percent over the same period. The Citizens' Research Foundation estimated that $138 million was spent on the presidential campaigns in 1972; the entire cost of electing all 435 Members of the House of Representatives and a third of the Senate was only $98 million.[5]

The costs of presidential campaigns grew much more rapidly than those of other campaigns because the underlying causes of the growth acted most directly on presidential campaigning. The advent of television as a campaign medium is usually accorded the most blame, though it was actually only one element in a more general transformation of campaign technology—and political conditions—that drove up campaign expenses. Television became an important campaign tool at a time when party organizations had already suffered a long-term decline in vitality; it rose to dominance in a period when an increasing number of voters were detaching themselves from the parties as well. The atrophy of parties encouraged—and was encouraged by—the development of professional campaign management. Like other professionals, campaign-management experts set about rationalizing their field of operation as much as possible. They adapted modern techniques of market research, advertising (especially broadcast advertising), and personnel management for use in political campaigns. They augmented the customary campaign arsenal with professionally conducted polls, computerized data processing, and individualized mailings; and they brought modern managerial approaches to bear on traditional campaign operations.[6] In doing so, they hastened the transition to ever more candidate-centered campaigns, making further inroads into the domains once dominated by parties. They also increased the cost of campaigning sharply; the entire package of new technology—not just television—is expensive.[7]

Because it is so expensive, modern campaign technology is not available to every candidate; in general, it is only practical in large campaigns. This is particularly true of television, which requires the candidate to pay for the audience reached regardless of whether or not its members are potential constituents. Only presidential campaigns can use network television efficiently, and even local television is of limited utility to most House candidates; it is much better suited to Senate and other statewide campaigns.[8] It is no surprise, then, that presidential-campaign expenses have grown most rapidly, or that the increase for Senate campaigns has been, based on the scanty evidence available, proportionately greater than that for House campaigns.[9] This latter difference is one reason for the divergent approaches to campaign-finance reform revealed by the actions of the two houses of Congress.

Technological and political changes are not the only sources of increased campaign costs. Economic growth over the same period made more money available; until 1972, campaign expenses were not growing any faster than either the Gross National Product or the national budget. Both the growth in federal spending and the extension of federal regulatory activity raised the political stakes enormously; decisions made by federal officials could have drastic effects on the prosperity of whole industries.[10] Campaign contributions that could assure favorable action—or even simple attention—became increasingly prudent investments. The supply as well as the demand for campaign money was on the rise; small wonder that campaign spending grew as it did.

The ever growing quantities of money seen as necessary to run competitive campaigns intensified the contradiction between democratic ideals and the actual system of campaign finance. Greater costs meant greater reliance on wealthy individuals and groups and therefore increased the threat of politics dominated by wealth rather than votes. A spate of millionaire candidates (mostly for the Senate) fed fears that politics would become a rich man's preserve. The potential for corruption escalated sharply; ironically, actual corruption reached its apogee in the financial dealings of the 1972 Nixon campaign, which *followed* (and was, in part, exposed by) the first major revision of campaign-finance regulation since 1925. The Watergate investigations revealed just how corrupt the process could become if exploited vigorously, systematically, and without an iota of self-restraint.

Reform Goals

Even before the appearance of such undeniable evidence that the old system was no longer tolerable, a consensus had developed that drastic changes were necessary. It was a comparatively simple matter to find agreement that the current policy was hopelessly misguided; it was hard to defend a regulatory scheme of which a congressman could truthfully say, "there is not a member of Congress, myself included, who has not knowingly evaded its purpose in one way or another."[11] Agreement could even be found on some general purposes of reform. The real difficulty lay in finding agreement on what exactly should be done to reform the old system in order to achieve ostensibly shared goals.

The fundamental purpose of reform was to ensure that money did not corrupt the political system, that elected officials were responsive to the people who elected them rather than to the people or interest groups who financed their campaigns. But it was equally important to assure candidates of access to adequate resources for waging competitive campaigns under current political conditions. A variety of means to achieve these objectives were suggested, adopted, and rejected. No change in the political rules is neutral; any change affects the distribution of political opportunity and influence, helping some and damaging others. Campaign-finance reform developed in a pattern that largely reflects the perspectives and interests of those participating in the policy-making process and their responses to rather immediate events and experiences. It is therefore essential to review the cast of participants.

Members of Congress

The most important makers of campaign-finance policy are, of course, Members of Congress. A peculiar regulatory situation thus exists: those most directly affected write the rules. Members have to live with whatever system of regulation is in force; they suffer from its defects and benefit from any advantages it confers. Their attitudes toward campaign-finance issues tend, for many reasons, to be equivocal. On the one hand, most intensely dislike the process of raising funds. Hubert Humphrey called it a "disgusting, degrading, demeaning experience";[12] his sentiments are not unique. Senator Pastore said he felt "embarassed and humiliated" when soliciting contributions; "it is not a pleasant thing to do. You almost feel like a beggar. . . . You are putting your self-respect on the line."[13] Senator Abourezk found the process "demeaning, corrupting, and absolutely without any redeeming value."[14] Even congressmen who find value in compelling members to generate financial support admit that it "can be difficult and occasionally embarassing."[15]

On the other hand, incumbents raise campaign funds much more easily than do their opponents; data from the 1972, 1974, and 1976 elections indicate that they typically outspend challengers almost two to one.[16] One scholar cites the exemplary case of a congressman who "said that he had had great difficulty raising money when he first ran for Congress, but . . . now, after nine terms, he did not need to solicit at all. In fact, he found that he got larger contributions if he just waited for people to send them than if he asked for them."[17]

Yet the money they do raise is not always without strings, and this is another source of unease. Senator Scott thought that "every person in the Senate . . . realizes that every time a contribution is made, some sort of obligation is implied at least by the general public, some sort of obligation is very often felt by the recipient, some sort of obligation may be in the mind of the donor. The obligation may be slight, . . . some minor favor. On the other hand, the donor may expect benefits which he has no right whatever to expect."[18]

Members argue endlessly about how much of a problem this really is. Everyone knows instances of direct quid pro quo exchanges; favorite examples, however, are from the executive branch: ambassadorships granted in return for large contributions or, later, Watergate. It is a touchy point. Members who argue that campaign gifts are corrupting are challenged to give specifics; their adversaries aver that certainly *their* contributors want nothing more than to support the broad principles the candidate shares. In response, those supporting the corruption thesis are forced to argue that the mere *appearance* of corruption is sufficiently damaging to public confidence in political leaders and institutions to require reforms that would deal with it, apparent or real. Senator Stevenson, for example, took the position that "financing campaigns now compels us . . . to accept large contributions from individuals, also from entities which have interests in Government. Those interests, either deliberately or quite innocently, are rewarded. And on the basis of circumstantial evidence, the public can draw only one conclusion—and they are drawing that conclusion."[19]

Congressional Perspectives on Reform

Members of Congress maintain a variety of notions about how far campaign-finance reform ought to go and, no less important, how reforms are to be administered. From their point of view, many diverse and frequently conflicting considerations are involved. They are, first of all, incumbents; they have succeeded at the game and have little interest in altering its rules in any way that threatens further success. They are also partisans and therefore attentive to the affects of policy changes on balance of advantages and resources between Democrats and Republicans. Their partisan attachments are, with very few exceptions, to the two major parties, so they also have a stake in maintaining a two-party system against the possible inroads of additional parties. Ideological perspectives, which coincide imperfectly with partisan divisions, add another dimension.

Furthermore, all members are experts on campaigning and on campaign finance. All have raised and spent money in successful political campaigns. But they are experts through experience in a wide variety of quite different electoral environments; each has a fund of idiosyncratic knowledge that may or may not have general relevance. Senate contests are run under extremely diverse circumstances, and not only because states vary so much in population and physical size. So are House contests; compare a campaign for North Dakota's single House seat to one for New York's 20th District on the West Side of Manhattan. And difference in primary-election rules and customs supply another set of variables.

The Incumbency Factor

Of these considerations, incumbency is without doubt the most important. For one thing, incumbency has become the dominant factor in congressional elections, particularly those for the House. The familiar figures on the decline of competition for House seats have spawned an extensive literature documenting and explaining the phenomenon.[20] For present purposes it is sufficient to note that the decline has occurred and that incumbents are not only winning with striking frequency (usually well over 90 percent of those running are reelected; the figure has been as high as 97 percent), but they are winning by even wider margins than in the past; there are fewer marginal (that is, competitive) seats.[21] Incumbency has also become more important in Senate elections, but Senate incumbents have never been so consistently successful as House incumbents and still remain twice as vulnerable on election day—another source of House-Senate differences on campaign-finance issues.[22]

Incumbency is also important because of the different ways campaigning—and campaign spending—affect the electoral fates of incumbents and nonincumbents. Incumbent members of Congress have supplied themselves with an extensive and steadily growing list of official resources. A recent estimate is that Representatives enjoy salary, staff, communications, travel, and office allowances "worth between a half million and a million dollars over the course of a two year term"; even more is provided Senators.[23] Most members freely use these resources to pursue reelection.[24] They advertise themselves, their accomplishments, and their views on a continuous basis, so that the additional campaigning that takes place during the formal campaign period has comparatively little impact on their overall level of support.

For challengers and other nonincumbents, however, the campaign period is crucial. They have no chance whatever if they cannot get the attention of voters; they need to make themselves known, and they must also take care to ensure that they are perceived in the best possible light. Money is a critical resource in this project; it buys access to the means of reaching voters—radio, television, newspapers, billboards, telephones, mailings, bumper stickers, rallies, and so forth—and supports the campaign organization as well. Nonincumbents' finances have an important effect on how well they do.

I have reported the evidence for this conclusion in detail elsewhere and so will only summarize it here.[25] In both House and Senate elections, the data show clearly that the more challengers spend, the better they do. Controlling for other factors (their party, the strength of that party in the constituency, their opponent's spending), House challengers typically gain about 1 percent of the vote for every $10,000 they spend. Incumbents actually do *worse* the more they spend, but only because they spend more in response to a serious challenge; with challengers' spending controlled, incumbent spending has little or no statistical affect on the outcomes of these elections. The pattern for Senate elections is similar. These findings stand even when the potential problem of reciprocal causation is taken into account; it is not simply that challengers receive more money when expected (correctly) to do well; rather, they do better the more they spend largely *because* of the spending.[26]

The implications of these findings are plain. Measures that increase campaign spending help challengers; those that restrict it help incumbents. Any increase in spending by *both* candidates favors challengers; any decrease favors incumbents. And it is, of course, incumbent congressmen who write campaign-finance legislation. Mayhew, who makes a very persuasive case that much of what congressmen do is best explained by the simple premise that they are "single-minded seekers of reelection,"[27] argues that "in a good many ways the interesting division in congressional politics is not between Democrats and Republicans, but between politicians in and out of office. Looked at from one angle, . . . it has the appearance of a cross-party conspiracy among incumbents to keep their jobs."[28] It would be remarkable indeed if the interests of incumbent Members were ignored when changes in campaign-finance policy are contemplated. They are not.

Partisan Considerations

The principal barrier to the exclusive dominance of incumbent-protection concerns is partisanship; although frequently diluted by incumbency considerations, partisan interests are never irrelevant and, in some important instances, have been decisive. Interested participants outside Congress—presidents, national party leaders, state and local partisans—have been quick to perceive potential gains and losses for their causes from changes in campaign-finance policy and have actively injected these concerns directly into the policy debate. Broadly speaking, partisans on both sides seek, first, to protect their own sources of funds (Democrats, for example, carefully avoid imposing new limits on what labor can do for them); second, to expand those sources; and third, to cut back on the resources available to the other party.

Other Active Participants and Their Concerns

Congress regulates campaign finance for presidential elections as well as for its own, so presidential politics is another constant factor in campaign-finance politics. Presidential involvement invariably takes on partisan overtones, but the president's role in making campaign-finance policy is comparatively limited. Congress has more than once shown itself quite willing to ignore or even act directly contrary to a president's wishes. And it has been much less hesitant to enact innovative legislation applying to presidential campaigns than it has been to revise its own campaign-finance practices.

Interested groups outside government have also involved themselves in campaign-finance reform. Spokesmen for the television networks and individual broadcasters have testified regularly on the many reform proposals dealing with broadcasting. Minor parties and independent candidates, labor unions and business groups, ideological organizations and "public-interest" lobbies have all taken part in the debates. A few groups deserve special attention, which they will be given later in this chapter.

One final participant must not be overlooked: the Supreme Court. The Court's involvement was inevitable. Campaign-finance policy impinges directly on political action and competition, on forms of communication and expression explicitly protected by the First Amendment. Opponents of reforms are sure to challenge their constitutionality. The Court's decisions have crucially affected the entire state of campaign-finance regulation.

First Steps Toward Reform: The 1960s

The beginning of the current cycle of campaign-finance reform can be plausibly marked by the April 1962 report of a commission appointed by President Kennedy to find better ways to finance political campaigns. The commission's recommendations were not original for the most part, but their support by so eminent a group of individuals placed them squarely at the head of the reform agenda. They are notable as much for what they omit as for what they include. Election costs were straightforwardly assumed to be necessary (the era of really spectacular growth in campaign spending was still ahead); the problem was to ensure that candidates enjoyed sufficient campaign resources without either being wealthy themselves or obligating themselves to wealthy donors. If enough people could be persuaded to contribute to candidates, campaigns would be adequately financed without the possibility of undue influence by specific contributors. Tax incentives—both credits and deductions—were recommended to encourage small individual campaign gifts. No subsequent debate on campaign-finance legislation has since passed without ritual mention of the need to broaden the base of political contributions; for reasons discussed later, measures designed to bring this about voluntarily seem destined to futility.

The other significant recommendation of the commission was for full disclosure of primary and general-election contributions and expenditures. This became a staple element in almost every reform package. It was the minimum step to be taken if *any* change in regulation were contemplated. Obviously, it would be essential to any more extensive regulation of contributions and expenditures. Conspicuously *absent* from the commission's recommendations were any limits on contribution or spending. Experience with the Corrupt Practices Act suggested that they would not work and that it was preferable to have full public knowledge of where candidates got their funds and how much they were spending. It would then be up to voters to judge whether the candidates were beholden to them or to special interests. A bipartisan commission (under the General Accounting Office) was recommended to administer the disclosure regulations.[29]

Other suggestions raised themes that appeared regularly in subsequent discussions of campaign-finance reform. One was suspension of the "equal-time" provision of the Communications Act of 1934 so that broadcasters could give time to major candidates for public office without having to give it to a host of minor candidates as well; from the beginning, campaign-finance questions were tied in with the problem of what to do about political television. Another was the first suggestion of matching grants; the commission recommended that if tax incentives did not serve their intended purpose, consideration should be given to matching all contributions of ten dollars or less with federal funds.[30]

Congress took no action on the commission's proposals—or on any other reform—until 1966. That year the first, and ultimately abortive, effort was made to provide public funds for presidential campaigns. President Johnson had included a call for campaign-finance reform in his State of the Union speech; his proposals were much like the commission's: tax incentives for small contributions, the removal of unrealistic spending ceilings, and full disclosure of contributions and expenditures. Committees in both Houses held hearings and reported bills, but no new legislation of this sort was enacted. What did pass, rather abruptly, was a proposal to allow tax-payers to check off one dollar on their tax returns (two dollars on joint returns) to be put into a special fund to finance presidential elections. The proposal was the brainchild of Senator Russell Long, chairman of the Finance Committee, who got it through as a rider to the Foreign Investors Tax Act. It came as a surprise to the administration, but Johnson eventually supported and signed the bill. It never took effect. It was officially suspended the next year until Congress could provide guidelines for distribution of money from the fund.

The handling of this legislation is revealing. The haste with which Long's proposal was pushed through contrasts sharply with the ponderous-ly slow and elaborate consideration of legislation applying to congressional elections. Debate on the bill also raised one of the fundamental difficulties with any campaign-subsidy scheme: what to do about third parties. Spending and contribution regulations can be applied equally to all candidates; subsidies, on the other hand, either discriminate against or encourage formation of minor parties. Long's bill discriminated against minor parties; in fact, any formula that does not provide equal funding for all parties is discriminatory. On the other hand, any subsidy system that does not discriminate against minor parties threatens to bring them into existence (just because the money is available) or at least to keep them going after the original purposes for which they were organized have disappeared. The American Independent Party, without George Wallace, would be a case in point.

The 1966 law was suspended because it had neglected to specify how the money might be spent and because the funds were to be given to the national parties, which would then decide how to use them in the presidential campaigns. Critics felt that this gave too much power to the national chairmen. All later subsidy proposals have required that most or all funds go directly to candidates. They would thereby diminish the role of parties yet further (as do some other elements of campaign-finance reform).[31] This has been of little concern to most members of Congress writing the legislation. Their own local parties rarely help—or, for that matter, hurt—their campaigns; it would scarcely occur to them to give parties control over public funds for congressional elections. In other mature democracies the issue is one of *party* finance; in the United States, it is one of *campaign* finance. The distinction is fundamental.[32]

Congress never took the promised action to determine how the funds that the checkoff would have produced were to be distributed, and no further changes in campaign-finance laws were made during the rest of the 1960s. The Senate did pass a major reform package (S1880) in 1967; but it was another year before the House Administration Committee acted on the measure, and the bill it eventually reported was killed by the Rules Committee. The House consistently showed less interest in reform than the Senate. Part of the problem was simply that Wayne Hays, chairman of the House Administration Committee, was a persistent and unabashed opponent of almost any change in the campaign-finance laws that did not flagrantly favor incumbents. At that time he had allies on his committee: northern Democrats who feared that new regulations would restrict labor contributions to their campaigns, and southern Democrats who did not welcome any law that would expose primary-election finances.

The main objective of opponents of this and other similar reforms was to prevent a bill from ever reaching the floor of the House. Since the old system could not be defended, and most Members were committed, at least publicly, to supporting campaign-finance reform, any reform package reaching the floor was almost certain to pass.[33]

Reform at High Tide: The Early 1970s

The struggle to reform campaign-finance practices finally succeeded in the early 1970s. Several of the reforms enacted were familiar remnants of earlier bills. But "reform" had taken on some new meanings as well; advocates of reform both in and out of Congress had altered their perceptions of both the problem and its preferred solution. This probably hastened the passage of fundamental changes, but it also shifted the purposes and consequences of those changes.

Earlier proposals, such as those of President Kennedy's commission, emphasized full disclosure and a broadened base of financial support as keys to a better campaign-finance system. The public-interest organizations involved—of which, because of its expertise and its unique collection of campaign-finance information, the Citizens' Research Foundation was most important—were basically interested in providing more campaign resources while allowing publicity to keep candidates honest and the public confident that they were. But subsequent public-interest lobbies that took up campaign-finance reform—first the National Committee for an Effective Congress, later Common Cause and the Center for the Public Financing of Elections—had a more radical agenda. They were willing to give strategic support to laws that deliberately limited campaign resources by imposing ceilings on campaign contributions and expenditures. These, it turned out, were the reforms Congress found most inviting.

The ultimate intention of these later reform groups was to put drastic limits on private contributions to political candidates, allowing only very small individual gifts and making up the difference with public funds. Strategically, pursuing limits on contributions and expenditures made good sense: it appealed to members of Congress; it reduced the flow of money into campaign coffers; it required complete reporting of all contributions and expenditures; and it increased the problems of raising campaign money to the point where public funding would become a much more attractive alternative. Common Cause, working through the courts as well as the Congress, was particularly effective in bringing about the changes it desired; its work to assure compliance with regulations once they were passed was especially important.[34]

Congress enacted major campaign-finance bills in 1970, 1971, and 1974. The 1970 bill was vetoed by President Nixon. Congress responded the next year with the Federal Election Campaign Act of 1971 (FECA), which was modified substantially, under the shadow of Watergate, by the FECA Amendments of 1974. The Supreme Court's decision in *Buckley* v. *Valco* overturned some provisions of the FECA and required further amendments, passed in 1976, to make some of its other provisions operative.[35] A major drive to enact additional changes—the most important being public funding of congressional campaigns—has so far been fruitless.

Each of these reform bills was actually a package of related regulatory provisions. It is therefore instructive to trace the separate development of major reform components: disclosure requirements and their enforcement;

spending restrictions; contribution restrictions; and provisions to increase campaign resources, including public funding.

Disclosure

Disclosure requirements were enacted with the least controversy. Full reports of all contributions, of the names of contributors of more than small sums, and of all campaign expenditures, were widely accepted as basic to any serious reform; and they were essential to any further regulation. Some civil libertarians and minor-party officials objected to the government's compelling people to reveal their political preferences by acknowledging their campaign gifts, but this objection was overwhelmed by the far more prevalent fear that secret contributions inevitably invited corruption.

The enforcement and administration of disclosure excited much more controversy. Public-interest reformers insisted that an independent commission with full regulatory authority was essential. Republican Members of Congress agreed. The alternative preferred by Democrats, particularly in the House, was to make the Clerk of the House and the Secretary of the Senate (and, for presidential candidates, the General Accounting Office) responsible for gathering and disseminating the data. The Democrats, not surprisingly, preferred to regulate themselves; they were hardly likely to suffer much inconvenience from officials who were dependent on them for their positions. Nor is it surprising that Republicans and reformers outside of Congress were skeptical about the vigor and impartiality of such regulators. The House, led by Wayne Hays, successfully resisted the creation of an independent agency in 1971; the Senate's proposal for a Federal Election Commission was dropped in conference.

Reformers did not give up on the issue. Common Cause led a continuing attack on what it considered weaknesses in the administration of the 1971 law and helped to resist proposed changes that would weaken disclosure further. It used both litigation and information available under the new law (data that Common Cause collected, analyzed, and publicized) to support its objectives.[36] In 1974, with the Watergate scandals still fresh, the FECA was amended to establish an eight-member Federal Election Commission (FEC) to enforce the law. The powers granted the commission were significant; they included authority to give advisory opinions, conduct audits and investigations, issue subpoenas, and sue for civil injunctions in court. Its structure was the result of a compromise: six voting public members, two each appointed by the Speaker of the House, the President of the Senate, and the president, with the Clerk of the House and the Secretary of the Senate serving ex officio (not voting). The Supreme Court eventually determined that the appointment procedures violated the constitutional separation of powers, and the FEC was reorganized in 1976 to conform to the Court's requirements. The bipartisan six-member FEC is now appointed by the president and confirmed by the Senate.

Although reformers won an independent FEC with substantial enforcement authority, Congress has not given over regulation of campaign finance entirely to the commission. Under the 1974 amendments, the House and Senate could, within thirty days of their promulgation, veto rules and regulations made by the commission; and they have done so. When the law was revised in 1976, this provision was altered to permit Congress to veto individual sections of FEC regulations, and other restrictions were imposed on the commission's authority. Members of Congress appreciate regulation no more than anyone else, and they are in a position to do something about it.

Reformers have succeeded in making disclosure work. Efforts to ease reporting requirements have failed; reports are now mandatory ten days before and thirty days after every election, on the tenth day after the close of each quarter (unless less than $1,000 was received or spent during the quarter), and at the end of every nonelection year. Publicity for the disclosed information has been less successful, mainly because, as a reporter observed, "the story is unreportable with disclosure, not because it is secret but because there is such a great volume of material."[37] But the information is there—for political opponents, for public-interest lobbies, for scholars; most other reforms depend on it, and this component of campaign-finance reform has unquestionably brought about significant changes in campaign-finance practices.

Disclosure regulations, particularly the requirement in the 1974 amendments that candidates designate a single committee to take responsibility for all financial aspects of the campaign, have clearly reinforced the trend toward more centralized, professional, candidate-oriented campaigns. The laws are complicated, the penalties for violating them can be severe, and candidates increasingly depend on lawyers and accountants to keep them out of trouble. Inexperienced candidates are most likely to find the regulations bothersome, and there are indications that voluntary individual participation has been discouraged by the new rules of the game.[38]

Spending Limits

It is not hard to fathom why Congress became interested in limiting campaign contributions and expenditures. The 50 percent increase in overall campaign costs between 1964 and 1968 obviously had something to do with it. So, too, did perceptions of where the money was coming from and how it was being spent. No fewer than twenty millionaire candidates competed for Senate seats in 1970.[39] The most conspicuous of their campaigns made lavish use of television advertising, and it is no coincidence that the first major reform passed had as its most important component limits on the amounts candidates for federal office could spend on broadcasting.

The Senate once again took the lead, and with even more reason than before. The perspective of incumbent senators is not hard to grasp. They were especially impressed by the few instances of wealthy candidates spending family fortunes on mass-media advertising to win instant prominence and statewide nominations. No matter that this extravagance rarely brought victory in general elections; it would be no pleasant thing to face such an opponent. It would seem to require an effort to match the mass-media spending as well as the campaign style of the opponent, and the potential effectiveness of both was doubtlessly exaggerated because they were new and unfamiliar.

Senators' feelings on the matter are plain from comments made during hearings and floor debates on the 1970 bill (S3637) to restrict broadcast spending. Senator Kennedy was moved to testify that "like a colossus of the ancient world, television stands astride our political system, demanding tribute from every candidate for public office, incumbent or challenger. Its appetite is insatiable, its impact unique."[40] And further, "the recent political landscape of America is strewn with the graves of incumbents and challengers, blitzed into defeat by an unlimited assault of television spending."[41] Senator Gore, about to be defeated in an expensive mass-media campaign, warned that "in the days of slogans, labels, image making mass communications, monopolizing the time of the television that goes into the homes of the American people is a great danger to the democratic process."[42] The examples could easily be multiplied. The dubious notion that candidates could be peddled like soapflakes was widely and uncritically accepted. One congressman even introduced a bill to ban all paid political broadcasts.[43] Broadcast-spending ceilings, at minimum, were deemed necessary to prevent wealth and Madison Avenue from destroying the political system.

The 1970 bill limited the amount candidates could spend on political broadcasting to 3.5¢ per vote (based on votes cast in the previous general election for the office) in primary elections, 7¢ per vote in general elections. It was vetoed by President Nixon. Among his stated reasons were that it was biased in favor of incumbents and other well-known candidates, that it discriminated against the broadcast media, and that more money would simply be spent on other forms of campaigning.[44] Congress responded the following year by passing the FECA of 1971, which, among other things, extended the limits to cover newspapers, billboards, magazines, and telephone banks. Candidates could spend no more than 10¢ per eligible voter (or $50,000, whichever was greater), and no more than 60 percent of the limit could be spent on broadcasting; television was still regarded as the basic menance. The bill passed both houses with huge majorities (334-20 in the House, 88-2 in the Senate).

The FECA Amendments of 1974 finally extended restrictions to cover total spending in all federal elections, primary and general. House candidates could spend up to $70,000 in a primary or general election, plus 20 percent more to raise the money; they could also receive an additional $10,000 from their parties. Senate candidates were limited to the greater of 8¢ per eligible voter or $100,000 in primaries, and 12¢ per voter or $150,000 in general elections, with similar provisions for fund-raising expenses and additional party contributions. Presidential-campaign spending was also restricted under a public-funding scheme enacted for those contests; this will be considered in detail later.

The growing emphasis on restricting expenditures and gifts to campaigns raised the question of how such reforms would affect competition for office. Spending restrictions are likely to have the least impact on presidential elections. Ironically, these best-financed of political campaigns probably depend less on direct expenditures to get the campaign message across—at least after the primaries—than any other federal campaigns. They are so thoroughly covered by the news media that even seriously underfinanced candidates (from their own perspective) will have a chance to reach the vast majority of potential voters. Congressional elections are an entirely different matter. Campaign spending does have an important effect on who wins these elections, and it is the amount spent by challengers and other nonincumbents that actually makes a difference. Spending limits, if they have any effect at all on competition, can only work to the detriment of challengers.

The question of whether or not spending limits would add to the already inordinate incumbent advantage was a central issue each time such restrictions were proposed. The argument that they would, in fact, favor incumbents, was given thorough presentation more than once in both houses. Representative Frenzel, almost single-handed, carried the point to the House. During hearings on the FECA of 1971, he declared,

What I am trying to find out from some witness is what is so bad about campaign spending. . . . I have tried to take a very unpopular position of being for a nonincumbent trying to take on the guy who has all the advantages of name recognition, popularity, access to the media, a limited franking privilege, etc., etc. This poor guy has to arise from nowhere and take on such distinguished people as you see before you. This is a very difficult task and history shows that they are very unsuccessful at it.

When you establish a spending limitation you literally insure that incumbents are not going to be defeated because the only weapon the nonincumbent has . . . is to get his name known.[45]

Senator Buckley made the same point most forcefully in the Senate. Elected as a Conservative, he remained very sensitive to the effects of campaign-finance legislation on electoral competition (he is, of course, the Buckley of *Buckley* v. *Valco*, of which more later). Buckley had the audacity to introduce an amendment to the 1974 bill that would have allowed challengers to spend 130 percent of the limits for incumbents. The amendment was debated, fittingly enough, on April 1; it lost, 66-17.[46]

Spending figures from 1972 congressional elections were available as evidence during consideration of the 1974 FECA Amendments; they showed clearly that challengers normally did well only if they spent a great deal of money—usually more than would be allowed under the formulas ultimately enacted.[47] Perhaps the strongest empirical testimony on the issue came from the several members of both houses who said in effect that had the proposed limits been in force, they never would have been elected in the first place.[48]

The reception accorded these arguments is revealing. Those making them were accused of wanting more incumbents to lose.[49] Evidence was countered by the claim that limits equalize spending and therefore give every candidate the same chance; by the argument that incumbent advantages are more than counterbalanced by political scars inflicted by controversial legislative issues; and by utterly specious comparisons to the low spending limits for British parliamentary elections. None of these arguments withstands serious analysis. Ultimately, however, demonstrations that the legislation would increase the already lopsided advantage enjoyed by incumbents were not carefully countered at all; they were simply ignored. If they were, in fact, convincing, it is of course possible that they helped gain support for restrictions rather than the contrary; few members were likely to admit such motives—except for Wayne Hays, who said, "It doesn't bother me since I am an incumbent."[50]

The actual limits were chosen somewhat arbitrarily. Bills were introduced with figures ranging from $30,000 to $190,000 as general-election spending ceilings for House candidates. Lacking any better information, each member generalized from his own campaign experiences. Each argued, in effect, that campaigns could be adequately financed with whatever amount it cost him to win his tightest contest.[51] A popular alternative position was that since congressmen were paid only $42,500 per year, as was true at the time, they should be allowed to spend no more than this to win the job.[52] For obvious reasons, this piece of wisdom did not appeal to the Senate, nor, indeed, was its application to presidential candidates ever considered. The Senate had to deal with the problem of the vastly differing populations of the various states; most suggested formulas provided a base amount to which more was added according to the size of the voting-age population. But campaigning evidently enjoys economies of scale, so that most formulas would not limit campaign spending at all in the largest states (where the most is spent), but would do so rather drastically in the smallest ones.[53]

The House consistently favored lower limits than the Senate; the limits in the House Administration Committee version of the 1974 bill were actually reduced on the floor. Only the Senate conferees' insistence that they be raised (in return for dropping public funding for congressional campaigns and making other concessions) prevented the 1974 bill from blatantly favoring House incumbents. The limits set by the 1974 amendments were probably high enough to give challengers a fighting chance, *provided* they spent the amount allotted for the primary campaign; those who stuck to the general-election limits would be underfinanced.[54] These limits were overturned by the Supreme Court in the *Buckley* decision on the grounds that they interfered with rights of free expression guaranteed by the First Amendment. The Court's position did, however, appear to permit the imposition of campaign-spending limits on candidates whose campaigns were publicly funded. And this is plainly one of the principal attractions public funding holds for members of Congress.

Contribution Limits

The FECA and its 1974 amendments not only put ceilings on campaign spending, but also sought to control and restrict contributions to political campaigns. Common Cause and some of its allies in Congress took the attitude that campaign contributions were inherently dangerous—that, as Senator Stevenson argued, "even if all of the dollars were honestly contributed and honestly spent, they would still have a corrupting influence on our politics."[55] Liberal Democrats were most likely to share this belief, more for traditional ideological reasons (money is always suspect) than from any clear conception of self-interest; a brief look at the available data would have shown that among the more prominent beneficiaries of lavish campaign contributions had been liberal Democrats opposed to the Vietnam War.[56] Their intention was to prohibit all but small, individual contributions to political campaigns, banning gifts from committees and organizations entirely.

Congress as a whole showed no interest in going this far, but limits on the flow of funds into campaigns were extended with each new reform law. The 1970 bill did not limit contributions. The FECA of 1971 restricted only gifts by candidates and their families to the campaign; the limits were $50,000 for presidential and vice-presidential candidates, $35,000 for Senate candidates, and $25,000 for House candidates. Congress was obviously reacting to the rash of millionaire candidates active in the 1970 elections. Or, as Wayne Hays said with characteristic hyperbole, "How do you balance the scales with no limit for some millionaire who moves into my district and decides he wants to go to Congress and is willing to spend a couple of million dollars of his own money to do it with? I don't want someone spending $2 million to buy a seat in the House."[57]

More extensive limits on contributions were defeated on the floor of the Senate. Republicans opposed them most vigorously, arguing that disclosure was sufficient. However, with the Watergate revelations as a spur, much more comprehensive limits were included in the 1974 amendments. This time the limits were actually reduced on the floor of the Senate. Individuals could give no more than $1,000 to a candidate for a primary or general-election campaign; the limit for multicandidate organizations was $5,000. Limits on contributions by candidates to their own campaigns were retained, and no individual was permitted to spend more than $1,000 on behalf of a candidate independently of the campaign.

Corporate and Union Contributions

The regulation of group contributions was a particularly sensitive area. Corporate and union gifts to political campaigns had been forbidden by federal law since 1907, but this prohibition was no more effective than any other campaign-finance regulation. Contributions from these sources were particularly worrisome, not only out of concern for undue influence by powerful economic interests, but also because an individual could, in effect, be compelled to contribute to candidates against his will. Union dues and corporate profits were passed along to candidates regardless of the wishes of individual members and stockholders. The issue also encourages a sharp partisan division; as a rule, corporate contributions go disproportionately to Republicans, union gifts to Democrats. Each party was alert to changes in the rules that might alter the partisan balance of resources available from unions and corporations.

The FECA of 1971 permitted, and sought to regulate, corporate and union political activity. It continued the ban on direct corporate and union contributions to political candidates, but legalized the practice of establishing separate campaign funds to accept voluntary contributions from stockholders or members. Regular dues and profits could be used to administer these funds and to raise the money. The widespread violation of these regulations uncovered by the Watergate investigations led to a substantial increase in the penalties attached to these provisions under the FECA Amendments of 1974.[58]

Congress carefully adjusted the pertinent provisions of the FECA and its amendments to treat corporations and unions evenhandedly. In 1975, however, the FEC upset this delicate balance, prompting further legislation. The FEC interpreted the law to permit corporations to solicit contributions from *all* employees—including union members—as well as stockholders; corporations could also use payroll checkoffs for gifts to their political-action committees. Unions could only solicit their members and their families and were forbidden under the Taft-Hartley law from gathering funds through payroll checkoffs. Labor and its Democratic supporters took the opportunity provided by the need to revise the FECA after *Buckley* to undo this decision and would have shifted the balance just as strongly in the other direction had it not been for the threat of a presidential veto. A precisely balanced compromise was once again worked out: unions can now only solicit members and their families, and corporations their stockholders and executive and administrative personnel (carefully defined), except for twice a year, when each is allowed to solicit anonymous contributions, by mail only, from all employees otherwise proscribed. And unions may now use whatever means of solicitation the company uses—including check-offs—although they must pay their share of the cost of doing so. This law also included a provision designed to prevent a proliferation of corporate and union political-action committees (PACs) as a means for circumventing the $5,000-per-candidate contribution limit. All PACs from any one international union or any single company are treated as one committee for contribution purposes.[59]

Contributions by PACs to congressional campaigns increased dramatically between 1974 and 1976 (from $12.5 million to $22.6 million) as a direct consequence of the publicly funded presidential campaign. Money no longer needed—or permitted—in presidential campaigns was transferred to congressional contests.[60] The largest increase was in gifts from business, professional, and agricultural interests. This has worried some labor leaders; unions, however, are legally permitted to engage in activities that directly benefit the candidates they support but that are not covered by campaign-finance regulations. The most important of these are the "non-partisan" voter-registration and participation drives they may sponsor among their members; "in-kind" assistance of this sort favors Democratic candidates and is extremely difficult to regulate. One analyst has argued that the public funding of presidential campaigns has, for this reason, clearly enhanced the political influence of organized labor and that extending public subsidies to congressional campaigns would have the same effect.[61]

Contribution Limits after *Buckley* v. *Valco*

In *Buckley* v. *Valco* the Supreme Court declared unconstitutional restrictions on contributions by candidates to their own campaigns and on spending by individuals independent of any campaign, but upheld limits on individual and group contributions to candidates. The former are, like campaign spending itself, protected forms of political expression that therefore may not be limited. The latter are distinguished as imposing only marginal restrictions on political expression; the symbolic act of contributing can still be performed and "the quantity of speech does not increase perceptibly with the size of the contribution."[62] The Court also determined that Congress had a legitimate concern with preventing the corruption, or appearance of corruption, that unrestricted campaign gifts would foster.

The restrictions now in force have several consequences. They once again favor incumbents at the expense of challengers. Given the way campaign spending affects the outcomes of congressional elections, *any* measure that limits the money available to candidates benefits incumbents. Proponents of restrictions on contributions and spending argue that, since incumbents raise twice as much money as challengers, such restrictions actually help to even things up. But they do not, because what matters is the absolute, not relative, amount the challenger spends. Incumbents also raise money in small amounts more easily. Contribution limits make it more difficult for challengers to gather start-up money, the funds needed early in the campaign to make a show of being "viable," so that further contributions and other forms of support can be attracted. More time is spent raising money—it takes as much time to solicit a single $1,000 contribution as it does one of $10,000—so less time is spent campaigning.

A survey taken for the FEC after the 1976 elections found agreement among candidates that the regulations made it more difficult and more time consuming to raise money and, in general, that these rules operated to the benefit of incumbents.[63] Incumbent senators from the two largest states were reported to have "complained about the incredible amount of time they had to devote solely to raising money due to the limit which makes it difficult to get large chunks swiftly."[64] Perhaps the only candidates not bothered by existing regulations are those who are personally wealthy, a singular irony in light of the original inspiration for contribution limits. Candidates may spend as much of their own money as they wish (Senator Heinz put almost $2.5 million of his own fortune into his victorious 1976 race), while the size of the contributions their opponents may accept is strictly limited.

The apparent difficulty in raising funds under these restrictions has no doubt increased the appeal of some form of public funding for congressional campaigns—just as some of the supporters of regulation intended. It is simply not possible to finance most campaigns adequately with small individual contributions, and even those of the size now permitted provide insufficient funds for large, competitive campaigns. As Representative Anderson explained, "the rationale for partial public financing of campaigns is to fill the vacuum left by the elimination of large individual and special interest contributions while at the same time placing a premium on and incentive for raising small contributions."[65] So far, however, this rationale has proved insufficiently persuasive.

Additional Resources for Campaigns

Public funding is the ultimate step in a long line of proposals and enactments designed to generate broadly based funding for political campaigns. It is part of the larger effort to provide campaign resources free of obligation to well-heeled contributors. This goal has been pursued in a variety of ways. One important set of proposals has dealt with the problem of making broadcast time—particularly on television—cheaper and more accessible to candidates. Reformers have frequently suggested, for instance, that the equal-time provision—section 315(a) of the Communications Act of 1934—be repealed. Section 315(a) requires stations that give air time to any candidate to give the same amount of time to every other candidate for the same office. Its effect has been to keep most stations from giving any free time to any candidate in order to avoid also giving time to a host of minor-party and independent candidates who would demand their legal share. It was suspended for the 1960 presidential election, permitting the debates that year, but since then has been kept in force despite a number of attempts to alter or suspend it again.

The 1970 bill vetoed by President Nixon included a section repealing the equal-time requirement for presidential elections only; it was widely speculated that Nixon's true reason for vetoing the bill was to avoid a debate in 1972, which would have been difficult without 315(a). The Senate's versions of the 1971 and 1974 campaign-finance-reform laws also included repeal of 315(a), but for all federal candidates, not only those for president and vice-president. The House once again objected; its members (led by Wayne Hays) were loath to give broadcasters the discretion repeal would have allowed. They did not disguise their distrust of both local-station owners and the national networks. Republicans were unwilling to repeal equal time only for presidential contests, since it would help whoever challenged the Republic president; Democrats chose not to push for partial repeal for fear of inviting a veto. Conference committee therefore dropped repeal in both instances.

Broadcasters have supported repeal of 315(a) most strongly; they have found other proposals to ease access to broadcast media unappealing. The networks and local broadcasters disagreed over the section in the FECA that requires stations to sell air time to candidates at the lowest unit rate charged to any customer for an equivalent time segment. The networks supported it; local stations, which bear the cost, did not. It is the only reform so far enacted that actually assists congressional campaigning, but it was passed only in conjunction with the 1971 limits on broadcast spending.

Other proposals designed to allow candidates cheaper and easier access to the electronic media have gathered little support. The concept of "Voters' Time," large segments of television time set aside during presidential campaigns for use by major-party candidates, was advocated by the prestigious Twentieth Century Fund and attracted some attention in Congress, but it never became part of any major reform package. Vaguer suggestions that free time be provided all candidates for federal office have been made from time to time, but the complexities arising from the varying structures of media markets and the distribution of congressional districts have kept these proposals from receiving any serious attention.[66] In any case, members of Congress are unlikely to legislate free television time for their opponents.

Neither are they interested in supplying any other campaign assistance. For example, one universally recognized incumbent resource of great value is the frank. Some reform-minded congressmen have proposed extending the privilege of free mailings to all candidates in federal elections; this has not been a popular idea. During the 1973 House Administration Committee hearings, Representative Udall was asked why he had dropped a provision for free mailings from his campaign-finance bill. His reply: "On practical grounds. I got my head torn off in the House dining room."[67] Congress did restrict the use of the frank during the twenty-eight days prior to a primary or general election, later extending the restriction to sixty days; but this action was taken only in response to litigation that was bringing judicial scrutiny to bear on this perquisite.[68] Congress is evidently much more willing to limit than to expand campaign resources.

Tax Incentives for Individual Contributions

The enactment of tax incentives for campaign contributions appears to be an exception to this generalization. The actual effect of incentives, however, has been minimal. President Kennedy's commission proposed tax incentives as a means for broadening the financial base of campaigns. The question of what kind of tax incentives has drawn a strictly partisan response. Democrats prefer tax *credits*, which can be claimed by all taxpayers and which give each taxpayer the same benefit regardless of income. Republicans prefer tax *deductions* for contributions; these can only be taken by taxpayers who itemize, who fall disproportionately into upper income brackets. A compromise was arranged and attached as a rider to the Revenue Act of 1971: credits (of one-half of political contributions up to

$25, double that amount for a joint return) *and* deductions (of up to $50, again twice that for a joint return); these amounts were doubled in 1974.

So far, tax incentives have proven ineffective. In 1972, only 2.5 percent of taxpayers took the credit option, only 1.3 percent the deduction.[69] The proportion of citizens contributing to political campaigns has not increased at all. There is actually little reason to think tax incentives should make much difference. From the perspective of most potential contributors, the victory of the preferred candidate or party is a "public good"; they enjoy the fruits of victory whether or not they have borne any of the cost necessary to achieve it. Since their small contribution would have no discernible effect on the outcome of the election, it is irrational for them to incur the cost of making it (on the assumption that it is irrational to bear any cost from which no benefit is possible).[70]

Small contributions are rational only if the act of making the contribution provides sufficient psychological satisfaction in itself to be worth the cost. Candidates who generate strong emotions—ideologues of the left and right, those associated with issues like abortion or gun control or, earlier, the Vietnam War—are best able to raise money from many individuals in small amounts.[71] Tax policies designed to encourage small contributions have little effect in either case. Insofar as candidates must rely on small individual contributions to finance their campaigns, the more extreme candidates are favored.

Matching incentives for campaign contributions are subject to the same criticism, but it is less obvious here because matching grants effectively stimulate *candidates* to more intense pursuit of small contributions. Matching grants come from public funds, however, and that raises quite another set of issues.

Public Financing of Campaigns

Public financing of all federal election campaigns, the ultimate goal of many reformers, is in some ways the logical conclusion of the current cycle of campaign-finance reform. The 1974 amendments established public funding for presidential campaigns, and in 1976 the first publicly subsidized presidential contests were held. Contrary to expectation, however, public funding has not been extended to congressional campaigns; and there are signs that the tide of reform is receding before this final step can be taken.

The successful drive toward public funding of presidential campaigns began with the revival of Senator Long's income-tax checkoff idea. A section allowing individuals to designate on their returns that one dollar of their taxes be placed in a special fund to finance presidential campaigns was attached to an important administration tax package, the Revenue Act of

1971. Division over the issue was strongly partisan, and with good reason. The Democrats were still $9 million in debt from the 1968 election, with only a year to go until the next. Republicans, with plenty of money, not unreasonably saw the proposal as a scheme to bail out the Democrats. The immediate interests of both parties dovetailed nicely with their traditional rhetorical attitudes: Democrats could support the scheme as one that would keep wealth from corrupting politics; Republicans could attack it as an assault on individual freedom and a further intrusion of government into political life. Only two Republican senators supported the measure, and then only because an amendment was adopted permitting taxpayers to designate which party would get the money—a provision that was repealed by an amendment to the Debt Ceiling Act of 1973.[72]

President Nixon adamantly opposed the idea—no surprise in light of subsequent revelations—and to avoid a promised veto, Congress delayed the law's effect until after the 1972 election and required that the money be specifically appropriated from the fund before it could be distributed to candidates. Congress did exactly that through provisions in the FECA Amendments of 1974. That law provided full public financing of major-party general-election campaigns for president (the amount is adjusted to the Consumer Price Index; each candidate received $21.8 million in 1976) and matching-grant subsidies for primary contests. For primaries, candidates who raise at least $100,000 in amounts of at least $5,000 from twenty states in contributions of $250 or less have these contributions matched by funds from the checkoff up to a total of $5 million per candidate. The law also doubled the amount of the checkoff.

This legislation also was unpopular among Republicans and would not have become law had it not been for Watergate. In March 1974 President Nixon promised to veto any bill that included public funding; the House passed its version of such a bill just as Nixon was resigning. Gerald Ford also opposed this section of the FECA Amendments, but signed the bill anyway, saying that "the times demand this legislation."[73]

The income-tax checkoff generates enough money to finance presidential campaigns at the level legislated by Congress. It has yet to prove a great popular success, however, and this has probably worked against the extension of public financing to congressional campaigns. In 1972, the first year the checkoff was in effect, only 7 percent of those filing tax returns chose the option. When, under pressure from Congress and some reform groups, the Internal Revenue Service simplified and publicized the checkoff, participation rose to 15 percent. Since then it has remained in the range of 24-28 percent. If public funding were extended to congressional campaigns, the checkoff fund would probably be insufficient to cover the cost.[74]

Public Funding in 1976

The first federally subsidized presidential campaigns were conducted in 1976. Some aspects of the experiment were quite successful; others were less so, and experience with the new law did not justify any serene confidence that public funding would necessarily work smoothly and fairly in congressional elections.

Public funding did produce some of its intended consequences. Large contributors were excluded entirely from general-election financing and were much less important for primary-campaign finances than in previous years. Nothing even suggesting the Watergate scandals has emerged from the campaigns. A regional candidate, an "outsider" without access to traditional sources of Democratic money, won the Democratic nomination and the presidency. Of the one hundred or so candidates who originally registered with the FEC, only fifteen became eligible for public funds, and only fourteen—twelve Democrats and two Republicans—actually received matching grants.[75] The threshold requirements effectively screened out most hopeless candidates. The total cost was about $68 million. And the candidates did have enough money to conduct adequate general-election campaigns.

But the money was barely adequate. The general-election limit of $21.8 million is significantly below, for example, the estimated $30 million spent by the McGovern campaign in 1972; and the cost of living rose more than 30 percent between the two elections. Limited, centrally controlled spending stifled grass-roots activity, as did the complicated regulations. Traditional campaign paraphernalia—posters, bumper stickers, buttons, hats, and so forth—were much less in evidence. Campaigns relied more heavily on the mass media because they reach voters most efficiently, and efficient use of strictly limited resources was essential.[76] Most of these problems could easily be alleviated by raising the limits and loosening the restrictions on local party activity; other problems may prove more intractable.

Administrative difficulties were evident. Part of the fault lies in the uncertainties and delays caused by the Court's decision on *Buckley* and the sluggish pace set by both the Congress and the president in reconstituting the administrative apparatus necessary to carry out the law. Some delays may well have been deliberate, a disturbing implication that public funding is subject to manipulation to the advantage of particular candidates.[77] The volume of material the FEC dealt with was very large, suggesting that providing matching funds to congressional candidates would require a formidable and expensive bureaucratic operation.[78]

Another important administrative problem was, simply, partisanship. The FEC is bipartisan, not nonpartisan, and showed a clear tendency to divide along partisan lines on issues affecting the relative advantage of the parties.[79] It is hard to imagine how it could be otherwise, since those appointed to the commission have been partisan politicians. In any case, Congress is doubtless reluctant to set up a truly independent agency to regulate federal campaigns, so this source of conflict and occasional confusion is unlikely to disappear.

It is not yet clear how the new system has affected the power relationships among political groups. One argument is that labor has been the main beneficiary; Malbin estimated that union communication, registration, and get-out-the-vote activities, none of which fall under FECA limitations, were worth an additional $8.5 million to the Carter campaign.[80] He argues that publicly funded congressional campaigns would give labor—hence Democrats—the same advantage, a point not overlooked by congressional Republicans. He also suggests that the role formerly played by wealthy "fat-cat" contributors is now played by individuals who can raise money in small amounts from many people; fund-raising ability, rather than personal wealth, is the future key to access and influence.[81] The only unquestionable losers have been the political parties; public funding has continued and reinforced the long-term trend against them.[82]

Public Funds for Congressional Campaigns

Bills providing partial public funding for congressional campaigns were considered by both houses in 1977. Contrary to the expectations of many observers, neither house enacted public-funding legislation. The Senate bill (S926) was killed by filibuster; the House bill (HR5157) never got out of committee. Congress' failure to act was somewhat surprising because the ground seemed well prepared for this ultimate step in the transformation of campaign-finance policy. After nearly a decade of legislation, administrative rule making, and judicial intervention, the state of congressional campaign-finance regulation supports a solid case for some form of public subsidy. Campaigns are more expensive than ever. Contribution restrictions have made raising money more difficult and time-consuming. Wealthy candidates, who may spend unlimited amounts of their own money on campaigns, are at a conspicuous advantage. Since it is hard to raise money from individuals in small amounts (an especially acute problem in the more expensive Senate elections), candidates still depend heavily on contributions from interest groups. And interest groups, now largely shut out of presidential-campaign funding, have redirected their resources into congressional campaigns.

Public funding offers an attractive alternative source of the necessary money. It would reduce the pressure to raise money and the time devoted to this unwelcome task. It would diminish the need for group contributions. It would also allow Congress to impose expenditure limits and to restrict candidates' gifts to their own campaigns (at least according to the usual interpretations of *Buckley* v. *Valco*), a point of no small interest to incumbent members. The 1976 experience with presidential-campaign funding encourages confidence (perhaps unfounded) that such a policy could be effectively implemented.

Nonetheless, despite support from the Carter administration and a large majority of the dominant party in Congress (and, it should be noted, despite the departure of Wayne Hays from the House), public-funding legislation has foundered. During the decisive Senate filibuster, opponents of S926 offered a variety of now familiar arguments against the bill. It would beget a large and meddlesome bureaucracy; it would unfairly hamper minor parties; it would discourage voluntary participation and force involuntary contributions to candidates. The most telling arguments, however, dealt with the effects of the proposed bill on the competitive positions of candidates. It was on this basis that Republicans and southern Democrats cooperated to kill the bill.

The Republican position was that S926 favored incumbents—hence, mainly Democrats—because the spending limits that would accompany public funds would not permit challengers to conduct competitive campaigns. The argument that spending limits protect incumbents has been offered every time the issue has come up; the critical difference in 1977 was that Republican senators adopted it as their own, speaking, in effect, for Republican challengers rather than for themselves as incumbents. Twenty of forty Republican senators had supported the decisive cloture vote that kept public funding for congressional campaigns in the Senate's version of the 1974 bill; only two of thirty-six voted for cloture in 1977. No fewer than fourteen Republican senators switched to opposition between 1974 and 1977.

The reasons for this shift are easy to understand. Republicans cannot indefinitely ignore the diminishing strength of their party; more attention to the fates of Republican challengers seems essential if the party is not to disappear as a political force. Republican incumbents who have survived the two post-Watergate elections may feel relatively secure. Republican candidates raise money in smaller individual contributions more easily than do Democrats. The intense pressure to support reform generated by Watergate has dissipated. And senators can no longer depend on Wayne Hays to keep the House from supporting subsidies for congressional campaigns.

Democratic proponents of S926 argued that, on the contrary, subsidies and limits would make elections more competitive by equalizing expenditures. It would provide funds to candidates of modest means without tying them to wealthy interests and individuals—the familiar long-term reformers' goal. Incumbents now outspend challengers decisively and also win elections consistently; *any* policy that makes it easier for challengers to acquire funds and that cuts down on incumbent spending will increase electoral competition.

The southern Democrats who helped the Republicans sustain the filibuster did not disagree with this position, but took it as a basis for their opposition to the bill. They contended that S926 would inspire Republican opposition in what are still basically one-party states; candidates would run simply because the money was there. Furthermore—and more critically—they argued that public funding would inevitably be extended to primary elections, something they were obviously anxious to prevent.[83]

The Senate bill, S926, established a general-election spending limit of $250,000 plus 10¢ times the voting-age population of the state (the bill applied only to the Senate; each house writes its own legislation). Major-party candidates would immediately be eligible for 25 percent of this total as a flat grant; contributions of up to $100 per donor would then be matched up to the spending limit. A maximum of 62.5 percent of the limit might thus be publicly funded. Candidates accepting public money could spend no more than $35,000 of their own money on the campaign. Third-party and independent candidates are not eligible for the flat grant but would receive matching funds if they raised 10 percent of the spending limit or $100,000, whichever was less, in individual gifts of $100 or less. Primary elections would not be covered.

The major House bill, HR5157, required candidates to gather a minimum of $10,000 in private contributions of $100 or less per donor to be eligible for matching funds; contributions (again, of $100 or less per contributor) would then be matched dollar for dollar up to a total of $50,000 in public funds. Candidates accepting grants would be required to limit their total spending to $150,000, and they could spend no more than $25,000 of their own money. This law, too, would apply only to general elections.

Analysis of these two bills (by estimating their likely effects had they been in force in 1972, 1974, and 1976) suggests that both Republicans and southern Democrats correctly assessed their probable consequences. Challengers do find it difficult to raise money, and public funds would help them organize better-financed, thus more competitive, campaigns. But the spending limits that accompany the matching funds ensure that, while doing somewhat better, challengers would probably not win any more frequently and might actually win even less often than they do now.[84] Southern Democrats would face more formidable Republican challenges, to be sure, but challengers there and elsewhere would find it harder to defeat incumbents because of the financial constraints imposed on their campaigns. The analysis also indicates that campaign spending is, in general, more important for Republicans than for Democrats, a consequence of the GOP's minority status in most states and districts.[85]

For years, political scientists have argued that competitive campaigns require more rather than fewer campaign resources; they have consistently recommended financial floors rather than ceilings for campaigns, and they have presented solid data to support their suggestions.[86] Neither house has shown the slightest interest in this approach. There has been no Republican support for the alternative of public funds without limits on spending. Such a system would finance more vigorous challenges without inhibiting campaigning and would probably do the most to generate electoral competition. Although the incumbent-protection motivation so easily construed from previous campaign-finance reform legislation was not as obvious in 1977 (at least among Republicans), no sizable group of incumbents, not excepting Republicans, seems ready to vote for public funding without spending restrictions. It is more likely that many members support public funding as a way of imposing such limits.

Prospects for Further Changes

Congressional campaign-finance reform is now at an impasse. Campaigns are not getting any cheaper. Under current regulations, raising money will not get any easier. Most candidates will continue to look for additional and less bothersome sources of campaign money; the few wealthy candidates who have no financial problems will earn the envy of the rest. Public subsidies—and the restrictions they permit—will remain an attractive alternative. And the groups that have been pushing for this reform all along show no signs of having given up.

But the questions raised in 1977 by opponents of public funding are not likely to be resolved, either. It will not be easy to convince Republicans that public-funding policies will not hurt their party, or, indeed, that any reform now supported by the Democratic majority is not aimed directly at them.[87] Southern Democrats will continue to oppose any system that might breed Republican opposition in their states. Both these factions easily find support for opposing public funding in their traditional ideologies. The question of what to do about primary elections—and minor-party candidates—will also remain to complicate the issue. The flood tide of reform may have crested, with further fundamental changes much longer in coming than was so recently anticipated.

The significance of changes in campaign-finance policy that have been achieved should not be underestimated. Full disclosure of campaign finances, enforced by a special regulatory agency, is a truly fundamental reform. Whatever its limitations in exposing finance activities during campaigns, disclosure has given us data that, for the first time, permit detailed assessment of the role of money in campaigns and in the broader context of

American national politics. A more precise understanding of that role could now underlie any future reforms, although past experience gives no assurance that it will. Public funding of presidential campaigns, another fundamental change, is here to stay. Many of its consequences are still obscure, but there is no question that it has radically transformed the environment in which candidates pursue the presidency.

Other aspects of campaign finance remain uncertain. No law may limit spending by individuals or groups independent of particular campaigns, even if all campaigns were publicly funded. Independent expenditures were uncommon in 1976 (and would not have been welcomed by those running the campaigns); their potential is unknown.[88] Political-action committees have a great deal of unexploited potential for growth; their future remains unclear as well. Many years of litigation must be expected as the courts try to balance the values of free expression and political association with the need for unbought politicians and elections. Again, the outcome is cloudy.

What is clear is that campaign-finance issues are not about to disappear. They derive from basic tensions between the democratic ideal of political equality and the liberal ideals of free expression and individual autonomy. They divide the parties by both interest and ideology. They impinge directly on practical problems of political competition and organization, and they unite fundamental questions of democratic theory and practice.

Notes

1. Quoted in Jimmy Breslin, *How the Good Guys Finally Won: Notes from an Impeachment Summer* (New York: Ballantine Books, 1975), p. 14.

2. Alexander (1972), p. 10; Heard (1960), p. 34.

3. Alexander (1976b), p. 17.

4. Ibid., p. 17.

5. Ibid., p. 20.

6. For an extended account, see Agranoff (1972).

7. Senator Muskie made a revealing observation during the 1971 hearings on broadcast expenditure restrictions. In 1954 he ran with three candidates for the House and one for governor on a combined budget of $18,000; his last campaign (1966), he said, cost ten times that much (Senate Subcommittee on Communications, *Federal Elections Campaign Act of 1971*, p. 358). His intended message was about the dramatic rise in campaign costs, but equally pertinent is the contrast between the *party* campaign of 1954 and the *individual* campaign of 1966. If nothing else, parties permit some economies of scale.

8. A survey taken after the 1968 elections found that 73 percent of Senate candidates, but only 25 percent of House candidates, used television

heavily. Similarly, only 9 percent of the Senate candidates polled used no television at all, whereas the figure for House candidates was 46 percent (House Subcommittee on Communications and Power, *Political Broadcasting—1970*, p. 43).

9. John R. Owens, *Trends in Campaign Spending in California, 1958-1970: Tests of Factors Influencing Costs* (Princeton, N.J.: Citizens' Research Foundation, 1973), p. 61.

10. For example, the dairy industry's pledge of $2 million to Nixon's reelection campaign and other smaller gifts to key members of Congress helped win an increase in price supports for milk worth "at least tens of millions of dollars to the milk producers" (from the Watergate Committee report, quoted in Congressional Quarterly, *Dollar Politics*, vol. 2 [1974], p. 13).

11. Representative Jim Wright, quoted in *1966 Congressional Quarterly Almanac* (Washington, D.C.: Congressional Quarterly, 1967), p. 487.

12. Adamany and Agree (1975), p. 8.

13. Senate Subcommittee on Communications, *Federal Election Campaign Act of 1973*, p. 130.

14. Senate Subcommittee on Privileges and Elections, *Public Financing* (1973), p. 71.

15. Representative William Frenzel in Senate Subcommittee on Privileges and Elections, *Public Financing* (1973), p. 151.

16. Average expenditures by Senate and House incumbents and challengers were:

	Incumbents	*Challengers*
House of Representatives		
1972	$ 50,900	$ 32,100
1974	63,800	40,200
1976	79,300	49,200
Senate		
1972	$495,400	$244,100
1974	597,800	332,600
1976	649,800	433,300

These and other data on campaign spending in this chapter are from Common Cause Campaign Finance Monitoring Project (1974); *Congressional Quarterly Weekly Report* 33 (April 19, 1975):789-794; Federal Election Commission, *FEC Disclosure Series No. 9: 1976 House of Representatives Campaigns, Receipts and Expenditures* (Washington, D.C.: U.S. Government Printing Office, September 1977) and idem, *FEC Disclosure Series No. 6: 1976 Senatorial Campaigns, Receipts and Expenditures* (Washington, D.C.: U.S. Government Printing Office, April 1977).

17. Leuthold (1968), p. 84.

18. Senate Subcommittee on Privileges and Elections, *Public Financing*, (1973), p. 34.

19. Senate, Subcommittee on Privileges and Elections, *Federal Election Reform, 1973*, p. 195.

20. See, for example, Walter Dean Burnham, "Insulation and Responsiveness in Congressional Elections," *Political Science Quarterly* 90 (Fall 1975):411-435; John A. Ferejohn, "On the Decline of Competition in Congressional Elections," *American Political Science Review* 71 (March 1977):172-175; Morris P. Fiorina, "The Case of the Vanishing Marginals: The Bureaucracy Did It," *American Political Science Review* 71 (March 1977):177-181; Robert S. Erikson, "Malapportionment, Gerrymandering, and Party Fortunes in Congressional Elections," *American Political Science Review* 66 (December 1972):1234-1245.

21. David R. Mayhew, "Congressional Elections: The Case of the Vanishing Marginals," *Polity* 6 (Spring 1974):297-304; Albert D. Cover and David R. Mayhew, "Congressional Dynamics and the Decline of Competitive Congressional Elections," in *Congress Reconsidered* ed. Lawrence C. Dodd and Bruce I. Oppenheimer (New York: Praeger, 1977).

22. See Warren Lee Kostroski, "Party and Incumbency in Postwar Senate Elections: Trends, Patterns, and Models," *American Political Science Review* 67 (December 1973):1213-1234.

23. Lewis Perdue, "The Million Dollar Advantage of Incumbency," *Washington Monthly* 9 (March 1977):50.

24. For an extended account, see David R. Mayhew, *Congress: The Electoral Connection* (New Haven, Conn.: Yale University Press, 1974).

25. Jacobson (in press).

26. Ibid.

27. Mayhew, *Congress*, p. 5.

28. Ibid., p. 105.

29. President's Commission on Campaign Costs (1962).

30. Ibid., p. 31.

31. See Alexander (1975) and Ranney (1977).

32. See Jacobson (1977).

33. A poll of Members taken by Congressional Quarterly in 1966, for example, found 208 for and 30 against more thorough disclosure requirements, including requirements for primary campaigns (*1966 C.Q. Congressional Quarterly Almanac*, p. 486).

34. See Greenwald 1975; Joel B. Fleishman and Carol S. Greenwald, "Public Interest Litigation and Political Finance Reform," *The Annals of the American Academy of Political and Social Science* 425 (May 1976):114-123.

35. 424 U.S. 1 (1976).

36. Fleishman and Greenwald, "Public Interest Litigation," pp. 116-117.

37. Kayden (1977), p. 26.

38. Kayden (1977), pp. 26-38.

39. Fleishman and Greenwald, "Public Interest Litigation," p. 115.

40. Senate Subcommittee on Communications, *Federal Elections Campaign Act of 1971*, p. 172.

41. Senate Subcommittee on Communications, *Federal Elections Campaign Act of 1971*, p. 173.

42. *Congressional Record*, 91st Cong., 2d sess., 1970, p. 11596.

43. Senate Subcommittee on Communications, *Federal Election Campaign Act of 1973*, p. 474.

44. Congressional Quarterly, *Dollar Politics*, vol. 1 (1971), p. 43.

45. House Subcommittee on Communications and Power, *Political Broadcasting—1971*, p. 85.

46. *Congressional Record*, 93rd Cong., 2d sess., 1974, pp. 9089-9091.

47. *Congressional Record*, 93rd Cong., 2d sess., 1974, p. 27223.

48. Examples are comments by Senator Tower (*Congressional Record*, 91st Cong., 2d sess., 1970, p. 11606) and Representative Seiberling (*Congressional Record*, 93rd Cong., 2d sess., 1974, p. 27247).

49. Representative Hays, responding to the argument that limits help incumbents: "The whole thrust of what I understand you to say . . . has been that . . . there ought to be not so many incumbents reelected, . . . and we have got to get rid of more incumbents" (House of Representatives Committee on House Administration, Subcommittee on Elections, *Federal Election Reform* [1973], p. 194.

50. House Subcommittee on Communications and Power, *Political Broadcasting—1971*, p. 166.

51. Representative Frenzel was refreshingly candid: "I think that $150,000 makes more sense. I suppose, mainly because that is what it cost me to get elected the first time" (Senate, *Public Financing* [1973], p. 145). Representatives Hays and Dent, in contrast, claimed that $35,000 or $40,000 was plenty (House Subcommittee on Elections, *Federal Election Reform* [1973], pp. 128-129); Hays spent $32,285 winning reelection in 1974; Dent spent $32,074 in 1972, less in 1974. Representative Young, who had just spent $35,000 to win a primary and about $200,000 to defeat the incumbent in the general election, introduced a bill setting ceilings of $50,000 for a primary and $175,000 for incumbents, $190,000 for challengers, in a general election (ibid., p. 174). Representative Obey proposed a formula that would allow about $32,000 to be spent in a primary and $48,000 in a general election (ibid., p. 295); his 1972 spending was about $64,000 for both. Representative Thompson supported a limit of $75,000, since the most he had spent up to that time in ten elections was $72,000 (*Congressional Record*, 93rd Cong., 2d sess., 1974, p. 27261).

No one, however, can match Senator Allen's campaign parsimony.

"The last time I ran for the Senate . . . my campaign committee in the primary and in the general election in both races spent a total of $34,000. I feel campaigns can be run on small amounts. In the general election I did receive 95% of the vote. That is proof that campaigns can be run for a small amount" (Senate Committee on Rules and Administration, *Federal Elections Reform Proposals of 1977*, p. 202). They certainly can if, as in Allen's case, the only opponent is a Prohibitionist.

52. *Congressional Record*, 93rd Cong., 2d sess., 1974, p. 27260.

53. See the testimony of Professor Roy A. Schotland, Georgetown University Law Center, in Senate Committee on Rules and Administration, *Reform Proposals of 1977*, pp. 477ff.

54. Jacobson (1976), p. 14.

55. Senate Subcommittee on Privileges and Elections, *Federal Election Reform, 1973*, p. 185.

56. John Kerry ($279,746), Allard Lowenstein ($285,475), and Robert Drinan ($199,703), all "peace" candidates, were among the top spenders in 1972; Paul McCloskey, an antiwar Republican, spent $321,558.

57. House Subcommittee on Communications and Power, *Political Broadcasting—1971*, p. 176.

58. Edwin M. Epstein, "Corporations and Labor Unions in Electoral Politics," *The Annals of the American Academy of Political and Social Science* 425 (May 1976):48-49.

59. *Congressional Quarterly Weekly Report* 17 (May 15, 1976):1223.

60. Malbin (March 19, 1977), p. 416.

61. Malbin (March 19, 1977), pp. 412-416.

62. Alexander (1976b), p. 151.

63. *Impact of the Federal Election Campaign Act on the 1976 Election* (1977), pp. 71-84.

64. Senate Committee on Rules and Administration, *Reform Proposals of 1977*, p. 180.

65. House Committee on House Administration, *Public Financing of Congressional Elections* (1977), p. 11.

66. See White (1977).

67. House Subcommittee on Elections, *Federal Election Reform*, p. 239.

68. *1973 Congressional Quarterly Almanac*, pp. 722-725.

69. Adamany and Agree (1975), p. 126.

70. See Mancur Olson, Jr., *The Logic of Collective Action: Public Goods and the Theory of Groups* (Cambridge, Mass.: Harvard University Press, 1965), chapter 1.

71. Barry Goldwater, George Wallace, and George McGovern raised an extraordinary share of their funds in small contributions. Conservative Republican House candidate Robert Dornan raised $241,185 in contribu-

tions of $100 or less through Richard A. Vigurie's direct mail company in 1976 (Malbin [1977], p. 417).

72. Adamany and Agree (1975), p. 126.

73. Alexander (1976b), p. 142.

74. Alexander (1977), p. 11.

75. Alexander (1977), p. 11.

76. Kayden (1977), pp. 35-38.

77. See Fay (1977); Alexander (1977), p. 13.

78. Malbin, (March 26, 1977).

79. Alexander (1977), pp. 17-19; Malbin (1977b), pp. 469-470.

80. Malbin, (March 19, 1977), p. 412.

81. Ibid., p. 417.

82. Ranney (1977), pp. 14-21.

83. See, for example, Senator Long's comments in the *Congressional Record*, 95th Cong., 1st sess., 1977, p. 13057.

84. Jacobson (September 1977), pp. 13-14.

85. Ibid., pp. 15-16.

86. See Adamany's testimony in Senate, *Federal Elections Campaign Act of 1971*, p. 608, and that of Alexander in Senate, *Reform Proposals of 1977*, p. 320. See also Cole (1975), pp. 1-5.

87. Republican suspicions are well founded. In March 1978, House Administration Committee Democrats introduced some campaign-finance amendments that would have lowered the limit on national party contributions and direct spending for congressional candidates by 75 percent. At that time, Republicans had collected $6.2 million for the 1978 campaigns, Democrats, $1.5 million. See David S. Broder, "Democrats Tilt Reform Bill," *The Hartford Courant*, 11 March 1978, p. 18.

88. Kayden (1977), pp. 40-42.

References

Books

Adamany, David W. *Campaign Finance in America*. North Scituate, Mass.: Duxbury Press, 1972.

Adamany, David W., and Agree, George E. *Political Money: A Strategy for Campaign Financing in America*. Baltimore, Md. and London: The Johns Hopkins University Press, 1975.

Agranoff, Robert, ed. *The New Style in Election Campaigns*. Boston: Holbrook Press, 1972.

Alexander, Herbert E., *Financing the 1964 Election*. Princeton, N.J.: Citizens' Research Foundation, 1968.

_____ . *Financing the 1960 Election*. Princeton, N.J.: Citizens' Research Foundation, 1970.

_____ . *Financing the 1968 Election*. Lexington, Mass.: D.C. Heath and Company, 1971.

_____ . *Money in Politics*. Washington, D.C.: Public Affairs Press, 1972.

_____ . *Financing the 1972 Election*. Lexington, Mass.: D.C. Heath and Company, 1976a.

_____ . *Financing Politics: Money, Elections, and Political Reform*. Washington, D.C.: Congressional Quarterly Press, 1976b.

Congressional Quarterly. *Dollar Politics*, vol 1. Washington, D.C.: Congressional Quarterly, 1971.

_____ . *Dollar Politics*, vol. 2. Washington, D.C.: Congressional Quarterly, 1974.

Crotty, William J. *Political Reform and the American Experiment*. New York: Thomas Y. Crowell, 1977.

Domhoff, William G. *Fat Cats and Democrats: The Role of the Big Rich in the Party of the Common Man*. Englewood Cliffs, N.J.: Prentice-Hall, 1969.

Dunn, Delmer. *Financing Presidential Campaigns*. Washington, D.C.: The Brookings Institution, 1972.

Heard, Alexander. *The Costs of Democracy*. Chapel Hill, N.C.: University of North Carolina Press, 1960.

Heidenheimer, Arnold J., ed. *Comparative Political Finance: The Financing of Party Organizations and Election Campaigns*. Lexington, Mass.: D.C. Heath and Company, 1970.

Hershey, Marjorie Randon. *The Making of Campaign Strategy*. Lexington, Mass.: D.C. Heath and Company, 1974.

Huckshorn, Robert J., and Spencer, Robert C. *The Politics of Defeat: Campaigning for Congress*. Amherst, Mass.: University of Massachusetts Press, 1971.

Leuthold, David A. *Electioneering in a Democracy: Campaigns for Congress*. New York: John Wiley and Sons, 1968.

McCarthy, Max. *Elections for Sale*. Boston: Houghton Mifflin Company, 1972.

Nichols, David. *Financing Elections: The Politics of an American Ruling Class*. New York: New Viewpoints, 1974.

Overacker, Louise. *Money in Elections*. New York: Macmillan, 1932.

Peabody, Robert L.; Berry, Jeffrey M.; Frasure, William G.; and Goldman, Jerry. *To Enact a Law: Congress and Campaign Financing*. New York: Praeger, 1972.

Shannon, Jasper B. *Money and Politics*. New York: Random House, 1959.

Thayer, George. *Who Shakes the Money Tree? American Campaign Finance Practices from 1789 to the Present*. New York: Simon and Schuster, 1973.

Articles, Reports, and Papers

Adamany, David. "Money, Politics, and Democracy: A Review Essay." *American Political Science Review* 71 (March 1977):289-304.

Adamany, David, and Agree, George. "Election Campaign Financing: The 1974 Reforms." *Political Science Quarterly* 90 (Summer 1975):202-211.

Alexander, Herbert E. "The Impact of Election Reform on the Political Party System." Paper prepared for delivery at the 1975 Annual Meeting of the American Political Science Association, San Francisco, Calif., September 2-5, 1975.

_____ . "Election Reform in its Second Stage: Momentum Passing from Reformers to Power Brokers." Paper prepared for delivery at the conference on "Political Money and Election Reform: Comparative Perspectives" at the University of Southern California, Los Angeles, Calif., December 10, 1977.

_____ , ed. "Political Finance: Reform and Reality." *The Annals of the American Academy of Political and Social Science* 425 (May 1976).

Bental, Benjamin; Ben Zion, Uri; and Moshel, Yair. "Money in Politics—An Empirical Study." Mimeographed. Revised working draft, February 1977.

Ben Zion, Uri, and Eytan, Zeev. "On Money, Votes, and Policy in a Democratic Society." *Public Choice* 17 (Spring 1974):1-9.

Berg, Larry L., and Eastland, Larry L. "Large Campaign Contributors in California: Personal Characteristics, Motivations, and Beliefs." Paper prepared for delivery at the conference on "Political Money and Election Reform: Comparative Perspectives" at the University of Southern California, Los Angeles, Calif., December 10, 1977.

Biden, Joseph R., Jr. "Public Financing of Elections: Legislative Proposals and Constitutional Questions." *Northwestern University Law Review* 69 (March/April 1974):1-70.

Cole, Roland J. "Campaign Spending in Senate Elections." Report to the Campaign Finance Study Group of the Institute of Politics, John F. Kennedy School of Government, Harvard University, 1975.

Common Cause Campaign Finance Monitoring Project. *1972 Congressional Campaign Finances.* 10 vols. Washington, D.C.: Common Cause, 1974a.

_____ . *1972 Federal Campaign Finances: Interest Groups and Political Parties.* 3 vols. Washington, D.C.: Common Cause, 1974b.

_____ . *1974 Congressional Campaign Finances.* Washington, D.C.: Common Cause, 1976.

Fay, James S. "Publicly Financed Elections: The Perils of Reform." Paper prepared for delivery at the conference on "Political Money and Election reform: Comparative Pespectives" at the University of Southern California, Los Angeles, Calif., December 10, 1977.

Fleishman, Joel L. "Freedom of Speech and Equality of Political Opportunity: The Constitutionality of the Federal Election Campaign Act of
1971." *North Carolina Law Review* 51 (January 1973):389-483.
_____ . "Public Financing of Election Campaigns: Constitutional Constraints on Steps Toward Equality of Political Influence of Citizens."
North Carolina Law Review 52 (December 1973):349-416.
Greenwald, Carol S. "The Use of Litigation by Common Cause: A Study
of the Development of Campaign Finance Reform Legislation." Paper
prepared for delivery at the 1975 Annual Meeting of the American
Political Science Association, San Francisco, Calif., September 2-5,
1975.
Hodson, Timothy, and McDevitt, Roland D. "Congressional Campaign
Finance: The Impact of Recent Federal Reforms." Paper prepared for
delivery at the 1977 Annual Meeting of the American Political Science
Association, Washington, D.C., September 1-4, 1977.
Jacobson, Gary C. "Practical Consequences of Campaign Finance Reform:
An Incumbent Protection Act?" *Public Policy* 24 (Winter 1976):1-32.
_____ . "The Electoral Consequences of Public Subsidies for Congres-
sional Campaigns." Paper prepared for delivery at the 1977 Annual
Meeting of the American Political Science Association, Washington,
D.C., September 1-4, 1977.
_____ . "Reforming Congressional Campaign Finance: The Incumbency
Dilemma." Paper prepared for delivery at the conference on "Political
Money and Election Reform: Comparative Perspectives" at the Uni-
versity of Southern California, Los Angeles, California, December 10,
1977.
_____ . "The Effects of Campaign Spending in Congressional Elections."
American Political Science Review, (June 1978):469-491.
Kayden, Xandra. "Report of a Conference on Campaign Finance Based
on the Experience of the 1976 Presidential Campaigns." Report to the
Campaign Finance Study Group of the Institute of Politics, John F.
Kennedy School of Government, Harvard University, 1977.
McKeogh, Kevin L. *Financing Campaigns for Congress: Contribution Pat-
terns of National-Level Party and Non-Party Committees, 1964.* Study
no. 17. Princeton, N.J.: Citizens' Research Foundation, n.d.
Malbin, Michael J. "Labor, Business, and Money—A Post Election Anal-
ysis." *National Journal*, 19 March 1977, pp. 412-417.
_____ . "After Surviving Its First Election Year, FEC is Wary of the Fu-
ture." *National Journal*, 26 March 1977, pp. 469-473.
Nicholson, Marlene Arnold. "Campaign Financing and Equal Protection."
Stanford Law Review 26 (April 1974):815-854.
O'Connor, Robert J., and Sorzano, Jose S. "Normative and Empirical As-
pects of the Campaign Finance Reform Act." Paper prepared for

delivery at the 1975 Annual Meeting of the Southern Political Science Association, Nashville, Tennessee, November 6-8, 1975.

Owens, John R. *Trends in Campaign Spending in California, 1958-1970: Tests of Factors Influencing Costs.* Study no. 22. Princeton, N.J.: Citizens' Research Foundation, 1973.

Penniman, Howard R., and Winter, Ralph K., Jr. *Campaign Finance: Two Views of the Political and Constitutional Implications.* Washington, D.C.: American Enterprise Institute, 1971.

President's Commission on Campaign Costs. *Financing Presidential Campaigns.* Washington, D.C.: U.S. Government Printing Office, April, 1962.

Ranney, Austin. "The Impact of Campaign Finance Reforms on the American Presidential Parties." Paper prepared for the Conference on Political Money and Election Reform: Comparative Pespectives, Davidson Conference Center, University of Southern California, Los Angeles, December 10, 1977.

Rose, Richard, and Heidenheimer, Arnold J., eds. "Comparative Political Finance: A Symposium." *Journal of Politics* 25 (November 1963).

Rosenthal, Albert J. *Federal Regulation of Campaign Finance: Some Constitutional Questions.* Study no. 18. Princeton, N.J.: Citizens' Research Foundation, 1972.

Schwartz, Thomas J. *Public Financing of Elections: A Constitutional Division of Wealth.* Chicago: American Bar Association, Special Committee on Election Reform, 1975.

Silberman, Jonathan, and Yochum, Gilbert. "Campaign Funds and the Election Process," Mimeographed, n.d.

Stout, Richard T. *Money/Politics: A Report of the Citizens' Research Foundation Conference Held in February, 1974, in Washington, D.C.* Study no. 24. Princeton, N.J.: Citizens' Research Foundation, 1974.

A Study of the Impact of the Federal Election Campaign Act on the 1976 Elections. Paper prepared for the Federal Election Commission by Decision Making Information and Hart Research Associates, 1977.

Tufte, Edward, ed. "Symposium on Electoral Reform." *Policy Studies Journal* 2 (Summer 1974).

Twentieth Century Fund Commission on Campaign Costs in the Electronic Era. *Voters' Time.* New York: Twentieth Century Fund, 1969.

Twentieth Century Fund Task Force on Financing Congressional Campaigns. *Electing Congress: The Financial Dilemma.* Background paper by David L. Rosenbloom. New York: Twentieth Century Fund, 1970.

United States. Congress. House of Representatives. Committee on Interstate and Foreign Commerce. Subcommittee on Communications and Power. *Political Broadcasting—1970.* 91st Cong., 2d sess. Hearings June 2, 3, and 4, 1970.

_____ . Congress. Senate. Committee on Commerce. Subcommittee on Communications. *Federal Election Campaign Act of 1971.* 92nd Cong. 1st sess. Hearings March 2, 3, 5, 6, 31, and April 1, 1971.

_____ . Congress. House of Representatives. Committee on Interstate and Foreign Commerce. Subcommittee on Communications and Power. *Political Broadcasting—1971.* 92nd Cong., 1st sess. Hearings June 8, 9, 10, 15, and 16, 1971.

_____ . Congress. House of Representatives. Committee on House Administration. Subcommittee on Elections. *To Limit Campaign Expenditures.* 92nd Cong., 1st sess. Hearings June 22, 1971.

_____ . Congress, Senate. Committee on Commerce. Subcommittee on Communications. *Federal Election Campaign Act of 1973.* 93rd Cong., 1st sess. Hearings March 7, 8, 9 and 13, 1973.

_____ . Congress. Senate. Committee on Rules and Administration. Subcommittee on Privileges and Elections. *Federal Election Reform, 1973.* 93rd Cong., 1st sess. Hearings April 11, 12, June 6 and 7, 1973.

_____ . Congress. Senate. Committee on Rules and Administration. Subcommittee on Privileges and Elections. *Public Financing of Federal Elections.* 93rd Cong., 1st sess. Hearings September 18-21, 1973.

_____ . Congress. House of Representatives. Committee on House Administration. Subcommittee on Elections. *Federal Election Reform.* 93rd Cong., 1st sess. Hearings October 2, 10, 16, 25, November 14 and 29, 1973.

_____ . Congress. Senate. Select Committee on Presidential Campaign Activities. *Election Reform: Basic References.* Pursuant to Senate Resolution 60. Committee Print, 93rd Cong., 1st sess. Washington, D.C.: U.S. Government Printing Office, 1973.

_____ . Congress. Senate. Select Committee on Presidential Campaign Activities. *Final Report.* Pursuant to Senate Resolution 60, February 7, 1973. S. Rept. 93-981. 93rd Cong., 2d sess. 1974.

_____ . Congress. Senate. Committee on Rules and Administration. *Federal Election Reform Proposals of 1977.* 95th Cong., 1st sess. Hearings May 4, 5, 6, and 11, 1977.

_____ . Congress. House of Representatives. Committee on House Administration. *Public Financing of Congressional Elections.* 95th Cong., 1st sess. Hearings May 18, 19, June 21, 23, 28 and July 12, 1977.

_____ . Federal Election Commission. *FEC Disclosure Series, Nos. 1-.* Washington, D.C., various dates.

Valco, Francis R.; Haley, Roger K.; and Ortiz, Patrick T. *Federal Election Campaign Laws.* Prepared for the Subcommittee on Privileges and Elections of the Committee on Rules and Administration, United States Senate. Washington, D.C.: U.S. Government Printing Office, 1975.

Welch, William P. "The Economics of Campaign Funds." *Public Choice* 20 (Winter 1974):83-97.

———— . "The Allocations of Political Monies: Parties, Ideological Groups, and Economic Interest Groups." Working paper no. 72. Department of Economics, University of Pittsburgh. September, 1977.

White, George. "Access to Television for Lower-Level Campaigns." Report to the Campaign Finance Study Group of the Institute of Politics, John F. Kennedy School of Government, Harvard University, 1977.

Zinser, James E., and Dawson, Paul A. "The Rationality of Indigenous Campaign Contributions." Paper prepared for delivery at the Annual Meeting of the Public Choice Society, New Orleans, La., March 11-13, 1977.

Zinser, James E.; Dawson, Paul A.; and Hausafus, Kurt F. "The Rational Analysis of Voter Participation: A Recursive Model of Household Behavior with Applications to Voter Turnout." Paper prepared for delivery at the Annual Meeting of the Midwest Political Science Association, Chicago, Ill., April 29-May 1, 1976.

8 Our Two Congresses: Where Have They Been? Where Are They Going?

Roger H. Davidson

The United States Congress has a persistent image problem. The other branches of government have nothing quite comparable to the comic image of Senator Snort, the florid and incompetent windbag. Pundits and humorists—from Mr. Dooley to Johnny Carson, from Thomas Nast to Pat Oliphant—find Congress an inexhaustible source of raw material. The general public also displays ambivalence toward the institution. Since the mid-1960s, public approval of congressional performance has been notoriously low, surging upward briefly at the time of President Nixon's resignation in 1974. In a recent Harris survey, three times as many citizens gave Congress a negative rating as gave it positive marks.[1]

The view of congress held by serious commentators—seasoned journalists, scholars, and old Washington hands—is often scarcely more flattering than the public image. Thomas E. Cronin persuasively argues that we have long been mesmerized by the awesome image of the omnicompetent "textbook president," a combination of Superman and secular saint.[2] If so, we are equally plagued by a stereotype of the "textbook Congress": an irresponsible and slightly sleazy body of (mostly elderly) men approximating Woodrow Wilson's caustic description of the House of Representatives as "a disintegrated mass of jarring elements."[3] Legislators themselves often contribute to this shabby image by portraying themselves to their constituents as gallant warriors against the dragons back on Capitol Hill: as Richard F. Fenno, Jr., notes, they "run *for* Congress by running *against* Congress."[4]

Criticisms of Congress, of course, shift with the political winds. During much of the post-Roosevelt era, the presidency stood for progressive interventionism in domestic affairs and internationalism in foreign policy. True to their electoral base in the pivotal urban states, presidents were more attuned than their congressional counterparts to the forces of urbanism, minority rights, and the social-welfare state. Meanwhile, malapportionment and the seniority system lent Congress a more conservative atmosphere, often redolent of magnolia blossoms and honeysuckle. Liberals naturally allied themselves with the presidency, deploring the parochialism and obstinacy of the legislative branch, which one journalist characterized as that "obstacle course on Capitol Hill."[5]

The winds shifted radically in the late 1960s. The Nixon presidency dedicated iteself to playing out the Vietnam tragedy, while struggling on the home front to contain liberal social programs. On Capitol Hill, meanwhile, the factional balance was tilting leftward. The moderate-to-liberal wing of the Democratic party was ascendant, gradually loosening the conservatives' grasp on congressional leadership posts. By the early 1970s, loyalty to domestic social programs and opposition to foreign adventurism became the orthodox position of Hill Democrats, who took up—at first hesitantly, then with growing confidence—the challenges laid down by the Nixon administration. Those same liberals who had championed presidential leadership a generation earlier now spoke darkly of the evils of the "imperial presidency." No less a reformer than Ralph Nader proclaimed that "nothing compares with Congress as the hope for America."[6] For their part, conservatives discovered new virtues in vigorous White House leadership.

Notwithstanding its reputation for inertia, Congress now is arguably the most basically altered of all our major government institutions The changes have rendered obsolete much of what scholars and journalists have written (and sometimes still write) about the House and Senate. They have affected virtually every nook and cranny on Capitol Hill—its membership, structures, procedures, folkways, and staffs. If Sam Rayburn or Lyndon Johnson were to return to visit the chambers they served with such distinction, they would doubtless be astounded at the transformations that have been wrought—even though both men had a hand in bringing about those transformations.

In assaying the present state of Congress and its future development, we must try to comprehend the meaning of the past few years' changes. This is no simple task. Some changes resulted from pressures built up over many years; others occurred suddenly and almost offhandedly. Nor are the changes part of a whole cloth, but rather fragments of a puzzling patch work.

The Two-Congresses Thesis Explained

In pondering the momentous changes that have overtaken our national legislature, it is useful to remember that there is not one single Congress, but two. They are analytically and even physically distinct, yet inextricably bound together. What affects one sooner or later affects the workings of the other.

One of these two bodies is Congress as an institution. It is the Congress of the textbooks, of the "how-a-bill-becomes-a-law" accounts. It is Congress acting as a collegial body, performing its constitutional duties and deliberating on legislative issues.

Casual visitors to Capitol Hill are often disappointed when, on searching, they fail to find this Congress. As a large institution with a demanding workload, Congress functions more often in subgroups than as a single body. The late Representative Clem Miller once remarked that "Congress is a collection of committees that come together in a Chamber periodically to approve one another's actions."[7] Yet its many work groups—of which there are now more than ever—are attending to the public's business; their products, whatever form they may take, affect the public as a whole.

Yet there is a second Congress, every bit as important as the Congress of the textbooks. This is the Congress of 535 individual senators and representatives. They come from diverse backgrounds and have followed various paths to win office. Their electoral fortunes depend not on what Congress produces as an institution, but on the support and good will of voters hundreds or thousands of miles away—voters who are not shared by any of their colleagues on the Hill. A Washington pundit once remarked that "Congress is an extraterritorial jungle inhabited by tribesmen whose chief concern while there is with what is going on around the council fires back home." That is of course an exaggeration, but it contains the important truth that not all of what Congress represents is to be found in Capitol Hill chambers and committee rooms.

The two-Congressess notion has considerable empirical validity. For one thing, the dichotomy between institutional and individual activities surfaces in legislators' role orientations and daily schedules. Like most of us, senators and representatives suffer from a shortage of time in which to accomplish what is expected of them. No problem has plagued the two houses more than that of balancing constituency work with legislative work (that is, committee and floor deliberations). Despite scheduling innovations for partitioning Washington and constituency work, Tuesday-Thursday Capitol Hill schedules persist. Legislators themselves acknowlege the primacy of the twin roles of legislator and constituency servant, although they assign different weights to these roles and budget their time differently to cope with them. In general, legislators' margins of victory in the last election are the best predictors of how much emphasis they assign to the constituency-servant as opposed to the legislative role.[8]

Second, citizens view the Congress in Washington through different lenses than they do their own senators and representatives. Congress as an institution is perceived mainly as a legislative body. It is evaluated largely on the basis of citizens' generalized attitudes about policies and the state of the union: Do people like the way things are going, or do they not? By contrast, citizens view their own representatives as agents of local interests, evaluating them on the basis of such factors as their ability to serve the district materially, their communication with constituents, and their "home style."

In a nationwide survey a few years ago, respondents were asked to rate their own representative's performance and explain the reasons for their rating. The vast majority of the answers dealt with the representatives' personalities or their abilities to serve their districts in material ways. About three out of every five responses concerned some aspect of the legislator's district service; one out of five cited the Member's personal characteristics or reputation. Only about one out of every ten responses dealt in any way with policy issues—foreign, domestic, or defense. When rating Congress as a whole, a large majority of these same respondents placed greatest emphasis on generalized policy matters.[9]

Divergent public perceptions of Congress as an institution on the one hand and a collection of individual representatives on the other imply diverging incentives: Congress is assessed in terms of substantive policies, albeit vaguely perceived, while individual legislators are assessed in terms of constituency factors. Here is concrete evidence for Richard F. Fenno's observation that we denigrate Congress at the same time that we love our congressmen.[10]

What changes have overtaken our first Congress, Congress-as-institution? What changes have affected the second one, Congress-as-career-entrepreneurs? In what ways have alterations in one had an impact on the other? What are the current problems of each, and what innovations are likely to be invoked in coming years to alleviate these problems?

Congress-as-Institution

Our age has been called antiparliamentary, and this is surely caused by the staggering, ever shifting challenges emanating from the larger political and social environment. These may take the form of rising public expectations, fast-moving events, competing institutions, or simply an exploding workload. In country after country, parliamentary forms have been overrun by military dictatorships or bureaucratic regimes after failing to cope with rapidly changing events or escalating political demands. Our Congress is more nearly a legislature in the strict sense of the word than is any other national assembly in the world. Yet many people question whether, realistically, Congress can continue to exert meaningful control over the government's activities, given the complex, technical and highly interdependent character of current problems.

Like most of the world's legislative bodies, Congress confronts a prolonged crisis of adaptation. Most analysts are agreed on this point, although they may differ over the exact causes and outline of the crisis. Some students trace the crisis to the downfall of Speaker Cannon early in this century, others to the rise of big government in the New Deal era. The crisis is typified by executive ascendancy, as Congress increasingly relies on the president and the bureaucratic apparatus for its legislative agenda and as it delegates ever larger chunks of discretionary authority to bureaucrats. Whatever the ultimate sources of the crisis, it is acutely felt on Capitol Hill as it stretches legislative structures and procedures to their limits, and sometimes beyond.

Origins of the Crisis

Without attempting an exhaustive listing, it is instructive to recount briefly the major factors in Congress's external environment that contributed to the crisis.

1. Government, and Congress in turn, is asked to resolve more problems than ever before. In absolute terms, House and Senate workloads are enormous and rapidly growing. Popular journalistic images of idleness on Capitol Hill are simply false. One study showed that the average House member works an eleven-hour day; by every measure—hours in session, committee meetings, floor votes—the congressional workload has just about doubled in the past twenty years.[11]

2. Relative to the magnitude of these demands, resources for resolving them in politically attractive ways have dwindled. It is vexing enough to shape policies for an affluent society; in an era of limits, the task is excruciating. Rather than distributing benefits, politicians find themselves having to assign costs. In political scientists' terminology, this represents a shift from distributive to redistributive politics—a discouraging prospect for policy makers.

3. The advance of the executive-branch establishment causes acute stresses on Capitol Hill. On the one hand, legislators expect sure-handed White House leadership and grumble when it is not forthcoming; on the other hand, they chafe under vigorous leadership, sensing a threat to legislative initiative and control. The Nixon administration represented a critical period in the constitutional struggle between White House and Capitol Hill, with the president's challenges in impoundment, executive privilege, war powers, dismantling of federal programs, and even abuse of the pocket veto. Nixon's actions left the Democratically controlled Congress in a politically compromising position, since the President could, and did, argue that he was acting in the public's behalf to curb legislative lassitude or irresponsibility.

4. Today's problems do not come in familiar packages or allow for traditional solutions. Many of them transcend traditional categories and jurisdictions, not to mention two-year legislative time clocks. President Carter's 1977 energy package embraced some 113 separate legislative initiatives, referred to five different House committees plus one ad hoc body.

Nearly every House and Senate committee handles some phase of energy policy. What is true of energy is equally true of other broad-gauged issues, such as health, welfare, and international economics.

5. Long-standing trench warfare rages between authorizing committees and the taxing-spending committees over federal spending levels. Although partly a byproduct of external stresses—for example, criticism from the Nixon White House—this conflict also stems from a clash of committee norms.[12]

6. A final impetus for change—external in the sense that it emanates from electoral decisions—is the shifting partisan and factional structure manifested in the House and Senate. The Democratic party seems to have donned the mantle of permanent rule on Capitol Hill. Within the party, however, dramatic changes have taken place: in both House and Senate, the Mason-Dixon line has become blurred, with the party's councils coming to be dominated by the progressive wing. The old coalition of conservative Democrats and Republicans has faded.

Institutional Innovations

In the wake of these shifts in its external environment, Congress has been forced to adopt a variety of innovations. Several of these are particularly noteworthy: adjustments in the congressional workload, committee and subcommittee proliferation, the growth of staff bureaucracies, and the "democratization" of the two houses in reaction to the seniority system.

Workload Adjustments. Congress has adjusted its workload by restricting its scope of decision making—mainly by delegating more decisions to executive-branch agents and shifting its own role to that of monitor, vetoer, and overseer. The proliferation of reporting requirements, not to mention oversight activities, is testimony to this strategic shift. Sometimes, as in the 1973 War Powers Act, the innovation takes the form of lending formal recognition to de facto shifts if the constitutional blend of powers. In searching out changes, students of politics often fail to look beyond formal innovations—reorganization, strictly speaking; yet these more subtle shifts in workload structure are of equal or greater importance.

Heightened dependence on executive initiatives has not occurred without resistance from conscientious legislators or from those simply opposed to the drift of legislation. Congress counters by striving to regain control it senses has been lost. Today, in the wake of the Watergate and Vietnam crises, we are witnessing a vigorously reactive phase, in which legislators of all persuasions proclaim their fealty to the concept of oversight, and some even put the concept into practice. Predictably, cries of congressional "meddling" are heard from the nether reaches of Pennsylvania Avenue. The emphasis on this critical but seemingly unrewarding function is laudable. However, some of the more ambitious oversight schemes, such as "sunset" legislation, may so badly overload Congress's institutional capacities that the inevitable result would be failure followed by renewed waves of disillusionment.

Committee and Subcommittee Proliferation. Perhaps the most significant organizational phenomenon on Capitol Hill is the proliferation of work groups. The Legislative Reorganization Act of 1946 was enacted largely because it promised to streamline the committee structure, by paring down eighty-one panels to thirty-four. The shift was primarily cosmetic, however. Subjects were consolidated but not actually rearranged, and subcommittees quickly sprang up in place of many of the abolished committees.

This growth continues. In the 88th Congress, the House of Representatives had 156 committees and subcommittees, with the average Member holding down 4.3 committee and subcommittee seats. By the 95th Congress the number of House work groups had risen to 184 (actually, the number changes from week to week), with the average Member serving on 6.1 of them. Early in the 95th Congress, the Senate succeeded in paring its 175 subcommittees to about 120. This was achieved by coupling the consolidation with limits on the number of subcommittee assignments and chairmanships each senator could hold, thus assuring a more equitable distribution of committee posts.[13] The average number of assignments per senator was cut from approximately 18 (4 committees, 14 subcommittees) to approximately 10 (3 committees and 7 subcommittees).

Still, Congress boasts a very large number of work groups, and only someone unfamiliar with the ways of the Hill would expect the number to remain stable. Senators and representatives are overcommitted; virtually any day the houses are in session, a large majority of legislators face conflicts in their meeting schedules. Members are tempted to committee-hop, quorums are hard to maintain, and deliberation suffers. Committee specialization and apprenticeship norms have been diluted, casting doubt on the committees' continued ability to give in-depth consideration to detailed measures that come before them.

Jurisdictional competition among committees is the order of the day, resulting in Member complaints about the need for tighter scheduling and coordination. Attractive issues often cause an unseemly scramble for advantage that sometimes breaks into open conflict and more frequently simply escalates decision-making costs by necessitating complicated informal agreements or awkward partitioning of issues.

The Growth of Staff Bureaucracies. The most lasting legacy of the 1946 act was its commitment to equip Congress with more adequate staff resources to cope with rising workload and compete with executive-branch expertise. No visitor to the Hill these days can fail to be impressed by the hordes of people who work there. More than 13,000 staff aides now work for Members and committees, some 25,000 more in congressional support agencies like the Congressional Research Service, the Office of Technology Assessment, and the Congressional Budget Office.[14] Simply housing them is a major, unsolved logistical problem.

The Capitol Hill bureaucracy has grown in ways that betray the character of Congress as a decentralized, nonhierarchical institution. Congress has begotten not one bureaucracy but many, clustered about centers of power and, in a sense defining those centers. Efforts to impose a common framework on the staff apparatus have so far been stoutly resisted.

Considering its origins in the Wayne Hays-Elizabeth Ray scandal, it was at least reasonable to assume that the House Commission on Administrative Review (the Obey commission) would propose certain broad job descriptions (for example, what it is or is not permissible to ask a congressional employee to do); minimal hiring and pay standards (for example, comparable pay for comparable services); and at least a skeletal grievance process. The commission ventured only gingerly into this *terra incognita*; at that, its report was rejected.[15] Thus, congressional staffs continue to reflect the institution's feudal structure.

The "Democratization" of Congress. Democracy has at last blossomed in the House and Senate. Formal positions of power still remain, as do inequalities of influence. But the Senate boasts nothing to match its bipartisan conservative "inner club" of the 1950s, which so vexed the little band of liberal Democrats. In the House, the old committee barons have been replaced by a horde of committee and subcommittee baronets. The strong chairmanship might be said to have drowned in the Tidal Basin, for Wilbur Mills was the last of that colorful line of chairmen whose combination of knowledge, shrewdness, and plain ruthlessness gave them iron control over their domains.

The war over the seniority system has been recounted both in academic studies and in the mass media.[16] One characteristic of seniority is that it records past electoral triumphs, rewarding a party's centers of strength as they existed a generation or so earlier. If the party's factional balance is shifting, the seniority system distorts the leadership ranks, causing a generational gap between leaders and backbenchers. Such a gap—in region, district type, ideology, and even age—lay at the heart of the Democrats' seniority struggles. Historically southern-dominated, the Democratic party was transformed into a truly national coalition only by the Roosevelt revolution. The transformation did not take place overnight, but in stages. By the late 1960s, internal contradictions within the congressional party were too glaring to continue; inevitably, they were resolved in favor of youth and liberalism. In the House, the revolts were spasmodic and occasionally bloody, punctuated by a series of intracommittee revolts against recalcitrant chairmen; dispersion of power into the subcommittees (1971 and 1973); and, finally, overthrow of several unpopular committee chairmen (1975). In the Senate the transformation was more gradual and peaceful, hastened by the "Johnson rule" for spreading desirable committee assignments, not to mention the benign leadership of Mike Mansfield.

Republicans experienced similar tensions, although they were more generational than ideological. For the GOP, however, seniority has never been the burning issue it has been among Democrats. Because of the GOP's prolonged minority status, its seniority posts are simply less valuable than those of the Democrats. Moreover, lacking the incentive of chairmanships, senior Republican Members have been more willing to retire, producing a surprisingly rapid generational turnover.

The seniority reforms have by no means eliminated seniority. As H. Douglas Price has remarked, "seniority, like monarchy, may be preserved by being deprived of most of its power."[17] But that is only part of the story.

Seniority has been preserved also by extending its benefits to far more Members.[18] At the latest count, 57 Democratic senators and 156 representatives were committee or subcommittee chairmen. That adds up to 92 percent of all Senate Democrats and 54 percent of House Democrats. Thus, there are more seniority leaders in the House and Senate than ever before. If Woodrow Wilson were around to revise his classic book, *Congressional Government*, he would no doubt be constrained to observe that "Congressional government is subcommittee government."

These changes have made the House and Senate more democratic bodies and have given Members more channels for participating. What the past generation of reform has not solved, however, is how to orchestrate the work of the separate and semiautonomous work groups into some semblance of a coherent whole. Indeed, the advent of subcommittee government has compounded the dilemmas of congressional leadership. The next generation of reform politics will have to direct its energies to unifying what the last generation of reforms has dispersed.

The Future Agenda

Post-World War II shifts in congressional organization and procedures—shifts that came to a head in the early 1970s—have reinforced the historic decentralization in the House and Senate. Congressional history is a struggle of the general versus the particular, in which the particular seems the most powerful force. This particularism—so characteristic of Congress from its beginnings, and with rare exceptions ever since—has been underscored by recent developments.

Two related problems of coordination will form the pivots for tomorrow's reform efforts: strengthening the central leadership and realigning the committee system.

The Struggle for Leadership. Most critics argue that stronger central leadership is required to orchestrate the activities of the scattered committees and subcommittees, schedule consideration of measures, and provide more efficient central services. Vigorous central leadership might also help Congress solve its image problem, by giving the media and the public a handle for identifying what is to most people a confusing and faceless institution.

Today's congressional leaders are stronger—on paper—than any of their recent predecessors, even the legendary Rayburn and Johnson.

The Speaker of the House has significant powers conferred on him by the Democratic Caucus. He chairs the Democratic Steering and Policy Committee and appoints nearly half its members. He now nominates all Democratic members of the Committee on Rules, subject to ratification by the caucus.

For the first time since the days of Speaker Cannon, the Rules Committee serves as a veritable leadership arm in regulating access to the House floor.[19] An additional proposal by Representative Richard Bolling's (D-Mo.) Select Committee on Committees (93rd Congress), to give Rules an important jurisdictional review function, was turned down by House Democrats, perhaps because they had not yet fathomed the new role of this traffic-cop committee.[20]

The Speaker also exercises crucial new powers under the House rules. He may now make joint, split or sequential referrals of bills to two or more committees with jurisdictional claims. In sequential referrals, he may also lay down time limits on the committees' deliberations. In addition, he is empowered to create ad hoc legislative committees to handle bills claimed by two or more committees. Such a committee helped the House process the Carter energy package; other panels deal with such topics as outer-continental-shelf lands and welfare reform. These new powers have often been called into play: a Congressional Research Service study indicated that the new referral options had been used more than 700 times during the first session of the 94th Congress alone.[21]

On the Senate side, although leadership trends have been less clear, there are signs of new vigor. That tireless mechanic of Senate procedure, Senator Robert Byrd (D-W.Va.), has parlayed his mastery of procedures and meticulous attention to detail into unprecedented controls over floor procedure. New Senate rules also give the majority leader added leverage over bill referrals and committee coordination. The precedents established in halting the 1977 filibuster over natural-gas deregulation, if institutionalized, will give the majority leader and the presiding officer potent weapons in combatting dilatory tactics.

Nevertheless, central leadership is suspect, and for the time being decentralizing forces predominate. The next few years will see the reform battle lines forming around leadership prerogatives.

The ghosts of "Uncle Joe" Cannon still stalk the Hill, for legislators are reluctant to entrust too much power in their leaders. And because a majority of Members in both houses now have immediate stakes in preserving the present decentralized structure, further efforts to centralize leadership will be hazardous. Among the Bolling committee's proposals rejected by the House were those dealing with administrative management and the jurisdictional review mechanism which would have been vested in the Rules Committee. Three years later, when the Obey commission proposed administrative management in the House, it was summarily turned down. Senate leaders have refrained from implementing the bolder administrative powers recommended in 1976 by the Stevenson committee and the Culver commission (the Commission on the Organization of the Senate). Reaction against Senator Byrd's role in ending the 1977 gas-deregulation filibuster was another manifestation of Members' antipathy toward strong leadership.

Leaders, for their part, seem not to know which way to turn. Often they seem reluctant to accept new prerogatives, preferring to rely on informal powers like those that formed the basis of the vigorous leadership of Sam Rayburn and Lyndon Johnson. Yet House and Senate leaders sense that, although publicly held responsible for congressional performance, they lack the power to coordinate or schedule the legislative program. That is why virtually every leader since Sam Rayburn has supported reforms that promised to increase their leverage on the legislative process.

Committee Realignment. Reorganization efforts have so far failed to recast House or Senate committees to dovetail with contemporary categories of public problems. The wide-ranging House committee realignment proposed by the Bolling committee in 1974 fell victim to intense lobbying by committee leaders who opposed curbs on their jurisdictions, not to mention those alliances known as "iron triangles" (composed of committee members and staffs, lobbying groups, and executive agencies), which feared that structural shifts would unwire their mutually beneficial alliances. The Bolling plan was ambushed by a reverse-lobbying process, in which committee members and staffs, seeking to preserve their positions, mobilized support from groups that had previously benefited from committee decisions.[22] The Obey commission's 1977 bid to revive committee reorganization was struck down summarily, partly because of the same forces.

The Senate was markedly more successful when a 1977 realignment package proposed by the Stevenson committee was accepted, with modifications. Like the 1946 realignment, the Stevenson package left jurisdictional lines almost untouched, concentrating instead on consolidating several obsolete committees. The scheme was accepted because, by limiting assignments and leadership posts, it succeeded in spreading the workload more equitably among the Senate's more junior members.

Committee-system modernization is politically the roughest reorganization challenge. It severely upsets the institution's internal balance, for it threatens not only individual legislators' committee careers but also their mutually supportive relationships with powerful outside groups.

Nevertheless, senators and representatives profess to be profoundly dissatisfied with the present committee system. In a survey of 101 House and Senate Members conducted during the 93rd Congress, the Murphy commission (Commission on the Organization of the Government for the Conduct of Foreign Policy) discovered that 81 percent of the legislators were dissatisfied with "committee jurisdictions and the way they are defined in Congress." Only 1 percent of the legislators were "very satisfied" with the jurisdictional situation, while 13 percent were "very dissatisfied."[23] In the House study conducted recently by the Obey commission, committee structure was the most frequently mentioned "obstacle" preventing the House from doing its job. "Scheduling" and "institutional inertia" were next in line.[24]

In short, legislators are fully aware of the committee system's disarray, although they cannot yet bring themselves to pay the price for remedying the problem. Since the costs of living with the present structure are bound to escalate, we will certainly hear much more about the question.

A related problem is the need to coordinate fiscal decision making—now scattered among the revenue committees (Senate Finance, House Ways and Means), House and Senate appropriations committees, and now House and Senate budget committees. The edifice proposed by the 1946 Legislative Reorganization Act crumbled before it was even erected. Later, prodded by President Nixon's budgetary thrusts, Congress enacted the Budget and Impoundment Control Act of 1974 (P.L. 93-344). A precarious compromise between competing committee interests in the two houses, the congressional budget process is a controversial set of innovations whose eventual fate cannot yet be predicted. The coming years will witness continued competition among the committees to influence fiscal decisions, with coordination being difficult to achieve.

For an institution reputed to be slow and tradition-bound, Congress has launched a surprisingly large number of major reorganization efforts in the past generation. There have been two joint committee investigations (1945 and 1965), two major committee-reform efforts (the Bolling and

Stevenson committees), two administrative-review bodies (the Culver and Obey commissions), and a major budgetary reform. The agenda of innovations is lengthy, and pressures for further institutional innovation will persist. This is the most eloquent testimony to the continuing nature of Congress' Crisis of adaptation.

Congress-as-Career-Entrepreneurs

Other pressures for change emanate from individual Members of Congress concerned with their careers, activities, and goals. Senators and representatives make their own claims on the institution—claims that must in some measure be satisfied if Congress is to attract talented men and women, provide a workplace where their talent can be utilized, and command loyalty from its members.

Individual legislators habor a variety of goals.[25] All Members, or virtually all, want to get reelected; some have no other interest. But men and women—even politicians—do not live by reelection alone. They seek opportunities to contribute, to shape public policy, to see their ideas become reality, to influence others, and to work in dignity and sanity. In a body of 535 politicians, this jostling of individual goals and careers is bound to cause friction.

How fares this second Congress, the Congress-as-career-entrepreneurs? Here, the careful analyst faces a combination of puzzling and seemingly inconsistent developments. No less than the institution itself, the individual careers that converge on Capitol Hill are subject to new stresses and strains. Yet they do not add up to a consistent picture, and there is reason to wonder if congressional careerism has not reached some sort of turning point.

Trends in Congressional Careers

Without attempting to be exhaustive, it is useful to recite several of the leading factors (well known to students of politics) that impinge on legislators' careers.

1. Of all the factors affecting today's politicians, one of the most conspicuous is the long-term decline of political party organizations. In only a minority of areas do party organizations still serve as sponsors and anchors for political careers. Nor do voters rely as heavily as they once did on party labels to guide their choices. Hence, politicians are thrust into the role of individual entrepreneurs, relying on their own resources for building and nurturing supportive constituencies. This yields a politics closely resembling a series of cottage industries—a situation very much at odds with the na-

tionalized interdependencies that mark other sectors of our social and economic life.

2. Historically, congressional careers have grown ever longer. This trend began in the nineteenth century, when Washington was very much a transient community, and seemed to reach its peak in the post-World War II era.[26] After about 1970, however, careerism seemed to wane. This phenomenon does not appear to be caused by competition at the polls.

3. Rising constituency demands have inundated individual legislators and their staffs. The average state now numbers some four million people, the average House district close to half a million. Educational levels have risen; communications and transportation are easier. Public-opinion surveys show unmistakably that voters expect legislators to "bring home the bacon" in terms of federal largesse and services, and to communicate frequently with the folks at home. In 1976, the House post office logged 53 million pieces of incoming mail—three and one-half times the 1970 figure. Surveys suggest that future constituency demands will, if anything, be greater.

4. Citizens' traditional ambivalence toward politicians turned into overt cynicism in the 1970s. Politicians of all persuasions felt a backlash following the Watergate scandal, not to mention the Vietnam War and the perceived ineffectiveness of government domestic programs. A number of congressional careers were halted by scandal—perhaps because a "new morality" spotlighted practices that previously would have escaped censure. Campaign-financing and ethical standards were singled out by such reformist citizen groups as Common Cause and Ralph Nader's Congress Watch.

"The Incumbency Party"

At first glance, senators' and representatives' careers would seem to be thriving. Certainly incumbents are doing well at the polls. In the eleven elections held between 1956 and 1976, an average of 94 percent of the House Members and 83.5 percent of the senators running in the general elections were successful.[27] In 1976, 97 percent of the House Members and two-thirds of the senators who ran in the general elections were returned to office.

Partisan swings are less pronounced than they once were, and it appears that the Democratic party is installed as the "permanent majority" on Capitol Hill, with the GOP relegated to the role of "permanent minority." Electoral competition also seems to be on the downswing, although the picture in the Senate is somewhat mixed. In any given election year, only about 15 percent of the congressional races are "marginal"—that is, won with 55 percent or less of the vote. Little wonder, then, that political observers have remarked that it is not the Democratic or the Republican party, but rather the "incumbency party," that controls Congress.

Why is competition so low in congressional races? Academic sleuths have been hard on the trail of "the vanishing marginals," and a number of potential culprits have been identified.

Gerrymandering is one possibility: reapportionment, it is argued, gives incumbents great leverage over the drawing of district boundaries, and in fact some redistricting laws seem to have protection of incumbents uppermost among their objectives.[28] Other students believe that party deterioration explains incumbents' advantages. Party loyalties have loosened during the past generation, and voters may rely less on partisan cues and more on incumbency factors.[29] Some investigators, like David Mayhew, point to incumbents' resources, such as staff and office perquisites, which allow office holders to advertise themselves more effectively.[30] Still others, like Morris Fiorina, argue that the rise of big government accounts for incumbents' advantage, allowing them to play the role of *ombudsmen* in helping citizens cope with the massive and dismaying bureaucracy.[31]

It is hard to choose among so many likely suspects. Actually, the solution resembles Agatha Christie's ingenious plot in her famous mystery, *Murder on the Orient Express*. As you may remember, the solution in that celebrated case, as uncovered by the master detective Hercule Poirot, was that *all* the potential murderers did it! All had motives for the killing and each, in complicity with the others, did the deed.

Such is also the case with the vanishing marginals. A variety of factors have undoubtedly played an interdependent role in producing today's incumbent advantages and low levels of competition.

Recent survey findings lend weight to the thesis that incumbents' resources, particularly communications and casework, reap rich electoral dividends. A 1977 Harris survey found that 15 percent of all citizens (or members of their families) had requested help from a Member of Congress. By more than a two-to-one margin (69 percent to 31 percent), the citizens were satisfied with the service they had received.[32]

On balance, then, constituency service is a profitable enterprise for legislators and their staffs. No fewer than two-thirds of the respondents in this same survey claim to have received some communication from their Member of Congress; half could correctly identify his or her name. As we have noted, citizens see their own representatives in a more favorable light than they do the Congress as a whole. This is all circumstantial evidence, to be sure; but it points unmistakably in the direction of incumbency resources as a source of electoral success.

Legislators, especially House Members, have always been expected to run errands for constituents. In an era of limited government, however, there were few errands to run. At the turn of the century, for example, constituency mail was pretty much confined to the topics of rural mail routes, Spanish War pensions, free seed, and an occasional legislative matter. A single clerk was sufficient to handle correspondence.

The constituency-service role has been quantitatively and qualitatively transformed within the past generation. Responding to perceived constituency demands, senators and representatives have set up veritable cottage industries for communicating with voters; responding to constituents' requests; and even generating these requests through newsletters, targeted mailings, and hot lines. Staff and office allowances have grown, district offices have sprouted all over the landscape, and recesses are now called "district work periods." This apparatus extends the legislators' ability to communicate with their constituents, and it provides badly needed *ombudsman* services for citizens for whom coping with the federal bureaucracy can be a bewildering and frightening experience.

One estimate places the monetary value of this apparatus to the average representative at $567,000 annually—all provided by taxpayers.[33] This includes $388,000 in staff salaries and office space, $143,000 in communication (mostly franked mail) and travel, and $36,000 in miscellaneous benefits. The biennial advantage for an incumbent would thus exceed $1 million—and the figure would be even higher for a senator. Not included in this accounting are such ancillary services as reduced rates for radio and television recording studios and use of such informational services as the Congressional Research Service.

We may ask which came first, the congressional apparatus for performing constituency-service functions, or the public's expectation that such functions should be performed. This is the subject of a lively scholarly controversy. It can be plausibly argued that legislators are responding to what they perceive as strongly held and legitimate voter expectations. There is no question that voters expect legislators to serve the constituency in material ways and to communicate with the folks at home, and that voters give scant attention to legislative stewardship in Washington. Many legislators, perhaps a majority, evince mixed feelings about their heavy involvement in constituency service, no matter how necessary they may consider this role. Whatever their feelings, legislators have profited from their investment. Indeed, constituent activity is a key ingredient of the advantage that incumbents enjoy in popular assessments and in electoral fortunes.

Constituency service is not the only source of advantage for today's incumbent legislators. Senators and Representatives receive free publicity through press coverage—respectful or even awestruck in tone—within their home constituencies. And the legislators are favored by campaign contributors, both individuals and political-action committees (PACs). In three recent election years for which we have complete data, incumbents have outspent their challengers by 1.7 to 1 (1976), 2 to 1 (1972) and 3 to 1 (1974). In the 1976 races, the 385 House incumbents spent an average of almost $80,000; the 370 challengers (25 incumbents were unopposed) spent an average of about $49,000. Incumbents often receive more than they really need for their campaigns, given their other advantages: in 1976, the average House incumbent had a *surplus* of more than $11,000—to be bankrolled for future electoral wars.[34]

Incumbency, then, would seem to be another instance of the rich getting richer. Nevertheless, there are signs of wear and tear in the congressional career.

Congressional Careerism in Trouble?

Congressional careerism—a phenomenon mainly of the twentieth century—has recently taken a slight downturn. Since 1969 a tide of new Members has come to Capitol Hill, following two decades of uncommonly low turnover levels. When the 95th Congress convened in 1977, in fact, 54 percent of senators and 60 percent of representatives were first elected in 1970 or later.

This is not primarily the result of electoral competition. In 1976, for instance, the total House turnover was 15 percent (64 Members). But three-quarters of these were voluntary retirements (47 Members, or 11 percent). Only 17 retirements were involuntary, the result of defeat at the polls—3 in primaries and 14 in general elections. Thus, the *electoral* turnover was only 4 percent. The Senate is more hazardous. In 1976, the turnover rate was 18 percent, less than half of which was voluntary. Considering that only a third of the Senate seats are contested in any one election year, the actual turnover rate was much higher.

What has happened is that, despite generally low levels of electoral vulnerability, voluntary retirements are on the rise. Legislators, it used to be said, "never go back to Pocatello." Apparently that is no longer true. In unusually high numbers (for modern times), Members are in fact choosing to retire from Congress or seek other jobs. Voluntary retirements have risen in every election year since 1966. In 1976, fully 10 percent of Congress' membership—47 representatives and 8 senators—voluntarily elected to retire, a thirty-year peak. In 1978 retirements topped even that figure.

Interestingly, a number of these retirements occurred in midcareer, when the legislator could look forward to years of service on Capitol Hill. Especially intriguing is what appears to be an outbreak of "kamikaze runs" by representatives running for other offices that are, at best, long-short chances. In 1976 this category of retirees included, according to my rough estimates, about a third of those who ran for other offices—none of whom, incidentally, succeeded in their bids.

Congressional retirements are by no means a bad thing. Indeed, turnover during the past generation had been uncommonly low; and in the absence of meaningful competition in many states and a large majority of

House districts, voluntary retirement may be the main avenue for achieving turnover. Nonetheless, the number of voluntary retirements suggests that congressional life is no longer as satisfying as it once was.

Scattered evidence suggests that senators and representatives are weary and alienated. In a survey of House Members in the mid-1960s, a generally high level of satisfaction with the institution's performance was discovered—an attitude characterized as "a vote of aye—with reservations."[35] A survey conducted a decade later yielded not even such tempered optimism. That study, which focused on foreign policy, uncovered widespread discontent among Members of both houses. Dissatisfaction was expressed by four-fifths of the legislators and extended to all groups and factions on Capitol Hill.[36]

In a more recent survey of House Members, conducted by the Obey commission, only 12 percent of the representatives thought the House was "very effective" in performing its principal functions. Discouragement is especially acute among Republicans, who have no realistic hope of controlling Congress and thereby ascending to leadership posts.[37]

Some might argue that testimony from retired legislators is suspect as rationalization; but comments from sensitive, productive ex-Members are too numerous to ignore. James W. Symington (D-Mo., 1969-1977) said that leaving Congress is "a release from a kind of bondage." Thomas Rees (D-Calif., 1965-1977) exulted that he no longer had "to listen to some hysterical person who calls me about an issue that I care nothing about."[38] Otis G. Pike (D-N.Y., 1961-1979) retired reportedly because he was "tired of wasting time on drivel."

Perhaps lateral mobility—a phenomenon notably absent in the 1960s—has at last proved attractive. It is no coincidence that three of President Carter's original Cabinet-level appointees were former House Members. New congressional retirement benefits, enacted in 1972, have undoubtedly made retirement more attractive than before.

Another source of trouble could be increasing incompatibility between the legislative and constituency roles, given the steep escalation of expectations in both areas. Findings from the Obey commission's Member survey (1976-1977) convey the distinct impression that Members are experiencing severe conflicts between these two roles. On the whole, Members *want* to spend more time on legislation than they do. Typically, they rate legislative tasks as more important than constituency service. But legislators cannot escape constituency demands, even if they wanted to do so. While 42 percent of the legislators in the Obey commission's survey described constituency service as "very important," no less than 70 percent of the general public put it in that category.[39]

Nor are public demands likely to abate. We are fast approaching the day when 90 percent of all adults will have received a secondary education and perhaps 50 percent a postsecondary education. Thus, political activity is likely to remain at a high level or even to increase—not the old-style activity of the political-party cadres, but dispersive involvement in myriads of special-purpose groups and causes. These activists will expect their elected representatives to be responsive. In the Harris survey cited earlier, citizens expressed the most dissatisfaction with legislators' efforts at public education and communication. Nine out of every ten respondents said that Congress should do more to inform the public about its activities.

Less obvious is the impact of constituency activities on the institutional life of Congress. It is at least arguable that ever more demanding *ombudsman* functions have helped to erode the legislative and institutional folkways identified by observers in the 1950s and early 1960s—especially the folkways of specialization, apprenticeship, and institutional loyalty. At the very least, it has placed added demands on Members' time and energies. Although most *ombudsman* activities are actually carried out by staff aides rather than by representatives or senators themselves, there are inescapable costs to the Members' own schedules. Large staffs, while helping Members extend their reach of involvement, require supervision and have a way of generating needs of their own. And with high (and apparently still rising) constituent expectations, there are inescapably a large number of symbolic functions that cannot be delegated to staffs—situations that require Members' personal intervention and face-to-face presence.

Post-Watergate morality also weighs heavily on the legislators. Details of their lives are exposed, their motives are suspect, and they are often treated to snickering comparisons with the Elizabeth Ray affair or the "Koreagate" scandal. Disclosure and ethics rules have become more stringent. Stung by press and public criticism and wishing to justify a congressional pay increase, both House and Senate passed new ethics codes (H. Res. 287; S. Res. 110) in early 1977. The codes limited the amount that any Member may earn from a job outside of Congress to 15 percent of his or her salary. The time-honored practice of Members' earning income by making public speeches was curbed; unofficial office accounts were barred; and public disclosure of the amount and sources of Members' incomes was mandated.

The new codes have exacted a price in legislators' morale. The regulations are controversial (at least on Capitol Hill); reactions in both houses have been bitter, accounting directly for the House's rejection of the Obey commission's final report late in 1977. One may argue whether or not legislators' reactions are warranted; but there is little doubt that senators' and representatives' self-esteem has been damaged. Several Members have cited the new codes in explaining their retirement from public life.

The past generation of career problems centered around Congress' low turnover rates and unrepresentative membership. This situation has been alleviated. Turnover has risen—more from voluntary than from involuntary retirements. Today's membership is more diversified; blacks, women, minorities, young people, and nonlawyers are better represented (although still not proportionately) than in prior years.

The next-generation problem may well be how to maintain the attractiveness of the congressional career. With other careers becoming relatively more attractive, with leadership within Congress more easily and rapidly attained, with congressional life betraying new stresses and strains, tomorrow's critics could conceivably be talking about a problem no one would have taken seriously in the 1960s: how to make certain that the jobs of senator or representative remain attractive enough so that top-flight individuals are attracted to them and so that their loyalty is commanded once they are there. At the same time, it would be healthy if a greater degree of electoral (or involuntary) competition could be fostered.

Conclusions

Are the two Congresses ultimately compatible? Or are they diverging, each detrimental to the other? The burden placed on both Congresses is vastly heavier than it was only a generation ago. Congress-as-institution is expected to resolve all sorts of problems—not only in processing legislation, but also in monitoring programs and serving as an all-purpose watchdog. By all outward signs of activity—such as numbers of committees and committee assignments, hearings, votes, and hours in session—legislators are struggling valiantly to keep abreast of these demands.

At the same moment, Congress-as-career-entrepreneurs is busier than ever. Partly because of the sheer scope of modern government, partly because of constituents' higher awareness, citizens are insisting that senators and representatives communicate more often, benefit their states or districts materially, and play the role of *ombudsmen*. Scholars and journalists sometimes imply that legislators' errand running is a calculated plot to ensure reelection at public expense. To be sure, legislators have been quick to grasp the advantages of constituency service and have profited handsomely from it. However, the evidence points to a further conclusion: legislators have built up staffs and services because they sense, correctly, that citizens expect them to run errands—not because they really enjoy doing so. It is a function legislators have accepted and profited from, but not without misgivings and not without detriment to their legislative tasks.

The heightened demands on the two Congresses may well lie beyond the reach of normal men and women. Reflecting on the multiplicity of presidential duties, Woodrow Wilson once remarked that we might be forced to pick our leaders from among "wise and prudent athletes"—a small class of people. The same can now be said of senators and representatives. And if the job specifications exceed reasonable dimensions, how can we expect reasonable human beings to volunteer for the jobs?

Notes

1. Louis Harris and Associates, Study no. 2651 (January 1977).

2. Thomas E. Cronin, *The State of the Presidency* (Boston: Little, Brown and Company, 1975), chap. 2.

3. Woodrow Wilson, *Congressional Government* (New York: Meridian Books edition, 1956), p. 210.

4. Richard F. Fenno, Jr., "U.S. House Members in Their Constituencies: An Exploration," *American Political Science Review* 71 (September 1977):914.

5. Robert Bendiner, *Obstacle Course on Capitol Hill* (New York: McGraw-Hill, 1964).

6. In Mark J. Green, James M. Fallows, and David R. Zwick, *Who Runs Congress?* (New York: Bantam Grossman, 1972), p. 4.

7. Clem Miller, *Member of the House*, ed. John W. Baker (New York: Charles Scribner's Sons, 1962), 110.

8. Roger H. Davidson, *The Role of the Congressman* (Indianapolis: Bobbs-Merrill Pegasus Books, 1969), chap. 4.

9. Louis Harris and Associates, Study no. 1900 (December 1968). Glenn R. Parker and Roger H. Davidson, "Bases of Public Assessments of Governmental Performance: The Content of Congressional Evaluations" (unpublished paper, 1970).

10. Richard F. Fenno, Jr., "If, As Ralph Nader Says, Congress Is 'The Broken Branch,' How Come We Love Our Congressmen So Much?" in *Congress in Change*, ed. Norman J. Ornstein (New York: Praeger, 1975), pp. 277-278.

11. House Commission on Administrative Review (1977), pp. 16-23.

12. Allen Schick, "The Appropriations Committees *versus* Congress" (Paper presented to the 1975 Annual Meeting of the American Political Science Association, San Francisco, September 1-5, 1975).

13. See Senate Committee on Rules and Administration, *Committee Systems Reorganization of 1977*, S. Rept. 95-2 (95th Cong., 1st sess.).

14. Fox and Hammond (1977), pp. 168, 171.

15. House Commission on Administrative Review (1977), pp. 81-122.

16. Two reliable accounts of facets of the change are: Norman J. Ornstein, "Causes and Consequences of Congressional Change: Subcommittee Reforms in the House of Representatives, 1970-1973," in idem (1975), pp.

88-114; and David W. Rohde, "Committee Reform in the House of Representatives and the Subcommittee Bill of Rights," *Annals of the American Academy of Political and Social Sciences* 411 (January 1974):43ff.

17. H. Douglas Price, "Congress and the Evolution of Legislative 'Professionalism,'" in Ornstein (1975), p. 19.

18. Norman J. Ornstein, "Seniority and Future Power in Congress," in idem (1975), pp. 72-87.

19. See Matsunaga and Chen (1976), pp. 52-54, 60ff. et passim.

20. This proposal is detailed in: U.S., Congress, House of Representatives, Select Committee on Committees, *Committee Reform Amendments of 1974*, H. Rept. 93-916 (93rd Cong., 2nd sess., 1974), pp. 55-61.

21. Walter J. Oleszek, "Joint Referrals in the House of Representatives" (Congressional Research Service, unpublished paper, 1976), p. 2.

22. Roger H. Davidson and Walter J. Oleszek, *Congress Against Itself* (Bloomington: Indiana University Press, 1977).

23. Commission on the Organization of the Government for the Conduct of Foreign Policy (1975).

24. U.S., Congress, House of Representatives, Commission on Administrative Review, "Congressional Attitudes toward Congressional Operations and Procedures," Wave I (January 1977, photocopied).

25. Richard F. Fenno, Jr., *Congressmen in Committees* (Boston: Little, Brown and Company, 1973), chap. 1.

26. Nelson W. Polsby, "The Institutionalization of the U.S. House of Representatives," *American Political Science Review* 62 (March 1968):146-147.

27. Rhodes Cook, "Midterm Elections: Past Trends Indicate Small Democratic Loss," *Congressional Quarterly Weekly Report* 36 (March 25, 1978):755.

28. Edward R. Tufte, "The Relationship between Seats and Votes in Two-Party Systems," *American Political Science Review* 67 (June 1973):540-554.

29. Robert S. Erickson, "The Advantage of Incumbency in Congressional Elections," *Polity* 3 (Spring 1971):395-405.

30. David Mayhew, "Congressional Elections: The Case of the Vanishing Marginals," *Polity* 6 (1974):295-317.

31. Fiorina (1977).

32. Louis Harris and Associates, Study no. 2651 (January 1977).

33. Cook, "Midterm Elections," p. 754.

34. Rhodes Cook, "House Races: More Money to Incumbents," *Congressional Quarterly Weekly Report* 35 (October 29, 1977):2299-2311.

35. Davidson, Kovenock, and O'Leary (1966).

36. Commission on the Organization of the Government for the Conduct of Foreign Policy (1975).

37. See U.S., House of Representatives, "Congressional Attitudes."

38. Ann Cooper, "Ex-Members of Congress: Some Go Home, Many Don't," *Congressional Quarterly Weekly Report* 35 (September 17, 1977):1970-1971.

39. Louis Harris and Associates, Study no. 2651; and House Commission on Administrative Review, "Congressional Attitudes."

References

Books

Davidson, Roger H.; Kovenock, David M.; and O'Leary, Michael K. *Congress in Crisis*. Belmont, Calif.: Wadsworth Publishing Company, 1966.

Davidson, Roger H., and Oleszek, Walter J. *Congress Against Itself*. Bloomington: Indiana University Press, 1977.

Dodd, Lawrence C., and Oppenheimer, Bruce I. eds. *Congress Reconsidered*. New York: Praeger, 1977.

Fenno, Richard F., Jr. *Home Style*. Boston: Little, Brown and Company, 1978.

Fiorina, Morris P. *Congress: Keystone of the Washington Establishment*. New Haven, Conn.: Yale University Press, 1977.

Fox, Harrison W., Jr., and Hammond, Susan Webb. *Congressional Staffs*. New York: The Free Press, 1977.

Mansfield, Harvey, ed. *Congress Against the President*. New York: Praeger, 1975.

Matsunaga, Spark M., and Ping Chen. *Rulemakers of the House*. (Urbana: University of Illinois Press, 1976.

Mayhew, David R. *Congress: The Electoral Connection*. New Haven, Conn.: Yale University Press, 1974.

Orfield, Gary. *Congressional Power: Congress and Social Change*. New York: Harcourt Brace Jovanovich, 1975.

Ornstein, Norman J., ed. *Congress in Change*. New York: Praeger, 1975.

Peabody, Robert L. *Leadership in Congress*. Boston: Little, Brown and Company, 1976.

Rieselbach, Leroy N. *Congressional Reform in the Seventies*. Morristown, N.J.: General Learning Press, 1977.

Articles, Reports, and Papers

Commission on the Organization of the Government for the Conduct of Foreign Policy, *Report*, vol. 5 (Washington: U.S. Government Printing Office, 1975), appendix M.

Davidson, Roger H., and Oleszek, Walter J. "Adaptation and Consolidation: Structural Innovation in the U.S. House of Representatives." *Legislative Studies Quarterly* 1 (February 1976):37-65.

United States. Congress. House of Representatives. Select Committee on Committees. *Committee Reform Amendments of 1974*, H. Rept. 93-316. March 21, 1974.

_____ . Congress. House of Representatives. Commission on Administrative Review. *Administrative Reorganization and Legislative Management*, H. Doc. 95-232. September 28, 1977.

_____ . Congress. Senate. Commission on the Operation of the Senate. *Toward a Modern Senate*, S. Doc. 94-278. December 1976.

_____ . Congress. Senate. Temporary Select Committee to Study the Senate Committee System. *The Senate Committee System*, Committee Print. July 1976.

**Part III
Conclusion**

9

Primrose Paths to Political Reform: "Reforming" versus Strengthening American Parties

Kenneth Janda

According to Webster's *New World Dictionary*, "reform" means "improvement; correction of faults or evils, as in politics." Proposals for political reform therefore arise from the perception of political malpractice. What constitutes malpractice in politics depends on the polity, for perceptions of political evil vary substantially across different cultures. What may be acceptable and even admirable political behavior in the United States may be seen as a heinous crime against the people if practiced in China. Thus political reform must be interpreted with reference to space and time, country and era.

Within the United States, and perhaps within the Western world generally over the past hundred years, political reform has acquired an implicit meaning that is narrower than the dictionary definition. Not only are political reformers the correctors of political evils by definition, but the *type* of evil against which they fight is also specified. In this comprehensive analysis of political reform in America, Crotty notes that the reform experiments have demonstrated "a line of progression" which leads "toward an ever increasing democratization of political power." Observing that reform is in the American tradition, Crotty concludes:

> The trend and direction is clear and persistent. The emphasis is, and has been, on increasing the individual citizen's power over and responsibility for the collective political destiny.[1]

Political reformers in America wear democrats' robes and are entitled to all the rights and priviledges they symbolize. To resist political reform is, by definition, to resist the correction of evil—to resist the democratization of political power. Such semantics mean that those who claim the mantle of political reform also inherit the positive ideological symbols of our culture. Political reformers are granted license to display the mace of democracy as authority for their proposals. Like Mother's Day, political reform is difficult to criticize.

It is much easier to criticize "political engineering," which is Sartori's term for induced political change.[2] Not only is political engineering un-

309

shielded by democratic values, but its *cognitive* basis is emphasized by the term "engineering," which indicates that the state of knowledge of cognition—is critical to its success. Everyone knows that *physical* engineers, with all that precise mathematics, sometimes fail to build properly. What crazy results, we fear, might be produced by *political* engineers? Lacking an ideological defense and showing gaps in their theoretical flanks, political engineers are everyone's favorite intellectual opponents.

Political reform also has an engineering component, but its causal assumptions are usually obliterated by a surrounding halo of value symbols. It is not enough, however, to envision an improved state of affairs; one must know how to change social institutions to elicit the behavior desired. An assortment of assumptions about human behavior exists in every proposal for reform. But this cognitive or engineering component is seldom the focus of debate, which centers instead on implementing the value change, on the politics of replacing evil with good.

Because they are rooted so weakly in causal understanding, reform movements often are unproductive. Mindful of this problem, the Citizens Conference on State Legislatures, a competently staffed and well-funded group organized to study and improve the functioning of state legislative institutions, warned that "good-government" movements, even with the best of intentions, have had dubious results.

> Their most common characteristic has been their addiction to the single-cure formula: If only we change this, or adopt that, all problems will be solved. The legislative reform movement itself has not been entirely free of this affliction. . . .[3]

Striving to avoid such causal simplicity in their own study, the Citizens Conference undertook a fourteen-month study, assembling "for the first time, a massive body of valuable information concerning the systems and operations of the 50 state legislatures."[4] The result was a series of recommendations intended to improve state legislatures and "to enable them to fulfill the expectations of the citizens of a democratic society."[5] The Citizens Conference concluded that this could be done through the development of more "professional" legislators, and they therefore recommended increasing legislators' salaries, increasing expense allowances, establishing retirement benefits, providing individual offices, and furnishing secretarial assistance—five of their seventy-three recommendations.[6]

These recommendations were made in 1971. There is some evidence that many of the reforms advocated by the Citizens Conference have been implemented in the years since.[7] But it appears that the impact of these recommendations has spawned another reform movement, also committed to developing more democratic legislatures. In 1978, the State Bar Association in Illinois (a state whose legislature ranked third on the Citizens Conference evaluation scale) issued a report which proposed to counter the trend toward "full-time professional legislators" with the formation of a "citizen legislature" composed of part-time members more responsive to the public's needs.[8] Further contradicting the recommendations of the Citizens Conference, *this* reform proposal would eliminate annual sessions and limit the length of biennial sessions to six months. Although both proposals were advanced in the name of political reform and both purport to improve popular responsiveness, they offer diametrically opposed recommendations that reflect vastly different understandings of the workings of political institutions.

The basic point is that reforms may not only be unproductive but may actually be counterproductive. As Crotty warns,

> The results have not always been happy. "Reforms" over the years have had a curious way of rewarding the "elect"; that is, further institutionalizing the political and economic power of "them that has."[9]

Crotty further cautions that reforms also "in turn, can, and most often do, lead to totally unanticipated consequences."[10] If political reforms are often ineffective, if they usually produce new problems through unanticipated consequences, and if they sometimes actually impair the values they were intended to advance, why bother to promote the cause of political reform? Of course, the idea of reform—that man has the capacity to change his political environment—is rooted in the philosophy of the Enlightenment.[11] Rather than wring one's hands in the face of political evil, one is moved to do something about the situation. Reformers are optimistic enough to believe that what they do will improve rather than harm the situation. The extent to which their beliefs are realized, however, is the subject of some dispute.

The more cautious advocates of political reform recognize its limitations and even its dangers. They persist in their advocacy because they reject the passive, accepting role assigned to the citizen by Burkean conservatism, which holds that existing institutions are the best institutions. Instead, their preference is for action over inaction. Crotty says that the relevant questions to ask of an existing institution are: "Why does it perform in the manner it does? Who benefits and who loses? What can, or should (or should not) be done about it?"[12] The less cautious advocates of political reform ask the same questions, but they find answers more quickly. They are attracted to prevailing value symbols in the liberal-democratic tradition and tend not to look beyond those symbols to underlying causal structures. Eager to right wrongs, impatient with theory building and testing, responsive to value symbols, they are too easily led down the primrose path of political "reform" that is ineffective, unpredictable, or counterproductive.

This chapter warns against the seductive appeal of political reform. It does so by examining the simplified assumptions about human behavior that are commonly involved in reform movements. It then selects party reform for closer analysis, illustrating how reformers have failed to deal with the theoretical incompatibility of different values in their reform agenda. It argues that reformers, in their zeal for "democratizing" individual parties, have actually infringed on the democratic functioning of the party system. Finally, it proposes some political engineering for the American party system that is unlikely to be recognized as party reform in the contemporary sense of decentralizing control but is nevertheless intended to correct a fault or evil of our political system that interferes with popular control of government.

Simplifying Assumptions in Reform Proposals

All attempts at understanding human behavior in any systematic or theoretical fashion involve simplifying assumptions. Standard criteria in the philosophy of science even favor theorizing from a parsimonious set of simple assumptions. But the philosophy of science also recognizes a tradeoff between parsimonious theory and empirically accurate theory.[13] Reform movement, however, tend to emphasize simplicity while slighting empirical consequences. This simplicity can be detected in reformers' assumptions about human behavior (the cognitive component of reform) as well as in their assumptions about the values they are pursuing (the normative component).

True to their roots in Enlightenment philosophy, reformers tend to have faith in the capacity of human beings to better their conditions. In the realm of politics, this leads to an idealized conception of the citizen, who is seen as a rational person acting with a thorough knowledge of issues, candidates, offices, and government operations. In the terminology of contemporary "rational-choice" theory, such reformers assume that individuals act so as to maximize their preferences in a world of "perfect information."[14] Accordingly, reformers have an individualistic, "direct-democracy" orientation, favoring proposals that enlarge the decision-making opportunities and responsiblities of individual citizens. This orientation conforms to the reform movement's emphasis on democratization; therefore, to oppose proposals that enlarge the decision-making opportunities for individual citizens is to be against "reform."

But the world as we know it is not one of perfect information. And as Downs has pointed out, the modification of this single condition can have profound consequences for political behavior. In the real world of imperfect information, Downs observes that "citizens do not always know what the government or its opposition has done, is doing, or should be doing to serve their best interests."[15] Moreover, information needed to overcome this ignorance is costly to acquire. Those with greater resources can acquire more information and thereby gain political power. Thus reforms provide options to citizens who may neither employ them equally nor employ them equally well. The net result is that "democratizing" reforms may not have democratic consequences in the sense of making government more accountable to the people.

This result may be illustrated with reference to one of the most sacred principles of the liberal-democratic tradition: election of public officials. The keystone of democratic theory is that popular control of government is achieved through direct election of government leaders. As rational actors in a world of perfect information, voters are expected to judge the actions of their government, determine who is responsible for which outcomes, and selectively vote to reward and punish those officials who do and do not behave according to their preferences. In this world, there is no limit to voters' abilities to exercise these judgments, and—assuming no behavior costs in the process—direct election may extend to all government officials without adverse consequences for popular control of government.

The legacy of direct democracy and the assumptions of perfect information and rational voters can be seen in American state-and local-government institutions. Voters are given the opportunity, or saddled with the responsibility, of electing scores of public officials. It is not atypical to have separate elections for governor, lieutenant governor, secretary of state, treasurer, attorney general, and other state executive offices; at the county level, it is common to elect separately the sheriff, treasurer, clerk auditor, coroner, assessor, and other obscure but important officials. In a world of perfect information, voters could be expected to make rational judgments about the performance of all these public officials. But in a world of imperfect information, more elections often mean more confusion and less control of government, as public officials entrench themselves in office because of family connections, ethnic identities, sports prowess, good looks, or some other non-task-related mark of distinction, while government responsibility becomes divided and actually divorced from targets for public retaliation.

Reformers often fall prey to the seductive maxim that if some is good, more must be better. If direct election of public officials is the key to democracy, so this logic goes, then more elections mean more democracy. This leads to the second type of simplifying assumption in reformism: value maximization. United in their support of a given value, reformers are inclined to absolutist thinking in the pursuit of that value. When "democratization" or "participatory democracy" are watchwords of the movement, its logic—and the social dynamics among militants within the movement—

demand that actions be interpreted with respect to the attainment of this value. There is little room for value relativism, in which the movement's objective is thoughtfully evaluated within a matrix of competing values and decisions about what constitutes goal achievement. In the language of rational-choice theory once more, a "maximizing" mentality takes precedence over a "satisficing" mentality. In fact, the dynamics of the movement's leadership ensure that the maximizing mentality will drive out the satisficing mentality. One way to lose stature within any movement is to be seen as "soft" on the issue. As George Wallace reportedly said in the 1960s, after a political defeat by a segregationist in Alabama, he would never be "out-seg'd" again.

The perfect-information and value-maximization assumptions tend to assure that activist reformers are not outflanked by others on the value of democratization, interpreted as decentralized control and direct participation in government. But a special issue arises when the movement becomes attached to any second value. The imperative of value maximization implies that this value too is to be pursued without limit; but limits arise when, as inevitably occurs, both values cannot be maximized simultaneously.[16] It is usually easy to construct a hypothetical situation that pits any given value against another; but hypothetical conflicts are not likely to trouble the comitted activist, who does not want to choose between cherished values if it is unnecessary. Yet real-world situations can also generate genuine conflicts, although they may not be noticed. If they are noticed, they require soul searching and some form of resolution, which may lead to modification of the movement and also to individual defections. If unnoticed, genuine value conflicts are certain to produce ineffective, unpredictable, or dysfunctional impacts of the movement. Such value conflict is inherent in many of the reforms proposed by American political parties.

The Record of Party Reform

It cannot be said that party reform has been ineffective in the sense of having had little impact on party politics. On the contrary, the record of party reform during the past century reveals a pattern of extensive activity resulting in substantial changes in party practice. But however great the impact, the results have tended to be different from the intentions of the reformers. Ranney's extensive study of party reform in America concludes that "the actual consequences of party reform are, in the future as in the past, likely often to disappoint their advocates, relieve their opponents, and surprise a lot of commentators."[17] In part, this is due to the ambivalent attitudes that Americans hold toward political parties. Although they recognize that party competiton is indispensible to democratic government,

Americans have nonetheless been suspicious of parties acting as private organizations in pursuit of the public interest. Ranney states that as parties became especially important after the Civil War, reformers sought to "put them in their place" through legal regulations, a process that peaked in intensity during the Progressive era of the late 1890s and early 1900s. "By 1920 most states had adopted a succession of mandatory statutes regulating every major aspect of the parties' structures and operations."[18]

The antiorganizational bias of party reform was obvious among the Progressives, who saw parties as interfering in the direct relationship between citizens and their government.[19] To varying degrees, this bias extends throughout the history of party reform, with antiorganizational sentiments resurging to Progressive peaks during the late 1960s and early 1970s. Wilson reminds us, "The phrase 'New Left' came to mean, in part, a commitment to political change that would be free of the allegedly dehumanizing consequences of large organizations."[20] Madron and Chelf observed that a central belief of this reform philosophy was that "the ills of society and government, including whatever ails our parties, will be cured by massive doses of direct democracy, or, in the terms of the modern-day populist, participatory democracy."[21]

Thus it is incorrect to say that party reform failed to deliver on its intentions because it was not guided by an overall theme. In fact, there was an underlying theme to much of the party-reform movement during our history. That theme was the familiar one of greater democratization, greater opportunities for involvement of individual citizens in party affairs. In their Twentieth Century Fund study of parties as avenues for citizen participation in politics, Saloma and Sontag hailed the Progressives' efforts to "advance citizen participation through a direct attack on the power of the party 'organization'" but lamented their failure to offer a solution to the problem of participation in the parties:

> They gave citizens a broad new kind of access through the direct primary but they provided no incentives for citizens to participate in the work of the party organizations themselves and in fact consciously undercut party functions and organizational effectiveness.[22]

Saloma's and Sontag's own prescription for reform some eighty years later is the creation of "citizen parties" that feature "broad citizen participation in politics and continuing citizen influence in the direction of government."[23]

Under the dominant antiorganizational orientation of party reform, parties came to be valued not as social *organizations* of political activists but as inanimate *vehicles* for citizen participation. Parties were regarded as aggregations of individuals rather than as true social groups. This orientation clearly conforms to the individualism in American culture and the pluralism of American politics, but it also denies the potential for political parties to be organizational forces in politics and raises questions about the role that parties should play in government.

Debate about the proper role for parties in American politics crystallized years ago with the publication of "Toward a More Responsible Two-Party System," a report of the Committee on Political Parties of the American Political Science Association (APSA).[24] The report criticized the existing parties as being too fragmented and decentralized, and it contained proposals to restructure the parties to produce *responsible* party government, meaning that voters would be able to hold the party in charge of the government accountable for governmental policies. After its appearance in 1950, the APSA report gave rise to a substantial body of literature, most of it critical of the APSA proposals, not to mention its scholarship.[25] Those who criticized the desirability of the responsible-party model as an alternative to the existing party system saw virtue in the fragmentation and decentralization of existing parties, defending our existing parties in terms of a "pluralist" party model. Pomper's study of the APSA report's critics notes "their relative satisfaction with the state of the nation, a satisfaction derived from their pluralist bias. . . ."

> Defenders of the American parties believed that the party system had achieved not only stability, but also some measure of justice through the "invisible hand" of pluralist politics.[26]

Times have changed. In the present era of the politics of scarcity, political scientists are less supportive of pluralist politics—the free play of groups competing for government favors—and notions of the responsible-party school are being revived within the context of party reform.[27] But unless party reformers come to grips with the theoretical issues that they have avoided over the years, future attempts at party reform are also likely to have unpredictable and unsatisfactory impacts.

Four Theoretical Problems in Party Reform

Why is the record of party reform so poor in achieving its intended results? In an important sense, of course, party reform *has* been successful: the organizational aspects of political parties have declined in importance, and their aggregative character has heightened. Wilson finds that "Parties, as organizations, have become, if anything, weaker rather than stronger" and concludes that "Parties are more important as labels than organizations."

> Sometimes the right to use that label can be won by a candidate who participates in no organizational processes at all—as when a person wins a

primary election by campaigning as an individual rather than as an organizational representative.[28]

Pomper concurs: as the party became "the vehicle for individual ambition rather than collective efforts," the devotion to the party as an entity decreased."[29] It may even be that we are approaching the culmination of the Progressives' dream, as Burnham sees us nearing *the liquidation of the political party as an action intermediary between the voter and the candidate.*"[30]

But if the decline of party organization is a victory for party reform, it is a Pyrrhic victory, for other values have fallen in the battle for democratization. Ladd states, "In fact, the changes seem more to have deformed than reformed the parties. They have left the system on the whole less representative, less competitive, less able to govern."[31] Kirkpatrick believes that party reform has advanced the "class interests" of the reformers, those with greater education, higher incomes, and professional occupations.[32] Most importantly, the decline of parties as organizational forces frustrates, rather than enhances, popular control of government. Burnham states the argument succinctly:

> It seems fairly evident that if this secular trend toward politics without parties continues to unfold, the policy consequences will be profound. To state the matter with utmost simplicity: political parties, with all their well-known human and structural shortcomings, are the only devices thus far invented by the writ of Western man which with some effectiveness can generate countervailing collective power on behalf of the many individuals powerless against the relatively few who are individually—or organizationally—powerful.[33]

Few seem satisfied with the weakened state of American parties after decades of party reform. Citizen participation in politics seems no better without strong parties than with them. The quality of public policy, of citizen influence on government, seems unimproved. Something is missing.

Indeed, something has been missing from the theory of party reform throughout most of its history and it is this omission that leads to the empty feeling arising when one surveys the wreckage of party organization. The theory of party reform simply did not provide adequately for the importance of party organization, and centralization of *power*, within the framework of democratic government. Lost in the pursuit of democratization, in the "opening up" of parties, in the decentralization of power within the parties, was consideration of how parties were to be *effective* in their government roles. To engineer for effectiveness, however, requires specifying authority patterns, creating positions of power, and entrusting power to officials. Such topics, however, do not fit with the democratizing ideology of party reform, especially when reformers, such as Saloma and Sontag, viewed the "traditional parties" as

> effectively closed political organizations whose operations frustrate broad citizen participation in politics. For the most part a handful of party notables, key officeholders and party professionals actually control the party organizations within the states and at the federal level.[34]

When the watchword is opening up the party, when the problem is seen as too much centralization of power, the movement does not invite considerations of organizational effectiveness.

Under the pluralist party model, of course, extreme decentralization of power is compatible with party effectiveness. This model attaches little significance to "party" beyond its function as a label for the use of individual candidates. With the rise of mass media and new campaign technologies, even the campaigning functions of parties are no longer important, and a party can be suitably "effective" to a candidate simply by lending its label and not interfering in the election process.[35]

There is evidence, however, that party reformers do *not* embrace this pluralist model but favor political parties that take clear positions on issues and seek to carry out their policies. In short, they favor aspects of the responsible-party model that stress the policy orientation of political parties. This side of the contemporary reform movement can be seen in analyses of reformers as party "amateurs" rather than party "professionals."[36] While party amateurs focused primarily on what they, along with Saloma and Sontag, saw to be the closed nature of American parties and advocated reforms aimed at opening the parties, Soule and Clarke state that amateurs also were concerned with party policy:

> Internal party democracy and the acceptance and encouragement of the largest possible base for participation were given unequivocal acceptance by amateurs. In this sense, intra-party democracy was a salient factor in the motivation of amateur Democrats. Policy goals for the party were conceived to be largely programmatic and were intended to offer clear alternatives to the opposing party. The amateur placed his highest political priorities on intra-party democracy and the party's commitment to specific substantive goals. . . .
>
> In contrast to the amateur, whose chief rewards for political participation tend to be somewhat abstract and intangible, the conventional or professional party activist wanted to win elections and thus provide the inducement which followers require for participation.[37]

According to this standard conceptualization of reformers as amateurs, party reformers were committed to not one but two goals: (1) intraparty democracy and (2) programmatic parties.[38] The potential for conflict between these two values gives rise to the first, and most important, of four theoretical problems confronting party reformers.

Programmatic Parties versus Intraparty Democracy

Maximizing intraparty democracy, especially in the sense used by reformers, inevitably conflicts with the development of a programmatic party, which can be defined (following Lawson) as one that "sets out an integrated long-range plan of action, addressing itself to both present needs and future goals."[39] To be effective, and thus to survive as an organization, a programmatic party must also demonstrate concerted action to implement its program in government decisions. Such cohesion in government can be realized only if one of two conditions prevails: Either party members in government share a high degree of consensus on the policies to be promoted, or party leaders have the capacity to elicit compliant behavior from party office holders through organizational inducements.

It is obvious that American parties do not qualify as programmatic, but this is less the result of ambiguity in their convention platforms than of the knowledge that the parties will not, or cannot, deliver on their campaign pledges. Studies by Pomper and Tufte, among others, indicate that the Democrats and Republicans do adopt distinctive ideological positions on many social and economic issues in their party platforms.[40] But both fail as programmatic parties because of their inability to command behavior from party office holders in support of party positions.[41] Given the highly factionalized nature of both parties,[42] party-supportive behavior will not come automatically from a high degree of consensus on policies to be promoted. It must come, if at all, through organizational inducements, through a greater degree of centralization of power within the party as a social organization—precisely what most reformers have abhorred.

The conflict between decentralized authority (as an expression of intraparty democracy) and political effectiveness is an established proposition in party theory. A quarter of a century ago, Duverger observed:

> Democratic principles demand that leadership at all levels be elective, that it be frequently renewed, collective in character, weak in authority. Organized in this fashion, a party is not well armed for the struggles of politics.[43]

In contrast, Duverger noted that the "democratic centralism" of Marxist parties equipped them especially well "for very careful control by the centre of the implementation of decisions."[44] More recently, Blondel has generalized the point: "centralization increases with the programmatic character of the party."[45]

Findings from a cross-national study of political parties support the basic theory.[46] Two components of the strength of party organization—complexity of organization and centralization of power—were correlated with two components of programmatic parties—legislative cohesion and doctrinism—for a sample of sixty-two competitive parties operating in democratic nations. These two pairs of components were correlated in a canonical model, which computes the maximum correlation between the best linear combination of the organization variables and the best linear combination of programmatic variables.[47] The results are given in table 9-1, which shows that the more complex the party organization *and* the greater the centralization of power, the more likely it is that parties will display high legislative cohesion *and* be guided by some established body of principles in their character.

Although both theory and data indicate that organization and centralization are instrumental to programmatic parties, American party reformers avoid acknowledging the relationship or acting on its implications. Data collected at the 1972 Democratic and Republican conventions were analyzed for differences between proreform and antireform delegates, who were distinguished by their warm or cold feelings toward "leaders in party reform activity."[48] As reported in table 9-2, proreform delegates in both parties were more likely than the antireform delegates to be strongly in favor of selecting a nominee who was strongly committed on the issues, and

Table 9-1
Canonical Analysis Relating Components of Strength of Organization to Components of Programmatic Parties

	Canonical Coefficients	
Components of strength of organization:		
Complexity of organization[a]	0.95 ⎱	Canonical
Centralization of power[b]	0.35 ⎰	correlation
		between both
Components of programmatic parties:		sets of component
		variables = 0.62
Legislative cohesion[c]	0.43 ⎱	(sig. 0.001)
Extent of reliance on party doctrine[d]	0.80 ⎰	N = 62

[a]Complexity of organization was measued by a six-item scale with a reliability of 0.82.

[b]Centralization of power was measured by an eight-item scale with a reliability of 0.83.

[c]Legislative cohesion was measured by a single score estimating the average cohesion of the party in accordance with the Rice index, for which 100 means that 100 percent of the party's legislative delegation voted together and 0 means that the delegation usually split 50-50.

[d]Reliance on party doctrine was measured by a single five-point item which estimated the extent to which the party appealed to a written body of doctrine or principles in party decisions.

Table 9-2

Comparison of Non-Reform- and Reform-Oriented Delegates to the 1972 Democratic and Republican National Conventions

Attitude Item	Democratic Delegates		Republican Delegates	
	Anti-reform (%)	Pro-reform (%)	Anti-reform (%)	Pro-reform (%)
Percentage who strongly favored "selecting a nominee who is strongly committed on the issue"	36	73	32	47
Percentage who expressed great interest in "decisions on the party's platform"	44	59	52	67
Percentage who favored "minimizing the role of the party organization in nominating candidates for office"	28	64	12	27

Note: The numbers of antireform and proreform delegates vary from item to item, but the percentages are based on approximately 175 antireform and 900 proreform Democratic delegates. For the Republicans, there are about 180 antireform and 150 proreform delegates. See note 48.

also more likely to register great interest in decisions on the party's platform. However, they were also more than twice as likely to favor minimizing the role of the party organization in nominating candidates for public office.

Despite the importance reformers attach to the party's role in promoting issues, they are reluctant to equip the party with an organizational capacity to mobilize support for issue positions among office holders. This reluctance is rooted in a belief that organizational power is incompatible with intraparty democracy, which is the *second* theoretical problem confronting party reformers.

Democratic versus Centralized Parties

In keeping with the tradition of pluralist democracy in the United States, American reformers tend to interpret party democracy primarily in terms of the decentralization of power.[49] In this view, democracy is equated with a partitioning of authority, expressed in such institutions as the separation of powers, plural executives, and staggered terms of office. But there is an alternative conception of democracy, majoritarian democracy, which not only allows for the centralization of government authority but actually requires it. Under the majoritarian conception, government institutions must be able to carry out the will of the majority once it is clearly expressed. Extreme partitioning of political authority, as practiced in the United States, clearly runs counter to the theory of majoritarian democracy, however well decentralization accords with pluralist democracy.

It is peculiarly American that reformers have chosen to advance party "democratization" by weakening the party organization. Wright has interpreted the normative issue concerning the proper role of party in government in terms of two alternative models—the *rational-efficient* model and the *party democracy*—that correspond to the "pluralist" and "responsible" party models that we have already discussed.[50] The rational-efficient model, favored by Americans, is briefly summarized as having "exclusively electoral functions" and being "pragmatically preoccupied with winning elections rather than with defining policy." In contrast, Wright sees the party-democracy model, which views parties as "more policy-oriented, ideological, and concerned with defining policy in an internally democratic manner involving rank-and-file member participation," as favored by European social scientists.[51]

Despite their commitment to party democracy, Europeans seem to be able to bring into harmony the values of policy orientation, member participation, and party organization. Wright states, "In the Party Democracy model, organization is of crucial importance; in the Rational-Efficient model, organization is of much less importance."[52] Organization becomes important in the rational-efficient model only to the extent that it is related to the mobilization of voters at election time and the winning of elections. But the party-democracy model involves members continually in party activities beyond campaigning, as members seek to provide input to party policy making. Party organization then bcomes critical in providing for intraparty communications, procedures for reaching decisions, techniques for carrying out party policy, and recruitment of party leaders.

Note that this party-democracy model does not necessarily imply decentralization of power. Just as majoritarian democacy relies on majority rule—and enough centralization of government power to carry out the will of the majority—party democracy in this sense allows for centralization of power within the party. While an important requirement in the party-democracy model is membership involvement in party policy making, the model also presumes that the party organization will have the power to execute decisions once made. Otherwise, there is no point to participation in policy making.

It is clear that American party reformers value rank-and-file participation in policy making. Proreform delegates to both 1972 national conventions strongly favored "encouraging widespread participation in making most party decisions" by a margin of more than two to one over the antireform delegates.[53] But reformers seem not to have thought as far as the next step. How are party decisions, reached through mass participation, going to be executed? It would be hoped that party members who opposed the final party decision would accept the outcome and cooperate in its execution. Yet even a mass-participation party cannot trust voluntary cooperation alone; it must have some power to induce cooperation. By neglecting to provide such powers to the party organization, reformers negate their efforts to provide for mass participation. It is as if they believe that mass participation is a *sufficient* condition for party democracy. A broader conception of party democracy, however, would provide for the execution of the decisions as well as participation in the decisions.

If execution of party decisions requires strong party organization, the reform movement would rather not discuss it. *D*ecentralization of power has become such a positive symbol that it has become equated with intraparty democracy, and proposals for strengthening party organization have not been wlecome within the movement. So long as reformers interpret intraparty democracy in terms of decentralization of power, they will not develop parties that are able to execute the policies that reformers themselves work so hard to shape in party platforms. Hawley's critique of nonpartisan politics puts the issue squarely before us:

> *The Problem, then, is to strengthen parties and to democratize them at the same time. . . .*
>
> While it is necessary to make some trade-offs between a broadly based open party and one with substantial unity and discipline, being self-conscious about the duality of the goals of party reform may bring us closer than before to viable strategies for accommodating these two essential elements of a change-including party system[54]

Reformers' emphasis on decentralization of power as the prime requisite of intraparty democracy may be thought to reinforce the value of "representativeness," another desideratum of the reform movement. But again, reformers seem not to recognize the conflict between decentralization of power and representativeness; this constitutes the third theoretical problem confronting party reform.

Centralization of Power versus Representativeness

A major concern of the reform movement since the 1960s has been the unrepresentativeness of American parties, especially as reflected in the delegations to the nominating conventions. Comparing delegates to both party conventions in 1968 with characteristics of the total population and party voters, Parris notes that the "convention delegations did not accurately reflect the composition of either the national electorate or party voters" and contends:

This demographic pattern is unfair. If the political parties are quasi-public institutions . . . , then they should reflect better their own constituencies. The major social characteristics of the delegations should more nearly correspond to those of the electorate and the party's own voters.[55]

Ranney's study of the reform movement attributes considerable clout to this "representative party structures" school, which—in contrast to the responsible-party school—holds that "the parties' greatest need is not more centralization or cohesion but more accurate *representation* of their rank-and-file members."[56] Within the Democratic party, of course, this value achieved expression in the Guidelines for Delegate Selection to the 1972 Convention, which required state parties to take "affirmative steps" to ensure that minority groups, young people, and women be represented at the convention "in reasonable relationship to their presence in the population of the State."[57]

It is common knowledge by now that the representation of minorities, youth, and women increased significantly for both parties between the 1968 and 1972 conventions.[58] The increased demographic representativeness within the Democratic party was attributed to state-party compliance with the national-party guidelines, while the Republican party's smaller increase was considered to be primarily a reaction to Democratic initiative.[59] We need to look more closely, however, at just *how* this increased representativeness was achieved. Did the increased demographic representation come about from *de*centralizing power to open up the party at the base, or did it actually result from a greater centralization of power at the national level?

The argument that demographic representation could be increased by opening up the party at the base assumes that the target groups—minorities, youth, and women—were prevented from participation in the past *because of* the existence of a power structure that kept them out. As Kirkpatrick put it, the assumption was, "*if there were no institutional barriers to their participation in party governance*, blacks, women and youth would be elected to the party's governing councils in rough proportion to their presence in the population." That is, their low representation in the past was not due to "such other attributes as ambition, interest, and skill."[60] Under this assumption, there is no conflict between decentralization of power and greater demographic representation. It is ironic, however, that the guidelines were implemented and greater demographic representation achieved as a result of an unprecedented acquisition and exercise of centralized power by the Democratic national party over the state parties, which faced refusal of seating at the convention for noncompliance.[61]

Contrary to the belief that decentralization of power within a social organization promotes demographic representation within party councils or among party candidates, there is strong evidence that *centralization* of power produces greater representativeness. Of course, the results achieved by the Democratic National Committee in delegate selection for the 1972 convention themselves provide clear evidence of centralized power exercised to improve representation, but there is more. Impressionistic evidence to support the relationship can be recalled from practices of party machines in "balancing the ticket" to ensure the presence of the Irish, Italians, Jews, and other groups on the ballot. Perhaps more convincing support comes from a study by Jackson and Hitlin of the members of the Sanford commission, charged with formulating a charter for the Democratic party, and the delegates to the 1974 Democratic Mid-Term Conference. Jackson and Hitlin noted that the Sanford commission members, who were centrally selected by outgoing Democratic chairperson Jeanne Westwood and incoming Chairperson Robert Strauss, were somewhat more demographically representative of the population than the delegates to the mid-term conference, who were selected at the district level but *without* operation of the McGovern-Fraser guidelines. Jackson and Hitlin remark, "the implication is that one can more readily obtain a demographically balanced delegation using a centralized elite selection process rather than a pluralistic, uncoodinated process."[62] Finally, a study by Scott of the occupational composition of the legislative delegations of the thirty-two political parties in fourteen nations found a correlation of .57 between the centralization of power within the party and a measure of the extent to which the occupational composition of the party's legislators reflected the occupational composition of its rank-and-file supporters.[63] The more centralized the party, the more accurately its parliamentary delegation reflected the occupations of its supporters.

Although it may seem counterintuitive that the presence of organizational control over the selection of party delegates or candidates can lead to more representativeness, the causal mechanism is readily understandable. Consider an extreme situation of very little party control over candidate selection, such as exists under the direct primary method of nominating party candidates for the U.S. Congress. The direct primary, which is virtually unique to the American political system, allows the maximum amount of individual initiative in seeking and obtaining party candidacy.[64] Ranney even ranks the direct primary as "the most radical of all the party reforms adopted in the whole course of American history," which "in most instances has not only eliminated boss control of nominations but party control as well."[65]

In the absence of party control, what factors come into play in securing the nomination? Personal characteristics become important, to be sure, and characteristics of a particular kind: wealth, social standing in the community, accommodative occupation. These are the factors that serve the ambitious contender for office in a situation of individualistic competition. It should be no surprise that lawyers and businessmen have fared well in seeking party nominations for congressional elections. Over 80 percent of all members of the House of Representatives have for years come from one of these two occupational groupings, with lawyers alone usually accounting for 50 percent of the membership—by far the highest percentage in any of the twenty-two democracies studied by Pedersen.[66]

The growing importance of the mass media, particularly television, has even increased the importance of the individuals' social status in winning the nomination. As Joslyn's study of the impact of television on partisan politics observes:

> Recruitment, for example, is much less the party organization's business when an aspiring politician can appeal directly to the voters in whatever way desired (provided he or she has the money). The presence and expense of political television insures that the availability of wealth will be a factor rivaling ideological orthodoxy, previous party service and demographic characteristics in important when it comes time to select a party's nominee.[67]

Noting that reformers themselves tended to be socially privileged in terms of education, income, and occupation—coming mainly from the professions—Kirkpatrick concluded that party reform "rewarded persons with the skills, styles, and values of the reformers at the expense of others."[68] When the party has a more direct hand in determining candidacy, on the other hand, personal ambition, leisure time, and high social status become less important, and candidates can be recruited on the basis of policy commitment or other social attributes. Hence, weakly organized and decentralized parties tend to favor the selection of those who are equipped by wealth, education, and occupation to win out in direct appeals to party voters. This is not a formula for ensuring equal representation.

However important the value of representativeness is to the reform movement, its exact relationship to the function of political parties in government has not been clearly specified. The goal of equal representation has been accepted as an article of faith by party reformers, and little thought is given to any negative consequences of increased representativeness of either party. This failure to analyze thoroughly the effect of maximized representativeness on the party system gives rise to the *fourth* theoretical problem in party reform.

Representative Parties versus Programmatic Parties

It was never settled in the reform literature whether the party's leadership was to be representative of its membership or of the population in general.[69] The difficulty in basing representation on party members lies in the unusual nature of American parties, which unlike most other parties do not have a formal membership basis.[70] The psychological concept of party identification offers an alternative means of identifying the characteristics of party supporters, but its measurement is too problematic to serve as a standard for judging representation. Moreover, as American parties have come to be viewed as quasi-public institutions involved in "state action,"[71] there is reluctance to regard them in the European tradition as "organizations to further the interests of their members, particularly in class or economic terms."[72] In any event, the McGovern-Fraser guidelines called for representativeness of convention delegates in proportion to the presence of minorities, women, and youth in the total population of the state, not among Democratic party supporters.

What is the effect of such highly representative parties on the programmatic character of political parties? It can be argued that demographic representativeness, especially when it is achieved for both parties in the system, works against the emergence of programmatic parties, since parties then lose their social basis of distinctiveness. It is a working theory of political science that parties advance issues favored by the groups that support them.[73] If the reform movement within each party were to succeed in maximizing demographic representation, so that each party was equally representative of the major social groupings with respect to ethnic composition, sex, age, and other key categories like education and religion, what would be the social basis for distinguishable party positions on issues? Would it be possible to produce anything more than Tweedledum and Tweedledee parties if they did not differ in their social bases? If the two parties mirrored the social composition of the national population equally well, one would expect them also to converge on the issues. By reflecting the heterogeneity of society, the parties would become catch-all parties which, as Kirchheimer contends, become vague on the issues—the antithesis of programmatic parties.[74]

The conflict between representative and programmatic parties is only the last of the four theoretical problems confronting party reformers. It joins the other difficulties—the conflict between programmatic parties and intraparty democracy, the confusion between democratic and decentralized parties, and the conflict between decentralized parties and representativeness—to confound the efforts of reformers to improve the practice of partisan politics in the United States. By failing to grapple explicitly with the theoretical issues underlying the realization of their values, the reform movement has wrought much change in party operations but little progress toward popular control of government.

Strengthening American Political Parties

In my view, the party-reform movement, throughout most of its history, has incorrectly diagnosed the disease in the body politic and has dispensed the wrong medicine for the illness. To the extent that party reformers have prescribed doses of decentralization of power, their treatment was akin to bleeding a patient whose problem was loss of blood. The evidence is strong that American parties not only are characterized by their decentralization but are among the most decentralized parties in the world.[75] In contrast to the antiorganizational orientation of most party reform, what is needed is more organization and more centralization of power within the national parties. This is why I speak of *strengthening* the parties rather than "reforming" them.

It is true that aspects of the recent reforms within the Democratic party can also be seen as centralizing power within the national organization and strengthening the national party in comparison with the state parties. Surely this was the thrust of the guidelines for the selection of delegates to the 1972 Democratic convention, when the national party was far more successful in obtaining state-party compliance than most observers thought possible.[76] Moreover, the new charter for the Democratic party, adopted at the 1974 midterm convention, constituted the first genuine constitution for a major American party.[77] Reviewing the reforms in the Democratic party since the 1968 Convention, Crotty concludes:

> More was attempted, and accomplished, than can truthfully be said to have been envisioned in the decades since the Progressive movement of the early 1900s. . . . In contrast to earlier attempts at political change, the intent was to strengthen and preserve an institution of incomparable value to the American political system rather than to destroy or replace it.[78]

Other students of American parties, however, emerge with a different evaluation of the reform movement, contending that the reforms sought to "wreck"[79] or "dismantle"[80] the party. On balance, the reforms in question probably did little to wreck or dismantle the party organization any further, simply leaving it as weak as ever. Even Crotty concedes this, stating, "The party charter's early contributions suggest only marginal differences in the way the national party is operating."[81] And Charles Longley's careful assessment of party nationalization in America (chapter 5 in this volume) sees much change but little difference:

> The conventional wisdom concerning national parties is no longer accurate—nor is it wholly inaccurate. Allied with the highly visible "practical" problems already noted, there remain the systemic constraints fostered by the separation of powers and federalism. In sum these considerations argue against a wholesale revision of our understanding of American party politics.[82]

Where reform proposals had a *real* opportunity to change the character of American parties, they were not adopted. Rejected at an early stage in the charter were proposals to create formal dues-paying party membership and to require local, regional, and national conventions to set party policy. At the 1974 conference itself, the proposal to elect the national party chairman for a four-year term (instead of allowing the presidential nominee to choose the chairman at the convention) was defeated, and even the proposal for mandatory midterm conferences was rejected.[83]

Whether because of the recent reforms or in spite of them, party politics in the United States remains characterized by personalities and interest groups, both of which neither promote popular control of government nor produce coordinated public policies for dealing with the social and economic problems arising under emerging conditions of scarcity. Strong parties, not weak ones, are called for. Huntington's remarks about politics in developing countries apply with equal force to the United States:

> . . . the development of a strong party substitutes an institutionalized public interest for fragmented private ones . . . .

> The evils attributed to party are, in reality, the attributes of a disorganized and fragmented politics of clique and faction which prevails when parties are nonexistent or still very weak. Their cure lies in political organization.[84]

Would the development of stronger parties amount to retrogression in the democratization of political power, identified earlier as the direction of political reform in America? Assuming that democratization ought to be judged by the degree of popular control of government policy rather than by the degree of opportunity for citizens to participate as individuals in election campaigns, I think that stronger parties would actually increase citizens' power over and responsibility for the collective political destiny. I think this because I recognize that the real world is *not* one of perfect information and no behavior costs, that most people do not or cannot take advantage of individualistic opportunities to participate in nominating and electing candidates, and that to view party reform in terms of decentralized and individualistic participation at the election stage is to slight values of democratic government at subsequent stages.

How could stronger party organizations promote popular control of government and coordinated public policies? It should first be noted that I do not subscribe to the *maximization* of organizational strength. Second, one should be reminded that complexity of organization and centralization of power are continuous rather than dichotomous concepts. The choice is not between organized or unorganized parties, nor between centralized or decentralized parties. One should analyze organizational strength by assessing the mixture of degree of organization and centralization of power as variable properties of parties. It turns out that in the United States, both

major parties display a greater degree of party organization than centralization of power in comparison with European parties.[85] My prescription is
primarily to increase the centralization-of-power component of organizational strength for American parties, not to maximize it.

I realize that a proposal that specifies no distinct target (for example, 9
units of centralization out of a possible score of 15 units) suffers from ambiguity; this is one reason why proposals couched in maximization language
are more readily understood and command greater fervor. I have no answer
to the ambiguity charge other than to note that ambiguity pervades our entire existence, and it is better to admit its presence than to assume its
absence. The thrust of my prescription is that American national parties,
which are among the most decentralized in the world, should be entrusted
with increased organizational power. The purpose of my prescription is to
promote popular control of government and coordinated public policies
through the capacity of the electorate to hold the parties accountable for the
policies they advocate.

Given stronger national party organization, party members in government positions or party candidates in government positions would have to
reckon with party policies in their actions and promises. The party
organization would be able to provide some constraints on the behavior of
party members in government as well as some inducements to ensure cooperation with party policies. Granted, party influence on the behavior of public
officials runs counter to the American tradition of freewheeling politics and
individual independence; increased party influence is a hard notion for
some to accept. But it is pure folly to contend that most American public officials are now autonomous actors and that party influence would seriously
compromise that autonomy. In reality, American senators, congressmen,
governors, sheriffs, and even presidents have political debts to hidden
groups that periodically collect these debts by influencing the behavior of
officials on government matters that touch their interests.[86] Increases in the
degree of party direction of government activity would only replace these
camouflaged patterns of influence with open links of party direction. An
argument for strengthening these party links should not be reduced to ab-
surdity by interpreting it as a proposal for iron-clad party control. Hawley
considered this objection and concluded:

> Thus, while I am not unmindful of the possibility that elected officials can
> become mere fronts for party leaders, the lack of dependence of elected of-
> ficials on the party seems the more serious problem for democracy.[87]

The question seems to be, how can the parties be strengthened enough to
provide a meaningful degree of central direction and control?

One school of thought contends that the American parties cannot be changed very much, because they are products of their environment. As Keefe says, "The parties are less what they make of themselves than what their environment makes of them."[88] And a good deal of the criticism directed at the APSA proposal for more "responsible" parties argued that the American political environment, especially federalism and the separation of powers, ensured that the parties would be decentralized and pragmatic rather than centralized and programmatic regardless of efforts to change them.[89] However, little systematic research has been done in the past to assess the parameters of environmental effects on party characteristics. Recent research by Harmel and Janda has shown that while the environment definitely affects party character, there is considerable potential for change at the party level as well.[90]

Studying ninety-five competitive parties in twenty-eight democratic nations, Harmel and Janda found that the country as a variable explained 57 percent of the variance in complexity of organization and 65 percent of the variance in centralization of power. As for federalism and the separation of powers as theoretical factors operating behind the identity of the country,

Table 9-3

Effects of Environmental Variables on Party Organization and Centralization

	Complexity of Organization	Centralization of Power
Percentage of variance explained by the identity of the country[a]	57	65
Percentage of the total variance explained:		
by federalism[b]	0	8
by separation of powers[c]	3	5
Percentage of the country environmental variance explained:[d]		
by federalism	0	12
by separation of powers	5	8

[a]The entries are based on the E^2 statistics computed from a one-way analysis of variance using the country identification as the independent variable. The dependent variables are the scales described in table 9-1. The analysis involved 95 parties and 28 countries.

[b]This analysis is based on 88 parties with data available on federalism and separation of powers. A total of 58 parties were in unitary states, 17 in effectively federal states, and 13 in states with mixed power distributions. The percentage of variance explained was determined through an analysis of variance.

[c]This analysis is based on 71 parties in parliamentary systems and 17 parties in presidential systems. Analysis of variance was used.

[d]These entries were computed by dividing the total variance that could be explained by the country by the percentage of variance explained by federalism and separation of powers. There was no significant interaction between the two factors and thus little overlapping explained variance.

federalism and the separation of powers together accounted for no more than 20 percent of the variance that can be attributed to the country environment.[91] The results are given in table 9-3.

It seems that although environmental variables have effects as theorized, there is substantial room for party-level reforms to affect party character. Moreover, it is not the case that party reform needs only to deal with party-level variables. In fact, the progressive reforms that instituted the direct primary did alter the political environment, and the impact of the delegate selection guidelines within the Democratic party was to revise state legislation on delegate selection, increasing the number of primaries for both parties.[92] Thus, even if parties are what the environment makes them (which is only about 60 percent true in the case of degree of organization and centralization of power), the environment itself is not immune to party reform. In any event, one cannot use these data to argue a convincing case of environmental determinism against proposals to strengthen party organization.

Although changes in the political environment are not beyond the reach of party reform, some aspects of the environment are more difficult to change than others. Obviously, proposals for wholesale constitutional change—such as replacing the presidential system with a parliamentary one—are not politically viable, even if they were desirable. In general—and with good reason—the more sweeping the proposal for change, the more political opposition. Some relatively specific changes, like nominating party candidates by party conventions or committees rather than through direct primaries, would tend to eliminate the extremes of decentralization but would also be politically intractable because of popular commitment to primaries and the need for statutory action in the individual states. Proposals for strengthening the parties are more likely to be adopted if they are relatively specific and capable of implementation at the center of national politics. The one proposal that appears to have the most political viability and the greatest promise for accomplishing its purpose deals with campaign financing.

Campaign financing has justifiably been a subject of great concern to political candidates and the public alike. Campaign costs have risen greatly since the 1950s, and there is no reason to expect the trend to be reversed. Candidates worry about raising enough funds to conduct effective campaigns, and the public worries about the political debts that candidates will contract in search of adequate funds. Scholars have written voluminously about money in politics, and numerous reforms have been proposed for raising and spending campaign funds.[93] Reflecting this agitation, Congress has responded recently with major campaign-financing legislation in 1971, 1974, and 1976—as explained by Jacobson in chapter 7 of this volume.[94]

Until recently, those attracted to the problem of campaign financing have shown a reformers' bias against strong parties. The relationship between weak parties and the influence of money in politics has seldom been a central part of their analysis, and their specific proposals for reforming fund raising and spending rarely involved the party organizations directly in the control process.[95] In contrast, scholars who advocate strengthening our party system have turned to the control of campaign financing as a key factor in enhancing the parties' role in the political process.[96]

In our pluralist political system, sizable contributions are funneled into party politics from numerous individuals and interests. These funds are normally raised for the financing of specific election campaigns rather than party activities in general. Lawson describes the time-honored process:

> Funds are gathered from contributors with widely varying political philosophies, with the tacit or expressed understanding that no issue will be dealt with in a way inimical to any of their interests. Funds are spent on communications media which lend themselves to the superficial, repetitious, huckstering campaign messages that characterize our parties' appeal to the electorate. After victory, each elected official is free to interpret his party's "program"—to the extent that such an amorphous entity has emerged—exactly as he wishes, even if this means voting against the majority of his party in Congress.[97]

Also, as Hess points out, "trouble arises because candidates seek funds in large amounts from people or interests who then wish preferential treatment from the government."[98] This *quid pro quo* quality is enhanced when contributions are given directly to the candidates rather than mediate through the party organization. This tendency for direct contributions to candidates has increased in recent years with the growth of candidates' ad hoc campaign organizations. The result of this more direct link between the candidates and their sources of funds is an increase in elected officials' independence of the party organziation. If a candidate arranges for his own campaign financing, he can afford this independence. But again, his increased independence of the party is purchased at a cost: he sacrifices some of this autonomy to his large contributors, which amounts to trading in visible links for invisible ones.

The evils of money in politics are usually expressed in terms of trading financial support before election for government influence after election. This danger is ever present in interest-group politics, and it is intensified in a form of party politics that makes the candidate the direct recipient of campaign funds. This point has been grasped by several recent critics of our weak party system who urge the development of more responsible parties. Broder proposes

> channeling virtually all funds for general election campaigns, from the Treasury or from many small givers, through the party organization, rather

than continuing the irresponsible practice of forcing each candidate to forage for himself among the big givers. Leashing the undisciplined power of money in politics remains a high-priority element in any program for reviving responsible party government.[99]

To the extent that public subsidies are provided for election campaigns, Hess also suggests that "they be given directly to the political parties, rather than directly to the candidates."[100] In possession of funds to support candidates of their choosing, the national parties would acquire some significant increase in organizational power.[101] As a result, the ability of the parties as organizations to induce support of party policies should be increased.

The study by Jacobson (chapter 7 of this volume) reviews the role assigned to the parties in public financing of electoral campaigns. It is a small one. The 1966 law, suspended by Congress the following year, would have given public funds directly to the national parties, but worry developed over placing too much power in the hands of the parties and the national chairman. All later subsidy proposals gave money directly to candidates. Jacobson states, "In other mature democracies the issue is one of *party* finance; in the United States, it is one of campaign finance. The distinction is fundamental."[102] Indeed it is, and the distinction is underscored by Herbert Alexander, the foremost student of money in politics. After noting that in other democracies across the world, public financing is directed toward political parties rather than candidates, Alexander states:

> Accordingly, ways should be thought through in which candidate-funding at least in general elections, can be channeled through the parties. Ultimately, the way to get more accountability and responsibility in political finance would seem to be through democratically reformed, adequately funded political parties, not through increased candidate independence.[103]

As for the actual effect of public financing on congressional campaigns, Hodson and McDevitt's study of the 1972 and 1976 senatorial elections found that funding of senatorial campaigns directly by political parties decreased not only proportionately but also in dollar figures between 1972 and 1976. They attach special importance to this finding because parties are more likely than other sources to target their giving to competitive races, and they are also the only major source of funds not strongly favoring incumbency.[104]

It seems feasible to propose that public funds be given directly to political parties rather than to candidates, yet this avenue has not been explored very far in the history of congressional legislation. The source of opposition is easy to identify. Incumbent members of congress have gotten where they are through successful competition in the current interest-group system. Public funding of political parties suggests that future office holders submit to a greater degree of party control than at present, which is unlikely to gain their favor. In their recommendations for election financing, the Committee on Economic Development stated that:

> resistance to change is deeply imbedded in custom and reinforced by vested interests. Perhaps the chief obstacle lies in the fact that the machinery of government—at all levels—is in the hands of those who have gained their positions under the prevailing system. They are thoroughly familiar with the operational details involved in nominations and elections, however obscure these may be to the average citizen or to potential opponents. A system that has placed men in power is likely to hold attraction for many of them.[105]

The same observation applies for any set of proposals to strengthen American political parties, for stronger parties would inevitably restrict the extraordinary independence that members of Congress enjoy under our system of partitioned government authority and weak parties.

Conclusion

The normative argument of this chapter is that American political parties need to be strengthened rather than reformed. It envisions a place for parties in the political system akin to that recommended in the 1950 American Political Science Association Report, *Toward a More Responsible Two-Party System*, but with some important differences. First, the idealized state of "party government" that inspired the report is not regarded as compatible with the separation of powers in the American constitutional system. Moreover, the party-government model puts a high premium on ideological differentiation between the parties, which may be forthcoming but is not essential. My view of "responsible parties" is closer to that of James, who distinguishes between the party-government and responsible-party models by noting:

> The principal mechanisms of Responsible Parties are the possibilities of shared involvement and risks under the party label. From this sharing should follow collective responsibility, simplification of electoral control by the general public, and party competition—without any need to specify the ideological or programmatic content of this competition.[106]

My proposal for strengthening American national parties also puts more emphasis on the centralization of power within the national committees in the financing of election campaigns with substantial support from an organized party membership. Other centralizing tendencies will no doubt follow, but the continued practice of candidate nomination by direct primaries, the fragmenting effects of federalism, and Americans' traditional suspicion of political parties are expected to resist this centralizing trend and to prevent any situation of extreme centralization of power. The argument is that the American political system not only can stand some degree of party centralization but also needs it. American government and politics are not being well served by our current national parties, which are so extemely *de*centralized that they stand virtually alone among parties in Western democracies and competitive parties throughout the world.

Who would be served by such a party system? Much of the writing in favor of stronger, more programmatic parties issues from liberal academicians who look to responsible parties as a means for accomplishing social change and redistributing wealth within society. Viewed in this light, proposals for developing responsible parties can be seen as an argument directed primarily at liberal Democrats for implementation within the Democratic party. But this view has several blind spots. First, the restructuring of opportunities within society is not exclusively a concern of liberal Democrats. Conservative Republicans have their own opinions about the most efficient and effective ways of allocating society's goods. There is also the important need to control social change as well as to create it. Sample surveys have shown that vast numbers of Americans are worried about dealing with social change, which is reflected in their strong responses to the "social issue."[107] These are preferences that any democrat, Republican or Democrat, needs to respect.

Finally, conservative Republicans as well as liberal Democrats have urged their own versions of a programmatic Republican party. This is often discussed in terms of a realignment of the party system along liberal-conservative lines. Many Republicans see a conservative majority in the United States that is divided unfortunately between the Democrats and Republicans so that Democrats have a party majority within the country, thus submerging the true conservative majority. William A. Rusher has grappled with this political conundrum. According to Rusher, the biggest obstacle faced by conservatives in America is " . . . simply to get, somehow, into a single party."[108] "Somehow," but how?

American parties are highly institutionalized, and party loyalties cannot be changed by wishing. There must be some inducement for change. These inducements are most likely to come from concrete party actions taken to show that the parties mean to deliver on their promises by directing the behavior of their members in government. If the Republican party were to become a force behind its programs, perhaps the conservative majority—as Rusher sees it—would be drawn to a party that meant what it said. If the Democratic party were to acquire more organizational authority, perhaps its presidents might be able to get their party proposals through a Congress controlled by their own members.[109]

Who would be served by a system of responsible parties? Eventually the public should benefit from mass inputs into party decisions, decreases in private influences on government decisions, increases in coordination of government policies, and creative competition between the parties in developing imaginative programs for public evaluation and choice with the knowledge that party programs were likely to be carried out.

Notes

1. William J. Crotty, *Political Reform and the American Experiment* (New York: Thomas Y. Crowell, 1977), pp. 267, 293.

2. Giovanni Sartori, "Political Development and Political Engineering," in *Public Policy*, vol. 17, ed. John D. Montgomery and Albert O. Hirschman (Cambridge, Mass.: Harvard University Press, 1968), pp. 261-298.

3. Citizens Conference on State Legislatures, *The Sometimes Governments: A Critical Study of the 50 American State Legislatures* (Kansas City, Mo.: Citizens Conference on State Legislatures, 1973), p. 11.

4. Ibid., p. xiv.

5. Ibid., p. 152.

6. Ibid., pp. 160, 165.

7. See the changes in American state legislatures since the mid-1960s as recounted in William J. Keefe and Morris S. Ogul, *The American Legislative Process: Congress and the States* (Englewood Cliffs, N.J.: Prentice-Hall, 1977), pp. 450-454, which credits the reform movement for the results.

8. "Bar group proposes a citizens' legislature,'" *Chicago Tribune*, 26 June 1978.

9. Crotty, *Political Reform and the American Experiment*, p. x.

10. Ibid., p. 271.

11. Charles Frankel, "The Philosophy of the Enlightenment," in *A History of Philosophical Systems*, ed. Vergilius Ferm (New York: The Philosophical Library, 1950), pp. 266-279. Dante Germino interprets the philosophical shift from "theocentric humanism" to "anthropocentric humanism" as emphasizing the use of reason to manage social relationships while obtaining desired goals. Man would "for the first time create history instead of serving forces beyond his control." See Germino, "The Contemporary Relevance of the Classics of Political Philosophy," in *Handbook of Political Science*, ed. Fred I. Greenstein and Nelson W. Polsby, vol. 1: *Political Science Scope and Theory*, (Reading, Mass.: Addison-Wesley, 1975), p. 242.

12. Crotty, *Political Reform and the American Experiment*, p. xi.

13. See James A. Caporaso, "A Philosophy of Science Assessment of the Stanford Studies in Conflict and Integration," in *Quantitative Interna-*

tional Politics: An Appraisal, ed. Francis W. Hoole and Dina A. Zinnes (New York: Praeger, 1976), pp. 354-382.

14. See Dennis J. Palumbo, "Organization Theory and Political Science," in Greenstein and Polsby (1975), vol. 2, *Micropolitical Theory*, p. 323, for a succinct statement of the major assumptions in rational choice theory.

15. Anthony Downs, "An Economic Theory of Political Action in a Democracy," *Journal of Political Economy* 65 (April 1957):139. Downs argues that the consequences of imperfect information include government bias in favor of producer and against consumer interests, the effectiveness of lobbying in legislative policy making, and even political apathy. He concludes: "Clearly, rational behavior in a democracy is not what most normative theorists assume it to be. Political theorists in particular have often created models of how the citizens of a democracy ought to behave without taking into account the economics of political action" (p. 149). Palumbo, "Organization Theory and Political Science," also notes the unreality of the assumption of complete information (pp. 332-334).

16. See Brian Barry and Douglas W. Rae, "Political Evaluation," in Greenstein and Polsby, eds., *Handbook of Political Science*, vol. 1: *Political Science Scope and Theory*, p. 341. They interpret the problem as one of "internal consistency" among valued alternatives, which cannot be ensured "unless all the criteria used to rank them can be reduced to a single consideration."

17. Austin Ranney, *Curing the Mischiefs of Faction: Party Reform in America (Berkeley: University of California Press, 1975), p. 191.*

18. *Ibid., p. 81.*

19. *Ibid., pp. 80-81.*

20. *Wilson (1973), p. 4.*

21. *Thomas W. Madron and C.P. Shelf, Political Parties in the United States* (Boston: Holbrook Press, 1974), p. 335.

22. Saloma and Sontag (1972), p. 8.

23. Ibid., p. 22.

24. American Political Science Association, Committee on Political Parties, "Toward a More Responsible Two-Party System," *American Political Science Review* 44 (September 1950):supplement.

25. See Evron M. Kirkpatrick, "'Toward a More Responsible Two-Party System': Political Science, Policy Science, or Pseudo-Science," *American Political Science Review* 65 (December 1971):965-990.

26. Gerald M. Pomper, "Toward a More Responsible Two-Party System? What, Again?" *Journal of Politics* 33 (November 1971):917-919.

27. Ibid., p. 939. See also the argument below in this chapter.

28. Wilson (1973), p. 95.

29. Gerald M. Pomper et al., *The Performance of American Government: Checks and Minuses*. (New York: The Free Press, 1972), pp. 76-77.

30. Walter Dean Burnham, "The United States: The Politics of Heterogeneity," in *Electoral Behavior*, ed. Richard Rose (New York: The Free Press, 1974), p. 716.

31. Everett Carll Ladd, Jr. "'Reform' Is Wrecking the U.S. Party System," *Fortune* (November 1977):178.

32. Jeane Jordan Kirkpatrick, *Dismantling the Parties: Reflections on Party Reform and Party Decomposition* (Washington: American Enterprise Institute, 1978), p. 13.

33. Walter Dean Burnham, *Critical Elections and the Mainsprings of American Politics* (New York: W.W. Norton, 1970), p. 133.

34. Saloma and Sontag (1972), p. 6.

35. In his study, *The New Style in Election Campaigns* (Boston: Holbrook Press, 1972), Robert Agranoff finds: "The candidate organization, the news event, the computer-generated letter, and most importantly the electronic media are the prevalent means of getting messages across in the modern campaign. The rise of the candidate volunteer and electronic media has enabled the candidate to bypass the party and appeal directly to the voters" (p. 5).

36. Robert A. Hitlin and John S. Jackson III, "On Amateur and Professional Polticians," *Journal of Politics* 39 (August 1977):786-793, finds that reforms of the delegate-selection process promoted the representation of amateurs in the Democratic conventions. The equation of "amateur" with "reformer" is not complete, however, and at least one major student of party reform characterizes reformers as "purists" rather than "amateurs." See Ranney, *Curing the Mischiefs of Faction*, p. 142.

37. John W. Soule and James W. Clarke, "Amateurs and Professionals: A Study of Delegates to the 1968 Democratic National Convention," *American Political Science Review* 64 (September 1970):888. Reprinted with permission.

38. The Soule and Clarke conceptualization of amateurs and professionals followed the theory initially advanced in Peter B. Clark and James Q. Wilson, "Incentive Systems: A Theory of Organization," *Administrative Science Quarterly* 6 (September 1961):129-166, and developed later in James Q. Wilson, *The Amateur Democrat* (Chicago: University of Chicago Press, 1962). Comparative studies of amateurs and professionals in different conventions are undertaken in John W. Soule and Wilma E. McGrath, "A Comparative Study of Presidential Nomination Conventions: The Democrats 1968 and 1972," *American Journal of Political Science* 19 (August 1975):501-517, and by Hitlin and Jackson, "On Amateur and Professional Politicians." These studies have applied the conceptualization without questioning the extent to which the two goals of intraparty democracy and programmatic parties actually coincided within the same individuals. A study by C. Richard Hofstetter, "The Amateur Politician: A Problem in Construct Validation," *Midwest Journal of Political*

Science 15 (February 1971):31-56, tried to apply the concepts to party leaders in central Ohio, with suspect results. Hofstetter writes, "If it were true that amateurs and professionals could be arrayed along a single dimension with regard to attitudes about party functioning, as Wilson's characterization of the amateur-professional attitude syndromes suggests, then a single factor should emerge from the factor analysis of role perceptions. An orthogonal rotation by Varimax criteria, however, demonstrates that two independent and theoretically meaningful factors emerge from the analysis rather than one factor. Since each of these factors accounts for a considerable proportion of the total covariance, it is concluded that the assumption of unidimensionality of role perceptions is incorrect" (p. 41). Soule and Clarke, in "Amateurs and Professionals", also did not find unidimensionality among the ten items they created to measure amateurism (they found four factors), but they did not choose to draw distinctions within the concept (p. 890).

39. Lawson (1976), p. 137. According to the intensity of issue orientation, Lawson places programmatic parties just after *issueless* parties, which avoid specific pronouncements altogether, and *pragmatic* parties, which deal with immediate practical problems only. More intense on issues are *ideological* parties, which formulate issues in an abstract, future-oriented way, in strict accordance with a known doctrine of thought.

40. See Gerald M. Pomper, *Elections in America: Control and Influence in Democratic Politics* (New York: Dodd, Mead and Company, 1975), chap. 7; and Edward R. Tufte, *Political Control of the Economy* (Princeton, N.J.: Princeton University Press, 1978), pp. 71-76.

41. While Pomper's study of the fulfillment of American party platforms finds that party members in Congress tend to show somewhat greater unity in voting on measures that are related to issues on which the parties have adopted *conflicting* platform positions, the pattern is mixed, with party members sometimes averaging *less* cohesion on votes dealing with conflicting platform positions than on all votes during a presidential term. Moreover, the overall indexes of cohesion tend to be low overall, seldom exceeding 67 except for *bipartisan* votes. See Pomper, *Elections in America*, pp. 195-197.

42. A study of the "coherence" of American parties in comparison with parties in European democracies finds that the American parties rate significantly lower on a five-item coherence scale measuring legislative cohesion and four manifestations of party factionalism: leadership, issue, ideological, and tactical. See Kenneth Janda, "A Comparative Study of Party Organizations: U.S., Europe, and the World," in *The Party Symbol*, ed. William J. Crotty (San Francisco: W.H. Freeman. 1980) pp. 339-358.

43. Duverger (1959), p. 134.

44. Ibid., p. 58.

45. Blondel (1969), p. 124.

46. See Kenneth Janda, *Political Parties: A Cross-National Survey* (New York: The Free Press, 1980). The full study involves 158 parties operating in a stratified random sample of 53 countries from 1950 through 1962.

47. For a lucid discussion of canonical analysis, see Mark S. Levine, *Canonical Analysis and Factor Comparison Techniques* (Beverly Hills, Calif.: Sage University Papers in Quantitative Applications in the Social Sciences, 1977).

48. These data were made available by William Crotty, who participated in the original study. Delegates who rated "leaders in party reform activity" at 30 degrees or below on a "feeling thermometer" were scored as antireform, while those who rated "leaders in party reform activity" at 80 degrees or above were counted as proreform, with the remaining delegates regarded as neutral. According to this operationalization, 12 percent of the Democratic delegates and 26 percent of the Republican delegates were designated as antireform in comparison with 59 percent Democrats and 19 percent Republicans as proreform. As might be expected, more Republicans (55 percent) than Democrats (29 percent) were neutral toward party-reform leaders, for reform was not the issue at the 1972 Republican convention that it was at the Democratic convention.

49. This interpretation of democracy has been associated most closely with various writings of Robert A. Dahl. See his "Pluralism Revisited," *Comparative Politics* 10 (January 1978):201-203, for an explicit discussion of centralization and decentralization in the context of pluralism. See also William Alton Kelso, *American Democratic Theory: Pluralism and Its Critics* (Westport, Conn.: Greenwood Press, 1978).

50. Wright (1971), p. 7.

51. Ibid.

52. Ibid., pp. 39-40.

53. Among the Democrats, 78 percent of the proreform delegates strongly favored "widespread participation in making most party decisions" as opposed to 38 percent of the antireform delegates. The respective figures for Republican delegates were 67 percent and 32 percent.

54. W.D. Hawley, *Nonpartisan Elections and the Case for Party Politics* (New York: Wiley, 1973), pp. 150-151.

55. Judith H. Parris, *The Convention Problem: Issues in Reform of Presidential Nominating Procedures* (Washington, D.C.: The Brookings Institution, 1972), pp. 60-61.

56. Ranney, *Curing the Mischiefs of Faction*, pp. 45-46.

57. Commission on Party Structure and Delegate Selection to the Democratic National Committee, *Mandate for Reform* (Washington, D.C.: Democratic National Committee, 1970), p. 40.

58. Jeane Kirkpatrick, "Representation at National Political Conventions: The Case of 1972," *British Journal of Political Science* 5 (1975):280-281.

59. Ibid., p. 280.

60. Ibid., p. 277.

61. Crotty writes that "the movement to force fifty state parties and the District of Columbia's party to accept rules promulgated by a national party body" was an undertaking that was "unparalleled in the history of American party politics. It was bound to be difficult. Yet, in less than three years, the McGovern-Fraser Commission wrought a political miracle." See William J. Crotty, *Decision for Democrats* (Baltimore: Johns Hopkins University Press, 1978), pp. 104-105.

62. John S. Jackson and Robert A. Hitlin, "A Comparison of Party Elites: The Stanford Commission and the Delegates to the Democratic Mid-Term Conference," *American Politics Quarterly* 4 (October 1976):452.

63. Paul Scott, "Political Parties and Reflective Representation: Organizational Effects on Its Distortion, A Cross-National Study" (unpublished Master's Paper, Department of Political Science, Northwestern University, 1976).

64. See Austin Ranney, "The Direct Primary: A Uniquely United States' Institution," *News for Teachers of Political Science*, a publication of the American Political Science Association, March 1978, pp. 20-21.

65. Ranney, *Curing the Mischiefs of Faction*, pp. 121, 129.

66. Morgens N. Pederson, "Lawyers in Politics: The Danish Folketing and United States Legislatures," *Comparative Legislative Behavior*, ed. Samuel C. Patterson and John C. Wahlke (New York: John Wiley and Sons, 1972), p. 28.

67. Richard A. Joslyn, "The Impact of Television on Partisan Politics" (Paper prepared for delivery at the Annual Meeting of the American Political Science Association, Washington, D.C., 1977, p. 21.

68. Kirkpatrick, *Dismantling the Parties*, p. 13.

69. Kirkpatrick, "Representation at National Political Conventions," p. 280.

70. Data on a sample of the world's parties operating from 1957 to 1962 reveal that 84 percent have some membership requirements, with almost 60 percent requiring their members to pay dues as well as formally enroll in the party. See Janda (1980), p. 127.

71. *Harvard Law Review* 88 (April 1975):1155-1163. Most of the issue is on "developments in the law—elections," but the section cited deals with party activities as state action. This issue is a rich source of information on national and state law related to parties and elections.

72. Joseph A. Schlesinger, "Political Party Organization," in *Handbook of Organizations*, in ed. James G. March (Chicago: Rand McNally, 1965), pp. 765-766.

73. Blondel (1972), begins his analysis of party goals by saying, "The goals of political parties relate to their social bases" (p. 87).

74. See Otto Kirchheime, "The Transformation of the Western European Party Systems," in LaPalombara and Weiner (1966), pp. 177-200.

75. See Janda, "A Comparative Analysis of Party Organizations: U.S., Europe, and the World" in *The Party Symbol*, ed. WIlliam Crotty (San Francisco: W.H. Freeman, 1980), p. 355.

76. Crotty reports that knowledgeable observers were doubtful of the outcomes of the reform movement, presuming that both the delegate-selection committee and the national party to be impotent for enforcing state-party compliance. Nevertheless, the final report on implementation of the guidelines for delegate selection to the 1972 convention revealed significant change in every state party. "An incredible 97 percent of the guidelines had been enforced, an unequalled record of success." See Crotty, *Decison for the Democrats*, pp. 139-142.

77. Crotty's analysis of the charter holds that it relegated "state party rules and state laws to an inferior position, recognizing their force only when they did not conflict with national party by-laws. . . . " Ibid., pp. 242 and 244.

78. Ibid., p. 254.

79. Ladd, "Reform is Wrecking the U.S. Party System."

80. Jeane Kirkpatrick, "Dismantling the Parties."

81. Crotty, *Decision for the Democrats*, p. 251.

82. See Charles Longley, "Party Nationalization in America," chap. 5 in this volume.

83. *Democratic Review*, February/March, 1975, pp. 38-39.

84. Huntington (1968), pp. 405-406.

85. According to a test of the significance of differences between means, the mean score of the American parties on a six-item scale of party organization is not significantly different from the mean for forty-two European parties, but the American parties rate substantially and significantly lower on an eight-item scale of centralization of power. See Janda (1980), p. 352.

86. Lowi even argued that the most important difference between Republicans and Democrats "*is to be found in the interest groups they identify with*" (emphasis in the original). See Theodore J. Lowi, *The End of Liberalism* (New York: W.W. Norton, 1969), p. 72.

87. Hawley, *Nonpartisan Elections*, p. 163.

88. William J. Keefe, *Parties, Politics, and Public Policy in America*, 2d ed. (Hinsdale, Ill.: Dryden Press, 1976), p. 1.

89. See Murray S. Stedman, Jr., and Herbert Sonthoff, "Party Responsibility—A Critical Inquiry," *Western Political Quarterly* 4 (September 1951):454-486.

90. See Robert Harmel and Kenneth Janda, *Parties and Their En-*

vironment: Limits to Reform? (forthcoming). Also see Harmel, "Relative Impacts of Contextual and Internal Factors on Party Decentralization: A Cross-National Analysis" (Unpublished Ph.D. dissertation, Northwestern University, 1977).

91. These findings are based on the x^2 statistic generated from a one-way analysis of variance using the country identification codes as nominal variables predicting to party scores on scales of degree of organization and centralization of power. This analysis was performed to assess the maximum amount of "environmental" effects on party characteristics, assuming that system-level factors in each country combined in some unique configuration that could only be captured completely by treating each country as a variable. The next step in theory and research is to probe beneath the country label to account for common system-level sources of variance in party characteristics. Having done this for a measure of party decentralization, Harmel arrived at four system-level factors—areal size of the country, its degree of democracy, its decentralization of power within the polity, and its autocratic tendencies—which accounted for 34 percent of the variance in decentralization scores for 114 parties across the world. The system-level variables accounted for more variance than the best party-level variables—ideological position and restrictive party strategy—which added only an additional 4 percent of explained variance in a block-hierarchical regression analysis. Ibid.

92. See Richard L. Rubin, "Presidential Primaries: Continuities, Dimensions of Change, and Political Implications" (Paper prepared for delivery at the Annual Meeting of the American Political Science Association, Washington, D.C., 1977), p. 9.

93. Alexander Heard wrote the 1960s classic, *The Costs of Democracy* (Garden City, N.Y.: Doubleday and Company, 1962). A great deal of research has been produced since. For a recent assessment, see Herbert Alexander, *Financing Politics: Money, Elections, and Political Reform* (Washington, D.C.: Congressional Quarterly Press, 1976).

94. See Gary C. Jacobson, "Campaign-Finance Regulation: Politics and Policy in the 1970s," chap. 7 in this volume.

95. See, for example, Committee for Economic Development, *Financing a Better Election System* (New York: Committee for Economic Development, 1968), and D.D. Dunn, *Financing Presidential Campaigns* (Washington, D.C.: The Brookings Institution, 1972).

96. For example, see Joyce Gelb and Marian Palley, *Tradition and Change in American Party Politics* (New York: Thomas Y. Crowell, 1975), pp. 238-239.

97. Lawson, *Comparative Study of Political Parties*, pp. 175-176.

98. Stephen Hess, *The Presidential Campaign* (Washington, D.C.: The Brookings Institution, 1974), p. 82.

99. David S. Broder, *The Party's Over: The Failure of Politics in America* (New York: Harper and Row, 1972), p. 236.

100. Hess, *The Presidential Campaign*, p. 89.

101. Hawley would concur: "If, then, we could put the parties back into the campaign funding business we could also strengthen the parties' role in candidate selection and campaign management," in *Nonpartisan Elections*, p. 161.

102. Jacobson, chap. 7 in this volume.

103. Herbert E. Alexander, *Campaign Money: Reform and Reality in the States* (New York: The Free Press, 1976), p. 10.

104. Timothy A. Hodson and Roland D. McDevitt, "Congressional Campaign Finance: The Impact of Recent Reforms" (Paper prepared for delivery at the Annual Meeting of the American Political Science Association, Washington, D.C., 1977), pp. 4, 14. Also see Gary C. Jacobson, "The Effects of Campaign Spending in Congressional Elections," *American Political Science Review* 72 (June 1978):469-491, who finds that ceilings on spending tend to help incumbents over challengers.

105. Committee for Economic Development, *Financing a Better Election System*, p. 19. Reprinted with permission.

106. Judson L. James, *American Political Parties in Transition* (New York: Harper and Row, 1974), p. 19.

107. Scammon and Wattenberg describe the "social issue," as "a set of public attitudes concerning the more personally frightening aspects of disruptive social change." More specifically, these frightening aspects include crime, racial conflict, dissent, and changing lifestyles. See Richard M. Scammon and Benjamin J. Wattenberg, *The Real Majority: An Extraordinary Examination of the American Electorate* (New York: Coward, McCann, and Geoghegan, 1971), p. 43.

108. *New York Times*, 23 June 1975.

109. It should be recognized that presidents too would have to adjust their behavior given the development of stronger national parties, which is why they have not worked to strengthen the national organization while in office. See Harold F. Bass, "Presidential Responsibility for National Party Atrophy" (Paper prepared for delivery at the Annual Meeting of the American Political Science Association, Washington, D.C., 1977).

References

Books

Blondel, Jean. *An Introduction to Comparative Government*. New York: Praeger, 1969.

_____ . *Comparing Political Systems*. New York: Praeger, 1972.

Dahl, Robert A., ed. *Regimes and Oppositions*. New Haven, Conn.: Yale University Press, 1973.

Duverger, Maurice. *Political Parties*. New York: John Wiley and Sons, 1959.

Epstein, Leon. *Political Parties in Western Democracies*. New York: Praeger, 1967.

Huntington, Samuel P. *Political Order in Changing Societies*. New Haven, Conn.: Yale University Press, 1968.

Janda, Kenneth. *Political Parties: A Cross-National Survey*. New York: The Free Press, 1980.

La Palombara, Joseph, and Weiner, Myron, eds. *Political Parties and Political Development*. Princeton, N.J.: Princeton University Press, 1966.

Lawson, Kay. *The Comparative Study of Political Parties*. New York: St. Martin's Press, 1976.

Rose, Richard, ed. *Electoral Behavior*. New York: The Free Press, 1974.

Saloma, John S., and Sontag, Frederick H. *Parties: The Real Opportunity for Effective Citizen Politics*. New York: Alfred A. Knopf, 1972.

Sartori, Giovanni. *Parties and Party Systems*, vol. 1. Cambridge: Cambridge University Press, 1976.

Triska, Jan F., ed. *Communist Party-States*. Indianapolis, Ind.: Bobbs-Merrill, 1969.

Wilson, James Q. *Political Organizations*. New York: Basic Books, 1973.

Wright, William E., ed. *A Comparative Study of Party Organization*. Columbus, Ohio: Charles E. Merrill, 1971.

Articles, Reports, and Papers

Epstein, Leon D. "Political Parties." In *Handbook of Political Science*, edited by Fred I. Greenstein and Nelson W. Polsby, vol. 4, pp. 229-277. Reading, Mass.: Addison-Wesley, 1975.

Harmel, Robert. "Relative Impacts of Contextual and Internal Factors on Part Decentralization: A Cross-National Analysis." Unpublished Ph.d. dissertation. Evanston, Ill.: Northwestern University Department of Political Science, 1977.

Janda, Kenneth. "A Comparative Study of Party Organizations: The United States, Europe and the World." In *The Party Symbol*, edited by William Crotty. San Francisco: W.H. Freeman, 1980.

Schlesinger, Joseph A. "Political Party Organization." In *Handbook of Organizations*, edited by James G. March. Chicago: Rand McNally, 1965. Pp. 765.

Scott, Paul. "Political Parties and Reflective Representation: Organizational Effects and Its Distortion, A Cross-National Study." Unpublished Master's Paper. Evanston, Ill.: Northwestern University Department of Political Science, 1976.

Indexes

Index of Names

Index of Subjects

About the Contributors

Greg A. Caldeira received the Ph.D. in politics from Princeton University and is assistant professor of political science at The University of Iowa. He is the author or coauthor of several book chapters and of articles in a number of journals, including *Law and Society Review, Judicature, Iustitia, Political Science Quarterly, Justice System Journal, Polity,* and *American Journal of Political Science.* His present research is on the politics of budgetary choice in criminal justice in America and on the changing nature of the Supreme Court as an institution.

Paul T. David is Professor Emeritus, University of Virginia, and currently visiting professor of public affairs, Sangamon State University. His most recent book, with coauthors, is *Proportional Representation in Presidential Nominating Politics.*

Roger H. Davidson is professor of political science and associate dean of the College of Letters and Science at the University of California, Santa Barbara. He is the author of several books and numerous articles on national policy making and congressional politics and has served as a special consultant to major committee realignment efforts in the U.S. Senate and House of Representatives.

Jack Dennis is professor and chair of the Department of Political Science at the University of Wisconsin, Madison. He has pioneered in the study of public attitudes toward politics and political parties and in the socialization of individuals to democratic norms. His published works are extensive and include *Children in the Political System* (as coauthor) and *Socialization to Politics* as well as articles in major American and international journals on the trends in mass support for public institutions.

Gary C. Jacobson is associate professor of political science at the University of California, San Diego. He is the author of *Money in Congressional Elections* and coauthor of *American Parties in Decline.* His articles have appeared in *American Political Science Review, Public Opinion Quarterly, Journal of Politics,* and other journals and compilations. He has also collaborated in the preparation of a report for Congress on the impact of the Federal Election Campaign Act.

Kenneth Janda is professor of political science at Northwestern University. His long-standing major interest is the comparative analysis of political parties. His most recent book, *Political Parties: A Cross-National Survey,* studies 158 parties in 53 countries. He is currently engaged in analyzing the effects of environment on party organization and activities.

Michael R. Kagay teaches courses in public opinion and mass political behavior at Princeton University and serves as polling consultant to *The New York Times*.

Charles H. Longley is professor of political science at Bucknell University. He has written extensively on party nationalization and party reform in both the Democratic and Republican parties, and his published works include contributions to a number of compendiums, including the recently published *Party Renewal in America*. Professor Longley has also participated in party politics in a number of elected and appointed positions and has served as editor of *The Informed Delegate*, published by the Center for Political Reform.

Lawrence D. Longley is associate professor of government at Lawrence University and is the author or coauthor of more than twenty articles and books on American politics and political institutions, including *The Politics of Broadcast Regulation*. In the area of electoral-college reform, he has written *The Politics of Electoral College Reform* and *The People's President: The Electoral College in American History*. He is a consultant to the U.S. Senate Judiciary Committee and has testified or contributed research findings to U.S. Senate hearings on electoral-college reform in 1973, 1977, and 1979. Professor Longley was himself a presidential elector nominee in the 1972 presidential election.

About the Editor

William J. Crotty is a professor of political science at Northwestern University. His particular interests concern party organizational development, party reform, and changes in presidential-nominating patterns. He was a consultant to a number of reform commissions, and his published works include *Decision for the Democrats, Political Reform and the American Experiment*, and *American Parties in Decline* (as coauthor).